Fighting to the End

Fighting to the End

The Pakistan Army's Way of War

C. CHRISTINE FAIR

OXFORD
UNIVERSITY PRESS

UNIVERSITY PRESS

Oxford University Press is a department of the University of Oxford. It furthers
the University's objective of excellence in research, scholarship, and education
by publishing worldwide. Oxford is a registered trade mark of Oxford University
Press in the UK and certain other countries.

Published in the United States of America by Oxford University Press
198 Madison Avenue, New York, NY 10016, United States of America.

First issued as an Oxford University Press paperback, 2018

Library of Congress Cataloging-in-Publication Data
Fair, C. Christine, author.
Fighting to the end : the Pakistan Army's way of war / C. Christine Fair.
pages ; cm
Includes bibliographical references.
ISBN 978–0–19–989270–9 (hardcover : alkaline paper); 978–0–19–068616–1 (paperback : alkaline paper)
1. Pakistan. Army.   2. Pakistan—Military policy.   3. National security—Pakistan.
4. Pakistan—Foreign relations.   5. Islam and state—Pakistan.   I. Title.
UA853.P18F35 2014
355'.03355491—dc23
2013036644

1 3 5 7 9 8 6 4 2

Printed in Canada on acid-free paper

For Jeff

CONTENTS

LIST OF TABLES

ACKNOWLEDGMENTS

This project has been many years in the making. There are numerous persons and institutions to thank. I have had the privilege and honor of being mentored by the finest minds in the study of South Asia's security. Many of these persons I have now known for nearly two decades, and most are among my dearest friends, colleagues, and collaborators. These *ustads* have offered generous insights into this effort and have been a constant source of guidance in this and almost every other project I have undertaken. I owe the deepest gratitude to (in alphabetical order) Ahsan Butt, Christopher Clary, Stephen P. Cohen, Sumit Ganguly, John (aka "Jack") Gill, Tim Hoyt, K. Alan Kronstadt, Peter Lavoy, Doug Makeig, Polly Nayak, David O. Smith, Ashley Tellis, Marvin Weinbaum, and Rob Williams.

I owe a particular recognition to a series of US Army South Asia Foreign Area Officers with whom I have met over the years. These include Brian Hedrick, Richard Girven, Gregory Ryckman, Scott Taylor, Scott Zurschmit, and Rick White as well as Gill and Smith.

In addition, Ayesha Jalal, Paula Newberg, and Shuja Nawaz provided thoughtful feedback early in this project. Thomas Johnson and Thomas Barfield critically read the fifth chapter of this volume with particular care. In addition, I'd like to thank the two anonymous reviewers who provided helpful critiques on the first draft.

Many Georgetown colleagues read parts of this manuscript and gave me insightful guidance and advice from the proposal to the drafting stages. Many thanks go to Daniel Byman, David Edelstein, Bruce Hoffman, and Kathleen McNamara in particular.

I am also indebted to the many Pakistanis in and out of uniform with whom I have had the benefit of interacting over many years, including Mahmud Ali Durrani, Husain Haqqani, Farahnaz Ispahani, Jahangir Karamat, Maleeha Lodhi, Sherry Rehman, Commodore Zaffar Iqbal, and Ehsan ul Haq as well as numerous defense attachés like Brigadier Butt and many more men in uniform than can be possibly named here for space and prudence. In past years, personnel from

Pakistan's Interservices Public Relations facilitated travel and meeting requests and answered questions. Khalid H., ostensibly from the Ministry of Information, was especially helpful as he accompanied me during travels to South and North Waziristan, Swat, Khyber Pakhtunkhwa, interior Sindh, and other locales. He also personally delivered several *Pakistan Army Green Books* in a paper bag to me while I recuperated from a concussion at an Islamabad "nail saloon."

I am also beholden to Georgetown University's Graduate School as well as the Edmund A. Walsh School of Foreign Service, which provided various kinds of support that enabled this project, ranging from small research grants to a junior faculty research leave in fall 2012. In addition, the American Institute of Pakistan Studies enabled me to do research in Islamabad at the end of 2012, and the American Institute of Afghan Studies permitted fieldwork in Helmand and Kabul in August 2010.

Much of the data collection was done at the fine South Asia collections at the University of Chicago and the University of California, Berkeley as well as the New York Public Library. Without those resources, this project would not be possible. I am also appreciative of the brief access that I have had to the National Defence University Library in Islamabad as well as the library at the Institute for Strategic Studies Islamabad.

I have also profited from the contributions of several fabulous research assistants. Much of the quantitative work that I have done with the Pakistan Army data would not be possible without Anirban Gosh. Michael Hardin provided survey and other data analytical support. Son Lee and Cheng He presented valuable assistance with mapping programs. Finally, Sarah Watson Jordan has been my right-hand woman for two years now. It has been an honor to work with her, and I wish her the best as she leaves Georgetown and moves forward to what will be a highly productive career.

Jacob N. Shapiro and Neil Malhotra have been my collaborators for several years. We fielded two large surveys of Pakistanis in 2009 and 2012. I incorporate some of these findings in this volume. It has truly been a pleasure to work with them as they are genuinely ingenious yet profoundly wonderful human beings.

I thank my husband (Jeff) and family (Joe, Whitney, Mallory, Logan, Pork, Ashley, Pickles and Cam, Bob and Bug), who endured holidays and weekends without me. My dear friends Hannah Bloch, Lisa Curtis, Simbal Khan, and Praveen Swami have provided endless support as well as advice. My students have been fun sources of enthusiastic encouragement. Of course, my canine associates—Ms. Oppenheimer, Vega Pussoise, and Emma—helped ensure that I did not become obese during this process by insisting upon lengthy walks and bouts of vigorous belly rubs and "derriere scratches." Ms. Oppenheimer has been my constant companion since 1999. Although I know I must, I cannot imagine undertaking a project without her support and pit bull spirit of surmounting.

Finally, I thank David McBride at Oxford University Press for supporting this project. Without him, all of this would be pointless.

Despite the collective help and wisdom of all of these generous folks, I alone am responsible for errors of fact or interpretation or a failure to be creative and thoughtful.

Introduction to the Pakistan Army's Way of War

Pakistan was born an insecure state in 1947, and it remains so to date. To the east, Pakistan continues to reject the Line of Control cutting through Kashmir as its international border with India. Pakistan views its eastern neighbor, India, as an eternal foe that not only seeks to dominate Pakistan but also to destroy it if and when the opportunity arises. In its quest to manage its external security perceptions, Pakistan has pursued guerilla warfare, proxy warfare, terrorism, low-intensity conflict, and full-scale wars with India. To coerce India to make some concession to Pakistan on the disposition of Kashmir, Pakistan has supported an array of Islamist militant proxies that operate in Kashmir and throughout India (Ganguly 2001). Despite Pakistan's varied exertions to wrest Kashmir through force or coercion, India has not budged. In fact, its position has hardened. India long ago abandoned the proposition that the people of Kashmir should ratify their inclusion within India through an internationally monitored plebiscite. The official policy of the Indian government now is that there will be no more changes to India's international borders.

Even though Pakistan has failed to make even modest progress toward attaining Kashmir, Pakistan's revisionist goals toward India have actually increased rather than retracted in scope.[1] Since the early 1970s, Pakistan has sought to resist, or possibly outright retard, India's inevitable if uneven ascendance both in the region and beyond. Despite the fact that India decisively defeated Pakistan in the 1971 war, with half of Pakistan's territory and population lost when East Pakistan became Bangladesh, Pakistan continues to view itself as India's peer competitor and demands that it be treated as such by the United States and others. In fact, former president and army chief Pervez Musharraf boldly declared that India must accept Pakistan as an equal as a precondition for peace (*Daily Times* 2006). Pakistan's conflict with India cannot be reduced simply to resolving the Kashmir dispute. Its problems with India are much more capacious than the territorial conflict over Kashmir.

Pakistan's conflicts with its western neighbor, Afghanistan, also began at independence. Afghanistan sought to use British decolonization as an opportunity both to denounce the Durand Line as the boundary dividing Afghan and Pakistani territories and to make irredentist claims on large swaths of Pakistani lands abutting Afghanistan. In addition to these territorial disputes with Afghanistan, Pakistan fears that India—working alone or with the Afghans—can destabilize Pakistan's obstreperous western border areas. This has driven Pakistan at various times to restrict India's political and physical presence in Afghanistan. To manipulate Afghanistan's domestic affairs and to create a regime that will forge foreign policies favorable to Pakistan and limit India's actions in Afghanistan, Pakistan has employed Islamist proxies there since 1960, if not earlier (Fair 2011b; Haqqani 2005; Hussain 2005; Jamal 2009; Swami 2007).

Policymakers, diplomats, and analysts puzzle over Pakistan's ostensibly inexplicable behaviors. Why does Pakistan continue to challenge the status quo in Kashmir? Why does it support a fleet of jihadi groups despite the fact that some of these groups have turned against their patrons? Why does Pakistan persist in repudiating India's ascendance as the principle power in South Asia and insist upon being treated as India's equal? After all, Pakistan is a weak state with enervated governmental institutions. It is chronically unable to assert its writ throughout much of the restive and insurgency-prone areas of Balochistan, Khyber Pakhtunkhwa, and the tribal areas. Ethnic and sectarian violence is a recurring menace in Pakistan's rural and urban areas alike. In the last decade, terrorists operating under the banner of the Tehreek-e-Taliban-e-Pakistan (TTP, or Pakistan Taliban) have sustained a campaign against military, intelligence, police, bureaucratic, and political institutions and personalities as well as Pakistan's citizens. Adding to this litany, Pakistan is noted for enduring praetorianism and anemic democratic institutions, abysmal human development indicators, and chronic shortages of power, water, and gas.

Not only do Pakistan's internal resources seem inadequate for the endless quest of seizing Kashmir, resisting India's rise, and orchestrating Afghan affairs, but Pakistan also has few allies and none that support its maximalist agenda with respect to India (Kux 2001; Pande 2011). Pakistan seems to be on an interminable downward spiral. However, India has launched itself on a path of steady economic growth despite its own numerous internal security challenges, not all of which can be blamed on its western neighbor (Sahni 2012). In recent years India has enjoyed sustained economic growth, even during the global recession, which has enabled it to enact steady defense modernization while still keeping defense spending under 3 percent of its gross national product.[2] As India's domestic sources of national power have expanded, India has cultivated strategic partnerships with the United States, the European Union, Israel, Iran, Saudi Arabia, and Qatar, among numerous others, and it has maintained its historically robust ties with Russia. The country has been able to generate substantial support for a permanent seat at the United Nations Security Council (Ganguly 2012; Pant 2009a, 2009b).

The instruments that Pakistan has developed to pursue its anti–status quo goals have incurred the wrath of the international community and, more deleterious for Pakistan, have imperiled the very viability of the state itself. Pakistan's conflict acceptance, coupled with and enabled by its rapidly expanding nuclear program and history of nuclear proliferation, conjure fears of a nuclear conflict in South Asia between nuclear-armed India and Pakistan. Because Pakistan relies upon a menagerie of Islamist militant groups—for example, Afghan Taliban, the Haqqani Network, Lashkar-e-Taiba (also known as Jamaat-ud-Dawa and the Filah-i-Insaniat Foundation), and Jaish-e-Mohammad—as instruments of foreign policy toward India and Afghanistan, the United States has periodically considered declaring Pakistan to be a state sponsor of terrorism. Since Pakistan is perpetually dependent on various financial bailouts provided under the auspices of the International Monetary Fund as well as bilateral aid programs, such brinksmanship is breathtakingly risk acceptant. Furthermore, Pakistan has paid—and will continue to pay—a heavy price for its revisionist agenda. Pakistan's army, which dominates foreign and defense policy, has commandeered control of the state and its resources to sustain this competition with India (Jaffrelot 2002b; Pardesi and Ganguly 2010).

Not only has Pakistan's reliance upon Islamist proxies created external security challenges for itself, but also in late 2001 these proxies began to turn against the state following then President and General Pervez Musharraf's decision to support the US-led war in Afghanistan. Since then, Pakistani terrorists operating under the banner of the Pakistani Taliban have killed thousands, if not tens of thousands, of Pakistanis (National Consortium for the Study of Terrorism and Responses to Terrorism 2012; Pakistan Institute for Peace Studies 2008, 2011; South Asia Terrorism Portal 2012).[3] In addition to waging a bloody campaign against Pakistan's citizenry, Pakistani Islamist terrorists have assaulted military, intelligence, police, and political actors and institutions (Fair 2011b; Hussain 2010).

In light of all these factors, Pakistan should have come to some accommodation with India long ago. Developing a modus vivendi with India may also have allowed Pakistan to endure Afghanistan as a neighbor rather than to ceaselessly seek to cultivate it as a client state. After all, as the power differential between the two antagonists continues to widen, the longer Pakistan defers this ultimate concession the more costly its eventual concession will be. Indeed, Pakistan's policy choices and actions do not align well with the scholarly expectation that "strategies that fail to attain a state's objectives will, in all probability, evolve or be abandoned" (Glenn 2009, 533). Ashley Tellis, a prominent South Asia analyst and consultant to the US government, insightfully opined:

> Pakistan has to recognize that it simply cannot match India through whatever stratagem it chooses—it is bound to fail. The sensible thing, then, is for Pakistan to reach the best possible accommodation with India

now, while it still can, and shift gears toward a grand strategy centered on economic integration in South Asia—one that would help Pakistan climb out of its morass and allow the army to maintain some modicum of privileges, at least for a while. *The alternative is to preside over an increasingly hollow state.* (Cohen et al. 2009, emphasis added.)

Because the power differential between India and Pakistan continues to increase, the longer Pakistan defers the inevitable acquiescence, the more costly the eventual concession will be.

The Argument: Explaining Pakistan's Persistent Revisionism in the Face of Repeated Defeats

Given the ostensible centrality of the Kashmir dispute to Pakistan's behavior in the region, some analysts (e.g., Rubin and Rashid 2008) believe that the only way to bring peace to India, Pakistan, and even Afghanistan is by resolving the Kashmir dispute. They argue that Pakistan will cease its adventurism in Afghanistan and India and will abandon its dangerous reliance on Islamist militant proxies only when the Kashmir issue is given closure in some way that accommodates Pakistan's preference. Unfortunately, this appreciation of the problem and the best resolution of it dangerously misstate the underlying structure of Pakistan's struggle with India. Even if at some point in the past Pakistan's existential struggle with India could have been mitigated through a mutually agreeable resolution of Kashmir, this is certainly no longer true. In this volume, I show that Pakistan's revisionism persists in regards to its efforts not only to undermine the territorial status quo in Kashmir but also to undermine India's position in the region and beyond. Pakistan will suffer any number of military defeats in its efforts to do so, but it will not acquiesce to India. This, for the Pakistan Army, is genuine and total defeat.

Because Pakistan's apprehensions about India are more ideology than security driven, understanding the nature of this security competition should influence how the international community seeks to manage this dispute. Namely, it is possible that any efforts to appease Pakistan through territorial concessions on Kashmir may actually encourage Pakistan's anti–status quo policies rather than temper them. This argument, drawing from the work of Glaser (2010), suggests that Pakistan may be a purely greedy state. Glaser defines such greedy states as "fundamentally dissatisfied with the status quo, desiring additional territory even when it is not required for security" (5). Purely greedy states pursue revisionist policies to increase their prestige, spread their ideology, or propagate their religion. Whereas efforts to ameliorate the threat perceptions of states concerned, about their security may be helpful, such appeasement strategies are counterproductive and dangerous for purely greedy states because their "non-security goals result in a fundamental conflict of interests that makes competition the only strategy with which a greedy state can achieve its goals" (ibid.). If Pakistan is such a greedy state determined to pursue its revisionism for ideological and even religious goals, as my research suggests is the case, the world should prepare for a Pakistan that is ever more dangerous and adjust multilateral and bilateral policy approaches appropriately.

To build these varied arguments, I mobilize a body of data, namely, Pakistan's own defense literatures. Curiously, this important resource has been poorly exploited to date, with the exception of Cohen (1984). I analyze these texts as well as the contexts of their production, consumption, and circulation to draw out the characteristics of the *strategic culture* of the Pakistan Army. As I detail in Chapter 2, for purposes of this effort the strategic culture of the Pakistan Army is more or less interchangeable with that of the country because with few notable exceptions the army has set the country's key foreign and domestic policies. I use Alastair Johnston's (1995a, 1995b) definition of strategic culture. He describes strategic culture as a system of symbols or discursive tools that help a state form enduring strategic preferences both by shaping how the state evaluates the role and utility of military force in international affairs and by endowing these understandings with an "aura of factuality" that makes these strategic preferences seem self evident and uniquely efficacious (Johnston 1995b, 46).

The strategic culture of the Pakistan Army encompasses the collectivity of its corporate beliefs, values, and norms as well as the accumulating weight of its historical experiences. Taken together, the army's strategic culture serves as a lens through which the Pakistan Army understands its (domestic and foreign) security environments, formulates appropriate responses to these challenges, and ultimately makes decisions about which options are most suitable to these threats as the army understands them (Rizvi 2002).

Unlike some armies that primarily concern themselves with external security challenges, the Pakistan Army also involves itself in managing domestic affairs of the state. This means that in the strategic culture of the Pakistan Army there is an inherent linkage between internal and external security challenges. This primarily occurs because the Pakistan Army sees itself as responsible for protecting not only Pakistan's territorial frontiers but also its ideological frontiers. The ideology, as repeatedly stated by virtually every Pakistani army chief, is Islam: the founding logic of the state and the ideology that successive military leaders have used to achieve a degree of national coherence across a multiethnic country and to garner support for the army's endless conflict with "Hindu" India. Even though the specific interpretations of Islam have shifted over the years, the Pakistan Army embraces protecting the ideology of the state as a core function.

Having read decades of the military's professional publications and accounts of senior officers, I conclude that the army's strategic culture shapes the way the Pakistan Army understands the kinds of threats it faces from Afghanistan and India; informs the particular ways that the army understands its principle foe, India; suffuses its conflicts within and beyond Pakistan's borders with various mobilizations of Islam; and influences the tools that Pakistan has developed to manage its varied security challenges within Pakistan itself and in South Asia. The strategic culture of the Pakistan Army produces a stable ensemble of preferences that has endured for much of the country's existence: resist India's rise; restrict its presence and ability to harm Pakistan; and overturn the territorial status quo at all costs. For the Pakistan Army, simply retaining the ability to challenge India is victory. However, to acquiesce is tantamount not only to defeating the Pakistan Army but also, fundamentally, to eroding the legitimacy of the Pakistani state. In this way, Pakistan has managed to snatch a redefined sense of victory from each of its otherwise defeats in its numerous conflicts and confrontations with India. The evidence that I derive from these publications and the strategic culture I infer from them offer little room for hope that Pakistan will abandon its revisionist goals for several nested reasons.

First and foremost, Pakistan's army sets and prosecutes major domestic and foreign policies of the Pakistani state. Since the army has controlled the state directly or indirectly for most of its history, it is well positioned to use the state to pursue its own institutional ends. Thus, it seeks to maximize as many of its own corporate interests as possible, even if it must do so at the expense of the state's interest. Because the army requires the state to enable its own existence, it must make appropriate adjustments along the way to ensure that its policies and preferences do not, in fact, destroy the state. In some general sense, the army has succeeded. However, as I argue here, the army's preferred policies have had enormous costs for the institution itself and for the state. The army's past ability to titrate the pursuit of its own interests against the general harm of the state does not necessarily mean that it will continue to be able to do so.

Second, as I argue in this volume, the army has been very effective at ensuring that civilian institutions and even ordinary Pakistanis share the army's strategic concerns and priorities; thus, the army generally sustains wide support for what it does, even when its preferences impose significant financial costs and opportunity costs upon the state and its people. Consequently, even if civilians manage to seize power from the army, it is not obvious that civilians would immediately pursue different security policies from those of the army.

Third, the army's concerns vis-à-vis India are not purely or even mostly security driven, as I illustrate herein. Pakistan does point to India's larger and growing military capability as evidence of India's intentions toward Pakistan. India's capabilities do warrant appropriate defensive investments. Curiously, while Pakistan could have framed its demands for Kashmir within the rubrics of water security and defensibility of its terrain, it has not done so with few recent exceptions.[4] As noted already, not all of the army's concerns are expressly tied to the territorial defense of the country. Since the earliest years of the state, Pakistan's army has assumed the role of protecting Pakistan's ideological frontiers and maintaining Pakistan's "Islamic" identity. This along with the army's commitment to defending it, which I detail in Chapter 4, locks Pakistan into a civilizational battle with India, which the army posits as universally Hindu despite the simple fact that India is a multireligious, multiethnic state. For the army, resisting India's rise is a necessary condition for the survival of Islamic Pakistan.[5]

Fourth, because the army's concerns and preoccupations are ideological as much as military in scope, the Pakistan Army views its struggle with India in existential terms. For Pakistan's men on horseback, not winning, even repeatedly, is not the same thing as losing. But simply giving up and accepting the status quo and India's supremacy, is, by definition, defeat. As a former chief of army staff explained to me in 2000, Pakistan's generals would always prefer to take a calculated risk and be defeated than to do nothing at all. Pakistan's army will insist on action at almost any cost, even that of presiding over a hollow state. After all, if the Pakistani state were to make such concessions to India, it would no longer be a state worth presiding over. By seeing victory as the ability to continue fighting, Pakistan's army is able to seize victory even from the jaws of what other observers would deem defeat.

Because the Pakistan Army drives the country's most disruptive policies, there is an urgent need for scholars, policymakers, and public policy analysts to understand the army's past and present views of its domestic and external challenges and the evolving ways it has considered dealing with both. As Stephen Cohen (2004, 97) wrote, "For the foreseeable future, the army's vision of itself, its domestic role, and Pakistan's strategic environment will be the most important factors shaping Pakistan's identity." Curiously, there have been few scholarly efforts to comprehensively understand the Pakistan Army's appraisal of its strategic environment and its evaluation of the best tools to manage this strategic environment. Some writers have focused on Pakistan's strategic culture in the context of nuclear weapons (Khan 2012a), while others have authored brief but insightful essays (Lavoy 2006; Rizvi 2002). There have also been important histories of the rise of authoritarianism in Pakistan (Jalal 1990; Rizvi 2000a, 2000b; Siddiqa 2007), accounts of the Pakistan Army as an institution (Cheema 2002; Cloughley 2002; Cohen 1984, 2004), narratives of battlefield encounters (Cloughley 2002; Nawaz 2008a, 2008b), and overviews of its ties to political Islam and Islamist militancy (Haqqani 2005).

These works offer glimpses into the strategic culture of the army, but this is not the primary focus of their authors. In this volume, I aim to inform scholarship about the Pakistan Army by focusing instead on how that institution appreciates and evaluates its actions and how these institutional perceptions are sustained and disseminated across successive cohorts of officers. I attempt to cast some measure of light on the army's strategic culture and the persistent revisionism that this culture encourages. I will do so principally through an examination of decades of professional military publications, most of which are available at various libraries in the United States; interviews with Pakistan military personnel; and multiple sources of data about army recruitment and public opinion regarding the army and its proposals for ensuring Pakistan's security. Understanding the strategic culture of the Pakistan Army, I argue, is the key to understanding what, if any, options the international community has for influencing this strategic culture and the strategic preferences it wields. Once I have identified and studied *strategic culture*, I modify Zionts' (2006) model to explain states' pursuit or abandonment of revisionist policies.

Understanding Pakistan's strategic culture, which is conservative but also evolving, has important implications for our understanding of regional dynamics. This empirical exercise provides further evidentiary support for Sumit Ganguly's (2001) explanation for the various conflicts between India and Pakistan. Ganguly draws on the work of Van Evera (1999) to argue that, even considering several predisposing factors (e.g., divergent ideological commitments, the ongoing territorial dispute over Kashmir, differing views on Partition) as well as specific precipitating and opportunistic events, Pakistan's confident initiation of several conflicts with India can be ascribed to "false optimism," particularly insofar as it led to a misreading of India's military strength and will. This derives in some measure from a chauvinist nationalism and related beliefs about the inherent superiority of the Pakistan Army—which is construed as "Muslim" and "Islamic"—over the Indian Army, viewed as "effete" and "Hindu." Of course the Indian Army also includes ethnic groups that many Pakistani soldiers, following the discredited British colonial paradigm, would consider warrior peoples or "martial races" (e.g., Sikhs, Rajputs). The Pakistan Army has intentionally inculcated this notion of Hindu India within and beyond the army in part to legitimize these reductionist conceptualizations of its nemesis. This volume provides ample textual evidence for the evolution and continuation of Pakistan's chauvinist nationalism, which is informed by stylized notions of Islam and informed by the accumulating weight of Pakistan's history.

A study of the strategic culture of a country dominated by civilians would have to focus on civilian institutions. However, when it comes to Pakistan, the army, which for the vast majority of the country's history has directly and indirectly influenced defense policy toward India and Afghanistan as well as military alliances with the United States and China, among others, is the most appropriate institution to study (Cohen 2004; Schaffer and Schaffer 2011). And because the ideology that the army has cultivated has deep resonance for Pakistan's polity as well as for civilian politicians and bureaucrats, even if the army were to one day suffer a loss of power, a change in strategy would still be unlikely.

The army's strategic culture is by no means static, but I show that it has been remarkably conservative and resistant to change since independence. The Pakistan

Army inherited some of the ways the British appraised the strategic environment of South Asia as well as several policy instruments to manage that environment and even British perceptions of the peoples of South Asia (e.g., understanding of Pakistan's western frontier and perceptions of the varied ethnic groups such as Pakhtuns, Baloch, and Punjabis, in particular).[6] The Pakistan Army still bears the imprint of British military recruitment policies and the ethnocentrism that undergirded the now nearly defunct notion of *martial races*. My analysis does not offer much confidence that the army will undergo substantial change in the near future. The United States, India, and others should abandon their hopes for transformation that have often undergirded engagement strategies. The international community should focus its attention on the implications of continuity rather than the minimal prospects for change.

Organization of This Volume

In this volume, I set forth my arguments over 10 subsequent chapters. The second chapter makes the case for Pakistan's persistent revisionism. It presents a framework of Pakistan's political structure, based on the work of Zionts (2006), to explain how both military and civilian regimes execute the army's preferences. The chapter also presents a discussion of the literature that I use in conjunction with Zionts' model to derive and detail Pakistan's strategic culture. To this end, Chapter 2 briefly reviews some of the lingering debates that divide scholars of strategic culture. Having put forth a definition of the Pakistan Army's strategic culture, I proffer a justification for reducing Pakistan's strategic culture to that of the army. I conclude with a review of data sources and analytical methods employed in this study. This work is primarily intended to be empirical. As a nonpolitical scientist trained in South Asian languages and civilizations, I do not attempt to adjudicate the varied disputes about state behavior in international relations theory. Instead, I use *strategic culture* as a heuristic tool to help explain Pakistan's enduring revisionism and proclivity for conflict. My principle sources of data are texts authored by Pakistani military personnel and, in most cases, printed and distributed by the army. I use these writings to infer how Pakistan assesses its strategic environment and its objectives within that environment as well as how Pakistan understands the use of force and its alliances to secure these interests.

In Chapter 3, I discuss the importance of colonial India's Partition and inheritance in shaping the Pakistan Army's strategic culture. Here, I offer a brief account of Pakistan's independence movement and the concomitant mobilization of communal politics as well as the ultimate division of the subcontinent generally and the army particularly. This separation gave rise to the enduring security competition over Kashmir. It also left indelible marks upon the Pakistan Army's perception of its nemesis, India, and its intentions. The independence movement is rooted in the arguments of the two-nation theory, the founding principle of the state. This movement spread communal conceptions of the religious Other, which deeply affected the Pakistan Army. The Pakistan Army believes it is its duty to protect Pakistan's ideology of Islam and the two-nation theory. In some sense the religious ideology that the army embraced was a product of the process of Partition.

Chapter 4 addresses the various roles of Islam in the Pakistan Army, particularly the concept of the two-nation theory. This theory holds that Muslims constitute a separate nation from Hindus and thus deserve their own homeland. This conception locks India and Pakistan in a civilizational struggle: Pakistan must defend Islam and the two-nation theory against what many Pakistanis believe to be an India dedicated to undermining it and thus the very legitimacy of the Pakistani state. These intertwined subjects of Islam—Islamism[7] and the two-nation theory—create considerable alarm beyond Pakistan and, on occasion, among Pakistanis, some of whom long for a state in which religion and state are more distinguished if not more distant. Anxiety about the role of Islam in the state and the army is exacerbated by the fact that Pakistan's army has long been associated with Islamist militant groups operating at its behest. In recent years, Islamist militants have infiltrated the army. Given Pakistan's track record on nuclear proliferation, rightly or wrongly analysts fear that Islamist militants could acquire nuclear weapons from the army through subterfuge or with the consent of some part of the organization.

Analysts and scholars who fear the influence of Islam in the Pakistan Army simultaneously understate and overstate the problem. Contemporary analysis minimizes the problem, suggesting that this concern is relatively recent, dating to the tenure of Zia ul Haq in the 1980s. In fact, the army was an ideological army almost from the beginning, and it instrumentalized Islam for a number of reasons. Analysts also exaggerate the army's mobilization of Islam because they do not understand the myriad and complex reasons behind it.[8] As I argue here, the army has long seen itself as the protector of Pakistan's Islamic ideology and has come to frame its conflict with India in civilizational terms. Understanding the various roles that Islam plays in the army is fundamental to understanding how Pakistan views the threats it confronts and the available tools at its disposal to confront them.

Chapter 5 identifies one of the most enduring derivatives of Pakistan's strategic culture: its obsession with forging strategic depth in Afghanistan, variously defined over time. While contemporary scholarship generally suggests that the army became interested in this concept in the late 1970s, I argue that in fact the Pakistan Army inherited this compulsion from the British. The entire British army was configured precisely to defend the empire from threats that were presumed to come into the subcontinent through Afghanistan. While Pakistan inherited the entire threat frontier, it had a meager fraction of the Raj's resources. This chapter traces the historical features of strategic depth prior to, during, and after Partition. This chapter also examines the behaviors that the Pakistan Army has pursued as a consequence of its presumed need for strategic depth in Afghanistan. This pursuit not only has had implications for the ways the army manages Afghanistan but also has profoundly shaped the state's policies toward and relations with ethnic Pakhtun and Baloch Pakistanis who live in the areas bordering Afghanistan.

Chapter 6 deals with the depiction of India and Indians in Pakistan's defense literature. Pakistan's defense publications consistently present highly stylized— if not outright faulty—versions of its engagements with India and the outcomes of these conflicts. What becomes apparent from a perusal of Pakistan's defense publications is that the Pakistan Army is neuralgically obsessed with India. Long before Indian strategists articulated a place for India on the international stage, Pakistani defense writers were doing so. Pakistan's apprehensions are not driven entirely by facts or empirical assessments; instead, its defense publications have sustained an ossified yet empirically erroneous account of its relations with India and even of India and Indians. Equally problematic, these narratives are thoroughly integrated into Pakistan's educational materials, public and private media, and elements of Pakistan's not-so-civil civil society. The result is that Pakistan's national discourse surrounding India and defense policy is informed by a deeply flawed historical understanding that is resistant to amelioration.

Chapter 7 focuses on the way Pakistan's relationships with the United States and China figure in Pakistan's strategic culture. Any frequent visitor to Pakistan will recognize the familiar refrain found in Pakistan's defense writings: the United States is a perfidious ally that uses Pakistan for its strategic ends and then abandons it. China, in contrast, is described as an enduring friend. Pakistan has other important partners, such as Saudi Arabia and North Korea. However, its professional military publications rarely mention them in any significant detail, much less dedicate entire articles to them. Many American scholars (including this one) have long believed that the army has developed this rhetorical strategy to exploit US government officials' relatively short memory of US–Pakistan relations to obtain lucrative rewards such as grant assistance; foreign military financing; access to desirable US weapon systems; and other financial, military, diplomatic, or political allurements. While this skepticism about Pakistan's objective and subjective assessments is certainly justified, it is also true that on the whole Pakistani military personnel believe this narrative even if specific individuals have a richer and more evidence-based understanding of US–Pakistan relations.

Chapters 8 and 9 explore the role of nuclear weapons in Pakistan's strategic culture, especially in enabling Pakistan to increasingly rely upon a raft of Islamist militants to prosecute the state's interests in India but also in Afghanistan. It is appropriate to treat the two subjects together because, as I demonstrate in Chapter 9, Pakistan's nuclear program enables its use of militancy in Kashmir and beyond.

These chapters both complement and expand on the work of Kapur (2007), who focuses on the Indo–Pakistan conventional crises that have been enabled by Pakistan's creeping nuclear umbrella. They do so, in part, by discussing the antecedent conditions for Pakistan's ability to expand the militant groups in terms of number, operational scope, and geographical area of operations as well as the contemporary Islamist militant landscape and the relationship that the state enjoys with the various actors therein.

Chapter 10 begins by asking which, if any, elements of this strategic culture could evolve over any policy-relevant future. It considers the various empirically demonstrated sources of change within the army and concludes with a discussion of the implications of these changes for the future of the institution and, by extension, the stability of Pakistan and of the region. This chapter also describes the geographical recruitment base of the army and how it has expanded from several districts in northern Punjab to include many districts in militancy-afflicted Southern Punjab, much of Khyber Pakhtunkhwa (KP), Sindh, the Federally Administered Tribal Areas (FATA), and even parts of Balochistan (Fair and Nawaz 2011).

The final chapter revisits the framework laid out in Chapter 2 of this volume and identifies the implications for Pakistan's behavior over the near term. It argues that Pakistan is a "greedy state" in the parlance of Glaser. Thus, policies of appeasement (e.g., helping to secure a resolution of Kashmir) may encourage further Pakistani revisionist pursuits rather than vitiate them. This chapter concludes with the ominous suggestion that the world must be ready for a Pakistan that is willing to take ever more dangerous risks because, in the view of the Pakistan Army, it has everything to lose by not doing so. For the army, to be defeated is not to lose on the battlefield; rather, defeat is to forego the opportunity or ability to keep resisting India and the agenda that Pakistan ascribes to its eastern nemesis.

CHAPTER 2

Can Strategic Culture Explain the Pakistan Army's Persistent Revisionism?

In this chapter, I first lay out the characteristics of Pakistan's persistent and even expanding revisionist goals.[1] Next, I present a framework of Pakistan's domestic politics derived from the work of Zionts (2006) to help explain how both military regimes and civilian governments alike pursue the army's revisionist agenda. Third, I briefly recount some of the salient debates in the scholarly literature about strategic culture and exposit how I apply Johnston's (1995a, 1995b) formulation of strategic culture to the Pakistan Army. Fourth, I offer a justification for reducing this puzzle of Pakistan's strategic culture generally to that of the army in particular. Then I give an overview of the Pakistan Army; this is fundamental to understanding how the strategic culture of the army is reproduced and sustained. I conclude with a brief discussion of methods and sources I use in this effort.[2]

Pakistan's Enduring and Expanding Revisionism

Pakistan is revisionist, or anti–status quo, in that it desires to bring all of the disputed territory of Kashmir under its control, including the portion currently governed by India.[3] As I describe in Chapter 3, while Kashmir never belonged to Pakistan in any legal sense, acquiring it is integral to Pakistan's national identity. Pakistan is revisionist in another sense in that it seeks to actively thwart India's rise in the region and beyond. Pakistan insists that India and the rest of world view and treat it as India's equal. Resisting India's rise is both an ideational and ideological goal of the Pakistan Army; however, doing so also has implications for how the army uses instruments of force and other elements of national power. For example, recent Pakistani reliance on Islamist militants in Afghanistan such as the Afghan Taliban, the Haqqani Network, and even Lashkar-e-Taiba has as much to do with limiting India's presence there as it does with shaping a regime in Kabul that is friendly to Pakistan. In contrast to Pakistan, India is territorially satisfied with the status quo, but it is mildly revisionist with respect to its place in the international system (Mohan 2004, 2006).

Pakistan first tried to seize Kashmir in 1947. As British decolonization of South Asia loomed, the sovereign of Kashmir, Maharaja Hari Singh, hoped to keep the country independent of either of the two new states, India or Pakistan. As Singh held out, marauders from Pakistan's tribal areas invaded the territory of Jammu-Kashmir in hopes of taking it for Pakistan and were supported extensively by Pakistan's nascent provincial and federal governments. This attack expanded into the first war between India and Pakistan. When it was over and the cease-fire line was drawn, Pakistan controlled about one-third of Kashmir, and India controlled the remainder. Although the war ended in a stalemate with international intervention, Pakistan may have rightly concluded that the strategy of using irregular fighters succeeded. After all, Pakistan had claimed at least some part of Kashmir, which it would not have had otherwise. Moreover, because of the war, Kashmir was the subject of several United Nations Security Council resolutions, and it was recognized as a "disputed territory" rather than a territory over which India exercised incontestable sovereignty.

Since 1947, Pakistan has remained locked in an enduring rivalry with India and has been steadfastly committed to seizing control of the entire territory of Jammu-Kashmir.[4] After the first war, Pakistan sustained a low-level proxy war in Kashmir in hopes of making India's possession of the territory so costly that India would simply abandon it altogether (Swami 2007). By the late 1950s, articles in Pakistan's professional military publications were already arguing for the viability of initiating and sustaining guerilla operations within the implied theater of Indian-controlled Kashmir.

Pakistan's second major military attempt to change the territorial status quo took place in 1965, when Pakistan dispatched regular and irregular troops disguised as local fighters to Indian-administered Kashmir in hopes of igniting an insurgency there and bringing international attention to the dispute. No uprising materialized, but the misadventure did slide into the second Indo-Pakistan war over Kashmir when India opened a second front across the international border. Indian and Pakistani accounts of their own performance diverge with respect to their losses of men and territory and the losses they inflicted upon the other (Nawaz 2008a). Scholarly accounts maintain that the war ended in what appeared to be a stalemate. However, there is strong evidence that India could have continued the war to deliver a decisive defeat to Pakistan had poor civil–military coordination not led India to accept the UN ceasefire prematurely (Raghavan 2009).

The war ended in a draw, but scholars note that Pakistan fared worse than India. For one thing, the war resulted in a cessation of American aid to both combatants. Pakistan was more dependent on American assistance than was India and thus was more adversely affected. Second, India "achieved its basic goal of thwarting Pakistan's attempt to seize Kashmir by force," whereas Pakistan "gained nothing from a conflict which it had instigated" (Kux 1992, 238). When the war ended, it was obvious that India was in a position to severely damage, if not capture, Lahore in Pakistan's Punjab, which "lay virtually defenseless" (Wolpert 1993, 375). In addition, India also controlled the strategically important Uri-Poonch bulge in Kashmir (Wolpert 1993). Lt. Gen. Mahmud Ahmed's account of the 1965 war, which General Headquarters approved for publication in 2002, describes it as a "watershed in the military history of the subcontinent. It marked the turning point in the balance of power in South Asia. After 1965, the Indian military power grew by leaps and bounds while Pakistan's strength declined appreciably" (530). This was, in his view, Pakistan's last opportunity to resolve the Kashmir dispute through military force in the twentieth century.

The 1965 war brought particular shame to the Pakistan Army in part because many Pakistanis were under the belief that their country was winning the war due to the misinformation broadcasted on Pakistani media throughout the conflict. During this war, Pakistan was under Gen. Muhammad Ayub Khan's military rule. Consequently, "once the euphoria produced by the official propaganda during the war had died down in Pakistan, people realized that Ayub Khan and the military leadership had failed the nation militarily" (Nawaz 2008a, 239–240).

In 1971 the third war between Pakistan and India began, but unlike the previous two conflicts, which were fought over Kashmir and in which Pakistan was the obvious aggressor, this one began as a civil war in East Pakistan. Pakistan's Bengali citizens there, frustrated with West Pakistan's extractive policies and unable to achieve full citizenship within a united Pakistan, eventually chose to secede. As refugees flowed into India, India seized the opportunity to intervene. When the war was over, Pakistan had lost East Pakistan, which emerged as independent Bangladesh. Pakistan's army was disgraced because it lost the war along with half of the country's territory and population, but also because the country was under military governance when the war took place. While Pakistan and India were relatively quiescent in the years following that war, Pakistan did not acquiesce to India's rise. Pakistan's "determination to protect its national identity and policy autonomy did not decline after the 1971 military debacle at the hands of India. If anything, its disposition stiffened" (Rizvi 2002, 314). Pakistan emerged committed to acquiring a nuclear weapons capability to steadfastly resist Indian hegemony.

In spring 1999, Pakistan again sought to change maps in Kashmir through military force, less than a year after Pakistan and India became overt nuclear states. In that conflict, known as the Kargil War, Pakistan dispatched Northern Light Infantry paramilitary personnel along with regular Pakistani Army personnel to seize territory in the Kargil–Dras sectors of Indian-administered Kashmir. By the end of summer 1999, India had vanquished the Pakistani intruders, albeit at a high cost in personnel and after introducing air power into the conflict. Pakistan emerged from this crisis as a reckless, conflict-prone, nuclear-weapon state. The army in particular fared poorly because its chief, Musharraf, did not fully inform Prime Minister Nawaz Sharif about the operation and its implications. Instead, he undertook planning for the operation because Sharif was prosecuting an important diplomatic effort with India's prime minister, Atal Bihari Vajpayee. In contrast, India received accolades for its forbearance and measured response to the outrageous maneuver. The Kargil War occasioned an important American shift away from Pakistan toward India and eventually paved the way for the US–India strategic partnership that unfolded during the tenures of US president George W. Bush and Indian prime minister Vajpayee (Fair 2009b; Lavoy 2009; Tellis et al. 2001).

Contrary to popular belief, Pakistan's efforts to antagonize India between official wars were not always restricted to fanning Islamist insurgency and terrorism. In the mid-1950s, Pakistan (as well as China) supported India's Naga rebels in northeast India through its own infrastructure in East Pakistan (Shekatkar 2009). In the 1960s Pakistan supported the Mizo rebels (Chadha 2009), also in India's northeast. Support to insurgents there became more difficult after the loss of East Pakistan in 1971. Beginning in the late 1970s and through the early 1990s, Pakistan supported the Sikh insurgency in India's northern state of Punjab (Fair 2004a, 2004c). By the mid-1980s, Pakistan's creeping nuclear umbrella emboldened it to pursue revisionist agendas.[5] In the late 1980s, Kashmiris in Indian-administered Kashmir began to rebel against New Delhi for a range of excesses including appalling electoral manipulation and its malfeasance in managing Kashmiri political expectations. While the rebellion began indigenously, Pakistan quickly exploited these developments. Pakistan redeployed battle-hardened militants from the waning Afghan war to Kashmir. By 1990, Pakistan and India were already behaving as if the other had an existential nuclear deterrent (Fair 2011b; Kapur 2007).[6] Within a few years, Pakistan transformed a conflict that began as an indigenous uprising in the late 1980s into a sustained campaign of proxy war in Kashmir (Evans 2000; Ganguly 1997).

As Pakistan continued to expand its nuclear program, and thus its confidence that India would be deterred from taking punitive action, it also increased its reliance on militant proxies in India (Tellis et al. 2001). Following the overt nuclearization of the subcontinent in 1998, Pakistan became increasingly aggressive in its use of low-intensity conflict, employing both official military forces (i.e., the Kargil War) and Islamist militant proxies. Pakistan-backed Islamist militants have conducted dozens of attacks throughout India, the most significant of which were the December 2000 attack on an intelligence operations center located near New Delhi's Red Fort; the December 2001 strike on the Indian Parliament, which brought the two countries to the brink of war; the May 2002 attack on housing for families of Indian army personnel at Kaluchak in Kashmir; a July 2006 coordinated bomb attack on Mumbai's commuter rail system; and the November 2008 notorious multiday siege of several sites across Mumbai. (The terrorist group

Lashkar-e-Taiba was responsible for most of these incidents, with the exception of the 2001 Parliament attack, which was carried out by Jaish-e-Mohammed. The 2006 attack was carried out by the Indian mujahideen with support from Lashkar-e-Taiba). These major assaults are in addition to many other smaller ones throughout India, which had fewer international and domestic consequences (Clarke 2010; Swami 2008). By expanding the conflict to the Indian heartland, Pakistan hoped to increase the cost of India's adamant commitment to the territorial status quo in Kashmir.

Despite the claims of some analysts (e.g. Rubin and Rashid 2008), Pakistan's antagonism with respect to India cannot be reduced to the bilateral dispute over Kashmir. As I show throughout this volume, Pakistan's defense literature clearly maintains that Pakistan's army also aims to resist India's position of regional dominance and its slow but steady global ascent, and more often than not this threat from India is described in ideological and civilizational terms rather than those of security (Mohan 2004, 2006; Pant 2009a, 2009b ; Scott 2009). Recently, Brigadier Umar Farooq Durrani (2010, 1) summarized Pakistan's resilience against India's "superiority complex" and refusal to deal with Pakistan "on an equal footing" by noting that some 60 years after independence, "Pakistan's lasting defiant posture has kept the Indian-dream [sic] from becoming a reality" and that Pakistan's nuclear program has made India only "more bitter and hostile." His essay opened the 2010 *Pakistan Army Green Book*, which is issued every two years by the army's Training and Evaluation Command and bears the imprimatur of the army chief himself.

The army's revisionist goals endure despite the accumulation of evidence that Pakistan's army cannot achieve them at present and is even less likely to succeed in the future. This is true for a number of reasons. For one, India's economic growth since the 1990s has allowed it to undertake significant defense modernization while keeping defense expenditures well below 3 percent of its gross domestic product (World Bank 2012). Second, India has forged strategic partnerships with the United States, Israel, Iran, and other regional and global actors and has even staged limited military exercises with China. Third, India's position in the international community is ascendant, with countries like the United States, Britain, and France formally backing its bid for a permanent seat on the United Nations Security Council (UNSC) within the context of UNSC reform (Thakur 2011).

In contrast, Pakistan's economy is shambolic, exhibiting weakness on virtually all measures (Economist Intelligence Unit 2012). The country has long been dependent on bilateral and multilateral development partners (Wahab and Ahmed 2011). Pakistan's heavy investment in the armed forces since 1947 has crowded out investments in other areas. According to the World Bank (2006, 1–2), "Due to regional tensions, military expenditures in Pakistan have consistently absorbed a significant proportion of the budget (about one-quarter to one-third of total revenue)....There remained very little fiscal space for basic government expenditures, or development expenditures." Shahid Javed Burki, a renowned Pakistani economist, argues that not only have Pakistan's priorities affected its spending decisions but also its security competition with India has resulted in enormous opportunity costs. In 2007, Burki calculated that had Pakistan not pursued revisionism in Kashmir,

> [its] long-term growth rate could have been some 2.25 to 3.2 percentage points higher than that actually achieved....A growth rate of this magnitude sustained over half a century would have increased the country's gross product by a factor of between 3.4 and 4.4. Indeed, had the country been at peace with India over the past decades, Pakistan's 2003–2004 GDP could have been three and a half times larger than it was—$330 billion rather than $95 billion—and its income per capita could have been $2,200 rather than $630 (25).

Pakistan's revisionist agenda not only has posed heavy costs upon the state but also in recent years has directly affected the security of Pakistan's citizens and even the state's own stability. Current members and direct descendants of many of the militant groups spawned by Pakistan's intelligence agencies now target Pakistan's civilian, military, and intelligence institutions as well as its citizens (Fair 2011b; Hussain 2010; Swami 2007). Assessments of the number of such incidents and of their victims vary between several thousands and several tens of thousands (Global Terrorism Database 2012; Pakistan Institute for Peace Studies 2012).

In short, Pakistan has doggedly attempted to revise the geographical status quo and roll back India's ascendency, and the very instruments it has used to attain these policies have undermined Pakistan's standing within the international community and even its own long-term viability. Looking to the future, Pakistan is even less likely to succeed either in altering the geographical status quo or in retarding India's ascent to regional and global power—yet it will continue to try to do so.

Pakistan should have abandoned its revisionism long ago. After all, scholars expect that "good strategy will...ensure that objectives are attained while poor strategy will lead to the ineffective execution of a state's power....It is also assumed that strategies that fail to attain a state's objectives will, in all probability, evolve or be abandoned" (Glenn 2009, 533). Despite numerous and ever-expanding obstacles, Pakistan remains staunchly revisionist, even though its position, already untenable and destabilizing, will become increasingly so in the future. Given India's upward trajectory and Pakistan's ever-sinking position in the global system, game rationality[7] suggests that it would behoove Pakistan to come to some accommodation with India today, as conceding defeat now will be less costly than doing so later, when the power differential between the two states is even greater.

Explaining Persistent Revisionism

The likelihood that Pakistan's military or even civilian leadership will abandon the state's long-standing and expanding revisionist goals and prosecute a policy of normalization with India is virtually nil. Even the 1971 catastrophic military defeat did not force Pakistan to revise its policies with regards to India. Pakistan's persistent revisionism can be situated within the more general scholarly puzzle as to why states are revisionist. Despite the challenges that revisionist states pose to international security, relatively few scholars have sought to explain why states *remain* revisionist, especially when such efforts consistently fail and even undermine the prospects for a state's very survival.[8]

Zionts (2006) sought to explain why some states refuse to abandon their revisionism in the face of clear policy failure. He does not deal with the question of why states are revisionist in the first place but rather seeks to understand a state's decision to persist with or abandon its revisionist goals. To do so, he posits domestic political structures as the crucial mediating variable.[9] Zionts examines several revisionist states and defines them as either *unreasonably* or *reasonably* revisionist. This judgment is based not on a normative evaluation of the goal pursued or contingent upon the success or failure of the goal, but rather on the feasibility of achieving that goal given a cost constraint. According to Zionts, the sine qua non of an unreasonably revisionist state is that the state fails to moderate its policies despite decisive defeats, even when the state's survival is at stake (634).[10]

Zionts (2006) cites Nazi Germany and imperialist Japan, both of which pursued their revisionism until they were destroyed. These states exemplify suicidally revisionist states, an extreme form of unreasonable revisionism that resulted in the regimes' demises. He describes Iran's actions during the Iran–Iraq war as those of a nonsuicidal but still unreasonably revisionist state. Despite Iraq's initial victories, Iran managed to repel Iraqi troops from its territory. When Saddam Hussein realized that he could not swiftly defeat his adversary, he pressed for peace and in June 1982 offered a ceasefire. Iran not only refused the offer but also actually attacked Iraq as part of its own effort to secure regime change. Despite severe casualties and economic hardship, Iran persisted in this policy for almost a decade. What made Iran's revisionism unreasonable, in Zionts' terminology, was its refusal to moderate its goals even though its assumptions proved time and time again to be false. Ayatollah Khomeini accepted a ceasefire only when he became convinced that failure to do so would mean the end of his Islamic revolution and of the Islamic Republic. But as unreasonable as Iran's revisionism was with respect to regime change in Iraq, it eventually relented. Pakistan, in contrast, has never moderated its revisionism since 1947.

Zionts (2006) distinguishes unreasonable states from those that are reasonably revisionist. States in this latter category drop their revisionist pursuits after having concluded that, given the low likelihood that they will prevail, the probable benefits of their revisionist activities are less than the probable costs. For Zionts, the actions of Israel during the 1982 war in Lebanon provide an example of reasonable revisionism. Israel invaded with the goal of destroying the Palestine Liberation Organization (PLO), ejecting it from Lebanon and installing a Maronite Christian-dominated leadership that would be positively disposed toward Israel. Israel succeeded in pressuring Lebanon to install Bashir Gemayel, an ally of the Israeli Defense Minister Ariel Sharon, as president in August 1982. Gemayel, however, was assassinated the following month. In response, Israel scaled back its goals in Lebanon, ceasing to seek an explicitly pro-Israeli government there. Note that Zionts does not frame Israel's revisionism within the larger context of its dispute with Palestinians or with other Arab states, and he does not use revisionism in the narrower sense of territorial revisionism but instead uses political revisionism.

Zionts (2006) argues that three variables (domestic structures, domestic politics, and elite ideology), "mediated by the structure of incentives and constraints" (639) facing leaders, explain the persistence of unreasonable revisionism. In terms of domestic political structures, Zionts distinguishes between democratic and autocratic states. In those that are democratic, the public's views will influence policymakers' decision to alter or sustain the state's foreign policy, if for no other reason than the need for democratic leaders to deliver popular policies or face defeat through democratic competition. In a closed system, however, the ideology of autocratic leaders will determine whether a state is reasonably or unreasonably revisionist. If leaders are ideological, they are likely to pursue a course of unreasonable revisionism, while pragmatic leaders are less likely to do so. This dynamic is captured in Figure 2.1.

The conceptualization Zionts (2006) presents of ideal types of domestic political structures and of their role in producing unreasonable revisionism offers some promise for explaining Pakistan's persistent commitment to reversing the status quo. Pakistan has been governed directly by the military for much of its history: from 1958 to 1969 by Ayub; 1969 to 1971 by Gen. Yahya Khan; 1977 to 1988 by Gen. Zia ul Haq; and 1999 to 2007 by Musharraf.[11] Even when not directly governing Pakistan, the army has wielded enormous influence over the country's domestic politics and dictated its foreign policies. Thus, even during periods of relative democracy, Pakistan still suffers under the weight of persistent praetorianism (Cohen 2004; Haqqani 2005; Jalal 1990; Siddiqa 2007). As recently as July 2013, the official commission established by the Pakistan government to investigate the US raid on Osama bin Laden's safe haven in Pakistan concluded that, while constitutionally setting defense policy is the responsibility of the civilian government, "in reality.... defence policy in Pakistan is considered the responsibility of the military and not the civilian government even if the civilian government goes through the motions of providing inputs into a policy making process from which it is essentially excluded" (Report

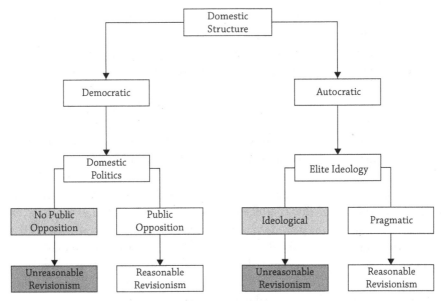

Figure 2.1 Domestic politics of unreasonable revisionism. Source: Derived from Zionts (2010, 639).

of the Abbottabad Commission 2013, 159). Over the expanse of its history, Pakistan—under military or even democratic governance—has distinct auto-cratic features.

Pakistan's military, specifically the army, has long justified its dominant role in running the state by arguing that it is uniquely well positioned to protect not just Pakistan's territorial integrity but also the very ideology of Pakistan, which centers on protecting Pakistan's Muslim identity from India's supposed Hindu identity (Haqqani 2005; Pande 2011). Oddly, civilians seem to have thoroughly acquiesced to this reality. The Report of the Abbottabad Commission (2013) observed that the civilian government did not evidence the slightest interest in exerting control over the nation's defense policy and further quipped that the Minister of Defense did not object to being "an irrelevance" (227).

For a number of reasons, Zionts' (2006) model ultimately cannot resolve the Pakistan puzzle in entirety. First, he looks at the decision to revise or sustain a pol-icy within the context of a single conflict (the Iran–Iraq War, or Israel's efforts to install a pro-Israeli government in Lebanon). Compared with Pakistan's 65-year history of initiating clashes with India, both of these episodes are relatively brief. In neither case does Zionts examine a state that persists in its revisionist goals for more than one decade. The Indo-Pakistan security competition has persisted for well over six decades despite the fact that Pakistan has either lost outright or failed to defeat India in every war they have fought. And unlike Zionts' case-study subjects, since independence Pakistan has actually expanded its revisionist goals beyond the territorial dispute over Kashmir to include resisting what it sees as Indian hegemony.

Second, Zionts (2006) does not define elite ideology. Nor does he attempt to account for how it is created; how it comes to control the views of other, less important, elites; or even how it shapes the views of the general public. (For Zionts, ideology is merely an intervening variable, one that he suggests explains the relationship between political structures and a state's decision to jettison or embrace its revisionist goals. For this reason he does not dilate upon this concept of ideology.) It is important to understand these processes because states like Pakistan vacillate between autocracy and weak democracy. Part of the Pakistan Army's ability to defend its preeminent position within the state stems from the success of its ideology, which permeates Pakistan's varied institutions and societal groups. Even during the periods of (invariably weak) democracy, civilian leaders and citizens alike embrace the elite ideology of the military: its strategic culture. It is entirely possible that civilians lack the adequate will or motivation to challenge the army rather than simply embracing its strategic outlook and assessments. However, it is impossible to disambiguate coercion and acquiescence on one hand from complicity and agreement on the other. Crucially, even if civilian elites were able to change the country's defense policy, it is unlikely they would do so because the military's defense policy is in line with popular preferences and because the army can simply oust the elected government as it has done repeatedly.

In this effort, I modify Zionts' (2006) framework to help explain Pakistan's persistent revisionism in several important ways (Figure 2.2). First, rather than retaining his language of reasonable or unreasonable revisionism as outcomes, I simply use *persists in revisionism* or *abandons revisionism* as the possible outcomes of state behavior. This language is preferable because it avoids any normative connotation suggested by Zionts' terminology. Second, I replace the army's *elite ideology* with *strategic culture*. Third, because there has yet to be a government that is genuinely controlled through constitutionally elected representatives and that sets domestic and foreign policies, I further modify Zionts' illustration to reflect the Pakistani reality of *army-controlled democracy* as the alternative regime type to military rule. Under periods of direct army rule, the ideological strategic culture of the Pakistan Army results in persistent revisionism. Zionts' alternative pathway of a *pragmatic elite ideology* is not germane to the Pakistan case. When Pakistan is under a notionally civilian governance regime, the army's preferences dominate in one or two ways. The civilian elites may share the strategic commitments of the army and thus continue the same policies as the army did when in power. Alternatively, if the civilians reject the army's strategic understanding and concomitant preferences, they may not wish to overturn the army's preferences for the purposes of staying in power. The outcomes are the same: revisionism persists. It is impossible to discern whether civilians pursue the army's preferred policies out of fear of the army, embrace of its strategic culture, or both.

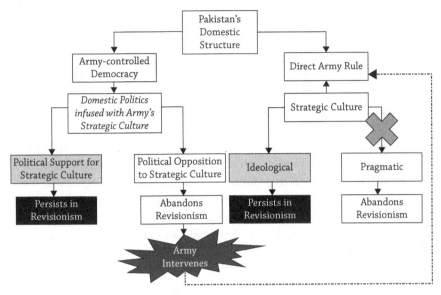

Figure 2.2 Domestic politics of Pakistan's persistent revisionism.

When civilians have reversed course on the army's preferred policies, the army has ousted them and resumed its preferred suite of policies. Lt. Gen. (Retd.) Kamal Matinuddin (1994) provides an account of this from 1971. Even though the Bengali and East Pakistan–based politician ,Sheikh Mujibur Rehman, and his party, the Awami League, swept the 1970 polls, the army refused to let him form the government. Twelve senior generals protested that if Mujib were in power he "would adopt a conciliatory attitude towards India, relegate Kashmir to the back-burner and direct funds from defence to economic development of East Pakistan" (156). The army's decision to disregard the results of Pakistan's general elections brought the country to the 1971 civil war in which India ultimately intervened to liberate East Pakistan. In 1988, Zia's prime minister Muhammad Khan Junejo signed the Geneva Accords to end hostilities in Afghanistan despite Zia's opposition to the terms of the agreement. As soon as Zia received the last tranche of US assistance, he sacked the government. In 1998, Prime Minister Sharif embarked on a major diplomatic overture to normalize relations with India. While Musharraf did not take over the government at that time, he simply undermined the peace initiative by planning what would become the spring 1999 Kargil War. When Sharif tried to rid himself of Musharraf in October 1999, Musharraf seized power. Either through cooptation or coercion, the preferences produced by the army's strategic culture dominate even during periods of civilian governance.

Strategic Culture Wars

Since the start of World War II, several waves of cultural theorists have argued for the importance of phenomena derived from historical or other ideational considerations to understand how states behave. As Alastair Johnston (1995b, 33) notes, much of this scholarship is consistent with the conclusions of Joseph Nye and Sean Lynn-Jones (1988), who argue that the strategic studies literature tends to be ethnocentrically American and that it demonstrates a concomitant neglect of other "national styles of strategy." Proponents of cultural explanations for state behavior contend that states facing otherwise similar conditions will adopt varying strategic preferences depending on their formative experiences. These strategic preferences are therefore influenced to varying degrees by cultural, political, philosophical, and even cognitive characteristics of the states' elites, if not the citizenry from which these elites emerge (Johnston 1995b; Desch 1998).

International relations scholars continue to debate the role culture plays in international politics (see, e.g., Chaudhuri 2009; Desch 1998; Duffield et al. 1999). Its proponents value the concept because they believe it helps explain the choices that states make to secure their national security objectives and may even inform how these objectives are formulated in the first place. While many scholars have deployed the concept to inform their empirical analyses, the intellectual underpinnings of "strategic culture" remain contested (see, e.g., Basrur 2001; Booth 1979; Chaudhuri 2009; Desch 1998; Farrell 2002; Foster 1992; Glenn 2009; Gray 1999; Johnston 1996, 1995a, 1995b; Kier 1995; Lantis and Charlton 2011; Lock 2010; Snyder 1977). Scholars disagree fundamentally about what strategic culture is and how it can be described. Some scholars contend that, even if one accepts the concept as intellectually justified, it is difficult to demonstrate that state behavior (the dependent variable) is causally influenced by strategic culture (the independent variable). Others note with concern that it is easy to overly essentialize the subject of inquiry and produce crude, if not racist or ethnocentric, caricatures (e.g., Larus 1979; Tanham 1992).

After robustly critiquing three generations of strategic culture theorists, Johnston (1995b) offers up a concept of strategic culture that has four key features. First, strategic culture must be observable and distinguishable from nonstrategic culture variables. Second, it must provide decision-makers with a "uniquely ordered set of strategic choices" (45) from which analysts can make predictions about state behavior. This set of ranked preferences must be consistent across the objects of analysis and even across time, and may be nonresponsive to noncultural variables (e.g., threat level, organization, technology).[12] Third, this strategic culture must be observed in strategic cultural objects (e.g., speeches, policy documents). Fourth, the transmission of this strategic culture must be traceable (46).

Johnston (1995b, 46) offers up a definition of strategic culture meeting these criteria that is derived from the work of Clifford Geertz (1973):

> Strategic culture is an integrated "system of symbols" (e.g., argumentation structures, languages, analogies, metaphors) which acts to establish pervasive and long-lasting strategic preferences by formulating concepts of the role and efficacy of military force in interstate political affairs, and by clothing these conception with such an aura of factuality that the strategic preferences seem uniquely realistic and efficacious.

Johnston's (1995b) system of symbols has two components. The first is the basic assumptions that both the institution in question and its stakeholders hold concerning the strategic environment. Do they view war as inevitable or aberrant? How do they view the nature of the adversary and the threat it poses? How efficacious do they judge the use of force to eliminate threats, and under what conditions do they believe the use of force is most likely to prevail? These assumptions about the strategic environment provide important shared information among key stakeholders and reduce uncertainty about the strategic environment. Importantly, they emerge from "deeply historical sources, not from the current environment" (46).

The second component of this system of symbols is an operational understanding of which means are the most efficacious for managing threats, contingent on how the institution understands its strategic environment. Johnston (1995a) argues that, while it is very difficult to relate strategic culture to specific behavioral choices in part because the evidentiary requirements are quite onerous, scholars should at least be able to demonstrate how strategic culture limits the options available to the institution in question (37).

How can we apply this system of symbols to the Pakistan Army? For purposes of this study, I first assembled a collection of defense writings—a sample—that was as comprehensive and specifiable as possible. These strategic cultural objects are described later in this chapter. I began systematically working through this sample, which included thousands of articles and dozens of books authored by senior officers, to understand how the Pakistan Army understands its conflict with India and other competitors and adversaries, how it appreciates the nature of these foes, and how it appraises the efficacy of the application of force or other means to manage the threat environment it faces. Several consistent and enduring themes emerged from this effort. First, the army understands Pakistan to be an insecure state born from an inherently unfair Partition process in 1947. For Pakistan, the business of Partition is unfinished. Second, the army believes that it inherited most of the threat frontiers managed by the British Raj but only a fraction of its resources. Third, the army believes that India is implacably opposed to the very existence of Pakistan and seeks to subjugate if not outright annihilate the state. This conviction was given further ballast by the 1971 war when India did in fact vivisect the young nation.

Fourth, the army is obsessed with various notions of strategic depth, whether geographical, territorial, or political. This concept of strategic depth has sometimes meant cultivating a physical space to place its military assets in the event of an Indian attack. Pakistan's territory lacks depth. Its main lines of control run parallel to the Indian border, and at several points along the main Karachi-Peshawar road it comes within 60 miles of either the international border with India or the Line of Control in Kashmir (Rizvi 2002). A few natural barriers, such as rivers and mountains, separate the two adversaries in the strategic planes of the Punjab. With the exception of the airfield in Quetta, there is no airfield farther than 150 miles from the Indian border. More often than this territorial concept, Pakistan has sought political strategic depth in Afghanistan. That is, the army has sought to cultivate a regime in Afghanistan that is favorably disposed toward Pakistan and that will deny India access to Afghanistan, from where it could harm Pakistan's interests (Rizvi 2002).

Where possible, I also sought to identify the second component in Johnston's (1995b) definition of strategic culture: namely, what are the more operational aspects of contending with this environment in light of how the army answers the previous questions? Distinguishing these elements is easier said than done. Nonetheless, I have identified several potential elements of this putative strategic culture and, most importantly, have traced the origins of the cultural and historical factors that shape the army's evaluation of the world in which it lives as well as the means it has cultivated to best manage that world. One such means is Islam, variously used. The army has cultivated Islam to contend with internal and external threats alike. Because the army has arrogated to itself the defense of Pakistan's ideology, which is essentially Islam, Pakistan's perceptions of its internal and external threats are inherently intertwined. The Pakistan Army believes that India seeks not only to undo Pakistan's territorial integrity but also to undermine the founding logic of the state and sow discord among Pakistan's varied ethnic and sectarian groups. As detailed herein, the label "Islam" is constant even if the content of that label have changed over time.

An equally enduring part of Pakistan's strategy to meet its security needs has been the cultivation of important partnerships with the United States, China, North Korea, and Saudi Arabia, among others. Pakistan has also invested heavily first in conventional defense assets and, from the late 1960s, also in nuclear assets, facilitated by its varied partnerships. From 1947 onward, Pakistan has used nonstate actors to wage proxy warfare and campaigns of terrorism in India and Afghanistan variously under the guise of *people's war, guerilla warfare,* or *jihad* (which some Pakistani writers alternatively spell *jehad*). Over time, Pakistan's military has masterfully used its nuclear deterrent to expand the scope of operations undertaken by nonstate actors on behalf of the state, confident that Pakistan's nuclear weapons will shield it from Indian or international retaliation.

The British handed down some of Pakistan's beliefs about its strategic environment and the tools available to manage them: for example, its management of its border areas with Afghanistan; its appreciation of martial races; and instrumentalization of religious and ethnic difference. However, these beliefs have been consistently reinforced as a consequence of Pakistan's efforts to apply those very tools. Other aspects of Pakistan's perceptions of its environment and enemies are of more recent vintage and stem from the Pakistan movement or from the processes of Partition.

This study presents considerable evidence that the Pakistan Army, based on its accumulating body of history and experiences, will prefer to challenge the territorial status quo and India's rise under virtually all circumstances. It will do so when possible in India, but when necessary it will do so by challenging India in the region—such as in Afghanistan. The tools that Pakistan has developed to do this include instrumentalizing religion at home and abroad, devising elaborate governance regimes within Pakistan to manage the western frontier, developing and supporting nonstate actors under its expanding nuclear umbrella, and forging rent-seeking relations with key external actors. Because the army defines defeat in terms of being unable to mount a challenge to India either territorially or politically, the army will prefer to take risks than to do nothing at all, which is synonymous with defeat.

Pakistan: An Army with a Country

Pakistanis and analysts of Pakistan have long remarked, with more truth than hyperbole, that while generally countries have armies, in Pakistan, the army has a country. This aphorism reflects the unfortunate history of Pakistan's floundering attempts at democratization. Brigadier (Retd.) Abdurrahman Siddiqi (1996, ii), detailing this phenomenon in his 1996 volume titled *The Military in Pakistan: Image and Reality*, observed the progressive subordination of Pakistan's "national identity and interest" to the "growing power of the military image." By way of explanation, he suggests that because "there is no other institution to rival the military in organization and discipline, above all, in its control of the instruments of violence, its image...reaches a point of predominance and power" (ibid.). Consequently, "A sort of Prussianism is born to produce an army with a nation in place of a nation with an army" (ibid.). Because the Pakistan Army is the largest and dominant service, *military dominated* in fact means *army dominated*, even though Pakistan does have an air force and a navy as well as an array of paramilitary organizations. Lt. Gen Chishti (1989, 65), who was a key general in the Zia coup of 1977 notes that successful *"coups d'état* in Pakistan have always been...led by the C-in-C Army or the COAS [Chief of Army Staff], and never a subordinate general or a junior officer...The Army generals would not do it, and it is beyond the capability of the Navy and the Airforce to do so."[13]

Pakistan's generals step in when they believe that the civilian order has failed disastrously and that their service to save the nation is required by virtue of their duty to the nation and because they believe that Pakistan's citizenry welcome the intervention. They are not entirely incorrect in their assessment that Pakistanis approve of the coup. Generally, Pakistanis have heaved sighs of relief when the generals oust the elected kleptocrats and install a technocracy, usually with the stated agenda of making Pakistan's system more suitable for democracy. Pakistan's encounters with military rule follow a similar pattern (International Crisis Group 1004, 2005, 2006a, 2007). The army chief seizes the government, suspends the constitution, issues a Provisional Constitutional Order (PCO), dismisses the parliament, and requires the Supreme Court to justify the coup under the principle of the doctrine of necessity (Wolf-Phillips 1979). The complicity of the Supreme Court is profoundly important. Justices who prefer to uphold their original oath to defend the constitution are simply replaced with justices who will acquiesce to the generals. Because the election commission draws from the superior judiciary, when elections are at last held they are conducted under the auspices of officials drawn from a highly compromised cadre of judges.

Perhaps reflecting the army's understanding of the democratic preferences of their citizenry, Pakistan's military leaders have all sought to govern with a patina of democracy, albeit under their control. Thus, within a few years of the coup the army chief, with the help of the intelligence agencies, cobbles together a "king's party," which draws from established mainstream political parties and new entrants seeking to take advantage of the military regime's patronage. In addition, the military uses its intelligence agencies to fashion an opposition of choice, usually composed of Islamist political parties. The Islamists become an important ally of the military government. Confident of an electable king's party and opposition of choice, the regime holds (inevitably flawed) elections that install the king's party in government. The ensuing pro-military parliament then enacts into law the various extraconstitutional orders issued by the army chief in his capacity as the president.

This is an interim move before the army regime collapses completely, partly due to the pressure from the military itself and partly due to the popular unrest and concomitant public distrust that develop toward the military government. The army retreats from formal power and permits a weak democratic restoration. In Pakistan, even though constitutionalism and democracy have never fully fructified, Pakistanis do not embrace military authoritarianism over long periods of time. The army is able to govern directly only for limited periods of time and only with the façade of democratic institutions. This is largely because the army fails to manage the state any better than the civilians it ousted and because army personnel themselves begin to resent the politicization of the force and missed promotions (and thus forced retirements) of senior generals arising from the army chief's refusal to leave his post. Eventually, the public demands a return to democracy—however imperfect or limited—and the army obliges in principle.

The army can be confident that democracy will remain under its thumb because Pakistan's military dictators have always left constitutional legacies that enable it to continue manipulating political affairs from the barracks. The army was hesitant to allow Benazir Bhutto to become prime minister after Zia's death. (Ms. Bhutto assumed leadership of the Pakistan People's Party [PPP] after Zia assassinated her father and founder of the party, Zulfiqar Ali Bhutto.) Nonetheless, the army was confident that it could keep her and her government in line due to a Zia-era constitutional measure: Article 58(2)(b) of the 1973 Constitution enacted with the Eighth Amendment. This provision allowed the president to dismiss the prime minister and the provincial chief ministers, dissolve the national and provincial assemblies, nominate judges to the superior judiciary, and appoint chiefs of the armed services. With the Eighth Amendment, Zia shifted the balance of power away from the position of the prime minister to that of the president. Throughout the 1990s, no parliament served out its term due to early dismissal by the president under 58(2)(b). This occurred with the connivance of the military (e.g., Bhutto's ouster in 1990 and Sharif's in 1993) and without (e.g., Bhutto's ouster in 1996 due to differences with President Farooq Leghari, also a member of the Ms. Bhutto's PPP). No civilian government could muster the two-thirds majority to repeal this amendment until 1997, when Sharif returned to power and jettisoned the odious 58(2)(b). Pakistan again returned to a parliamentary form of democracy, but the interregnum was brief: Musharraf restored 58(2)(b) when he seized the government in October 1999. It remained in place until the Eighteenth Amendment was passed in April 2010, which again returned Pakistan to a parliamentary democracy (Hoffman 2011; Jaffrelot 2002a; Shah 2003).

This antagonistic relationship between the military and the democratic parties is more reciprocal than may seem at first blush. When opposition political leaders request help with weakening their opponents, the military often obliges (Siddiqa 2007). As a consequence of this elaborate collusion between the military, politicians, judiciary, and bureaucracy, the first quasi-civilian government to serve out its entire five-year term since 1977 was elected under the auspices of Musharraf in October 2002. It should be noted that Musharraf had every incentive to keep this parliament in place as long as it more or less served his purposes. In June 2004, Musharraf dismissed Prime Minister Zafarullah Khan Jamali, who came into office following the October 2002 elections conducted under Musharraf's government. Musharraf replaced him with Shaukat Aziz, the American Citibank executive, who remained in that capacity until November 2007. In March 2013 when the previous PPP-led government stepped down to give way to a caretaker government and fresh elections in May, it was the first wholly civilian government to serve out its term and be replaced by a constitutionally elected new government.

It is a curious fact that, despite the generally democratic aspirations of the Pakistani people, the army has dominated the state since the early years of independence. Given the army's ability to bring down a civilian government through direct or indirect intervention, few politicians are willing to take on the army. Most prefer to defer to the military in exchange for the opportunity to remain in power (Haqqani 2005; Siddiqa 2007). Not only has the Pakistan Army directly and indirectly manipulated the domestic and foreign affairs of the state, but it also has had a preeminent role in shaping Pakistan's educational curricula, textbooks, and the publicly and privately owned media (Fair 2011c; Farooq 2012a, 2012b; Haqqani 2005; Kohari 2012; Sabri 2012; Yusuf 2011). Thus, the Pakistan Army is able to cultivate support for its strategic imperatives across a wide swath of Pakistan's diverse public.

Given the army's power to set Pakistan's foreign policy, as well as any domestic policy in which it is interested, it is reasonable to simplify Pakistan's strategic culture to that of the army. While some studies of strategic culture focus on the civilian decision-making institutions that shape a country's defense policy (Johnston 1995a, 1995b; Kier 1995; Snyder 1977), this effort focuses narrowly on the army. Critics may argue that this approach is overly reductionist and may counter that there have indeed been important periods in Pakistan's history when civilians took the initiative. One example of this is the democratically elected but highly autocratic government of Zulfiqar Ali Bhutto, who served as prime minister from 1973 to 1977 and as president and chief martial law administrator between 1971 and 1973. Bhutto was able to take advantage of the army's weakened position due to the national belief that it was responsible for the loss of East Pakistan. However, by 1978 the army was back in power (Siddiqa 2007). Another example is that of Prime Minister Muhammad Khan Junejo, appointed by Zia following the 1985 elections, which were held on a nonparty basis. Zia's amendments to Pakistan's constitution had weakened the prime minister's powers, bolstering his confidence that Junejo would be an easily controlled puppet. But Junejo infuriated Zia by demanding the end of martial law, refusing to let the parliament rubber-stamp Zia's various ordinances, and signing the Geneva Accords in April 1988, thus ending the conflict in Afghanistan without specifying who would govern Afghanistan after the Soviet departure. After having received the last tranche of assistance from the United States, in May 1988 Zia dissolved the parliament and dismissed Junejo (Haqqani 2005).

But notwithstanding these examples, the army has still dominated Pakistan's foreign policy (Schaffer and Schaffer 2011). Moreover, with the return of democracy following Zia's death in 1988 and Benazir Bhutto's election that same year, every prime minister has governed with the explicit understanding that the civilian government will not interfere in military or foreign policy. Prime ministers who reneged on this commitment have quickly found their governments dismissed (Khan 2012a; Shah 2004). Taken together, these facts justify speaking of Pakistan's strategic culture as identical with that of the army, at least to a first-order approximation.

Reproducing Culture: Recruitment in the Pakistan Army[14]

Pakistan's army is an all-volunteer force, with far more applicants for officer and other ranks than there are positions to fill. Like most militaries, "while [it is] composed of many, ever-changing individuals," the Pakistan Army has "distinct and enduring personalities of [its] own that govern much of [its] behavior" (Builder 1989, 3). Even though militaries are composed of individuals, one of their goals is to shape the behavior, comportment, and beliefs of the men (and in some cases women) in uniform. Like all militaries, the Pakistan Army does this by imposing recruitment standards, mandating consistent and regularized training at the country's military institutions for various levels of promotion and specialization, and constantly asserting selection pressure as enlisted men, noncommissioned officers, and officers come up for promotion. Krebs (2006), describing this general socialization process, explains that militaries may "socialize the rank and file and officers to national norms reflected in the military's manpower policy. Because the military is (often presumed to be) a 'total institution' and because soldiers generally serve during their 'impressionable years,' inductees may be nearly blank slates on which the military can inscribe values" (6). The Pakistan Army, like most modern armies, must bring together individuals of "various backgrounds in common cause and in a collaborative spirit, providing a setting seemingly well-suited to breaking down dividing lines based on race, ethnicity, religion or class" (7). As described throughout this volume (especially Chapter 4), the army sees itself as a site of nation formation, with soldiers and officers alike entering as Punjabis, Sindhis, Pakhtuns, or Baloch but becoming Pakistani.

Generally, enlisted personnel (also called *jawans* in Urdu, the national language of Pakistan, which translates as "young men") must have at least a tenth-grade education, be between 17 and 23 years of age, and meet a number of physical requirements. However, the army relaxes its educational and even physical standards in places where it hopes to expand recruitment. For example, in Balochistan, recruits with an eighth-grade education will be considered for all positions except as technicians, nurses, or military police. Recruits from Balochistan can be somewhat shorter as well, with a minimum height of 5 feet, 4 inches instead of 5 feet, 6 inches, among other relaxations of physical standards (Pakistan Army n.d.). While there are no recent, publicly available data for the recruitment of the enlisted ranks (*jawans*), Cohen (1984) found that they tended to come from throughout Pakistan but especially from remote districts with rural peasant backgrounds. These recruits are brought together at regimental training centers, which are the core of the army's training system. Some of these soldiers may be unaccustomed to bathrooms or latrines, fixed meals, or regular working hours. If necessary, before training commences recruits learn Urdu and receive supplementary primary education. All recruits learn a stylized version of Pakistan's history, and they are encouraged to "take pride in the fact that they are Muslims and part of a broader world community" (38; see also Schofield 2011).

Enlisted personnel train at a regimental center for 36 weeks, which is often a self-contained community, with its own hospitals, schools, recreational facilities, and housing. *Jawans* remain with their original regiment for much of their military career (typically eighteen years). Like most militaries, the Pakistan Army affords enlisted personnel numerous educational opportunities throughout their time in the service, and some enlisted men will eventually become noncommissioned officers (NCOs) or junior commissioned officers (JCOs). The latter serve as an important link between the enlisted personnel and the officers, who are often better educated and of higher socioeconomic status and who are increasingly likely to have urban roots (Fair 2012).

In contrast to the various regimental centers that serve to train *jawans*, the principal institution for training officers is the Pakistan Military Academy (PMA) at Kakul, in the town of Abbottabad in Khyber Pakhtunkhwa province—made famous when bin Laden was discovered in a safe house a short distance from the PMA. Admission to the PMA is very competitive. The Pakistan Army does not release public information about the number of applicants it receives, and scholarly estimates vary. Fair and Nawaz (2011) report that each year some 3,000 candidates apply for about 320 cadet places in each of two regular long courses at the PMA. Schofield (2011), however, claims that between 45,000 and 50,000 apply each year, of which the PMA accepts only 1,000.[15] Per her interview data, the PMA admits roughly 400 cadets for each of the two long courses, which begin in spring and fall. A few hundred others enter the PMA's one-year Technical Graduate Course as well as a six-month course that trains officers for the medical corps, education corps, judge advocate generals, and veterinarians, among other specialized fields. Personal biographical accounts of officers coming from the PMA (or, prior to Partition, Sandhurst or the Indian Military Academy) stress that they were called gentlemen cadets, which emphasizes that the entire program at the PMA stresses character development and the production of well-rounded, polished officers (ibid.).

The criteria for officer candidates are not particularly onerous. Aspirants must be single, hold at least an intermediate degree (i.e., 12 years of schooling), and be between 17 and 22 years of age. They must also obtain a score of at least 50 percent in their matriculation (tenth grade) or Fine Arts (FA), which one receives upon successfully completing twelfth grade exams (Pakistan Army n.d.). Applicants undergo initial testing and screening at eight regional selection and recruitment centers across the country, located at Rawalpindi, Lahore, and Multan (in the province of the Punjab); Hyderabad and Karachi (in the province of Sindh); Quetta (in the province of Balochistan); Peshawar (in the province of Khyber Pakhtunkhwa, formerly known as the North-West Frontier Province); and Gilgit (in the administrative area of Gilgit-Baltistan, previously known, with Pakistani Kashmir, as the Northern Areas). Those who meet the basic criteria next take an intelligence exam on which they must score at least 50 percent. (At various times, the Pakistan Army has relaxed standards for applicants from Sindh and Balochistan, provinces in which the army has had difficulty recruiting and in which educational standards are low.) If they score satisfactorily on the written exam, candidates undergo physical and medical tests and a preliminary interview at the recruitment centers (Pakistan Army n.d.).

Successful candidates continue on to screening at the Inter-Services/General Headquarters Selection and Review Board in Kohat or at satellite centers in Gujranwala (Punjab), Malir (Sindh), or Quetta (Balochistan). The screening process is arduous and includes four days of observation and testing to assess recruits' intelligence, psychological profile, leadership potential, and physical fitness. Successful candidates are then recommended for the PMA. Each year, Army General Headquarters determine the precise number of slots for the PMA using regimental reports of shortfalls. Officer selection is generally based on merit, with the exception of episodic efforts to enhance the prospects of cadets from provinces such as Sindh and Balochistan, which are considerably underrepresented in the officer corps (Fair and Nawaz 2011; Pakistan Army n.d.).

Gentlemen cadets come from all over the country as well as from every socioeconomic class. (Analysts of the Pakistan Army speculate, in the absence of hard evidence, that PMA cadets no longer come primarily from the upper middle class, as was once the case.) Some recruits may speak English well, while others have little English proficiency. The PMA aims to "bring them all up to the same cultural level" (Schofield 2011, 77). Apart from learning how to salute and march, PMA recruits—like their enlisted counterparts—are taught how to use a flush toilet, sit on the commode, care for their uniforms, perform physical exercise, and even use the proper dining etiquette (ibid.). After graduating from the two-year program, cadets are commissioned with the rank of second lieutenant (Fair and Nawaz 2011). Notably, the current recruitment procedures do not appear to differ markedly from those in the past, according to the 1976 account of Lt. Gen. Attiqur Rahman, a noted army historian who served as the martial law administrator of West Pakistan during Gen. Yahya Khan's military regime.[16]

The Pakistan Army, like other militaries, uses its selection process and criteria, its various educational and training institutions and opportunities, and regular evaluation for promotion to ensure cohesion and adherence to standards across the ranks of the force. South Asian Foreign Area Officers in the US Army as well as scholars of the Pakistan Army also note that in the Pakistan Army officers are also "judged on their personal behavior to a degree that is uncommon" in western armies.[17] Penetration by the military's values is likely to deepen as the period of service lengthens, in part because a soldier's professional trajectory depends on the military command's assessments of his performance. The Pakistan Army fosters an institutional body of knowledge by commissioning studies at the Command and Staff College, the National Defense University (previously National Defense College), and other training centers and through a massive body of military publications published either by the General Headquarters or through Inter-Services Public Relations, a military organization headed by a major general.

Methods and Sources of This Study

To illuminate the lineaments of the Pakistan Army's ostensible strategic culture, I explore six decades of the Pakistan Army's security discourse, through which the army articulates external dangers and "carve[s] out and maintain[s] a particular version of national identity for the state" (Nizamani 2000, 11). A fundamental assumption of this project is that these writings comprise an evolving *discourse* rather than a collection of prescriptions, descriptions, and assessments offered by disconnected authors at particular times. These essays reflect "expressions of particular interests and justifiers of a distinct regime of practices or truth" (ibid.). In this work, I use Nizamani's concept of *discourse analysis*, which he employed to understand the elite rhetoric surrounding nuclear weapons in India and Pakistan. Nizamani's notion of discourse draws on Foucault's earlier contention that "each society has its regime of truth, its 'general politics' of truth; that is, the types of discourse which it accepts and makes function as true; the mechanisms and instances which enable one to distinguish true and false statements; the means by which each is sanctioned; the techniques and procedures accorded value in the acquisition of truth; the status of those who are charged with saying what counts as true" (12). In Pakistan, as I have already discussed and will continue to demonstrate throughout this volume, the army has a privileged place in defining truth, determining how truth is described, and regulating who gets to articulate it. For most of Pakistan's existence as an independent state, the Pakistan Army has exercised its power to produce truth from its privileged position as the supreme manager of the state's affairs.

One of the ways the army has produced truth has been by exercising control over knowledge and information and developing, nurturing, and policing epistemic communities. Nizamani (2000), to explain the elite consensus in Pakistan and India on their nuclear weapons program, adopts this concept of epistemic communities from the work of Peter M. Haas (1992) and describes them as essentially networks of persons who are granted expertise on particular issues and who share fundamental worldviews or epistemes. As Haas notes, whereas some scholars associate "epistemic communities" with "scientific communities" in particular, in his formulation, they "need not be made up of scientists or of professionals applying the same methodology" (3). His conceptualization of epistemic community resembles Fleck's (1979) "thought collective" or a "sociological group with a common style of thinking" (3). Haas describes a number of other characteristics of epistemic communities: they share ways of knowing and patterns of reasoning and espouse a common "policy project drawing on shared values, shared causal beliefs, and the use of shared knowledge" (ibid.). Nizamani expands this concept of epistemic communities to include public intellectuals, media personalities, and retired and serving military and civilian personnel, who advance state preferences for nuclear weapons and build consensus for them among the citizens of the states of India and Pakistan.

With respect to the Pakistan Army, I argue that these epistemic communities are linked to the army through the creative activities of both active and retired military personnel who author personal memoirs, accounts of wars, treatises on Pakistan's history and policies, and essays for military journals or commercial publications such as *Pakistan Defence Journal* that are aimed at the military community. Many of these military-based commentators become public intellectuals and prominent voices in Pakistan's print, radio, and television media that help to shape Pakistani public opinion on a range of issues. When military officers retire, they are frequently granted senior leadership posts within private-sector enterprises but also government ministries. For example, during Musharraf's tenure, Lt. Gen. Javed Ashraf Qazi, who headed the Inter-Services Intelligence (ISI) between 1993 and 1995, served as Musharraf's communications minister (2000–2002) and then as education minister (2004–2007). When the country is under an army dispensation, the army dispatches numerous officers to run governmental offices. In 2008, when Gen. Ashfaq Kayani became the army chief, he ordered that army officers would be withdrawn from some 23 civil departments including the Ministry of Education, the Water and Power Development Authority, the National Accountability Bureau, and the National Highway Authority. This order did not affect retired officers who were so ensconced (Masood 2008). Retired and serving officers are also able to exert influence outside of Pakistan by participating in seminars throughout the world, sojourning at prominent think tanks and universities, and authoring books (recent examples include Khan 2012a, 2012b; Matinuddin 2009; Salik 2009; Walker 2006).

The military cultivates civilians including scholars, journalists, and analysts, providing them selective access to the institution and punishing them—either with physical harm (or the threat of it) to the author or her family members or simply with the denial of future access—should they produce knowledge that harms the interests of the army. Since access is perhaps the most valuable currency among those who wish to be and remain experts on the military, the army uses this implied transaction to produce sympathetic assessments of the armed forces and their actions and goals.[18] While it is easy to focus on the coercive ability of the army to shape and influence these epistemic communities, it should be noted that individuals who become part of them have agency and have personal and professional reasons to join them through either active consideration or passive acquiescence. However, remaining outside the circle of favored commentators itself imposes constraints on the ability to garner accurate and recent insights into the institution.

Pakistani media coverage of the military should also be read within the context of the army's management of knowledge about the institution and its role in managing security and domestic affairs of the state. While in recent years many commentators have praised Pakistan's press for its relative freedom, self-censorship is still very common, as is deference to the army's preferred narratives. The intelligence agencies' willingness to use lethal methods against intransigent journalists and other domestic critics has repeatedly earned Pakistan the dubious distinction of being one of the most dangerous places in the world for journalists (Committee to Protect Journalists 2011).

As Shuja Nawaz (2008a) explains, Pakistan's media was a willing participant in incorrect reporting on each of Pakistan's wars with India. Pakistan's media reassured Pakistanis that their military was succeeding up until the moment that the various ceasefires, and their terms, could no longer be concealed. Pakistan's media also depicted India as the aggressor, even when Pakistani actions clearly and directly precipitated the war. As I will show, Pakistan's defense journals also offer histories of these conflicts that are at odds with scholarly accounts of the same. Pakistani textbooks repeat the same highly stylized narratives (Sabri 2012).

Pakistan presents an example of how more than six decades of ossified historical inaccuracies and distortion can resist the sanitizing effect of the global information technology revolution and the resulting expansion of access to abundant—alas, low-quality—information. The endurance of these inaccurate accounts of Pakistan's history can be partly attributed to the prevalence of conspiracy theories as a means of framing and understanding events as well as Pakistan's relationships to those events. Weinbaum (1996) notes the reliance on conspiracy narratives in Pakistan and the resulting suspicions, which are "readily sustained in the absence of full, creditable information. [Conspiracy theories] offer disarmingly simple and not entirely implausible explanations, and no amount of evidence can refute them…. [The] more the evidence seems to disprove the theory, the deeper the conspiracy is conceived to be" (Weinbaum 1996, 649). A full exposition of the role of conspiracy theories in Pakistan is beyond the scope of this volume, but numerous scholars have explored this phenomenon, in Pakistan and elsewhere (see, e.g., Jamil 2011; Wood et al. 2012; Yusuf 2011).

In this volume I rely heavily on the Pakistan Army's professional publications, particularly those published either by the army's general headquarters or Inter

Services Public Relations (ISPR), which serves as the official publication clearinghouse for the armed forces. These official publications include *Pakistan Army Journal, Citadel* (the official publication of the Command and Staff College in Quetta), *Hilal* (an official ISPR publication), *Margalla Papers* (a key publication of the National Defence University and previously of the National Defence College), *Pakistan Defense Review, Defence Journal* (before it became a private entity), and *Pakistan Army Green Book*. Throughout this volume, I offer specific quotations from this literature either because the quote is exemplary of a particular genre of accounts or understanding of an event or concept or because the author of the quote in question has inordinate importance to the institution. For example, if the current army chief offers insights that are novel, I do not discount them because they do not echo views espoused earlier by other officers. If a particular view offered by a specific quote is not representative of the varied writings studied in this research, I note it as an exceptional offering. Thus, unless noted elsewhere, the specific pieces I cite here are representative of writings that dilate on particular themes I discuss or represent the views of seniormost leadership.

At times the essays in these volumes may strike the reader as being outright noncredible, such as India's posited commitment to destroying Pakistan, America's conniving to subjugate Pakistan, and even racist and xenophobic stereotypes perpetuated in their pages. However, it is important to note that these claims—however bizarre—are consistent across times, appear in numerous publications officially sanctioned by the army, and often, as in the case of the *Green Books*, are prefaced by the army chief himself. Thus, it would be imprudent to dismiss these writings. While these writings do not comprise doctrine per se, they represent an important body of literature in which the army presents to itself the way it understands the world in which it operates. (Unlike the US military, the Pakistan Army does not make public its various doctrinal documents.)

In addition to these official military publications, I also examine the memoirs of Pakistan's senior military leadership, the most recent being that of former Chief Pervez Musharraf. It should be noted that these memoirs are not always published with authorization from the army headquarters or ISPR. In some cases, the military officers have published their accounts to clear their name or to dissociate themselves from policies they found objectionable. In other cases, the officers believe that their life journey offers insights and lessons for Pakistanis generally. Even if these officers' memoirs are not always blessed by the military as an institution, they provide important insights into the military's strategic culture. I would be remiss if I did not mention that military history as a scholarly genre is virtually absent in Pakistan, despite its numerous conflicts in its relatively short existence. Even when officers discuss the varied wars in their autobiographies, their accounts read as personal essays about what they did and thought during the war in their private capacities as well as in their standing as men in uniform. These narratives rarely comprise critical historical accounts of the conflicts in question.

Matinuddin (1994) offers one reason for this lacuna of Pakistan military history. Speaking specifically about the 1971 war, he notes that there is little interest in writing about defeat. When a fellow officer suggested that he write about this war, Matinuddin at first demurred. He had little interest in expositing an ignominious defeat particularly because doing so would mean "treading on the toes" of senior colleagues with whom he developed personal friendships after retirement (17).[19]

I complement this documentary evidence with observations that I have made over more than 15 years of fieldwork in Pakistan, during which I have focused on civil–military affairs and related issues. However, unlike the aforementioned documents, interview subjects actively use interactions with foreigners to shape perceptions about the Pakistan Army and its objectives, needs, actions, and threat perceptions. Military personnel who are authorized to interact with foreigners generally know their briefs very well and do not deviate from script, which casts further aspersions on interview-derived data (Schaffer and Schaffer 2011). In contrast, military publications and officer memoirs reflect an evolving conversation within the institution and the epistemic community in which it is embedded and that it helps nurture. Because the professional defense publications are not intended for a readership beyond Pakistan's men—and occasionally women— in uniform, they offer the most accurate reflection of how the institution wants observers, both in and out of uniform, to view Pakistan's domestic and foreign affairs rather than an orchestrated effort to shape international perceptions. They reflect and perpetuate the culture and preferences of the army over time. These documents offer a pristine glimpse, untainted by a desire to influence external audiences, into how the army understands its strategic environment and what options are best to manage it.

These Pakistani professional military journals differ from US military publications in three important ways. First, during periods of war, US military journals devote significant space to topical discussions of contemporary battles, war-fighting strategies, and subjects that are salient to the conflict at hand (e.g., logistics, recruitment, coalition building, personnel). In contrast, Pakistan's journals are notable for the absence of such discussions. For example, even though Pakistan was embroiled in the so-called Afghan jihad throughout the decade of the 1980s, the journals are surprisingly silent on this conflict (with a few exceptions, discussed herein). Equally notable is the fact that many of the Pakistan Army journals have not discussed Pakistan's post-2001 operations in the tribal areas. This is peculiar because Pakistan has launched numerous campaigns in the tribal areas and even in settled areas such as Swat (Jones and Fair 2010a; Nawaz 2011; Tellis 2008). This reflects more generally what Schaffer and Schaffer (2011) note as a general institutional avoidance of self-criticism or efforts to derive lessons learned from past efforts.[20]

Second, when these journals do publish accounts of particular battles in wars, they are written as memoirs rather than as critical analyses. These essays tend to focus on the personal relationships that the author formed or the particular emotional experiences that the author underwent during the conflict. More often than not, these memoirs focus on battles in which Pakistan prevailed but within wars that Pakistan lost. This is most true of the 1971 war. Third, there is a persistent emphasis on religious themes, such as the nature of the Islamic warrior, the role of Islam in training, the importance of Islamic ideology for the army, and the salience of jihad. Pakistan's military journals frequently take as their subjects famous Quranic battles, such as the Battle of Badr. Ironically, the varied Quranic battles are discussed in more analytical detail in Pakistan's journals than are Pakistan's own wars with India. A comparable focus on religion in the Indian army (which shares a common heritage with the Pakistan Army) would be quite scandalous. It is difficult to fathom that any Indian military journal would present an appraisal of the Kurukshetra War, which features the Hindu god Vishnu and is described in the Hindu Vedic epic poem the *Mahabharata*. Judging by the frequency with which articles on such topics appear in Pakistan's professional publications, religion is clearly acceptable, and perhaps desirable, as a subject of discussion.

CHAPTER 3

Born an Insecure State

Many of the ways the Pakistan Army sees India and the rest of the world have been deeply shaped by the experience of Partition and the events that led up to Partition. Because the movement for Pakistan was based on Islam and the notion that Muslims and Hindus comprise separate nations, Islam became the ideology of the Pakistani state in a constructed opposition to "Hindu" India. The Pakistan Army, from the earliest days of independence until now, sees itself as the guarantor of both the ideological and territorial frontiers of the state. While some American analysts view the tenacity with which the Pakistan Army and Pakistanis more generally burden themselves with the weight of this fast-receding history, understanding the Pakistan Army and its strategic culture requires taking its experiences and its narratives of those experiences seriously. This is all the more important because Pakistanis—in and out of uniform—continue to identify the flawed process of Partition as the source of Pakistan's inherent insecurity vis-à-vis India and the region.

Pakistan's military histories, school textbooks, and popular cultural productions continue to rehearse the inherent inequities in the processes and personalities that begrudgingly acquiesced to Pakistan's independence. In this chapter, I chronicle the events of Partition as experienced by the Pakistan Army and the lasting security competition between India and Pakistan that is the noxious fruit of that complicated and bloodied process of untangling the Raj. Here, I briefly recount the history of the independence movement, the mobilization of communal politics, and the ultimate Partition of the subcontinent, with a particular focus on the impact of the division of the armed forces. I conclude with a discussion of the important legacies of this process, for the new state in general and its army in particular.

Cracking the Raj

By the end of World War II, decolonization of the Indian subcontinent appeared imminent. After two world wars, Britain was war-weary, and its exchequer was depleted. Colonial India was no longer a profitable concern, as it had become difficult to extract revenue from an increasingly noncompliant subject population. There was little domestic interest in reasserting the Raj, and the United States, along with much of the international community, was pushing for decolonization. In India itself, unrest was increasing, including via various civil disobedience movements and, beginning in 1946, a series of mutinies in the armed forces. Acquiescing to the inevitable, in early 1947, Britain announced that it would transfer power no later than June 1948. In the end, the British accelerated decolonization, announcing that Pakistan and India would emerge as independent states on August 14 and 15, 1947, respectively.

The British plan for Partition was hastily concocted and ill conceived. Populations in border areas, in anticipation of Partition, mobilized communal militias to undertake mass violence in hopes of cleansing their districts of minorities. The violence continued as millions of people made their way to their adopted homelands. Muslims were attacked by Sikhs and Hindus, while Sikhs and Hindus were attacked by Muslims. The violence was unprecedented in scope and scale: it included savage murders, rapes, abductions, mutilation of corpses, and other horrors. The British utterly failed to prevent the massive communal violence that seized the Punjab and Bengal because their energies were entirely focused on evacuating all British personnel from the subcontinent.[1] The two states that emerged from this bloodied birth "necessarily saw each other through the prism of the violence that had taken place and eyed each other warily across the expanses of the ruptured Punjab" (Khan 2007, 142).

Hundreds of thousands of people were killed in the communal violence that preceded and accompanied Partition. Some 12 million were displaced, becoming refugees in their adoptive countries. Partition, along with preceding events that made Partition unavoidable, bequeathed to both states notions of nationhood that were "carved out diametrically, in definition against each other" (Khan 2007, 9). Pakistan, as the smaller and seceding state, had comparatively fewer resources with which to confront these problems. Moreover, Pakistan had several grievances about its territorial award, grievances that persist today. Pakistan believes that it was deprived of key Muslim-majority areas in the Punjab as well as of the Muslim-majority princely state of Kashmir; thus, that Partition was and remains incomplete. As Tinker observed in 1977, while many countries remain embittered over lands lost, Pakistan is one of the few countries "with a sense of bitterness and grievance for territories that have never formed part of its polity" (695).

Imagining Pakistan

Pre-partition politics were largely dominated by the Indian National Congress (henceforth the Congress). By the early twentieth century, the Congress expanded its base and developed the machinery of a mass party.[2] With local units reaching down into the villages, it finally "attained the character of a popular party engaged in organizing millions in a struggle against the (British) Government and for the realization of self-government along democratic lines" (Greenberg 1942, 172). On December 31, 1929, the Congress, under the presidency of Jawaharlal Nehru, first hoisted the flag of an independent India and forthwith issued its demand for Purna Swaraj, or complete independence from the British. Despite various setbacks, such as the imprisonment of its leadership during World War II, the Congress not only maintained but also extended its presence throughout India (Greenberg 1942).

In 1906, the All India Muslim League (henceforth the Muslim League) was founded as a Muslim communal party. It would become the Congress' principal rival at the national level, and the fate of the subcontinent eventually rested in the outcome of their contest. The Congress Party and the Muslim League competed not only with each other but also with deeply entrenched provincial parties. As independence seemed ever more likely, the Muslim League leaders began to fear for the fate of South Asia's Muslim minority in a Hindu-dominated independent India governed by the Congress (Moore 1983). Their apprehensions became ever more acute as they perceived the Congress to have retrenched from its commitment to secular democratic principles (Riaz 2002). The Muslim League began considering the best options to secure Muslim communal interests; one of these was an independent Muslim state.

One of the important Muslim personalities was the philosopher and poet Muhammad Iqbal. Also known as Allama Iqbal, Pakistanis believe that he inspired the Pakistan movement, a point that can surely be debated with reference to his varied writings. Nonetheless, Iqbal's picture frequently appears alongside that of Mohammad Ali Jinnah in public spaces in Pakistan.[3] Jinnah is officially recognized in Pakistan as the founder of the nation and is referred to as Quaid-i-Azam (lit. "Great Leader," often shortened to "the Quaid"). But Pakistanis believe that Iqbal imagined Pakistan. Pakistan's first military dictator, Gen. Mohammad Ayub Khan (1960), described Iqbal as a philosopher who undertook a "careful study of human affairs, both East and West, and focused the light of his inquiry on the causes of economic and cultural subjugation to which the Muslims of India had been systematically subjected since their first abortive struggle for independence in 1857" (547). According to Ayub, he "spelt out the broad outlines of a plan under which the Muslims of India were led to aspire to an independent state in which they would be free to follow their own way of life" (ibid.).

While most Pakistanis herald Iqbal, along with Jinnah, as the forces behind an independent Pakistan, their positions were more complicated than contemporary perceptions suggest. For example, Jinnah had not always supported an independent Muslim state. In fact, until about 1946 he worked to preserve

Muslim interests within a united India. Before embracing a separate state for Muslims, Jinnah used Islam as "a cultural basis for an ideology of ethnic nationalism that was intended to mobilize the Muslim community in order to defend the 'minoritarian Muslims'" (Jaffrelot 2002c, 11; see also Jalal 1985; Moore 1983).

Iqbal's thinking was equally complicated. He was most certainly anxious about Muslims' future constitutional status as a minority in a future India, dominated by the Congress. He eventually concluded that the "only practical solution lay in Muslim self-government managed through territorial arrangement that involved the consolidation of 'a Northwest Muslim Indian State'" (Shaikh 2009, 25–26). This formulation of Muslim politics suggests a regional or even ethnic understanding derived principally from the Muslim communities that resided in the northwest of the Raj, rather than all of the Muslims in British India. Iqbal's solution called for an autonomous Muslim state "within the British empire or without" which further suggests that Iqbal first and foremost imagined "the immediate community of Muslims in the north-western provinces of India, comprising Punjab, the North-West Frontier Province, Sind and Balochistan" (26). This practical understanding of a Muslim political community that considered the importance of geography among other factors sat uneasily with his notion of a universal Muslim community (umma). More difficult to reconcile was Iqbal's discomfort with territorial Islam. In fact, he "harboured strong reservations about separate Muslim territorial statehood" because he understood it to be a "blow to communal solidarity" (33). Despite the complexity of Iqbal's imagination of India's Muslim communities and the best political order to best secure their interests (see Iqbal 2002), the Pakistan Army and other Pakistanis have tended to fetishize the "liberating thrust" of this vision that contributed to the ultimate emergence of Pakistan (Shaikh 2009). Pakistani defense publications frequently cite the poetry of Iqbal on a variety of themes ranging from the notions of faith and community to that of jihad.

The Muslim League was formed in 1906, but the appellation *Pakistan* (which translates literally as "Land of the Pure") came into use in 1933. The relatively late appearance of this moniker reflects the simple fact that, for much of the Muslim League's history, it focused not on communal separatism but rather on communal politics in which Muslims would receive affirmation of their difference and recognition of their nationhood (Moore 1983; Riaz 2002).[4] During a famous session of the Muslim League in Lahore in March 1940, Jinnah articulated his belief that Muslims and Hindus comprise separate nations, the so-called two-nation theory. According to Jinnah, "Islam and Hinduism are not religions in the strict sense of the word, but are; in fact, different and distinct social orders.... The Hindus and the Muslims belong to two different religious philosophies, social customs, and literatures.... To yoke together two such nations under a single State, one as a numerical minority and the other as a majority, must lead to growing discontent and the final destruction of any fabric that may be so built up for the government of such a state" (Jaffrelot 2002c, 12).

While this meeting is often described as witnessing the birth of the Muslim League's demand for Pakistan, in fact it saw no mention either of the word *Pakistan* or even of the necessary Partition of the subcontinent. Rather, the Muslim League simply called for all subsequent constitutional dispensations to be reconsidered in light of the claim that Indian Muslims constitute a nation. The Muslim League argued in vague terms that the Muslim-majority provinces of the northeast and northwest should "be grouped to constitute Independent States in which the constituent units.... [would] be autonomous and sovereign" (All India Muslim League Resolution of March 23, 1940, cited by Jalal 1990, 15). (The wording of this resolution would later be used by advocates of an independent Bangladesh, who argued that the resolution called for independent states, not a single independent state.)

Although the appeal of the notion of Pakistan continued to grow in both Muslim-minority and -majority provinces during World War II (1939–1945), the concept did not at first attract widespread support among Muslims. Muslims in the Muslim-majority provinces that would later become Pakistan had little interest in divisive rhetoric because they did not feel acutely threatened by Hindus and because many of their commercial and other interests depended on communal harmony. The idea of Pakistan resonated most intensely in the United Provinces,[5] where Muslims were a minority and thus most disquieted by Hindu numerical domination. These areas, however, remained within India (Jaffrelot 2002b, 2002c; Jalal 1990; Talbot 1980).

The Muslim League, by design, never clearly articulated what kind of state Pakistan would be (secular or Islamic), what modes of governance it would have, which territories it would occupy, or even what the basis of Pakistani citizenship would be. Jinnah deliberately preserved this ambiguity because he had opposing goals. He had to bolster support for the Muslim League and some notion of Pakistan at the national or all-India level. But the Muslim League and the two-nation theory had little appeal in the Muslim-majority provinces that would eventually become Pakistan. In areas like the Punjab, Sindh, and the North-West Frontier Province (NWFP, now known as Khyber Pakhtunkhwa), Jinnah had to forge political deals with provincial political elites to secure their support for the League as well as for some ill-defined notion of Pakistan (Talbot 1980). Conversely, the two-nation theory had the most appeal in north India's United Provinces where Muslims were a minority and feared Hindu dominance most acutely. Thus, Jinnah kept the idea of Pakistan vague as long as possible to cobble together a tentative coalition for the Muslim League and Pakistan made up of diverse constituencies with fundamentally different priorities and concerns (Jalal 1990).

The Congress, which hoped to inherit and govern a united India, opposed the idea of an independent Pakistan and strenuously fought the Muslim League.[6]

To secure the Muslim vote in the 1937 elections, Jinnah sought to link Muslim League concerns with those of Muslims in the critical Muslim-majority provinces, which would likely form the territory of any future Pakistan. With strong support in the Muslim-majority areas, and thus significant representation at the center, the league could safeguard the interests of Muslims in the Muslim-minority provinces. However, Muslims in the Muslim-majority areas had no reason to link their political futures to the Muslim League without concrete evidence that the British would in fact devolve sufficient power to make such an arrangement viable, and Jinnah's strategy failed to convince Muslims in either the Muslim-minority or -majority provinces. In the 1937 elections, the league won a meager 4.4 percent of the total Muslim vote. (This figure is all the more astonishing because, under the constitutional reforms of 1919, Muslims actually had separate electorates. Thus, Muslims could vote only for Muslim candidates.) Instead, most of the Muslim voters in the provinces voted for the candidates of provincial parties rather than of parties that had a presence at an all-India level. The Congress fared the best among the national parties, owing to its massive civil disobedience campaigns in the 1920s and early 1930s and its increasing grass-roots presence across India (Jalal 1990, Talbot 1990).[7]

By 1945, the Muslim League was still struggling to establish itself in the provincial legislatures. Muslim League governments in the North-West Frontier Province and Bengal had been ousted. The league had no support in the Punjab, which was perhaps the most important province from a strategic perspective. (Today, Pakistan's Punjab remains the "strategic heartland" of the country.) Only in Sindh did the league have a shred of support. With no political platform other than a demand for a nebulous Pakistan, Jinnah and the Muslim League fought to capture the Muslim vote in the 1945–1946 elections by negotiating deals with provincial power brokers. Stunningly, the league won all Muslim seats in the central assembly and captured three-quarters of the Muslim votes cast in elections for provincial assemblies. The league could finally legitimately claim to speak on behalf of South Asia's Muslims. Jinnah saw the vote as a referendum on the league's demand for a Pakistan "based on undivided Punjab and Bengal.... The stridently communal overtones of the League's election propaganda, specifically the role of local religious leaders in stirring Muslim passions, had embittered relations between communities beyond repair" (Jalal 1990, 20; see also Khan 2007).

The two-nation formula is not a forgotten part of Pakistan's distant history or merely part of a strategy for achieving an independent Pakistan. Despite the battering the concept has sustained virtually from the beginning, it persists as a strong ideological basis for contemporary Pakistan (Cohen 2004). The Pakistan Army's professional journals continue to refer to the two-nation theory as a critical element of the so-called ideology of Pakistan, of which the Pakistan Army is the defender. While the prominence of this concept is often attributed to the Islamizing efforts of Zia ul Haq, in fact its importance predates Zia. Khan (2006) explained in his biography that "[man's] greatest yearning is for an ideology for which he should be able to lay down his life....Such an ideology with us is obviously that of Islam. It was on that basis that we fought for and got Pakistan, but having got it, we failed to order our lives in accordance with it. The main reason is that we have failed to define that ideology in a simple and understandable form" (221–222). Khan devotes an entire chapter to laying out his understanding of Islam as an ideology of and for Pakistan and its role with respect to Pakistan's constitution (209–251). The evolution of this concept will be detailed at length in Chapter 4.

The Problem of the Princely States

In 1945, Clement Attlee's Labor party came into power in war-weary Britain and began to accelerate the end of British rule in India. On February 20, 1947, Prime Minister Attlee announced that Britain would transfer power by June 1948. However, the British ultimately expedited the timeline for departure. In June 1947, the British promulgated the Indian Independence Act of 1947, calling for the creation of two independent dominions, known as India and Pakistan, starting from August 15, 1947. It further elaborated that the "the territories of India shall be the territories under the sovereignty of His Majesty which, immediately before the appointed day, were included in British India except the territories which, under subsection (2) of this section, are to be the territories of Pakistan" (Indian Independence Act of 1947). The act stated that the territories of Pakistan would be composed of the provinces of East Bengal and West Punjab as well as the territories included in the province of Sind (as it was then known) and the chief commissioner's province of British Balochistan and, subject to a referendum, the territories of the North-West Frontier Province (Indian Independence Act of 1947).

These provisional territorial awards to India and Pakistan pertained only to those areas that were British territories. However, at the time of Partition, the South Asian subcontinent was home to two kinds of territories: those under British rule; and the more than 560 princely states, which were under the rule of Indian princes.[8] Taken together, the latter comprised nearly 41 percent of the Raj's territorial landmass, but they ranged widely in size; whereas the states of Kashmir and Hyderabad were the size of a large European country, others were mere fiefdoms, with no more than a dozen villages (Guha 2007; Ramusack 2003). While the rulers of these principalities exercised near autonomy in their internal affairs, they recognized the paramountcy of the Crown.[9] When the British tried to persuade them to join the All-India Federation, they demurred, opting for quasi-independence under the Crown in preference to the increasingly raucous provincial political environments (Copland 1991).

As independence loomed, Lord Mountbatten—at the urging of the Congress leadership—sought to persuade the princes to cast their lot with either India or Pakistan and to abandon any thoughts of independence. On July 25, 1947, Mountbatten addressed the Chamber of Princes,[10] telling his audience that the Indian Independence Act had released "the States from all of their obligations to the Crown" (Guha 2007, 41). However, while they were technically indepen-dent, he warned that chaos would "hit the States first" should they fail to act prudently (ibid.). Mountbatten advised them to join those states to which they were proximate, cautioning them that they "cannot run away from the Dominion Government which is your neighbor any more than you can run away from the subjects for whose welfare you are responsible" (ibid., 42). The princes were told that the instruments of accession to either state would cede their powers over defense and external affairs. But, Mountbatten reminded them, they would have access neither to modern weapons nor to the resources to post diplomats around the world. Thus, they would give up responsibility for those matters that they could not possibly manage while retaining internal authority (Guha 2007).

By August 15, almost all of the princely states had agreed to accede to one of the new countries, largely on terms similar to those they had previously rejected (Copland 1991). Three princely states remained problematic: Junagadh; Hyderabad; and Kashmir. Junagadh was on the Kathiawar peninsula in Western India, surrounded by India on three sides and with a long seacoast on the Arabian Sea. Even though the Muslim sovereign governed over a Hindu majority, he elected to join Pakistan and announced his intention to do so on August 14, 1947. Because Junagadh was a Hindu-majority area, Pakistan delayed responding to the request for weeks, finally accepting Junagadh's accession on September 13. Guha (2007, 50) suspects that Pakistan accepted this Hindu-dominated state in hopes of using it as a bargaining chip with India in the struggle for Kashmir. Soon there-after, under considerable pressure from India, the Nawab fled to Pakistan, leaving one of his courtiers to reverse course. The transfer of power to India took place on November 9, 1947. It should be noted that Junagadh is depicted as Pakistani terri-tory on many Pakistani maps.

The Nizam of Hyderabad, a Muslim sovereign who ruled over a Hindu-majority population of more than 16 million and a territory spanning more than 80,000 square miles, wanted to retain his independence after the British left. For the new Indian state, it was unthinkable that Hyderabad, which was nestled deep within Indian territory on the plateau of the Deccan, should remain independent. India began to apply coercive instruments, most notably an economic blockade intended to signal to the residents of Hyderabad that they were economically dependent on India but also to restrict the Nizam's ability to provide his army with weapons. As the threat of forceful annexation by India loomed, a militant organi-zation evolved. This organization, comprised of so-called *razakars* ("volunteers"), first assisted the Muslim political party, the Ittehad-ul-Muslimeen, in upholding Muslim interests in the state. However, they evolved into a serious militia with the intent of defending Hyderabad and Muslims against raids on Hyderabad's border or outright invasion. While the economic blockade was also intended to limit their ability to procure weapons, they were able to obtain them from the black market (Eagleton 1950). After Mountbatten resigned from post of governor general and the violence in Hyderabad deepened, the Indian government took decisive action to end the impasse. On September 13, 1948, it dispatched troops, which took full control of the state in fewer than four days. As with Junagadh, Pakistani maps still lay claim to Hyderabad, even though the prince never evinced any interest in joining Pakistan and fought tenaciously to remain independent.

Of the three problematic princely states, Kashmir proved the most enduring challenge: the conflict between India, Pakistan, and various Kashmiri groups over the state's disposition persists even today. With more than 84,471 square miles, the state of Kashmir was even larger than Hyderabad (Guha 2007) and was notable for the considerable heterogeneity of its 4 million thinly dispersed residents. Kashmir had five principal regions. Jammu, abutting the Punjab, had a slight Muslim majority (53 percent) before Partition. However, following a wave of panic sparked by Partition, many Muslims fled, leaving Jammu with a Hindu-majority population. The second major part of Kashmir was the so-called Valley of Kashmir. Unlike Jammu, it was dominated by Muslims. To the east of the valley was Ladakh, which bordered Tibet and was (and still is) populated largely by Buddhists. To the west were the territories of Gilgit and Baltistan. While Gilgit and Baltistan were Muslim majorities, their inhabitants were mostly Ismaili Shia, rather than Sunni Muslims, who dominated in the valley. These disparate regions came under the rule of a single sovereign, a member of a clan of Dogra Rajputs, in the mid-nineteenth century. What became known as "Jammu and Kashmir" shared borders with Tibet, China's Xinjiang region, and Afghanistan (Copland 1991; Guha 2007).

Kashmir's sovereign at the time of Partition was Maharaja Hari Singh. While he loathed the Congress party and feared that Nehru would carry out drastic land reforms, he was apprehensive about his future as a Hindu in the Muslim state of Pakistan. Like the Nizam of Hyderabad, he preferred independence. With Kashmir's accession in the balance, Lord Mountbatten actually counseled the maharaja not to act in haste but rather to ascertain the preferences of his diverse populace before committing. "With a view to keeping options open and under Jinnah's careful approach so as not to upset the delicate balance of accession of a number of key states that were still weighing their options... Pakistan signed a Standstill Agreement with the Maharaja of Kashmir" (Nawaz 2008b, 117). Singh's indecisiveness disquieted India's political leaders, who feared that the longer he dithered the more likely he would opt to remain independent or, worse, permit Pakistan to enter the state.

The disposition of Kashmir soon became entangled in a number of other crises, further complicating the maharaja's decision-making. After World War II, some 60,000 veterans from the area of Poonch in Western Jammu had returned from World War II and found that they were no longer subjects of the maharaja of Poonch but rather the maharaja of Kashmir. While the former was a benign ruler, the maharaja of Kashmir imposed onerous taxes. The Poonchis, who were also largely Muslim, did not take this well, and they were also incensed by the communal violence against Muslims in the Punjab and elsewhere. In August 1947, the Poonchis held a public meeting in which they demanded to join Pakistan. The maharaja dispatched his (Hindu) Dogra troops, who opened fire on the meeting. During the course of the ensuing rebellion, many Poonchis fled to Pakistan; one of them was Sardar Mohammed Ibrahim Khan, a lawyer and member of the state assembly. In Pakistan he met Colonel Akbar Khan of the Pakistan Army and sought his help in liberating Kashmir (Nawaz 2008b).

Khan was the director of weapons and equipment at General Headquarters in Rawalpindi. While Pakistan hardly had a surplus of weapons, he planned to condemn working weaponry and then use it to surreptitiously arm the rapidly growing group of men who wanted to fight to liberate Kashmir. Khan could not approach the Pakistan Army's chief (British General Sir Frank Messervy) with his scheme because Messervy may have communicated the plan with the Indian Army chief, Sir Robert McGregor Macdonald Lockhart, who was also British, or to Field Marshal Sir Claude John Eyre Auchinleck, the supreme commander of all British forces in India from Partition until early 1948. (As described herein, the Pakistan Army suffered from a severe officer shortage and was dependent on British officers who stayed on.) Thus, Khan worked clandestinely at first. Having found a way to arm the fighters, he next focused on organizing the men. As he could not employ active Pakistani military forces without the approval of the army chief, he planned to use ex-servicemen who had joined the Indian National Army (INA)[11] and who had not been reinducted after their release. Word of Khan's plan eventually reached Prime Minister Liaquat Ali Khan and Sardar Shaukat Hayat Khan, a minister in the Punjab government, but care was taken to ensure that Messervy was kept out of the loop.

Planning for operations in Kashmir became increasingly complex, with multiple centers of state and nonstate support at provincial and, increasingly, federal levels. Shaukat Hayat Khan, for example, wanted to use INA officers in the operations themselves rather than limit their role to training the militants. Col. Khan eventually approached the deputy director of military intelligence to get an assessment on the situation in Kashmir and arranged for another officer to collect and store the "condemned ammunition" on behalf of the fighters. Air Commodore Muhammad Khan Janjua, among others in the air force, offered help with logistics. Nevertheless, the plan was not well-conceived and continued to exclude higher army leadership as well as (officially) Jinnah. Shuja Nawaz (2008b), brother of a former Pakistani army chief and highly regarded American interlocutor for Pakistan's current military establishment, writes that the "higgledy piggledy" plan "for Kashmir was off to a less than illustrious start, with amateur enthusiasm leavened by some military fervor and a good deal of bickering among the principals" (121).

By October 1947, the Pakistan Army concluded that the maharaja's reluctance to join Pakistan meant that the Kashmir situation had reached a critical stage. However, it is not clear that the general headquarters of the Pakistan Army, which was operating far from the capital of Karachi and with a skeleton staff, had a well-thought-out strategy in place. After all, the prime minister continued to keep the British army officers, including the army chief, in the dark. Despite the many shortcomings of this approach, the prime minister ultimately approved the plan. Nawaz (2008b) suspects that, given the relationship between Prime Minister Liaquat Ali Khan and Jinnah, it is "unlikely that all of this planning was being done without Mr. Jinnah's tacit approval" although this remains a subject of debate in Pakistan (124).

Under Col. Akbar Khan's command (who took the nom de guerre of General Tariq), Khurshid Anwar (the commander of the Muslim League National Guards), with the assistance of the Kashmiri-born chief minister of the North-West Frontier Province, Khan Abdul Qayyum Khan, and Khwaja Rahim, the commissioner of Rawalpindi, put together a force of some 2,000 tribesmen from the North-West Frontier Province and tribal areas. They crossed into Kashmir through the Jhelum Valley early on October 23 (Nawaz 2008b). The following evening, Nehru informed Mountbatten that the tribesmen were arriving in Kashmir on military transports. With the tribesmen pouring into Kashmir, the maharaja sought India's help to repel them. India offered aid, but at the price of accession. Hari Singh signed the instrument on October 26, and Indian troops landed in Srinagar shortly thereafter.

By the time the Indian forces had reached Srinagar, Jinnah ordered General Douglas Gracey (the acting army chief while Messervy was on leave) to launch the Pakistan Army into Kashmir. Gracey refused, citing that he would have to secure Auchinleck's permission, which likely would have entailed the loss of British military officers in the Pakistan Army. Auchinleck issued stand-down instructions to all British officers in both militaries. By March, the Pakistan Army was fully in the fight, and the two sides waged a limited war for over a year until Nehru sought the United Nations' (UN's) intervention. After protracted negotiations, the UN succeeded in arranging a ceasefire, which came into effect on December 31, 1948. The ceasefire required Pakistan to withdraw its regular and irregular forces while it permitted India to maintain a minimum force for defensive purposes. Once these conditions were met, Kashmir's future was to be decided by plebiscite. Pakistan never withdrew, and the plebiscite never took place. The terms of the ceasefire left about three-fifths of Kashmir under Indian control, with the balance of the state going to Pakistan.

Oddly, many authors in Pakistan's military journals do not consider the 1947–1948 war to be a war at all, even though the army was clearly engaged and even though the operation had the backing of the senior most political leadership. While teaching undergraduates at the Lahore University for Management Sciences during summer 2010, I learned that those students, who came from throughout Pakistan, had never learned that a war took place in this period. Their textbooks had told them that the conflict in Kashmir was merely an extension of the violence of Partition. While this characterization is not entirely false, these students believed that the conflict involved only mujahideen and were incredulous that the army and civilian leadership were involved.

Untangling the Punjab

Pakistani concerns over the disposition of Kashmir unfolded in tandem with a growing conspiratorial understanding of how the departing British had constructed the new states of India and Pakistan. The Indian Independence Act called for the creation of two commissions: one to Partition the northern state of Punjab; and the other to Partition the eastern state of Bengal. The commissions were to be established after the Bengal and Punjab provincial assemblies voted to divide their provinces, which they did on June 20 and 23, 1947, respectively. The commissions, both chaired by Sir Cyril Radcliffe, were charged with dividing both Punjab and Bengal on "the basis of ascertaining contiguous majority areas of Muslims and non-Muslims. In doing so, [they would] also take into account other factors" (Ali 1967, 204–205). Radcliffe arrived in South Asia for the first time on July 8, 1947 (Y. Khan 2007; Wirsing 1998).

At Lord Mountbatten's urging, the various political leaders of erstwhile Pakistan and India—Jinnah and Nehru in particular—agreed to accept the boundary commission decisions before the awards were announced. The details of the Partition were not revealed until August 16, 1947, a day *after* the transfer of power. (Radcliffe himself left India on August 15 and never returned to South Asia.) While both sides accepted the outcome, as they had promised to do, they each had concerns about the manner in which the so-called Radcliffe line was drawn. India believed that it should have received some of the districts that were awarded to East Pakistan. Pakistan, however, was particularly unhappy with the award and thus was prone to seeing the commission's decision in conspiratorial terms, in part because India received seven Muslim-majority tehsils (an administration subdivision of a district, a larger administrative unit) in the Punjab (i.e., Gurdaspur, Batala, Ajnala, Jullundur, Nakodar, Ferozepur, and Zira) as well as a part of Kasur district. Pakistan, in contrast, did not receive a single non–Muslim-majority tehsil (i.e., one dominated by Sikhs or Hindus) (Ilahi 2003; Y. Khan 2007; Tinker 1977; Wirsing 1998).

The Pakistan that emerged in 1947 was thus not the country that Jinnah had imagined. Talbot (1988) remarked that the Pakistan created by the Radcliffe

Commission, which had awarded India the agricultural districts of East Punjab and West Bengal, was "moth-eaten" (388). In the minds of Pakistan's leaders, the emergent Kashmir impasse, a further blow to their hopes, was inextricably linked to the commission's division of the Punjab. The particular administrative unit of concern was Gurdaspur, which refers both to a district and the tehsil after which it was named. Pervaiz Iqbal Cheema (2000), an influential Pakistani scholar who has directed one of Pakistan's premier think tanks and who now holds a post at Pakistan's National Defence University, captures Pakistan's apprehensions about the division in Punjab using conspiratorial language to denounce the Gurdaspur award:

> The loss of Gurdaspur District was viewed as a major blow because it meant something much more than a simple award of additional territory to India. This was a decision which not only linked Kashmir to India but also facilitated India's forcible occupation of the State at a later stage. The district of Gurdaspur consisted of four tehsils (sub divisions), Gurdaspur, Batala, Shakergarh and Pathankot. Apart from Pathankot which had a Hindu majority, all the others were Muslim majority tehsils. If the principle of religious affinity had been applied then the whole district should have been awarded to Pakistan. Radcliffe decided to allot three-fourths of the district to India giving an access to the State of Jammu and Kashmir (8, citations omitted).

Pakistani skepticism about the commission's true affinities persists and has been fueled by the speculation of authors such as Lord William Birdwood, who served in the Indian Army for much of his career, including a term as commander in chief from 1925 to 1930. In 1952, Birdwood wrote that he did not believe that India would have fought a war in Kashmir had it not received Gurdaspur.[12]

The commission's decision to set aside its general guidance and award the two Muslim-majority tehsils to India could have been justified by legitimate apprehensions about the safety of Sikh and Hindu minorities who lived there as well as by concerns regarding the division of the canal waters (Ilahi 2003; Korbel 1954; Lamb 1967; Tinker 1977; Wirsing 1998). Indeed, no scholar has marshaled conclusive evidence to support Pakistan's contention that the British awarded Gurdaspur to India in an effort to influence the eventual territorial disposition of Kashmir (Ilahi 2003; Tinker 1977). Nonetheless, Pakistanis continue to harbor the belief that the award of Gurdaspur was meant to ensure that Kashmir had adequate land communication with India and thus to force the maharaja's hand (Ziegler 1985). In 2000, Cheema wrote that "the Radcliffe Award was indeed unjust and more political than judicial. The Award of two contiguous Muslim majority tehsils of Gurdaspur district to India not only deprived the Pakistanis [of] the legitimate Muslim majority areas but it also provided the valuable road and rail link from India to Kashmir" (23).

What is astonishing about this persistent claim is that it is so easily debunked with a closer examination of the Gurdaspur award itself. First, not all of Gurdaspur district went to India (Shakergarh went to Pakistan, becoming part of Sialkot district in the Punjab). Second, and most importantly, Pathankot had a Hindu majority and thus would have gone to India, even if the principle of communal majorities had been applied without consideration of other factors. As long as India had Pathankot it would have had access to Kashmir, as it was this tehsil that contained the important land links. The Indian railways ran to Pathankot, and Pathankot was the location of the bridge that spanned the Ravi River, the sole land route from India to Kashmir (Ilahi 2003).

The creation of the new states of Pakistan and India from the body of the Raj was accompanied by extensive violence and what is likely the largest migration in recent human history. While exact assessments of the number of displaced persons and the level of bloodshed do not exist, scholars believe that somewhere between 10 and 12 million people crossed the between India and Pakistan in 1947. Brass (2003, 75) says of the carnage:

> It has proven much more difficult to arrive at a consensus figure on the numbers of persons who died as a consequence of violence that occurred during the impending partition, the partition itself, and after it in the misery of the refugee camps. Estimates range from around 200,000 at the low end to a million and a half at the high end. A consensus figure of 500,000 is often used, but the sources that are most likely closer to the truth give figures that range between 200,000 and 360,000 dead.

These figures are all the more appalling given that these were "peacetime" deaths. Pakistan and India had not yet gone to war, although war over Kashmir was on the horizon (ibid.).

For a number of reasons, Bengal fared better than the Punjab during the crisis. First, Muslims were the predominant population in the eastern districts (which became East Pakistan), while Hindus dominated the western districts (which remained in India). Population distribution also made it obvious that Calcutta would go to India. Brass (2003, 78) remarks, "Once the decisions were made to partition the country as a whole, and Bengal as well, and once it was accepted that Calcutta could not be placed anywhere but in West Bengal, the demarcation of the boundaries between the two states was relatively simple. There was, therefore, no point in further large-scale violence nor any need or desire for cross-migrations that would be of no benefit to either side."

In contrast, partitioning the Punjab was far more complex, largely because it was home to an important third group: the Sikhs. While the Sikhs supported the

Partition of the Punjab, they did not want their communities or sacred sites to be separated by an international border. The boundary commission was to decide the boundary only on the basis of Muslim and non-Muslim populations, without reference to the Sikhs, who were classified as "non-Muslim." Although Sikh equities could be included in the "other considerations" that could inform an award, there was no way that the Punjab could be divided according to the location of Muslim populations without also separating Sikh communities and holy sites. The Sikhs, like the Muslims and Hindus, had a variety of militias and political organizations through which they could coordinate violence against religious minorities in their localities. Many of the gangs in the Punjab were even led by retired military personnel, who were widely available given the traditional British reliance upon the Punjab for recruitment (Brass 2003; Jha and Wilkinson 2012).

Breaking Up the Indian Army

With the looming division of the empire, the fate of the armed forces came into question. For some two centuries, the British had invested in the security of South Asia in an attempt to fend off Russian and other intruders. British security managers had hoped that this system could be perpetuated through some kind of joint defense arrangement that would preclude dividing up the armed forces. Field Marshal Claude Auchinleck, the commander in chief of the pre-independence Indian Army, was a strong proponent of keeping the armed forces undivided. He feared that a dismemberment of the army would cause such an administrative rupture that the subcontinent would be left defenseless (Cohen 1985; Jalal 1990; Rizvi 2000b). Jinnah, however, along with other Muslim League leaders, insisted on a separate military. Liaquat Ali Khan (a confidant of Jinnah and Pakistan's first prime minister) believed that without an army Pakistan "would 'collapse like a house of cards'" (Jalal 1990, 38). The Muslim League's leadership was more adamant about the division than were the Congress leaders because they feared that in any collective defense mechanism, Pakistan would be a junior partner, dependent on the Congress and India.

The British deferred a decision on dividing the army until it was unavoidable (Greenwood 1990). When it was finally determined that, by the time Pakistan and India became independent states (August 14 and 15, 1947, respectively), the new countries would have operational control of their own independent armed forces, the British had a mere 72 days to accomplish the gigantic task of dividing the army (Rizvi 2000b). On July 2, 1947, Auchinleck laid down the principles that would guide the reconstitution of the armed forces. The order had five main features. First, the armed forces of Pakistan and the Union of India would be predominantly composed of the two states' own subjects and would operate within their two separate territories and under their respective control. Second, administrative control of the armed forces would be unified at first, with a gradual devolution of authority to the two dominions as they became competent to manage their own forces (Khan 1963; Rizvi 2000b).

The reconstitution process also would unfold in two phases, the first of which was a crude division of the existing armed forces on a communal basis. This meant that the Muslim-majority units stationed outside of Pakistani territory would be moved to Pakistan, while similarly situated non-Muslim-majority units would be moved to India. In the second phase, every Indian officer and enlisted man would be classified as Muslim or non-Muslim and allowed to choose which state he would serve. There were some important restrictions on free choice, however. Muslims from the areas that would go to form Pakistan could not opt for India, and a non-Muslim in the territory that became India could not opt for Pakistan. There was no restriction on Muslims in India choosing Pakistan or non-Muslims in Pakistan going to India. A few non-Muslims opted to stay in Pakistan, and a comparatively greater number of Muslims chose to stay in India; however, the communal violence that marked Partition compelled some to reverse their decisions. British officers were encouraged to opt for service in either of the states, in the hope that their continued service would help ensure a successful reorganization (Jalal 1990, 39; Rizvi 2000b).

The British order also attempted to guarantee that there would be no fundamental change in the organization and nomenclature of formations, units, infrastructure, or the class composition of the units until after this process of division was complete. Finally, the three services' liabilities, such as pensions and annuities, up to August 14–15, 1947, would be borne by the new governments (Rizvi 2000b).

The colonial government established an armed forces reconstitution committee to execute this complicated task. This committee was to work in consultation with the Steering Committee, a subsidiary of the Partition Council, the body ultimately responsible for partitioning. The Armed Forces Reconstitution Committee was composed of the commander in chief, Auchinleck; the service chiefs of the air force and navy; the chiefs of the general staff; and one representative of each of the states in waiting. Phase 1, the division of the troops, was completed without much difficulty. By August 15, 1947, the future disposition of the various units had been decided (with the exception of troops that were either abroad at the time of Partition or serving in the Punjab Boundary Force, both of which were divided later). The ratio for division was 64:36 for India and Pakistan, excluding the Gurkhas, who were divided among the British and Indian armies. This was roughly the ratio of Muslims to Hindus in undivided India (Jalal 1990; Rizvi 2000b).

The assets of the Raj were also divided according to this ratio. As the smaller, succeeding state, Pakistan was always slated to receive substantially fewer personnel, stores, supplies, and facilities. However, Maj. General Fazul Muqeem

Khan (1963), who served in the army during Partition and who wrote *The Story of the Pakistan Army* while serving as the commandant of the Pakistan Military Academy, stated that in the end "Pakistan was forced by events to accept only one-third of the assets" (29). Pakistan inherited some 150,000 of the former Indian Army's 461,800 personnel. These men, including an officer corps, were distributed over 500 units of varying size, almost all of which were incompletely staffed (Cheema 2002; Cohen 1984). Pakistan received 6 armored regiments (compared with India's 14), 8 artillery regiments (compared with India's 40), and 8 infantry regiments (compared with India's 21) (Cohen 1984). As Khan (1963) wrote with dismay, the most immediate problem facing Pakistan was that India held the majority of the army stores, ordnance factories, and training institutions and thus stood to gain by delaying the division. Equally disconcerting for Pakistan's military and political leadership, Nehru insisted that India was the only successor state to British India and therefore that Pakistan should be treated as a dissident province seceding from the union (23). The beliefs that India never accepted the legitimacy of Pakistan and that Pakistan was deprived of its fair share of the Raj's assets are still articles of faith both within and beyond the Pakistan military.

Pakistan did get the short end of the stick in terms of the division of fixed assets, because the bulk of the infrastructure was located in India. All 16 working ordnance factories were located in India, and Pakistan failed to secure machinery for the two factories on its territory, which had not yet been completed. India eventually paid Pakistan compensation (Rs. 60 million) to set up an ordnance factory and a secure printing press (Rizvi 2000b). Training institutions became part of the state in which they were situated. For example, India retained the prized Indian Military Academy in Dehra Dun, among other important schools. Pakistan kept several army training centers, including the Staff College (Quetta, Balochistan) and the Royal Indian Service Corps (Kakul, Khyber Pakhtunkhwa), as well as several regimental training centers. Pakistan also inherited antiquated defense installations (British-era forts and outposts) in the Pakhtun areas and miscellaneous naval facilities at Karachi (Sindh) and Chittagong (East Pakistan) (Cohen 1984; Khan 1963).

Pakistan and India fought bitterly over the division of financial resources and military supplies. When India declined to give Pakistan its appropriate share (according to the division of assets called for by the partition plan), Pakistan had few means of redress because most of the stores were in areas that became part of India (Rizvi 2000b). The division and transfer of the movable assets became another early bone of contention. Again, Khan's (1963) words are both instructive and representative of Pakistan's defense writings on this subject:

> The division of manpower and units proceeded without any hitch or hindrance. Obviously there was nothing to be gained by objecting to such a division.... However, when the question of the division of real assets

and the sinews of the army—stores and factories—came up, the Indian attitude changed and all manner of difficulties began to appear, preventing or delaying the division. The Army sub-committee had unanimously recommended as early as the third week in August, that the ordnance stores must be divided in the proportion of thirty-six to Pakistan as against sixty-four to India, a proportion based on the communal percentage of strength of the army.... The Indian Deputy Prime Minister [after considerable stalling], who attended the Joint Defence Council for the Indian Union, maintained that the decision of the Partition Council only applied to personal equipment and not the stores. Auchinleck, who was responsible for drafting the principles of the division, which had been agreed upon by the Partition Council, was the best authority on the interpretation of these principles. He vehemently supported the Pakistan stand inside the Joint Defence Council and outside it. According to the Partition Council's decision, he was the trustee of all undivided stores and equipment; and [he] vigorously maintained the principle on which the AFRC was required to work was that all stores should be divided in proportion to the strength of the armies of both Dominions.... [Even though he opposed partition,] like a good soldier, he applied himself wholeheartedly to the impossible task of its division amicably (30–32).

India later conceded that it held up shipments of such assets, although it claimed that Pakistan owed India compensation for surplus stores that remained in Pakistani territory (Rizvi 2000b).

Not only did this experience with India cast a permanent shadow over Pakistan–India relations, but also some military writers have reduced the disagreement to religious stereotypes. A typical assessment of this type is afforded by the 1991 comments of Lt. Col. Anwar Shafiq Naqvi (1991) in the *Pakistan Army Journal*. He writes that while Pakistan tried to obtain as much as possible from the division of assets, India made equal efforts to deny Pakistan its fair share. What Pakistan did receive "was claimed, was broken and useless. Indian's negative attitude can be accessed from their Hindu mentality. Just after partition, India charged that Pakistan was making excessive and unrealistic demands" (27). As this volume demonstrates, this tendency to conflate India with *Hindu* is a common trope in Pakistani military writings, and writers rarely bother explaining what precisely they mean by such expressions as *Hindu mentality*. It is simply assumed that the readership will understand the negative connotations of such turns of phrase.

Pakistan encountered even greater difficulties than India in reconstituting and reorganizing the army because at the time of Partition there was not a single exclusively Muslim battalion. After the Indian Rebellion of 1857 (sometimes also called the First War for Indian Independence), for which the British blamed the Muslims, they resolved to prevent future such crises by eliminating all-Muslim units. Consequently, Pakistan did not receive any full-strength units because the non-Muslim soldiers had been removed. As Khan (1963) summed up the situation, Pakistan inherited a "paper army of 150,000 officers and men. It consisted of 508 units of various sizes. On August 14, 1947, 40 percent of these units were stationed outside Pakistan" (42). Indeed, many of the units with large Muslim representation were located in areas that would become part of India. Some of these Muslims could have chosen to move to Pakistan, but many remained in India. In contrast, virtually no Sikh or Hindu officers within Pakistan's territory elected to stay in the Pakistan Army. The Gurkhas were divided evenly between India and Britain (Cohen 1984).

To ameliorate this problem, Pakistan first amalgamated the regiments that had common recruiting areas, class composition, and traditions. The remaining gaps were filled with new recruits. It was therefore not uncommon to find regiments in which officers and soldiers had never met before and lacked the esprit de corps that the British regimental system sought to instill (Rizvi 2000b). Thus, the army focused on building morale and a sense of corporate cohesion. Equally problematic, it faced a dire shortage of officers, especially those with staff experience. The planned force size of approximately 150,000 required 4,000 officers, but only 2,500 were available. Pakistan had one major general, two brigadiers, and six colonels, but the army required 13 major generals, 40 brigadiers, and 52 colonels. While Pakistan needed 600 officers to fill engineer billets, only 100 were available, "most of them unqualified" (Cohen 1984, 7; see also Cheema 2002; Rizvi 2000a). To bridge the shortfall, the Pakistan Army retained 355 British officers already in Pakistan and recruited another 129 from England (Cohen 1984; Rizvi 2000a).

So the Pakistan Army—weak, poorly organized, and ill equipped—inherited most of the Raj's problematic frontiers "without the strategic depth of resources to withstand serious pressures from the northwest" (Cohen 1984, 7). Pakistan also was in a far more precarious financial situation than India. Pakistan had to fight tooth and nail to extract even modest foreign exchange reserves from India and needed to mint a new currency. Despite these institutional, financial, and geographic problems, from the first day of Pakistan's independence the new army was responsible for contending with the violence of Partition and the burgeoning refugee crisis. In addition, in connivance with provincial and national leaders and bureaucrats, the new army embroiled the country in its first war with India (Khan 1963; Nawaz 2008a; Rizvi 2000b).

In 1947, the Pakistan Army's commander in chief appointed a Nationalization Committee to study the best way of indigenizing the Pakistan armed forces by 1950. Competent officers from all the services obtained accelerated promotion, and many officers were recruited on an emergency or short-term basis. Several junior commissioned officers were promoted to the commissioned ranks. In addition, men who had been released from the army and were not employed in essential government service were asked to come back as enlisted personnel. The armed forces also issued a temporary stop-loss order. Finally, they instituted emergency commissions (generally in the case of specialist positions) and even began to accept qualified officers who had previously served in those princely states that opted for Pakistan (Rizvi 2000a). Pakistan also established new training institutions to replace those now located in India. The Pakistan Military Academy was set up in Kakul in January 1948 to replace the Indian Military Academy, the Air Force College for training pilots was resumed in Risalpur in fall 1947, and the navy established its own institutions (Cheema 2002).

Historical Legacies: A Punjabi Army

The culture and traditions of the contemporary Pakistan Army stem, in significant measure, from its colonial heritage. For example, one of the most important issues facing the Pakistan Army is the ostensible overrepresentation of Punjabis in the army. While the army recruits heavily from among Pakhtuns, the perception that the army is a "Punjabi-dominant" institution evokes great ire from non-Punjabi Pakistanis. Apprehensions that Pakistan has become "Punjabistan" are no doubt fueled by the Punjab's prominent role in Pakistani civilian politics but also the by domineering, extraconstitutional role that the army has played in Pakistan's governance. The belief that the army is a Punjabi army fuels distrust of the organization in places like Balochistan, where some locals see expanding army infrastructure as an effort to "colonize" it (A. Khan 2009). This perception that the army is Punjabi dominated reflects the population composition of Pakistan, where Punjabis are the largest ethnic group. However, it also is the result of a colonial concept of "martial races,"[13] which was inherited by the Pakistan Army (Talbot 2002). Despite the passage of some six decades since independence, the concept survives. However, it is of diminishing importance, and the Pakistan Army has made consistent efforts not only to address the perception that the army is Punjabi dominated but also to expand its catchment area (Fair and Nawaz 2011).

While Orientalist[14] scholarship has rightly derided the discourse of martial races as an example of British essentialism, the British appropriated and reified preexisting Indian categories of race, caste, religion, and other social groupings in complex ways (Titus 1998). By the late 1890s, a central concept in British recruitment was *class*, which embraced ethnicity as well as religion. The army organized companies and even regiments along class lines and recruited heavily from regions that produced martial races. The British believed that members of these races were natural fighters, as opposed to members of nonmartial races, who were seen as smaller, effeminate, and not suitable for military service. The so-called martial races included Punjabis (Sikhs, Hindus, and Muslims from contemporary East and West Punjab), Pakhtuns (from the North-West Frontier Province and the tribal areas), and the Gurkhas of Nepal. Conversely, the British considered South Indians and Bengalis to be nonmartial and sought to exclude them from military service. Because the British goal was to build an effective military to protect Britain's interests in the colonies rather than to develop an ethnically representative institution, they encouraged recruitment of members of martial races and discouraged the induction of members of nonmartial races (Peers 2008; Rizvi 2000a, 2000b).

The 1857 Indian Rebellion provided an additional impetus to this trend. First, the rebellion (sometimes also described as a mutiny) shook British (then the East India Company)[15] confidence in the troops, which were drawn from the rebellion-affected north-central areas.[16] The British were particularly unsure of Muslims from these areas because many British believed that Muslims had provoked the rebellion in an attempt to restore Muslim rule.[17] After the mutiny, the East India Company was abolished, and the crown ruled India directly. The British sought to avoid recruiting Muslims and others from the rebellion-affected areas and redoubled their focus on recruiting in the Punjab and what was then known as the North-West Frontier. Although those regions had been conquered much later than the north-central areas of India, their populations had supported the British during the rebellion. As an added safeguard, the British made sure that Muslims were not grouped together in all-Muslim units (while allowing all-Sikh and all-Hindu units) (Cohen 1984; Rizvi 2000a, 2000b).

After the rebellion, the British increasingly relied on the concept of martial races to identify those who ostensibly had the moral, mental, and physical faculties to become good, reliable soldiers. Lord Frederick Roberts, commander in chief of the Indian Army (1885–1893), systematically integrated the notion of martial races into military planning, remarking that apart from "Gurkhas, Dogras, Sikhs, the pick of Punjabi Mohammedans, Hindustanis of the Jat and Ranghur castes, and certain classes of Pathans, there were no native soldiers in our service whom we could venture with safety to place in the field against the Russians" (cited in Krebs 2005, 556). To this end, the army produced a number of handbooks meant to help familiarize British officers with the characteristics of the soldiers in their command. Lt. Gen. Sir George MacMunn penned a number of crude taxonomies of the peoples of India, underscoring his Orientalist obsessions with caste and race. The writings of such men as Roberts, MacMunn, and Rudyard Kipling contributed to the episteme of martial races (Peers 2008).

Apart from their beliefs about martial races, the British had geostrategic reasons for seeking to increase recruitment from the Frontier and the Punjab. These areas formed an invasion corridor long employed by marauders who entered South Asia from Central Asia. With the British continuing to concentrate on the

Russian threat, this region became an important component in the security architecture of the subcontinent.

In 1879, the Eden Commission "noted that the Punjab was 'the home of the most martial races of India'" and "'the nursery' of the best soldiers" (Rizvi 2000a, 38), and by 1909 the Government of India, reflecting on 50 years of Crown rule after the rebellion, could boast that the "proportion of soldiers drawn from unwarlike races has been greatly reduced while the proportion of Goorkha [*sic*] regiments and of soldiers from the martial races of northern India has been increased" (Peers 2008, 38). For the British, the concept of martial races retained its validity throughout their tenure in South Asia: during both World War I and World War II, Punjabi Muslims were the largest population within the Indian Army.

The composition of the Indian Army was also shaped by several important supply-side considerations stemming from the socioeconomic standing and the preferences of potential recruits. At the time the British entered the region, the Punjab peasantry was in difficult economic straits. Army service afforded peasants opportunities to augment family income and insulate themselves from the vicissitudes of a dependence on agriculture. Many of these recruits came from the Salt Range (Potwar, also spelled Potohar) regions of northern Punjab (e.g., the districts of Jhelum, Rawalpindi, and Attock) and areas adjoining the NWFP (Rizvi 2000a). The British encouraged peasant interest by granting recruits agricultural land in the Punjab as a reward for military service. When, in 1885, the British Indian government began developing a network of canals to irrigate the Punjab, these lands became even more productive and thus more attractive allurements into army service. This practice continued until independence, by which time nine Canal Colonies had been built on previously nonarable land. The British allotted plots within the Canal Colonies, especially to officers and former enlisted men, as rewards for service to the Raj. (Substantial land grants, for example, were made to World War I veterans.) Land grants were also made for purposes of breeding horses, camels, and other animals needed by the army. This practice made the army an extremely attractive profession for Punjabi peasants seeking to improve their socioeconomic standing (Rizvi 2000a).

During World War I, the British were compelled by the need for men to attempt to extend recruitment opportunities to nonmartial races; however, they largely failed to increase the diversity of their recruitment pool even though the areas populated by nonmartial races comprised some 70 percent of the empire's territory. Bengal, for example, which had nearly 45 million inhabitants, produced only 7,117 combat recruits. The Punjab, with a total population of only 20 million, yielded 349,689 recruits. In the Punjab, 1 of every 28 men was mobilized; in the rest of British India, only 1 of every 150 men was mobilized. In the late 1920s, the Punjab, the NWFP, and Nepal provided 84 percent of all troops in the British Indian Army. On average, the Central Provinces, Bihar, and Orissa provided only 500 troops, and Bengal and Assam produced none (Rizvi 2000a).

The British recruitment experience during World War II was similar: the Punjab and the NWFP produced 712,952 of India's 2,047,430 total recruits. In contrast, Bengal produced a mere 171,252 men. More than 60,000 Bengalis were recruited to pioneer (i.e., construction) units, but no regular Bengali Muslim unit was formed. Despite all efforts to effect change, the Punjab and the NWFP continued to dominate army recruitment until Pakistan's independence in 1947 (Rizvi 2000b). Given that the Japanese actually reached the Bengal border, the dearth of recruitment from that region is curious given the imminent nature of the threat.

This created a number of problems for the post-independence army. Pakistan's military was dominated by Punjabis and Pakhtuns from West Pakistan, while predominantly Bengali East Pakistan had virtually no representation in the military. In fact, East Pakistanis constituted less than 1 percent of the total strength of Pakistan's armed forces, a fact that exacerbated mounting ethnic and political tensions between Bengali East Pakistan and Punjabi- and Pakhtun-dominated West Pakistan. Nor was the army representative of the West itself: the Punjab and the NWFP continued to produce the majority of officers and cadres, while Sindh and Balochistan remained massively underrepresented. The districts of Kohat, Peshawar, Campbellpur (now Attock), Rawalpindi, Jhelum, and Gujarat were the main recruiting areas for the Pakistan Army, with nearly every second family having some kind of link to the military (Cohen 1984; Rizvi 2000, 2000b).

Liaquat Ali Khan, troubled by the extreme imbalance in recruitment, appointed a committee to investigate why the army had so few East Pakistanis (Bengalis) and to find ways of increasing its representativeness. Although neither the report nor its recommendations were made public, the army did take a number of steps to redress the situation. Most notably, it raised two battalions of a new East Bengal Regiment. Some of these recruits came from the pioneer units or were Muslims who had served in the Bihar Regiment of the pre-partition Indian Army, but others were junior commissioned officers from the Punjab Regiment. As Bengalis became available for service, the Punjabis were replaced. These regiments were unique in that they were exclusively Bengali. (No other regiments were made up of a single ethnic group.) In 1968–1969, the Army raised 10 more exclusively Bengali battalions and opened recruitment for all branches of the Pakistan military to East Pakistanis (Cohen 1984; Rizvi 2000b).

In 1959, General Ayub Khan reduced the physical standards for recruitment into the Army for East Pakistanis (but not West Pakistanis) in hopes of encouraging them to join the armed forces. Although the number of Bengalis serving in the army (as well as the air force and navy) did increase, Bengalis did not achieve a level of representation proportionate to their population distribution (nearly 50 percent of Pakistan's population).

The army resisted further expansion of Bengali representation, at least in part because many within army leadership harbored "considerable distaste for the quality of Bengali officers and other ranks" (Cohen 1984, 43). The maltreatment of Bengalis and their lack of representation within the military were festering problems that ultimately undermined the unity of Pakistan. Bengali officers and other ranks formed the backbone of the Bengali resistance during the civil war of 1971. Despite clear warnings that its policy of discriminating against Bengalis endangered the nation, the Pakistan Army remained ambivalent about "whether [Bengalis] should be taken into full partnership or completely eliminated" (ibid.).

The army's anti-Bengali preferences are well-known, but the lack of Bengalis in the army was not entirely driven by demand-side constraints (i.e., was not entirely the result of the army's official policies). Pakhtun tribesmen enthusiastically joined the army, as did others from West Pakistan. With the supply of willing recruits dwarfing the demand (for both officers and *jawans*), the army had its choice of candidates. Bengalis, who were often physically smaller (or least assumed to be by those in West Pakistan), could not compete with groups presumed to have greater martial prowess. If Pakistan had faced a shortage of recruits, perhaps the army and the other services would have been more interested in rethinking their facile assumptions about the connections between ethnicity and military competence. Furthermore, it is not clear whether Bengalis ever had the same level of interest in the military as those in West Pakistan. Certainly, the number of applications received from East Pakistan was a full order of magnitude smaller than those from West Pakistan (Rizvi 2000b).

Because the army ran the country for much of Pakistan's pre-civil war existence, the exclusion of Bengalis, who composed a majority of the population, was particularly problematic: arguably, the compulsion to have a nationally representative army is stronger when that army directly or indirectly governs a state. Thus, until 1971 the lack of representation of Bengalis was a preeminent concern. But similar doubts about the martial qualities of the Baloch and Sindhis have been in circulation since 1947. Both Balochistan and Sindh have hosted ethno-nationalist insurgencies of varying degrees of severity. In each case, Pakistan (under civilian and military leadership) pursued military responses, often using excessive force.

The loss of Bangladesh, the persistent complaints about Punjabi domination, and the underrepresentation of Sindhis and Baloch have occasioned concerns about the further disintegration of Pakistan (see Harrison 1980, 2009). Motivated by such concerns as well as by the need to become truly representative, the army has tried to expand the numbers of Baloch and Sindhis within its ranks, with modest success (Fair and Nawaz 2011).

Building a Modern Army

The Pakistan Army has grown steadily since 1947. During the 1950s, it received considerable assistance from Britain and the United States, with which it was variously allied through the Southeast Asian Treaty Organization (SEATO) and the Baghdad Pact—subsequently renamed the Central Treaty Organization (CENTO). This assistance enabled Pakistan to increase the size of the army, to expand the quantity and quality of its inventory, and to enlarge its cantonments to meet the growing Indian threat.[18] While the 1960s and 1970s were turbulent times for US–Pakistan ties, Pakistan again became closely allied with the United States in the 1980s, after the Soviet invasion of Afghanistan. Pakistan argued that US military assistance was required to expand the Pakistan Army, ostensibly because doing so would enable Pakistan to better counter the emerging Soviet threat, even though Pakistan sought this assistance to strengthen its position vis-à-vis India. Consequently, with US military and economic assistance, by 1989, the Pakistan Army had grown to nearly 450,000 and had become increasingly reliant upon US weapon systems.

Pakistan had to modify the army's organizational structure to keep step with its expanding size. At independence, all of the army's divisions were commanded directly from General Headquarters in Rawalpindi. As the army continued to grow and as it fought (and lost) several wars with India (in 1947, 1965, and 1971), its leadership realized the need to add additional corps headquarters. The first addition was I Corps (now located in Mangla), formed in 1957. The IV Corps (in Lahore) was formed in 1965. Several corps headquarters (II, V, X, and XI) were added in the 1970s, and several more (XII, XXX, and XXXI) were added during the 1980s. The current Pakistan Army is composed of nine corps and the Army Strategic Forces Command, created in 1999 to exercise control over Pakistan's nuclear arsenal and is thus treated as an equivalent to a corps command and has an end strength of 555,000 active-duty personnel (International Institute for Strategic Studies 2012). Table 3.1 lists each corps headquarters, its location, and the date on which it was founded.

Table 3.1 **Corps and Locations**

Corps	Headquarters	Date Formed
I	Mangla (Kashmir)	1957 (originally in Abbottabad)
II	Multan (Punjab)	1971
IV	Lahore (Punjab)	1965
V	Karachi (Sindh)	1975
X	Rawalpindi (Punjab)	1974
XI	Peshawar (NWFP)	1975
XII	Quetta (Balochistan)	1984/1985
XXX	Gujranwala (Punjab)	1986/1987
XXXI	Bahalwpur (Punjab)	1986/1987

Sources: Cloughley 2002; GlobalSecurity.org.

Implications for the Pakistan Army's Strategic Culture

The Pakistan Army that emerged in 1947 was substantially less well organized than was the Indian Army. It was plagued by an acute officer shortage, incomplete units, and a debilitating scarcity of Muslim officers with staff experience. This motivated the army to seek outside help to rebuild its military. The breakdown in trust that resulted from the contentious division of personnel and fixed and moveable assets, the gruesome communal violence that marred the cleavage of the new states, and the war of 1947–1948 all contributed to the emergence of an enduring Indian–Pakistani security competition that persists to this day.

As I will show in subsequent chapters, the way the army came into being continues to shape the way it sees itself and, equally important, India—which remains the perfidious foe seeking to undermine Pakistan's security, if not existence. The two-nation theory, which was the founding logic of independent Pakistan, remains one of the most important political concepts in Pakistan generally and is steadfastly defended by the army. This has imbued the army with an obligation to defend and instrumentalize Islam and to manage internal and security concerns.

While Partition no doubt has shaped the way Indians view Pakistan, with fewer assets and more problems, Pakistan bore the brunt of the crisis. India inherited a largely intact government structure with a national political party and regional (e.g., ethnic, caste, linguistic) groups that could aggregate interests. In contrast, British colonial parliamentary processes had not come to full maturity in the areas that became Pakistan due to the uneven "geography of early colonial parliamentarism" and the different schedules according to which different territories of the Raj were allowed to democratize (Jaffrelot 2002b, 253).[19] Pakistan was "moth-eaten," with two wings separated by the expanse of hostile India. Its government structure had to be built on the heterogeneous foundations of the provincial governments, which "had been suddenly deprived of their decision-making centre, Delhi, from which they had always taken their lead" (255). As Lord Mountbatten said of the administrative arrangements for the new states: "Administratively, it is the difference between putting up a permanent building, a nissen hut or a tent. As far as Pakistan is concerned we are putting up a tent. We can do no more" (1958, 70).

Pakistan felt cheated by Partition, from the Gurdaspur award to India's forceful annexation of Junagadh and Hyderabad and the ultimate injury of being denied Kashmir. For India and the Congress party, Partition was undesirable and even avoidable, but once it had occurred the process was complete. India was essentially a territorially satisfied state. For Pakistan, Partition is unfinished business (Tellis 1997). The Pakistan Army has never ceased trying to seize Kashmir, nor has it ever been able to fathom the notion of normalization with India. Neither the army nor the country's security managers have ever been able to see the events of Partition as Pakistan's past; rather, Partition permeates the present and casts a long shadow over the future.

CHAPTER 4

The Army's Defense of Pakistan's "Ideological Frontiers"

Because the Pakistan Army sees itself as securing Pakistan's ideological frontiers, Islam is an enduring feature of the army's strategic culture. However, the prominence of Islam within this organization disquiets policymakers, analysts, and scholars in the United States, Europe, and increasingly Pakistan.[1] Unfortunately, this speculation about the purported Islamization of the Pakistan Army rarely involves defining what the authors mean by *Islamization*.[2] This term is often associated with the potential for army personnel to support Islamist terrorism in the region and beyond as well as with deepening anti-Americanism within the army (Paris 2010). These apprehensions about the Pakistan Army take several forms. First, because it has relied on Islamists and Islamist militants to prosecute its interests in India and Afghanistan since 1947 and 1960, respectively (Haqqani 2005; Hussain 2005; Rubin 2002), some analysts and policymakers speculate that elements within the army may sympathize deeply with the worldview of its past and current clients.[3] Others suggest that a radical, rogue Islamist column may split off from the army. Such a rogue group, operating beyond the control of the army and intelligence agencies such as the Inter-Services Intelligence (ISI) directorate, Military Intelligence, and the Intelligence Bureau, might work to undermine the state or might support Islamist militancy (Roach 2013; Stratfor 2007). Third, some analysts fear that Islamist elements within the Pakistan Army may provide terrorists with nuclear materials, know-how, or perhaps even operational nuclear weapons (see, e.g., Grare 2006; Riedel 2011, 2012).[4] Thus, the mention of Pakistan in US—and, increasingly, Pakistani—policy discourse conjures up the horrific and intertwined specters of nuclear proliferation and international terrorism.

In this chapter, I posit that the fears of Islamization in the Pakistan Army are both under- and overstated. They are understated insofar as they posit that the Islamization of the army began in earnest only with Gen. Zia ul Haq's coup and the anti-Soviet jihad Afghanistan. The Pakistan Army was born an ideological army that specifically espoused Islam as its corporate ideology. Inheriting the

British practice of institutionalizing religion (as well as ethnicity) to serve corporate goals, the Pakistan Army quickly began to revise the traditions it inherited from the British Army to reflect the Islamic identity of the new state. Conventional wisdom about the Islamization of the army attributes a relative novelty to the phenomenon and thus underestimates its longevity. Yet these fears of the Pakistan Army and its alleged Islamization also *overstate* the problem because they lack an understanding of the reasons for which the army has embraced the concept of an ideological military, with Islam as the basis for that ideology. Moreover, these fears of Islamization derive from a widespread tendency to assume that deepening commitments to political Islam (Islamism) or increasing personal piety or even conservatism is coincident with a greater propensity to support Islamist militancy in Pakistan (Ahmed 2007).

In this chapter, I first delineate what Pakistanis typically mean when they refer to the *ideology of Pakistan*, which has been an elemental part of Pakistani identity from the state's earliest days. This ideology, which draws on the two-nation theory and on Islam as the founding logic of the Pakistani state, predates the emergence of Pakistan itself. Next, I detail the ways the Pakistan Army has championed Islamism as the ideology of Pakistan, beginning with the tenure of its first chief, Gen. Muhammad Ayub Khan, who went on to seize power in a bloodless coup in 1958. Third, I elaborate the ways the army has Islamized. Finally, drawing upon some six decades of army publications and officer memoirs, I explicate the specific ways the Pakistan Army instrumentalizes the ideology of Pakistan to unify the polity, to motivate the Pakistani people to support unending praetorianism and belligerence, and to bolster the troops' morale. I conclude with a discussion of some of the implications of the army's enduring espousal of Islam for the army itself as well as for regional and international security.

The Ideology of Pakistan

From the moment that Pakistan came into existence, its leadership was confronted with a serious existential problem. As I discuss in Chapter 3, most of the people who finally voted for the All India Muslim League and the nebulous notion of Pakistan in the 1946 elections did so without really understanding what Pakistan would be (Haqqani 2005). The entire campaign for Pakistan was based on a communal argument: Muslims comprise a separate nation from Hindus and could not live with dignity and security within a united India because they would be subjected to the tyranny of the Hindu majority and its antipathy toward Muslims. The communal violence that raged before, during, and after Partition seemed to prove the validity of this view. The concept gained even more salience as Indian political leaders either rejected the legitimacy of Pakistan's statehood outright or grudgingly accepted it out of fear that the British would otherwise refuse to transfer power or would provide the princely states with an option for independence, leaving India with a moth-eaten political geography of its own. In many cases, Indian leaders publicly stated their conviction that Pakistan would fail and be quickly absorbed into India (Cohen 2004; Haqqani 2005).

However, once Pakistan became independent these communal appeals became dangerous. Pakistan was home to many minorities, including Hindus, Parsees, Christians, and Sikhs. The divisive rhetoric that had pulled apart the subcontinent had to be tempered and subdued if Pakistan's varied peoples were to live harmoniously within a new nation with a precarious political geography and strained resources. However, Pakistan could not completely abandon the communal argument or its counterpart, the two-nation theory, divisive as they were, because they formed the basis of Pakistan's demand for Kashmir and provided the justification for the state's very existence. Despite the obvious tension between Pakistan's ideology and its reality, Pakistan's leadership retained the two-nation theory and the communal basis of identity as the founding logic of the state, hoping to manage the consequences of this choice (Nasr 2005).

As communal violence raged through out much of north India, Jinnah sought to stop the violence. In one of his late speeches, given before the August 11, 1947 meeting of Pakistan's Constituent Assembly, he declared:

> You are free, free to go to your temples; you are free to go to your mosques or any other places of worship in this state of Pakistan. You may belong to any religion or caste or creed that has nothing to do with the business of the state.... [You] will find that in the course of time Hindus would cease to be Hindus and Muslims would cease to be Muslims, not in the religious sense, because that is the personal faith of each individual, but in the political sense as citizens of Pakistan (Haqqani 2005, 12–13).[5]

The speech was and still is used by more secular Pakistanis as evidence that Jinnah wanted a Pakistan that was inclusive rather than an Islamic republic.

Unfortunately, when it came to Islam's role in Pakistan's constitution and governance structures, Jinnah often said different things to different audiences. This multiplicity of his statements has permitted proponents of one vision or another to selectively quote Jinnah's speeches in support of their position. Farzana Shaikh (2009) offers perhaps the best exposition of these multiple interpretations of Jinnah and his varied visions of the state. Jinnah, who died within a year of independence, never clarified his actual vision for Pakistan. This left his successors "divided, or confused, about whether to take their cue from his independence eve call to keep religion out of politics or to build on the religious sentiment generated during the political bargaining for Pakistan" (Haqqani 2005, 13). Pakistan's leaders had to find some way of managing the implicit contradiction between the clearly communal underpinnings of Pakistan and the imperatives of state consolidation and of securing a multiethnic and multireligious polity. They chose to do so by forming and promulgating what various civilian and military leaders alike have labeled a state ideology based on Islam.

There is a widespread belief that Zia ul Haq was responsible for promulgating this ideology, in part because Zia remains tightly associated with the project of Islamizing Pakistan. In reality, Pakistan's political and military leadership instrumentalized religion even before independence, and after 1947 it became the principal tool used to strengthen Pakistan's identity. Shortly after independence, the Islamists demanded an Islamic constitution. Their efforts, spearheaded by Maulana Shabbir Ahmed Usmani (a prominent Islamic scholar and supporter of the Pakistan movement), culminated in the Objectives Resolution, which Liaquat Ali Khan put before the first constituent assembly in March 1949. This vote was perhaps the first irreversible step in Pakistan's path to becoming an ideologically Islamic state. The resolution, which would become the preamble to the constitution, affirmed the commitment to making Pakistan an Islamic rather than a secular state, proclaiming that "whereas sovereignty over the entire universe belongs to Allah Almighty alone and the authority which He has delegated to the State of Pakistan, through its people for being exercised within the limits prescribed by Him is a sacred trust" (Objectives Resolution, n.d.). It also declared, over the objection of minority legislators, that "the principles of democracy, freedom, equality, tolerance and social justice as enunciated by Islam shall be fully observed. . . . the Muslims shall be enabled to order their lives in the individual and collective spheres in accordance with the teachings and requirements of Islam as set out in the Holy Quran and the Sunnah" (Objectives Resolution, n.d.; see also Shaikh 2009).[6]

Most members of the first constituent assembly, including Khan, were members of Pakistan's secular elite. Their decision to make Pakistan an Islamic state and to employ Islam as the ideology of the state (albeit vaguely defined and with a role that would vary widely over time) was motivated by the realization that Pakistan had multiple identities and that the adoption of Islam as the unifying ideology of the state offered the best prospect of dampening the divisive potential of Pakistan's diversity (Haqqani 2005).

After the loss of Bangladesh in the 1971 war, Prime Minister Zulfiqar Ali Bhutto sought to promote Islam as a unifying factor to mitigate fissiparous tendencies among the remaining ethnic groups in Pakistan. The government and Islamists alike viewed embracing Islamic ideals of governance and society as the most likely means of maintaining state cohesion. Bhutto deepened Pakistan's connections to the Arab states of the Persian Gulf, expanded the role of Arabic in the public school curriculum (creating new jobs for those who specialized in Islamic studies), declared Ahmediyas to be non-Muslims, outlawed drinking and gambling among other efforts to promote his notion of Islamic socialism, and enshrined Islamization within the 1973 constitution, which identified Pakistan as an Islamic state for the first time (Nasr 2001).[7] It should also be noted that Bhutto undertook these initiatives to bolster his sagging popularity and to co-opt Islamist groups who were rallying against him.

After he ousted Bhutto in 1977, Zia worked to enlarge the role of Sunni Islam within the Pakistani state and polity. His Islamization efforts were "regulative, punitive and extractive" (Rizvi 2000a, 170). Zia reconstituted the Council of Islamic Ideology to give conservative and orthodox ulema (Islamic scholars) more power to advise the government on Islamization, including efforts to review extant laws and bring them into greater conformity with the Quran and Sunnah. In 1979 Zia amended the constitution to establish a shariat bench within each of the four provincial high courts as well as an appellate bench in the Supreme Court. In 1980, he established a federal shariat court that replaced those benches (171). Also in 1979, Zia's government strengthened four laws (known as the Hudood Ordinances) that prescribed so-called Islamic punishments (amputation, stoning, and whipping) for sex-related crimes, possession of drugs and alcohol, and property theft, among other transgressions (ibid.; see also Nasr 2001). In addition, Zia introduced interest-free banking, based on an alternative system of profit and loss sharing, and a highly controversial compulsory Islamic tax, the zakat (Rizvi 2000a, 171–172). Shia Muslims, outraged by the imposition of zakat, which is contrary to their religious practice, mobilized to resist it. The tax became a flash point for sectarian strife in Pakistan, which was exacerbated by regional developments such as the Iranian Revolution, the Iran–Iraq War, and the anti-Soviet jihad.

Zia's government, with financial assistance from the Arab Persian Gulf states, founded a shariat faculty within Islamabad's Quaid-i-Azam University in late 1979 and later established a separate Islamic University in Islamabad. Zia, building on the efforts of Ayub and Yahya Khan, continued to instrumentalize school courses and syllabi, revising them to provide a greater emphasis on the ideology of Pakistan as well as on Islamic principles and teachings. Zia's government, like previous regimes, informed the electronic media and press that their content should reflect orthodox Islamic values. In addition, obligatory prayer breaks were imposed in government offices, and private-sector employers were encouraged to do the same (Nasr 2001; Rizvi 2000a, 171–172).

Zia came to depict Islamization as the justification for his imposition of martial law. This was an important contrast from Ayub, who viewed his takeover as revolutionary; Islam was a means of building the state Khan envisioned rather than of legitimizing his particular approach. Zia's reliance on Islamization intensified as his legitimacy began to wane. Public dissatisfaction with his regime deepened when he refused to hold promised elections and continued to enlarge his goals (Cohen 1984). Nonetheless, the effort to Islamize society was hindered by the military government's failure to appreciate the number and diversity of the Islamic schools of thought found in Pakistan, most of which had fundamental disagreements on various points of shariat. Thus, Zia's efforts to impose shariat devolved into an intersectarian struggle over which version would prevail.

In Pakistan, there are five main interpretative traditions of Islam (*masalik*, pl. of *maslak*). Besides the Shia maslak, which itself has multiple sects, there are four Sunni *masalik*: Barelvi; Deobandi; Ahl-e-Hadith; and Jamaat-e-Islami, which purports to be suprasectarian. Each maslak has its own definition of shariat and looks to different sources of legitimacy. Another hindrance to the emergence of a Pakistani Islamic orthodoxy was, and remains, the lack of a clerical hierarchy in Pakistan's Sunni tradition. This is an important contrast with Iran, to which Pakistan is often compared. Iranian Shia Islam has a defined hierarchy, which enabled a revolution led by a supreme leader and the subsequent consolidation of the clerical regime. The multiple interpretative traditions and lack of any clerical hierarchy diminish the likelihood of Pakistan emerging as a theocratic state along the lines of Iran.

Unfortunately, despite all of the ink that has been spilled about the purported Islamization of Pakistan, there is no way to empirically demonstrate the impacts of these various trends on Pakistanis' views on Islamism, militancy, or piety, much less on the views of personnel in the Pakistan Army in particular. Simply put, while historical accounts posit a slow but steady process of Islamization of Pakistani institutions—including the army and civil society—there are few means of validating these claims. This is because the existing surveys of Pakistani opinion that address Islamism (e.g., political Islam), piety, Islamist militancy, and related issues were all conducted after September 11, 2001. Thus, these data sources do not permit any assessment of trends prior to this date. In addition, many of the available surveys employ samples that are not representative of Pakistan's population distribution or that have very high nonresponse rates on sensitive questions. Equally problematic, none of these surveys permit identification of military households, much less specific officers, and none have the sample size that would allow analysis of the views of military households or officers, even if they included variables that indicated that either the respondent was an officer or whether the household included such persons (Fair et al. 2010; Shapiro and Fair 2009–2010).

The Army's Embrace of the Ideology of Pakistan

Cohen (2004) writes that it was in the 1960s that the army increasingly linked itself to the ideology of Pakistan and thrust itself into the role of protecting this ideology, the cornerstones of which were Islam and a perpetual hostility to India. Haqqani (2005) suggests that this process took place somewhat earlier, in the 1950s. Almost immediately after independence, "'Islamic Pakistan" was increasingly defined through the lens of "resistance to 'Hindu India'" (15). With respect to the army, Haqqani contends, in mild opposition to Cohen, that "notwithstanding the fact that the Pakistani army had been created out of the British Indian army and had inherited all the professional qualifications of its colonial predecessor, within the first few months of independence it was also moving in the direction of adopting an Islamic ideological coloring" (29).

But the Pakistan Army's adoption of a religious ideology did not, in fact, conflict with the British model. After all, the British had long made use of religion in their military training. The British emphasis on martial races compelled them to devise elaborate handbooks so that officers could identify and recruit such races, including the Punjabi Musalmans and the Sikhs. This attention to religion continued once the recruits had joined the force and resulted in the codifying of some forms of religious practice and even of appearance, such as the requirement that Sikhs keep their hair uncut and wear a turban (Gell 1996). The British also took care to enforce religious practice among its officer corps, as attested in some Pakistani officers' biographies. Brig. Mirza Hamid Hussain (2003), for example, who was a cadet at the Royal Indian Military College in Dehra Dun between 1926 and 1932, notes that the British required recruits to attend religious parades in uniform:

> We lined up according to our religious beliefs and marched to our respective places of worship. There were three main religions, that of the Sikhs, Hindus and Muslims and we fell in lie in accordance with the number of people in each religious group. This meant that if the Sikhs were more in number then they took the front position, the Hindus and Muslims, depending on whichever group was greater in numbers, occupied the second position....It always struck me as strange that the British who ran the school and were so very anxious to keep religion as far always as possible from the boys during the day, would in the evening, without fail, undertake this duty of separating us into various religious groups. This, I presume, was to impress upon us that we were really different people following different religions (72–73).

Given that the British made use of religion, it should not come as a surprise that the Pakistan Army continued to do so upon independence.

The army's role in defending Pakistan's ideological frontiers began with Mohammad Ayub Khan, who became the first Pakistani army chief on January 17, 1951, following the departure of Gen. Sir Douglas Gracey (Haqqani 2005). Britain's transitional role officially ended when Ayub became the chief of the army. In 1958 he took over the state in a bloodless coup, which he described as "the Revolution in October 1958" (M.A. Khan 2006, 15). There is no evidence that Ayub or his colleagues had any serious interest in Islamism or Islamic orthodoxy; in fact his autobiography, *Friends not Masters*, demonstrates contempt for religious leaders and evinces his desire for Pakistan to adopt a modern Islam, as detailed in his volume and elsewhere (M.A. Khan 1960, 2006).[8] Ayub sought to build a strong central government that would be reinforced by Islam.

Some of the strategies that Ayub employed included changing the significance of Pakistan's numerous Sufi shrines and the relevance of the saints attached to them. Ayub used these shrines as a means of modernization (Ewing 1983). He aimed to limit the direct participation of the ulema in politics but also to associate his government with Islam. He also wanted to restrict the role of the hereditary religious leaders (pirs) associated with Sufi shrines. Both the pirs and ulema had goals and views of Islam that were at odds with Ayub's own vision of a modern Muslim state. These pirs, along with their sometimes millions of followers, had long become embedded in politics. After all, they could easily deliver the vote banks of their followers.

Ayub sought to associate himself with this popular form of Islam to legitimize himself while also stripping the pirs of their political influence. To do so, he established the Department of Auqaf to oversee all of these shrines and other religious endowments. In this way he sought to demonstrate to the public that the government, rather than the pirs, was best equipped to take care of these shrines. Under Ayub, Auqaf sought to shift the activities of the shrines away from those rituals that directly involved the pirs and to remake the shrines as "centers of more general social welfare by building hospitals, schools, and other facilities for poor and rural people" (Ewing 1983, 261). Medical services were a particularly direct way of displacing pirs' traditional authority because they claimed spiritual powers of healing. Ayub's government also used the shrines to host agricultural and industrial exhibitions during Urs (lit. wedding) celebrations (ibid.) of the death of a saint and his union with his beloved god. Despite Ayub's efforts, the pirs remain an important political actor in Pakistan as evidenced by the many contemporary politicians who are hereditary spiritual leaders associated with shrines.

Under Ayub the army arrogated to itself the task of protecting Pakistan's ideological as well as physical frontiers. In a 1960 article for *Foreign Affairs*, Ayub reiterates his support for Pakistan's ideology and seeks to define it. In offering his definition, he draws heavily on the famed Pakistani Islamist political philosopher and poet Dr. Mohammad Iqbal:

> Pakistan was ... almost losing its ideology in the very act of trying to fulfill it .... Iqbal, one of the main creators of our ideology, had taken pains to define it in very clear terms: "In Islam the spiritual and the temporal are not two distinct domains and the nature of an act, however secular in its import, is determined by the attitude of mind with which the agent does it. It is the invisible mental background of the act which ultimately determines its character. An act is temporal or profane if it is done in a

spirit of detachment from the infinite complexity of life behind it. It is spiritual if it is inspired by that complexity.... The State from the Islamic standpoint is an endeavor to transform these ideals into space-time forces, an aspiration to realize them in a definite human organization." It is this sort of human organization which Pakistan aspires to become and *one of my endeavors is to clear at least a part of the way by liberating the basic concept of our ideology from the dust of vagueness and ambiguities it has accumulated over the years* (Khan 1960, 547–548, emphasis added).

The tenor and content of the article demonstrate the extent to which Ayub, his secular credentials notwithstanding, was willing to mobilize Islam in the name of protecting the nation.

The same article also attests to Ayub's immodest goals. He believed that his "revolution" could resolve Pakistan's foundational contradictions:

[Until the] advent of Pakistan, none of us was in fact a Pakistani, for the simple reason that there was no territorial entity bearing that name.... Prior to 1947, our nationalism was based more on an idea than on any territorial definition. Till then, ideologically we were Muslims; territorially we happened to be Indians; and parochially we were a con- glomeration of at least eleven smaller, provincial loyalties. But when sud- denly Pakistan emerged as a reality, we who had got together from every nook and corner of the vast sub-continent of India were faced with the task of transforming all our traditional, territorial and parochial loyalties into one great loyalty for the new state of Pakistan (Khan 1960, 549).

It is clear from both Ayub's autobiography and the *Foreign Affairs* essay that among the key elements of his conceptualization both of the ideology of Pakistan and of Pakistani nationalism were "Pan-Islamic aspirations and fear of Hindu and Indian domination" (Haqqani 2005, 42). In *Friends not Masters* he argues that the cause of Pakistan's most significant problems is India's "inability to reconcile herself to our existence as a sovereign independent State. The Indian attitude can only be explained in pathological terms. The Indian leaders have a deep hatred for the Muslims.... From the beginning, India was determined to make things difficult for us" (M.A. Khan 2006, 135).

Later in the same volume, Ayub, describing India's posited hegemonic impulses, its implacable hostility to Pakistan, and the intolerance of the Hindu priestly caste, the Brahmins, contends:

India was not content with her present sphere of influence and she knew that Pakistan had the will and the capacity to frustrate her expansionist designs. She wanted to browbeat us into subservience. All we wanted was to live as equal and honourable neighbors, but to that India would never agree. It was Brahmin chauvinism and arrogance that had forced us to seek a homeland of our own where we could order our life according to our thinking and faith.... There was [a] fundamental opposition between the ideologies of India and Pakistan (M.A. Khan 2006, 194–195).

Ayub's writings evince a belief that, should Pakistan's ideology fail, Pakistan would also fail. To ensure the success of this ideology, and thus of Pakistan, then, his government had to actively promote it and secure its legitimacy within Pakistan. This required the government to mobilize the same kinds of tools other states employ to socialize their citizens, such as public school curricula, print media, radio, and television. Ayub's government used these instruments to restrict public debate about the nature of the Pakistani state and its ideology. Under Ayub, "Pakistan began the process of official myth-creation in earnest. A large central bureaucracy was created to manufacture an ideology for Pakistan, one that glorified the army as the state's key institution" (Cohen 2004, 67).

There were several dimensions to this effort. While the remainder of this chapter focuses on how the military formulated and instrumentalized the so-called ideology of Pakistan, it is important to note that Ayub's government engaged the entire apparatus of the state to consolidate and protect Pakistan's ideology. Pakistan's educational system became an obvious tool of Ayub's government, and it remains an important means of propagating and protecting the ideology of the state. During his tenure, Ayub laid the foundations of Pakistan's current national educational system. His government undertook a massive review of educational policy, the results of which were compiled in 1959 in the Sharif Commission report. Reflecting Ayub's revolutionary mission, the commission's recommendations were aimed at developing a national consciousness along the lines of Ayub's ideology (Saigol 2003).

The Sharif Commission report had two overarching goals: achieving national integration and homogenization; and modernizing Pakistan's economy and society. "Consistent with the premise of the two-nation theory," the commission invoked religion "for the purpose of national integration. Since religion seemed to be the only common thread tying the different regions to each other, it was deployed as a strategy for national unification" (Saigol 2003, 5–6). The report also established a textbook board, whose primary task has since been to ensure that the country's textbooks align with the government's policies (Lall 2008). As has been described in depth elsewhere (see, e.g., Ahmed 2004; Aziz 1998; Lall 2008; Nayyar and Salim 2003), this curriculum offered—and continues to offer—deeply problematic histories of Islam in the region and xenophobic characterizations of India and Hindus and has over time come to emphasize Sunni Islam, to the exclusion of other Muslims and non-Muslims. Both "curricula and textbooks were standardized, presenting a version of history that linked Pakistan's emergence to Islam's arrival in the subcontinent instead.... Muslim conquerors were glorified, Hindu-Muslim relations were painted as intrinsically hostile" (Haqqani 2005, 40).

Although Ayub's government focused on the educational sector, he also mobilized other state apparatuses. The Ministry of Information and Bureau of National Reconstruction ensured that radio, television, magazines, books, newspapers, and films reflected the same message as the school system. By doing so, Ayub's regime was able to disseminate his ideology among adults, who were outside the direct reach of the school system (Cohen 2004; Haqqani 2005).

While Ayub may have been the first army chief to advocate a role for the Pakistan Army in defending Pakistan's ideological as well as physical frontiers, he was not the last. Zia contended that the "preservation of [the] ideology and the Islamic character of the country was.... as important as the security of the country's geographic boundaries" (Rizvi 2000b, 256). Equally noteworthy is the wording of the referendum on his rule that Zia put before the Pakistani electorate. Voters were asked whether they:

> endorse the process initiated by General Muhammad Ziaul Haq, the President of Pakistan, for bringing the laws of Pakistan in conformity with the injunctions of Islam as laid down in the Holy Qur'an and Sunnah of the Holy Prophet (Peace be upon him) and for the preservation of the Ideology of Pakistan, for the continuation and consolidation of that process and for the smooth and orderly transfer of power to the elected representatives of the people, and in case of answer "Yes," General Muhammad Ziaul Haq shall be deemed to have been duly elected President of Pakistan for a term of five years from the day of the first meeting of the Houses of Parliament in joint sitting (Pakistan Supreme Court, 2002).

Zia's approach to managing Islam, however, differed sharply from that of Ayub. Whereas Ayub sought to co-opt Sufi shrines and circumscribe the power of the pirs associated with them while limiting the political inputs of the ulema, Zia did not feel the need to associate his regime with Sufi Islam. During his period, he increased the direct participation of the ulema parties and involved them in the functions of the state. Whereas Ayub reappropriated the Urs festival of the saint associated with the shrine to promote modernizing programs, Zia gave these events considerably less promotion. (Note that Z. A. Bhutto adopted a very similar strategy to shrine management as Ayub before him.) While Zia was associated with attempting to reinstate "the original Islamic social order that prevailed at the time of the Prophet Mohammad," his government did not entirely disavow

Sufi saints and shrines (Ewing 1983, 263), but instead redeployed the identity of saints as models of piety. Zia continued the policy initiated by Ayub of turning "shrines into multifunctional religious and social welfare centers administered by the Auqaf Department," which represented the state (264).

President Gen. Pervez Musharraf, despite the praise he received for his ostensible personal secularism, also made use of Islam during his tenure. As with Zia's government, the ulema figured prominently. The bloc of Islamist parties, the Muttahida Majlis-e-Amal (MMA), constituted the opposition party of choice during his tenure at the center. The MMA formed the provincial government in the North-West Frontier Province, since renamed Khyber Pakhtunkhwa, and formed a coalition with Musharraf's party, the Pakistan Muslim League (Quaid-i-Azam Group) (PML-Q), in Balochistan. In his famed speech as army chief on September 19, 2001, Musharraf explained to Pakistan's citizens why he had agreed to support the United States in its war efforts in Afghanistan; he made ample reference to Islam. It is instructive to reproduce parts of this speech to understand the ways he mobilized Islam as the cornerstone of the state:

> Our forces are on full alert and ready for a do or die mission. In this situation if we make the wrong decisions it can be very bad for us. Our critical concerns are our sovereignty, second our economy, third our strategic assets (nuclear and missiles), and forth [*sic*] our Kashmir cause. All four will be harmed if we make the wrong decision. When we make these decisions they must be according to Islam.... It's not a question of bravery or cowardice. But bravery without thinking is stupidity. Allah has said that he who has 'hikmat' has a huge blessing. We have to save our interests. Pakistan comes first, everything else is secondary.... Some 'ulema' are trying to react on pure emotions. I want to remind them of Islam's early history. They moved from Mecca to Medina (hijrat). Was this (God forbid) cowardice? This was wisdom to save Islam.... Then when the Jews saw that Islam was getting stronger they started to conspire against the Muslims. When the Prophet (PBUH) saw this happening he signed a no war pact with his enemies in Mecca. I want to remind you of that pact. At the end of the pact, where his signature was required, the Meccans demanded that he cannot sign it as "Prophet Mohammed." The Prophet (PBUH) agreed.... The Prophet explained later that its [*sic*] best for Islam, and it's the right thing to do. And time proved him right. Six months later there was a war with the Jews and the Meccans did not support the Jews and the Muslim forces won. And some time after that Mecca also fell to Islamic mujahideen.... At this time, we have [to] make sure that our enemies do not succeed in their designs to harm us. Pakistan is

regarded as a fort of Islam. If this fort is damaged, Islam will be damaged (Musharraf 2006).

Thus, Musharraf argued that by acting to secure core state interests he was advancing the interests of Islam itself.

Despite some obvious similarities to the ways Zia and even Ayub used Islam to defend their actions, Musharraf's approach was also uniquely his own. This can be seen from the referendum he put before the people in 2002. In Musharraf's yes/no referendum question, he asked voters: "Do you want to elect President Musharraf as President of Pakistan for the next five years for: survival of local government system; restoration of democracy; continuity and stability of reforms; eradication of extremism and sectarianism, and the accomplishment of the Quaid-i-Azam's [Jinnah's] concept?" (Rouse 2002). To the casual observer, this question appears to lack Zia's cynical manipulation of Islam, and indeed Musharraf's instrumentalization of Islam is subtler than that of Zia. Nonetheless, Musharraf equated support for his government with support for accomplishing the Quaid-i-Azam's concept, which is an allusion to the two-nation theory and the protection of Islam as Pakistan's ideology.

Musharraf assigned himself the grand task of reconfiguring this ideology to best suit his vision of the state, which echoed the similar visions of Ayub and Zia. In 2004, before the opening of the annual meeting of the Organization of Islamic Cooperation, which was to be held in Islamabad, he unveiled his platform of Enlightened Moderation. He subsequently published an editorial called "A Plea for Enlightened Moderation" in the Washington Post, Egypt's Al-Ahram Weekly. The editorial and the concept was covered extensively in the Pakistani media. In this piece he ascribed Muslims' involvement with terrorism to economic and political oppression. He suggested Enlightened Moderation as a way of addressing this very real problem, describing it as "... a win for all—for both the Muslim and non-Muslim worlds. It is a two-pronged strategy. The first part is for the Muslim world to shun militancy and extremism and adopt the path of socio-economic uplift. The second is for the West, and the United States in particular, to seek to resolve all political disputes with justice and to aid in the socioeconomic betterment of the deprived Muslim world" (Musharraf 2004).

While Musharraf sustained some criticism for conceding Muslim involvement in terrorism and for what some saw as his naive belief that the United States and other Western nations would actually seek to resolve political disputes in the Muslim world with political, social, and economic justice, he earned accolades in the United States and beyond (Bano 2004).

Musharraf also garnered support abroad and among liberals at home for denouncing some groups of Islamist militants as terrorists. Unfortunately, his policies belied his public statements. He still adhered to a belief in good Islamist militants (freedom fighters or mujahideen) such as Lashkar-e-Taiba, the Haqqani Network, and the Afghan Taliban, and his government continued to support them and took umbrage at the suggestion that these groups were terrorist organizations. Under Musharraf, Pakistan negotiated several peace deals with the Islamist militants who were coalescing under the banner of the Pakistan Taliban, and he increasingly relied on Islamist politics to temper civil–military conflict (International Crisis Group 2003, 2006b; Nasr 2004). These policies contrasted with his government's generally supportive role in US efforts to contain al-Qaeda. Indeed, al-Qaeda made several attempts to kill Musharraf, among other military leaders.

Prior to stepping down as army chief, Musharraf promoted Ashfaq Parvez Kayani, the chief of ISI, to full general and made him the vice chief of army staff and thus Musharraf's selected successor as army chief. Musharraf ceded the post of army chief in November 2007. While a new parliament and prime minister was voted into power as a consequence of the March 2008 general elections, Musharraf remained as president until fresh presidential elections were held in August 2008. While Pakistan has nominally remained under civilian control since the restoration of democracy in 2008, Kayani has continued to play an important role in manipulating domestic politics in the country. Amid some controversy, in July 2010 he received an unprecedented three-year term extension. While Prime Minister Yousaf Raza Gillani announced the news, analysts of Pakistani civil military affairs widely understood the move to have been self-initiated or, worse, initiated by those in Washington, DC (Nawaz 2010).

Kayani, like many of his predecessors, often references the so-called ideology of Pakistan and the importance of protecting it. For instance, in May 2012 he invoked the concept while addressing a Rawalpindi audience consisting of military brass, Pakistani ministers, foreign defense attachés, and the relatives of Pakistan's slain soldiers on the occasion of Youm-e-Shuhada (Day of Martyrs): "I am hopeful that we will emerge from this stage victorious with the help and prayers of the nation. We would be successful when we have a strong belief in the ideology of Pakistan. Any doubt about this ideology would weaken the country" (Daily Times 2012a). On August 14, 2011, addressing crowds assembled at Pakistan's Military Academy in Kakul for the annual Azadi Parade (to celebrate independence), Kayani explained:

> 14th August 1947 was a historic day for the Muslims of the Subcontinent. This day is testimony to the indomitable will of the Muslims to establish a separate homeland under the inspiring leadership of Quaid-i-Azam Muhammad Ali Jinnah. Let us, on this day, humbly thank Allah Almighty. Let us pray together that He gives us strength and wisdom to preserve and protect the ideology, solidarity, integrity and a bright future for Pakistan. We must stay committed to the ideals of Pakistan

and remain ever ready to protect our motherland. I have no doubt that the challenges we face today, will only strengthen our resolve. Ladies and Gentlemen! The basis of our existence is the 'Ideology of Pakistan.' Therefore, each one of us must endeavour to pass it on to the future generations. We have a firm belief that by following the golden principles of Islam, we shall progress and win a respectable place in the comity of nations. We should never forget that Islam is the religion of peace. This great religion is the bond that binds us together and should not in any way divide us. (COAS 2011).

Given the army's ongoing struggle against Islamist violence, Kayani, like Musharraf before him, must strike a balance between reinforcing Islam as the "ideology of Pakistan" as a unifying force while rejecting Islamist terrorism. This is a more difficult line to walk than it may appear at first blush. As I show in subsequent chapters, the army's publications frequently deploy the concept of jihad both to describe the country's struggle with India and to cast this contest within a larger context of Islam's greatest battles against the nefarious designs of nonbelievers. How can the Pakistani state expect its citizens to sustain support for some notions of state-supported jihad while denouncing other self-proclaimed jihadi groups for committing what the state believes is terrorism? This is all the more difficult when one appreciates the degree to which the "good jihadis" and the "terrorists" are comingled within groups and within specific operations.

A superb example of Kayani's tightrope act is a speech he delivered in Urdu at the Pakistan Military Academy on August 13, 2012, during which he told his military audience: "Should extremists (*intahaiparast*) or terrorists (*dahashatgardi*) or the other militants we are battling prevail, we will be divided and move towards civil war. The army does not bear the sole responsibility for this struggle against extremists and terrorists; rather the entire nation must participate. We can only succeed if all are involved" (General Ashfaq Pervez Kayani Full Speech at PMA Kakul August 13th 2012, translated and paraphrased by author). However, not once did he use the word *jihadist*, which is the expression that these groups use to describe themselves. How are ordinary Pakistanis expected to understand the difference between these varied groups and support or denounce them in accordance with the state's preferences? In practice, many cannot.

Ultimately, Kayani must confront the same challenges as Musharraf. While Kayani has urged Pakistanis to publicly resist those terrorists that are undermining the state and terrorizing Pakistani civilians, the government has remained committed to using Islamist proxies as tools of foreign policy and Islamism as a tool of domestic politics. Because the Pakistan Army persists in deploying the two-nation theory as the ideology of Pakistan and the civilizational conflict that framework suggests, the state continues to see Islamist militancy and political Islam as the best tools for securing its regional interests. Because the groups that service its foreign goals have deep ties to those that service its domestic goals and those that have regrouped to target the state, Pakistan will likely find it ever more difficult to manage the portfolio of Islamist actors who are variously allied with or against the state.

The dual challenge of containing some militant proxies while instrumentalizing and supporting others is evidenced by Kayani's own engagement with these varied groups. When he was the ISI chief, he oversaw many of the controversial deals between the Musharraf government and the militants—none of which brought peace and most of which were broken before the ink had dried (International Crisis Group 2006b). However, Kayani was hesitant to declare full war on a set of militants who could one day work to advance Pakistan's goals in India or Kashmir. Pakistan, usually working with the American drone program, acquiesces to killing these Pakistan Taliban leaders only when it becomes abundantly clear that they would not make peace with the Pakistani government (Mazzetti 2013). Given the army's competing assessments of the relative costs and benefits of these varied militant groups, it is doubtful whether Kayani will be any more successful than Musharraf was at using Islam to contain the Islamist terror threat to the state while continuing to rely on Islam and Islamist militancy as tools of foreign policy and on "Islam" and the exclusive two-nation theory as instruments of social cohesion.

The Army's Methods of Islamization

Over time, the Pakistan Army and its leadership have engaged in a number of active efforts to Islamize the force. As noted in the preceding section, after the 1977 coup Zia sought to Islamize Pakistan generally and the army particularly. Immediately after becoming army chief in March 1976, Zia replaced Jinnah's motto of "Faith, Unity, Discipline" with "Iman, Taqwa, Jihad-fi-sibilillah" (Faith, Piety, holy war (or struggle) in the name of god[9]) (Kukreja 2003). Rizvi, however, argues that while the adoption of this motto reflected Zia's personal religious inclinations, it was not a major departure from the Pakistan Army's culture. Military education had always emphasized Islamic principles, teachings, and history as well as the careers of Muslim military heroes (Rizvi 2000a). It is likely that these concepts shifted over time. After all, such shifts are observable in the views of Islam espoused by generals Ayub, Zia, and Musharraf.

Zia, when he became army chief, set a qualitative new tone for the military and the role of religion in it. He was particularly sympathetic to Jamaat-e-Islami (JI) and used his authority to allow the party to distribute literature among officers and enlisted men. This allowed JI to make inroads into the army and other services, and many officers began to overtly affiliate with JI and its founder, Maulana Abul A'la Maududi (Nasr 2001). Zia also permitted other Islamic groups, such as the Tablighi Jamaat, to expand their presence among army personnel. (Tablighi Jamaat is a revivalist group, dedicated to proselytization, which claims to eschew political activity.) Such freedom would have been anathema to previous army chiefs. Zia was the first head of state to attend Tablighi Jamaat's annual meeting in Raiwind (in the Punjab, near Lahore), which encouraged several officers to openly associate with the group to demonstrate their piety (Rizvi 2000a, 246). Bhutto was reportedly dismayed by Zia's pro-JI activities, even summoning him before the cabinet to explain himself. During his trial before the Supreme Court, Bhutto remarked, "I appointed a Chief of Staff belonging to the JI and the result is before all of us" (Nasr 2001, 97).

Under Zia, Islamic training was introduced to the curriculum of the Command and Staff College. Cohen (1984) draws special attention to the lectures given there during the 1970s by Col. Abdul Qayyum; these were eventually printed in book format with a foreword by Zia. Qayyum encouraged officers to respect mullahs and maulvis and argued that these "clerical" figures—despite their widely varying degrees of religious scholarly achievement– could serve as a bridge that would unite an officer's "Westernized profession and his faith" (Cohen 1984, 95).[10] Qayyum urged students to make the Quran the base of their education.

Cohen considered the degree to which the Pakistan Army sought to part ways with the traditional practices of the Raj to achieve greater adherence to Islamic principles. He recounts that the regiments took on distinctly Islamic battle cries. The Pakistan Frontier Force, for instance, adopted "Nadar Hazar Ali!" (I am present before the Almighty). Signboards reminded recruits that "life and death are the same thing: and when the experiment of life is completed, then the eternal life—which we call death—begins." Other boards declared, "Fighting in the name of Allah, fighting in the name of truth, is the supreme sort of worship, and anybody who does service in the armed forces with the intention of doing this job in worship, his life is a worship" (Cohen 1984, 38–39).

Zia undertook several measures during his tenure that had far-reaching impact on the role of Islam in the army. First, he mobilized conservative Islamist groups to legitimize his ever more problematic rule, simultaneously encouraging Islamic orthodoxy within the army. Zia's government elicited popular support from Pakistanis by promulgating an ideology that linked both Islam and the country's destiny to that of military regime (Ahmad 1996). Zia adumbrated the original formulation of Pakistan's ideology, which emphasized the inherent relationship between Islam and the nation, by arguing that maintaining the military-led political establishment was "equally vital for the preservation of Islam and Pakistan. Thus [during Zia's tenure] Islam, Pakistan, and the military regime became united in an indivisible trinity" (382). Under Zia, subtle changes in recruitment patterns took place within the army. Officers increasingly came from middle to lower socioeconomic strata as well as from the urban areas and small towns, where conservative Islamic ideology is more prevalent than in rural Pakistan. Thus, the values that Zia promulgated in the army were in increasing alignment with those of the new Pakistani soldier (Rizvi 2000a).

Zia also upgraded the maulvis' status and required them to go into battle with the troops.[11] Prior to his tenure, maulvis had been somewhat comical figures both within and outside the army (Rizvi 2000a). A maulvi is technically a religious scholar who has completed a formal course, lasting eight or more years, at a madrasa. In reality, few of those calling themselves maulvis or mullahs have completed this rigorous course of study; many have only a few years of formal religious education, and others are barely literate in any language. Traditionally, maulvis or mullahs have not received a salary, living instead by the generosity of the community they serve. The maulvis' lack of genuine religious knowledge and social status encourages many Pakistanis—pious or otherwise—to see them as charlatans more worthy of derision than reverence. The persistent rumors of their pederast tendencies provide further fodder for the large number of jokes about them.

Under Zia, the degree to which officers evidenced a commitment to Islamic conservatism influenced their promotion paths, in part because he viewed faith as "an important part of the public profile of the in-service personnel" (Rizvi 2000a, 246). While officers' private lives had always come under scrutiny, under Zia an officer's piety and religious practice became a formal part of his assessment for promotion. This may have encouraged some officers to begin growing beards and to eschew alcohol—which had formerly been a feature of the officers' messes prior to Bhutto's banning of it from them (ibid.).

In addition, an increasing number of officers and enlisted men received temporary postings in the militaries of the Persian Gulf, exposing them to orthodox (often Wahhabist) teachings (Rizvi 2000a, 245). Unfortunately, very little has been written about military-to-military cooperation during this period. In 1967, Pakistan and Saudi Arabia signed a pact formalizing Pakistan's role in the defense of the kingdom. Pakistani pilots flew Saudi fighter jets through the 1970s, and in the same period there were some 15,000 troops stationed there (Khalid 1989b). Khalid's account differs from that of Lt. Gen. Faiz Chishti, who played a key role in Zia's 1977 coup as corps commander of the X Corps in Rawalpindi. According to Chishti, Zia first announced that he had secured the cooperation of Saudi Arabia to send troops there in 1979. Zia gushed that they would be handsomely compensated. Chishti claims that he protested vehemently to Zia and argued: "We are not mercenaries.... If they are sent, it will lead to the destruction of the Pakistan Army" (Chishti 1990, 99). Chishti believed that the impact of serving in Saudi Arabia would be "thoroughly harmful to the Pakistan Army. Substantial benefits from enhanced salaries bred jealousies, disinterest in service often grew after a tenure in Saudi and the Sunni-Shi'a rift opened up too" (ibid.). Chishti claims that Zia acquiesced and did not send troops to Saudi Arabia until after Chishti's retirement in 1980.

Rashid (1996) noted that in 1986 between 40,000 to 50,000 Pakistani military personnel were serving abroad, with the largest contingent stationed in Saudi Arabia. In the 1980s, Pakistan exported an entire armored brigade to Saudi Arabia,[12] and as of 1986 Pakistan had one division (approximately 13,000 men), two armored and two artillery brigades (approximately 10,000 men), and several naval and air force personnel stationed there.[13] In addition to these associations with Saudi Arabia, for a time Pakistani air force pilots could enhance their chances of promotion by flying with the United Arab Emirates Air Force.[14] At least through 1999, Pakistan continued to provide technical and training assistance to the United Arab Emirates, Saudi Arabia, Kuwait, Bahrain, and Qatar (Henderson 1999).

Pakistan does not publicize its foreign deployments (with the exception of United Nations peacekeeping missions). Thus, it is impossible to verify its current deployments in the Middle East using public sources. Recent reporting suggests that in 2010 Pakistan deployed a battalion of the Azad Kashmir Regiment to Bahrain to train local troops. Pakistan also sends retired officers to augment Bahrain's military capabilities. According to a recent report, Prime Minister Yousuf Gilani assured Bahrain's foreign minister in March 2011 that Pakistan would dispatch more retired manpower to quell the unrest by Bahrain's Shia majority against their Sunni rulers. This same report estimates that there are about 10,000 active and retired Pakistani military personnel currently in Bahrain (Husain 2011). The long association between the Pakistani armed forces and those of the Arab states of the Persian Gulf raises an important—if unanswerable—question: did exposure to these states, and to Wahhabism, encourage Islamism among Pakistani personnel posted there and among those who interacted with them, including their families? After all, those same individuals could have just as easily been put off by the decadence of their Arab hosts and the maltreatment of South Asians living in the Gulf.

The Pakistan Army's varied efforts to Islamize the force had some successes. Stephen Cohen (1984), who performed his fieldwork in the late 1970s and early 1980s, cites one senior officer who told him that "expressions like the 'ideology of Pakistan' and the 'glory of Islam,' normally outside a professional fighter's lexicon, were becoming stock phrases.... The Service Chiefs sounded more like high priests than soldiers" (87). One retired officer wrote that the cumulative effect of Zia's policies was the "rise to religious orthodoxy among a cross-section of the armed forces. For this small group, ideology can be stretched to radicalism and takes precedence over professionalism. Their attitude needs to be countervailed otherwise it will erode the very foundation of a cohesive, professionally competent, and technologically adept armed forces" (Rizvi 2000a, 247).

The changing ethos of the military must have influenced the recruiting pool of the Pakistan Army's officer corps and enlisted men. Individuals who rejected Zia's vision or who were unwilling to pretend to accept it may have been less likely to join the army in the first place. Thus, Islamization could have taken place via top-down efforts by the army leadership but also through supply-side pressures that altered the attributes and attitudes of those seeking to join the officer corps. Needless to say, there are no data that allow us to evaluate any of these possibilities.

Despite Zia's efforts, Cohen (1984) found that the changes in the officer corps, while important, were in fact quite modest. He also found a considerable difference of opinion about Islam within the officer corps, mirroring the divergence of views about the origins of the state and the role of Islam in it. Cohen did find officers who were dissatisfied with the dawdling pace of military Islamization: in particular, a number of officers criticized the Staff College and army regulations as having a "distinct aroma of subjugation suited to a colonial power" rather than "reflecting a true Islamic equalitarianism" (96).[15]

Some senior army leaders, who came after Zia, feared that his policies had led members of the force to substitute "professionalism and discipline with Islam-oriented activism" (Rizvi 2000a, 247). Gen. Asif Nawaz Janjua, the army chief between August 1991 and January 1993, and his successors tried to push back the elements of politicized Islam within the force and reinstate prior traditions of "keeping Islam and professionalism together and treating the former as a component of the latter" (ibid.). But Zia's successors still continued to acknowledge the role and importance of Islam within military ideology (ibid.).

Rizvi (2000a), anticipating contemporary concerns about the army, argued at the turn of the twenty-first century that the Pakistani military would face major challenges that millennium. First, it would have to ensure professional and cohesive disposition as the new breed of officers, who came up during the Zia years, take command. Second, it would have to maintain the delicate balance between Islam and service discipline as Islamic and Islamist groups continue to make inroads. No doubt Pakistan's active utilization of Islamist militant groups as tools of foreign policy has given heart to some personnel within the army for whom abandoning jihad is very difficult (ibid.).

The Army's Instrumentalization of Islam

Given the importance that successive military leaders have ascribed to the defense of Pakistan's ideology, it should not be a surprise that the army's professional publications regularly dedicate many pages to Islam, the ideology of Pakistan, and even jihad. At first blush, the prevalence of such topics in Pakistan's professional publications is disquieting, given concerns over the Islamization of the army and its support for an array of Islamist militant groups. Having read the bulk of these publications dating back to the late 1950s, I suggest that authors employ these themes to serve at least three tightly interrelated objectives.

First, the army employs Islam as a means of unifying the country via an identity that can supersede ethnic affiliations and the fissiparous tendencies stemming from Pakistan's ethnic diversity. Second, the army uses Islam to rally the citizenry in times of war and to prepare them to accept adversity as well as the army's continued domination of national affairs. Third, the army has used Islam to motivate soldiers by focusing on the purported supernatural advantages conferred by Islamic faith. Numerous authors writing in Pakistan's military journals suggest that a pious Muslim can defeat his adversary even if outnumbered. These writings also essentialize the enemy, reducing him to the category of *Hindu* despite the fact that India's armed forces include Sikhs, Muslims, Christians, and Parsees as well as Hindus. I discuss each of these objectives at greater length below, with reference made to specific essays in Pakistan's professional military journals.

UNIFYING A DIVERSE COUNTRY ACROSS ETHNICITY AND CREED

In Pakistan's defense literature it is evident that the army instrumentalizes Islam in effort to forge a coherent, national unity from a population rife with ethnic and sectarian dissonance. While conducting his seminal field research on the Pakistan Army in the late 1970s, Cohen (1984) observed that the army "moved immediately [after independence] to emphasize Islam as a unifying force" amid ethnic diversity and ethnic political demands (37). Six decades of Pakistan's defense literature provide ample evidence to support Cohen's claim. Indeed, the available evidence suggests that this goal continues to remain a crucially important reason for the army's resort to Islam.

Several essays from Pakistan's defense literature exemplify this belief that an Islamic ideology can build national character. That such themes dominate Pakistan's professional army publications attests to the institutional importance attached to this goal and the presumed centrality of the army's role in achieving it. One representative early example is Capt. Muhammad Bashir's 1961 essay in the *Pakistan Army Journal* titled "National Character," in which Bashir identifies several ills that stem from Pakistan's economic, political, and social cleavages. Echoing the writings of his chief, Ayub, Bashir argues that ideology is necessary because "A nation's ideology is its very soul; without it, it cannot exist.... [It] is an ideology which keeps a nation together and wards off disintegration" (52). He identifies Islam as the only possible ideology that could fill this role for Pakistan, because Islam alone "can bring people together and enable them to rise above provincial, racial and tribal jealousies. The cause of most of our troubles in the past has been that this idea which is the strongest unifying force, was relegated to the background" (52–53). Bashir argues that the ideal Pakistani citizen is the *momin*, or "man of unblemished character" (53), and he proposes developing this ideal citizen through imitation, fostering fundamental change in Pakistan's cultural environment, and reorienting the educational system.

Maj. S. S. A. Naqvi, in a 1973 essay titled "Motivation of Armed Forces Towards our Ideology," puts forth a similar argument when he contends that "the ideology for the country draws its strength from an Islamic system and Islam is a source of energy for our national goals" (58). Writing in the aftermath of the loss of East Pakistan, he attributes Pakistan's "recent decline" to the "erosion of the spirit which created Pakistan" (ibid.). Maj. Mohammad Ali's 1991 essay, "An Analytical Study of Situation in Sindh," offers a similar prognosis and diagnosis. As suggested by the title, the author both seeks to describe the nature of the violence that gripped Sindh in the later 1980s and early 1990s and propose some remedial approaches to stem it. Ali provides a commendable account of the province's numerous and daunting challenges, which include social disparities, historical underdevelopment, and an influx of illegal immigrants, many of whom "are associated with narcotics, weapons, smuggling, and other illegal activities" (85). After having suggested several sensible and practical remedies, such as law enforcement measures, increasing the independence of the judiciary, and redress of legitimate grievances, he ends with a clarion call for the "Revival of the spirit of the Pakistan movement" and the "adoption of Islamic strategy and avoidance of other state models" (87).

In 1991, Air Commodore Inamul Haq published an exhaustive volume titled *Islamic Motivation and National Defence* in which he emphasizes these points as well when he argues that "only the love for brotherhood in Islam can consolidate and create a strong homogeneous and unified society. Our ideology alone can contribute to greater unity" (27). Haq argues that Pakistan needs "a rejuvenation of our faith and ideology" for the purpose of "regaining our lost dignity, ensuring our territorial integrity and increasing our political and economic independence" (29).

In 2000, Lt. Col. Asif Mahmood offered a similar view in the *Pakistan Army Green Book 2000*, the first published following Musharraf's coup. The entire volume is dedicated to the role of the armed forces in rebuilding Pakistan. Mahmood's essay exemplifies the belief in the ameliorative role of Islam as an ideology, arguing that the political elites of Pakistan have failed to implement the ideology of Pakistan, to the nation's detriment. Indeed, the linked tropes of civilian ineptitude and military competence are recurrent themes in Pakistan's defense literature, particularly during periods of military rule. Mahmood dilates on the importance of Pakistan's Islamic ideology, which, he asserts, puts "forward a set of universal principles and cultural values, given by Islam for the guidance of mankind....Islam eliminates national, ethnic and racial differences" (113). Echoing decades of writers before him, he avers that "Islam and Pakistaniat should have served as the national philosophy and driving force for social integration, national resolve and preservation of national sovereignty. Unfortunately, up to the present, it has neither been interpreted nor implemented as such (114)."[16] For Mahmood, this is a serious problem because Pakistan's varied regions will remain unified only if Islam serves as the basis of Pakistani nationalism.

Pakistan's defense literature assumes an intimate connection between the quality of Pakistan's society and the quality of the troops, as already suggested. Pakistan's army is rooted in society; thus, the army must work to improve the qualities of the society from which it draws and also to exclude the less salutary attributes of that society. This recurrent theme across more than six decades of defense writings is captured in a 1992 essay by Brig. Jamshed Ali, in which he notes, "National culture and military performance and achievements are closely inter-linked. An army *mirrors the true state of its society* and is as good and as bad as the people who constitute it" (59). Given the numerous problems of the civilian world, "The armed forces must at all times maintain a state of cultural purity and mirror the idealistic virtues of an army steeped in Islamic military traditions. It must remain apolitical, isolated from societal ills and other pervasive malpractices" (ibid.). (The call for the force to remain "apolitical" is typical among writings in the early years of restored democracy; it recedes once the army again intervenes in politics.) Given the uncivilized world of the civilians, "It is only by maintaining an integrated, cohesive and puritanical military system that the armed forces can retain their pristine, tradition oriented military way in a liberal society" (ibid.).

READYING THE PEOPLE FOR ARMY DOMINANCE AND WAR

Pakistan fought wars with India in 1947–1948, 1965, 1971, and 1999 (in addition to numerous close calls and border skirmishes). With the possible exception of the 1971 war, Pakistan began each war and failed to decisively win any of them.[17] Despite this record, the military must cultivate Pakistani support for the drain it places on national resources, its involvement in politics, its dominance in foreign policy, its staunch anti–status quo position vis-à-vis India, and ultimately war. This is no easy task given the toll that belligerent policies have taken on ordinary Pakistanis. Because the Pakistan Army—like all armies—recruits from among the population, it is very sensitive to how the citizenry views the organization. In fact, Musharraf was so discomfited by the International Republican Institute's (IRI's) 2007 polls showing widespread opposition to his rule that his government began harassing the organization and its staff in Pakistan. The Pakistani government's intimidation worked: IRI no longer publishes the results of the surveys it conducts on behalf of the US Embassy (Sethi 2008).

Believing that Musharraf was responsible for degrading its standing, the army pressured him to step down as chief in an effort to preserve its corporate interests (Barker 2007; Gall and Sengupta 2007). When Kayani assumed the post he worked assiduously to improve army morale, which had taken a sustained beating during Musharraf's tenure, and to rehabilitate the army's image among ordinary Pakistanis, which had worsened dramatically during the same period. As one Pakistani journalist observed, under Kayani's leadership, "the Army has consciously been working to redeem itself by overt displays of professional, nonpolitical conduct. It's been given a fillip by its valorous operation against the Taliban in Swat and South Waziristan, its handling of the refugee crisis from Swat, and the rescue and relief efforts after the floods" (Ahmed 2010).

Articles in Pakistan's professional military journals also use Islam, the ideology of Pakistan, and the two-nation theory to sustain popular appetite for unending conflict with India and the army's continued dominance over Pakistan's internal and external affairs. This dynamic manifests itself in several ways. First, throughout some six decades of Pakistani professional military publications, much ink has been spilled on excoriating civilian leadership. The entire 322-page *Pakistan Army Green Book 2000*, written in the wake of Musharraf's military coup, is dedicated to celebrating the role of the military in saving Pakistan after civilian failures to do right by the nation. While the army clearly believes it is important to propagate this view among civilians, it is equally important to spread it among officers themselves, as most professional soldiers prefer to honor their oath to stay out of politics. Professional soldiers with whom I have interacted have often opined that managing the country distracts the army from its primary duty of war fighting.

In 1963, Maj. Gen. Fazal Muqeem Khan, who would go on to serve as Defence Secretary between 1973 and 1977, published *The Story of Pakistan Army*. Writing a mere five years after Ayub's coup, Khan endeavors to justify Pakistan's first break from parliamentary democracy. Unsurprisingly, he argues that the blame lay with politicians, many of whom "had been ignorant, vainglorious good-for-nothings, only able to influence the polling of votes—often by far from honest means" (193). Because these politicians were "devoid of any higher understanding of politics, their vision remained confined to their own limited spheres, and instead of striving for the greatness of the nation, they looked only for self-aggrandizement and personal gain" (ibid.). In contrast to these venal politicians, who sought to advance their own personal standing, the author depicts Ayub as hesitant to take control and resistant to the public's growing demands for him to do so. Ultimately, given the brewing tumult in East Pakistan and endless political troubles in West Pakistan, "the army was called in to take over the country as soon as possible" to "avoid...a catastrophe" (194), and Ayub, a loyal soldier, answered the calls of the citizenry.

Decades later, Maj. Gen. Asif Duraiz Akhtar (2000), writing in the *Pakistan Army Green Book 2000*, echoed Khan's sentiments. He contends that "our political leadership...has failed to provide requisite stability, show maturity and acumen. They could not capitalize on [the] Two-Nation Theory and consolidate the national integration" (1). In contrast, the "Army has tried to provide stability, pursued aggressive foreign policy…and developed a semblance of cohesion in the society based on Nationalism or Pan-Islamism" (ibid.). This undergirds his conclusion that the army's "enhanced participation in decision making on national issues, even during the elected government's tenure is considered to be *the moral obligation of the armed forces*" (ibid., emphasis added).

During periods of democracy, writers in Pakistan's professional military journals sometimes offer more critical reflections on the role of the army in governance. Writing in 1993–1994, after the restoration of democracy that followed the death of Zia ul Haq, Lt. Col. Mahmud Akhtar takes a more ambivalent view of the impact of the army's interventions. Assessing the causes of Pakistan's "disintegration," he identifies the early death of Jinnah, the assassination of the first prime minister, the demise of the Muslim League, the "mushrooming of various pseudo political parties at the behest of selfish politicians and bureaucrats; undemocratic policies and malpractices of governments in power and the delay in making the first constitution and last of all controversial role of judiciary and interference of armed forces in national affairs" (111). While he concedes that the absence of democracy and prolonged military rule have undermined the development of governance in Pakistan, he stops short of either criticizing the quality of governance provided by the generals or ruling out military interventions at all.

Islamic themes, the two-nation theory, and the ideology of Pakistan (Pakistaniat) were explicitly invoked to mobilize civilians as well as soldiers in Pakistan's wars in 1965 and 1971 (Rizvi 2000a). This was not overtly the case in the 1999 Kargil War, because the official Pakistani position during the war was that only mujahideen irregulars were involved in the conflict. Nonetheless, Pakistani media coverage of the conflict inspired national pride that a handful of ragged but plucky holy warriors could tie up the Indian (read as Hindu) Army and inflict such heavy causalities. It was only after the crisis had passed that Pakistanis learned that no mujahideen had been involved; rather, the invaders were Pakistan Army troops and paramilitary forces from the Northern Light Infantry (Fair 2009b).

Equally important, the military attracts public support by describing the foe—inevitably Hindu India or its agents—as nonbelievers (*kufar*, pl. of *kafir*) and casting the conflict nearly exclusively in religious terms. Thus, conflict with India is portrayed as a jihad against nonbelievers who threaten Pakistan. This assumes, of course, that all of Pakistan's wars have been defensive and that India is implacably dedicated to destroying it. This assumption is bolstered by Col. Syed Nawab Alam Barhvi in his 1991 essay titled "Iqbal's Concept of Jehad," in which he tells his readers that "Jehad is fighting against aggression, fighting to defend the territorial boundaries and national integrity, and to take up arms against aggressive enemies" (87; see also Naqvi 1973, 1994). Nor is this jihad merely a duty for soldiers; rather, "Jehad is a sacred duty.…It is obligatory for every man, woman and child. It has to be an all encompassing, cohesive effort of the entire nation, manifested through its Armed Forces" (Farooqui 1992, 23).

Unfortunately, because Pakistan's ideology is fundamentally rooted in this absolute opposition to India, the struggle appears set to be perpetual. Pakistan's military publications seem comfortable with this outcome. Maj. Qaisar Farooqui's 1992 essay, titled "Islamic Concept of Preparedness," exemplifies this concept of perpetual struggle: "if the conflict is everlasting between the believers and the non-believers, or in other words between the forces of light and darkness, the fight has to go on till one of the belligerent forces is completely wiped out" (15). According to the narrative established by the army and promulgated throughout Pakistani society, India is an inexorable foe. Hence,

> Preparation for war is thus a sacred duty not only of an individual but of the entire Muslim Ummah; the Quranic message (read out on every passing out parade in the Pakistan military Academy, Kakul) enjoins upon all Muslims to take to the highest standards of preparedness, as it says, "And make ready your strength, to the utmost of your power including sinews of war, to strike terror into the hearts of the enemies of Allah, and your enemies, and others besides them, whom you know not but Allah doth know. And whatever you expend in the cause of Allah shall be repaid until you and you shall not be treated unjustly." (Al Anfal-60)...Islam does not visualize the total annihilation or complete extinction of the non-Islamic forces and people but ordains the Muslims to keep their enemies either subjugated or restrained (16).

Under this view, the commitment to subjugating or restraining the non-Muslim enemy is not simply the purview of the military but rather the responsibility of all Muslims. Implicit in such writings is an exclusivist notion of Pakistani citizenship: how could Pakistan's non-Muslims participate in this project?

Farooqui (1992), writing during the 1990s when Pakistan was undergoing yet another fiscal crisis following the imposition of US sanctions, argues that Pakistan must continue to expend resources on the military so that the army can defend the nation against its irreconcilable foe. He deploys the language of jihad to make his case, arguing that the preparation for jihad must be continuous and never-ending. "The preparedness [of the nation] has also to be perpetual. At times, the defensive effort might have to be made at the expense of important, essential needs of education, health and general welfare. The nation has to be prepared, mentally, physically, psychologically and intellectually to back up its defenders" (22).

Consonant with the defense publications' consistent definition of jihad as a defensive duty of the Pakistan Army, the literature—buttressed by Pakistani school curricula and the media coverage of all wars—depicts India as the aggressor in all cases, irrespective of the conflict this creates with indisputable facts and scholarly accounts. It is useful to briefly recount here the claims for and narratives of the key Indo-Pakistan wars. With respect to the 1947–1948 war, it must be noted that many Pakistani military writers do not acknowledge that the conflict was an Indo-Pakistan war (see, e.g., Farooqui 1992; Rahman 1976). Curiously, many memoirs of senior generals—for example, Lt. Gen. Gul Hassan Khan (1993), Gen. Ayub Khan (2006), and Maj. Gen. Hakeem Arshad Qureshi (2002)—do not even mention this war, even though they cover events immediately before and after.[18] Many Pakistanis still do not concede the extensive involvement of civilian and military officials in the infiltration of lashkars into Kashmir, which began the 1947–1948 war. Those writers who acknowledge that there was a war tend to argue that it began after the Indians airlifted troops into Kashmir and forced Kashmir's accession to India. Pakistani writers generally accept no culpability for creating the conditions that motivated the maharaja to sign the instrument of accession to India or to request Indian troops.

A typical example of this characterization of the 1947–1948 war is the 1978 essay "The Pakistan Army." The anonymous author insists that the Pakistan government tried to find a peaceful solution to the emerging crisis on Kashmir but was frustrated at every turn by a belligerent and recalcitrant India, which wanted to foist a military solution upon Pakistan. In view of this imminent threat, the essay contends, "Pakistan decided in April 1948 to send a small element of Pakistan Army into Kashmir with orders to deter India from obtaining any decision by force of arms ("The Pakistan Army" 1978, 6). Pakistan's official account of this war not only focuses on India's aggression but also consistently celebrates the courage and valor of the Pakistani forces, which held their own against a larger, more prepared force. For example, Maj. Gen. Muqeem Khan declares that "the Pakistan Army had performed its task admirably. It had done much more than it was expected or ordered to do. It did not go to conquer Kashmir, but was sent there on a purely defensive mission. It had, against overwhelming superiority in men, material and weapons, thwarted Indian designs" (Khan 1963, 116; see also "The Pakistan Army" 1978; Sattar 2007).

The 1965 war is described with similar narratives. Many writers for Pakistan's military journals fully concede that Pakistan was vexed by India's contention that Kashmir was not in dispute and by its corresponding attempts to integrate the state into the federation. Given these evolving realities, Pakistan sought "to keep the flickering flame alive by throwing occasional crackers in occupied Kashmir. [The Pakistan Intelligence Bureau] conducted some minor sabotage activities there, but these attempts also proved futile" (Musa 1983, 2). Gen. Mohammad Musa (who commanded the Pakistan Army during the 1965 war with India) acknowledged that Pakistan erroneously believed the time was right to commence a sustainable civil war in Indian-administered Kashmir. Pakistani planners were encouraged to believe that an insurgency was possible when the *Moh-e-Moqadis*, a hair from the prophet Muhammad, was stolen from Srinagar's Hazratbal shrine in December 1963. When the public learned that the relic was missing, violent protests broke out throughout the state (*New York Times* 1963).

Musa (1983) describes Operation Gibraltar, which "envisaged, on a short-term basis, sabotage of military targets, disruption of communications, etc. and, as a long-term measure, distribution of arms to the people of occupied Kashmir and initiation of a guerilla movement there with a view to starting an uprising in the valley eventually" (35–36). (Operation Gibraltar was to be followed by Operation Grand Slam, which involved a full-scale assault in southern Kashmir employing regular troops, tanks, and support from the Pakistan Air Force.) Musa admits that the force that Pakistan infiltrated was large, consisting of some "7,000 Mujahidin from Azad Kashmir. Most of it was given some guerilla training within the short time available before it was launched. It was armed with light machine guns and mortars, besides personal weapons, and was equipped with wireless sets" (36). He even concedes the extent to which the Pakistan military regulars were employed in this operation. Pakistan's calculations were wrong in every respect. Not only did Operation Gibraltar fail to ignite an enduring insurgency in Kashmir, but India also responded against Pakistan's expectations by widening the war, launching an attack in the Pakistani Punjab. Despite fully acknowledging Pakistan's actions leading up to the war, Musa's account—like many others—ultimately blames the start of what he calls the first major Indo-Pakistan war on India.

Pakistani authors paint India as the aggressor. First, they characterize the limited skirmish in the Rann of Kutch as the result of Indian aggression. This incident took place over several months in late 1964 and early 1965, prior to the execution of Operation Gibraltar and the slide to war. The Rann of Kutch is a marshland adjacent to the Arabian Sea; India and Pakistan disputed the demarcation of the border in this area. Scholarly and journalistic accounts of this conflict describe skirmishes breaking out between the Indian and Pakistani forces patrolling the area, with fighting rapidly escalating to a brigade-sized battle. Most observers decline to declare India or Pakistan the clear and obvious aggressor (Chari et al. 2001; Lamb 1991; Nawaz 2008a; Schofield 2000). Others, such as Sumit Ganguly (2001, 41), argue that Pakistan initiated a limited probe in the disputed area to "test Indian mettle." However, in Pakistan's military publications India appears as the clear aggressor—as Schofield (2000) notes, Indian accounts make comparable claims about Pakistan. Most scholars agree, though, that the Indian response was tepid and that this likely bolstered Pakistan's unwarranted confidence that Operation Gibraltar could be launched without sparking a wider war.

In Pakistan's account, Indian aggression in the Rann of Kutch was but a harbinger of a larger intent to fight Pakistan. Pakistani accounts contend that the actual war did not begin until India moved across the international border. From Pakistan's optic, sending regular and irregular troops across the line of control in Kashmir to foment insurgency and to attack Indian forces did not constitute an act of war. According to the anonymous 1978 essay in the *Pakistan Army Journal*,

"The Indian Army has launched her ignominious, undeclared and blatant aggression against Pakistan on September 6, 1965 ... with a view [to] achieving surprise and catching the Pakistan Army unaware" ("The Pakistan Army" 1978, 7–8). The author describes the Indian move as "an undeclared attack [that] was a great shock to the entire nation as it was not only against all canons of international law, but also against the norms of international morality and military ethics" (8). Thus, for Pakistan there is no sanctity of the line of control. The only fair Indian response to Pakistani moves across the line of control is a counteroffensive that is limited to the line of control. For Pakistan, movement of regular and irregular fighters across the line of control is not tantamount to an act of war; rather, it is the expansion of the conflict across the international boundary that is the threshold for war. This seems to be an optic peculiar to Pakistan's military personnel: most international observers found Pakistan's Operation Gibraltar to have been an act of war.

Ayub's words on the first day of the Indian offensive across the Line of Control have cast a long shadow over Pakistani understandings of the war and the security competition with India. He told the Pakistani public that "Indian aggression in Kashmir was only a preparation for an attack on Pakistan. Today [the Indians] have given final proof of this and of the evil intentions, which India has always harbored against Pakistan since its inception" (Haqqani 2005, 48). Official Pakistani accounts of the 1965 war aver that nothing Pakistan did prior to India expanding the conflict across the international border could, in any way, be construed as starting the war.

Pakistan's account of the 1971 war also paints India as the clear aggressor. This position is not as indefensible as it is for the prior two wars. Most accounts of the war, such as *Hamoodur Rehman Commission of Inquiry into the 1971 War* (2001), Lt. Gen. Gul Hassan Khan's *Memoirs* (1993), Maj. Gen. Hakeem Arshad Qureshi's *1971 Indo-Pak War: A Soldiers Narrative* (2002), among numerous other essays in the professional journals, concede that consistent government malfeasance sowed the seeds of discontent in East Pakistan and that the crimes (of omission or commission) of Gen. Yahya Khan, Z. A. Bhutto, and Sheikh Mujibur Rahman made the war inevitable. Most also concede that West Pakistani political elites never reconciled to the principle of one man, one vote, because it would allow the ethnically and politically cohesive East Pakistan to dominate politics. Such frankness is typified in the account of Lt. Gen. A. A. A. Niazi, who was the last governor and martial law administrator of East Pakistan under Yahya Khan and the last unified commander of the Eastern Military High Command. (It was Niazi who ultimately surrendered to India.) Niazi (2009) describes these conditions and reveals the extent to which the Bengalis were reviled due to their supposed Hindu characteristics:

> The West Pakistanis ... were concerned that the Bengalis, if given major-
> ity representation to their population in the federal set-up, would

eventually edge them out. They were also apprehensive about the Hindu influence in Bengali politics. With twenty per cent of the population being educated Hindus, and given their dominance in all facets of life, who could have stopped them from dictating the national policies? The government would be formed by Bengalis, the iron fist in the velvet glove would be that of the Hindus. To ensure that the Hindu influence was nullified, the parity system was evolved, meaning equal representation between the two wings. This was aimed at protecting the interests of the West Pakistanis from exploitation by the Hindu-controlled Bengalis (34).

Pakistani military authors also admit that the military used excessive force in its effort to put down the growing insurgency, even though they differ on whether or not this use of force was ultimately justified.

However, even Pakistani military authors who are most candid about the chain of errors that brought about the war ultimately blame India for enabling the insurgents. This is in part because Bengalis were seen as nonmartial and incapable of mounting any sort of offensive on their own. Ali (1992) wrote with surprise that the "derided Bengalis performed well and much beyond expectations" (56). The author of the 1978 essay "The Pakistan Army" acknowledges that the roots of the war were indigenous to East Pakistan but claims that India exploited Bengali grievances for its own ends. On this point, the author is surely correct. The Indians did exploit the situation in East Pakistan. Lt. Gul Hassan Khan (1993) takes a similar approach when he notes that by September 1971 "India's intervention was a foregone conclusion, unless we managed to deescalate the conditions in East Pakistan," and he admits with chagrin that Pakistan's leadership did not "appreciate how seriously India would take it upon herself to get involved in our dilemma and ensure that the turmoil in the East be precipitated" (284–285).

These narratives of the wars with India distort the truth about which actions precipitated the wars, exculpate Pakistani military leadership for its disastrous planning, and sustain the myth of an innocent Islamic Pakistan perpetually targeted by an insolent Hindu India resolved to destroy it.

MOTIVATING THE ARMY FOR WAR

Pakistan's defense literature also seeks to use Islam, the ideology of Pakistan, and the trope of the two-nation theory to motivate its officers and men to fight an enemy that has always been conventionally superior. Pervaiz Iqbal Cheema (2002), in his discussion of officer training at the Pakistan Military Academy and other institutions, such as the National University of Science and Technology, notes that underlying these educational programs "is a strong grounding in general Islamic teaching including the concept of Jihad. This is inevitable in a Muslim country: the concept of Jihad is an important pillar of Islam" (82). In fact, to ensure that soldiers have a solid understanding of the "concept of Jihad," teaching it has become an "integral part of training in the armed forces" (ibid.). Cheema sees this as necessary because Pakistan confronts the larger, better equipped Indian Army and must therefore rely on a "great measure of moral superiority which encompasses a high degree of professional competence, in-depth study of modern concepts and doctrines of war, better leadership and inspired ideological orientations" (ibid.).[19] The use of Islam to debase and demean the enemy also bolsters the army's will to fight. During the civil war of 1971, the commander in chief and president of Pakistan, Yahya Khan, motivated his soldiers by calling the Mukti Bahini (the Bengali guerillas) a "Kaffir" army against which the Pakistan Army was waging a legitimate jihad (Cohen 1984, 87).

Cohen's (1984) and Cheema's (2002) observations are amply supported by the professional military journals studied for this effort. One of the important themes of this literature is that the conflict with India and the need for war is not simply about territory. Col. Saifi Ahmad Naqvi, in an essay for the 1994 *Pakistan Army Green Book,* devotes a section to the concept of "Motivation through Religion." Here he reminds his readership that Pakistan is an "ideological state based on the ideology of Islam," and thus "the existence and survival of Pakistan depends upon complete implementation of Islamic ideology in true sense. If the ideology is not preserved then the very existence of Pakistan becomes doubtful" (184). This is germane to the army's mission because the army is "responsible for defence of the country to safeguard the integrity, territorial boundaries and the ideological frontiers for which the country owes its existence" (ibid.). For this reason, Naqvi argues that "the indoctrination of the officers and men is an undisputed requirement. For this purpose knowledge of religion and propagation of its teaching should be imparted in an organized manner down to the soldier level...Its message raises the morale and cultural level of its followers, and promotes social order, unity and intellectual hygiene" (ibid.).

This was not a new message, as evinced by the 1973 publication of Maj. Syed Shahid Abbas Naqvi's essay "Motivation of Armed Forces: Towards Our Ideology." In this essay, the author argues that all soldiers should be taught "the fundamentals of Islam and the Muslim ideology. The syllabus for basic instruction should include 'why' and 'how' about Muslim rise and fall. They should know why battles like 'Uhad,' 'Khaibar,' and 'Khandaq' were fought" (61). After the soldier completes this basic "ideological training," soldiers should next be "infused with the spirit of Jehad. At this stage of training a grounding has to be given to the soldiers to develop their courage with a strong will to defend this country. They should be given a cause to fight for" (ibid.). (Naqvi apparently does not view territorial defense alone as adequate motivation.) In an attempt to reinforce the religious nature of the battlefield, Naqvi argues that "terminologies like 'Foxland'

and 'Blue Land' [akin to red teaming and blue teaming in the US context] should be replaced by terms like 'Kafirs' [nonbelievers] or 'Mushriks' [apostates] and 'Muslims'" (ibid.).

Many writers for Pakistan's professional publications use the notion of jihad to describe the defense of Pakistan's ideological and territorial integrity. Saifi Ahmed Naqvi (1994), however, reminds his readers that, beyond being galvanized to perform these defensive tasks, "the best motivation for a Pakistani soldier is to be a dedicated Muslim to fight for the cause of Islam and to preserve unity and sovereignty of the homeland which is considered to be the citadel of Islam" (185). Musharraf used similar language in 2001 when, dressed in full military regalia, he addressed the nation after the December 2001 Jaish-e-Mohammad attack on the Parliament in New Delhi and concomitant massive Indian mobilization of forces along the border. He attempted to reassure Pakistanis that their armed forces were prepared to successfully fend off any Indian aggression. In doing so, he described Pakistan as the fortress of Islam ("Pakistan Islam ka qila hai") (Ahmed 2013, 2). The selection of the word *citadel* is itself instructive. In both English and Urdu (*qila*), this word is by definition a garrison community peopled by soldiers and civilians alike who are prepared to launch an armed defense against aggressors. Citadels or garrisons were also established by empires to guard their frontiers (2–3). By evoking this language, Pakistani officers and soldiers are fighting not simply to defend the frontiers of Pakistan but that of Islam itself.

Consistent with this effort to impress Pakistani men in uniform with the conviction that they are serving national, ideological, and religious goals, the literature also seeks to situate Pakistan's men in arms within a larger tradition of great Islamic warriors (Chohan 1998; Haq 1991; Malik 1963, 1992a, 1992b, 1992c; Majeed 1994; Pathan 1963). Thus, Pakistan's martial traditions are described as drawing on thousands of years of great Islamic generalship and conduct of war, predating both the British period and independence. Ali (1992) explained:

> Islam plays a vital and extremely pivotal role in the military culture of our soldiers. Our country's ideological foundations have a dominant motivating impact on the soldiers. As a role model, they look up to the rich heritage and martial traditions of Islam as inherited from the Holy Prophet (P.B.U.H.). If properly channelised this aspect of our military culture is a big combat multiplier for it enjoins patritism [*sic*], honour and commitment to cause. The ongoing renaissance of Islam and the radical changes brought about since 1947 in our customs and traditions have had a salutary effect on our military culture. The Islamic heritage serves as a useful platform and framework for the junior and senior leadership to exercise their command functions (57–58).

Other authors echo these ideas. For example, Lt. Col. M. Safdar Iqbal (1966) advocates *terbiyat* (religious education) for the Pakistani soldier. He implies that such education comes naturally to a soldier, as his religious training begins at birth when he first hears the *azan* (the call to prayer). Iqbal believes that "under higher direction, this 'Terbiyat' in the armed forces, is being conducted in a more systematic and purposeful manner. The officers and the men, the leaders and the led are rediscovering greater meaning and significance, nobler aims and ideals" (12). Most importantly, the author concludes, *terbiyat* will prepare the Pakistani soldier to act in accordance with Islam even when he is outnumbered and confronted by a better equipped enemy. To emphasize this point, he includes a quote from the Quran (a frequent habit of authors in Pakistan's professional journals): "Those who fight in His way and get killed, do not call them dead! They are alive and get their victuals from their Allah, but you do not understand. Those who die in the way of the Lord, shall go to paradise and live there forever; those who survive shall be amply rewarded, both here and in the hereafter" (15). Maj. Gen. Askari Raza Malik, writing in the 1992 *Pakistan Army Green Book: The Year of the Senior Field Commander*, stresses that the "important character traits of the successful field commanders" derive exclusively from Islam. In fact, "physical courage is only a fruit of moral courage....For a Muslim, the concept of shahadat [martyrdom] has, to much chagrin of others, grown into such a strong institution that is both marvelous and awe inspiring. What can the enemy do to a person who is overanxious to embrace death" (78).

In a 1998 essay, Col. F. J. Chohan agrees that Islam should be the basis of the army's indoctrination. Moreover, "The love of Jehad and to be called a Ghazi or Shaheed is ingrained and embodied in the hearts of our Jawans" (55). For Chohan, motivation of the Pakistani military "is not a mere function of pay, good administration, training and equipment. The material aspects are...vital for the sustenance and maintenance of an individual but these are not the real energizers...behind the behavior of a Muslim. The main motivation of a Momin [faithful Muslim] comes from the strength of his own inner faith in Allah as well as his action as oriented in the light of the knowledge revealed through the exemplary behavior of our Prophet (Peace be upon him)" (61).

Frequently, references to early Muslim campaigns are used to bolster the morale of officers and men because in many cases the early Muslims were outnumbered by their foes. This has obvious relevance to the contemporary security competition with India. Col. Bashir Ahmad provides an illustrative example of this genre in his 1963 essay titled "Morale: From the Early Muslim Campaigns." The author explains that "there are no finer examples in history of the influence of morale on the decisions of battle than those found in the early Muslim campaigns" (6). One of the most frequent references is to the Battle of Badr,[20] where, according to the author, 313 Muslim civilians—the vast majority of whom had little experience with warfare—prevailed against 1,000 seasoned soldiers equipped with armor, 700 camels, and 100 horses. The author notes that "a force three times superior in number, ten times better equipped and far superior in battlecraft had been defeated by its opponents. Morale alone was the cause of this success. Success did not go to the side with larger numbers, better equipment, more experience and greater skill. It went to the belligerent with better morale" (7; see also Chohan 1998).

Ahmad (1963) analyzed several other battles in which the early Muslims took part and derived four lessons. First, in each battle, the Muslim contingent was inferior in strength, ill equipped, and poorly trained. Nonetheless, despite early setbacks and obvious disadvantages, in each case they won "due...to their moral qualities" (11). Second, each battle ended in their favor not simply because they defeated the enemy but because they destroyed the enemy's will to fight. In other words, "It is...the moral and not the physical condition of a force which is the decisive factor in war" (ibid.). Third, the Muslim combatants entered into each battle fully aware that they were outmatched. They came out onto the battlefield "only to defend the intrinsic values of their faith. They entered every battle completely sobre [*sic*] and cool. And to the end, even under the most adverse conditions, they continued to fight unruffled and with the same cool determination" (12). Fourth, he concludes that "the main-stay of the morale of these Muslims was...the identification of life with and its subordination to the ideal: a fundamental of the faith. An army equipped with this faith will always dominate the adversary" (13).

Similar lessons from Islam's martial history are offered throughout Pakistan's defense literature. In 1990, Brig. Ashfaq Ahmad examined Pakistan's geopolitical realities and its enormous security burdens: over 1,500 miles of border to defend against a "treacherous and numerically superior adversary while in the west the threat of a super power, having confluence of interests with India, continues to linger and weigh on the minds of our planners... [the] rapidly deteriorating political situation in Occupied Kashmir has further complicated and compounded the problem and increased the threat" (105). Ahmad argues that the only way to manage the threat posed by these more powerful enemies is to draw inspiration from Islam. Thus, "our limited numbers will definitely beat the heavy odds against them...more than once, in the Holy Quran...fully armed with the strength of character, a Muslim will prove superior to ten non-Muslims" (ibid.).

Haq (1991) devotes an entire chapter, titled "Quality vs. Quantity in the Muslim Military Campaigns," to this subject. He believes that the Quran demonstrates repeatedly that high-quality Muslim soldiers can defeat a numerically dominant foe since "no power on earth can subdue the valour of the Mujahidin" (43). A later chapter titled "Combat Motivation" instructs his readership in how Muslims use Islam to compensate for lack of numbers, mobilizing numerous Quranic verses to show that "the inferiority in numbers or weapons can be made up by superior moral stamina, patience and trust in Allah" (46).

It is worth noting that *The Pakistan Army Green Book 1990: Year of the Junior Leader* is festooned with Quranic verses extolling the mujahideen, encouraging readers to be ready for war, and advising them in conduct on the battlefield and the importance of prayer and perseverance, among other themes. It contains numerous essays on "Islamic Concepts of Leadership" (see, e.g., Ahmad 1990; G.M. Malik 1990; A.R. Malik 1990; Sarfraz 1990). Brig. Muhammad Sarfraz (1990), for instance, explains that once a man enters the army "he can begin to understand that his regard for his uniform must be a far different thing from what he felt about his civilian dress, since it is identified with the dignity of 'soldier of Islam'.... [The] edifice of our leadership must be built upon the true ideals of our religion" (23). Like numerous similar essays, Sarfraz's essay seeks to situate the Pakistani soldier within the historical and cultural contexts of the great soldiers of Islam.

Mobilization of Islam and early Islamic military history bolsters the confidence of the Pakistani fighter by reassuring him that, as a Muslim, he is an innately superior fighter. Pakistan's defense literature, however, also mobilizes Islamic martial history to denigrate the enemies of Islam, be they *kufar* (infidels) or *muratid* (apostates). There are several narrative means of achieving this, one of which is to denigrate the legitimacy of India's cause. For example, Iqbal (1966) ascribes the failure of the Hindus in the 1965 war to the fact that the Indians lacked a legitimate cause. For this reason, nothing could persuade the Indian soldier of the need to endure "the hardships of battle, the pangs of hunger and thirst, the merciless beating of hostile elemental fury and the extreme rigours and suffering, trials and tribulations and death and decay that had started with it" (8).

Another way of denigrating the enemy is to reduce the diverse Indian Army to a solely Hindu force. This is in keeping with the line that Pakistan's army has drawn between the civilizations of Hindu India and Muslim Pakistan and the frequent resort to characterizing the conflict with India as jihad. Perhaps one of the most important examples of such exposition was written by Brig. Javed Hassan (1990). Hassan, who would retire as a lieutenant general, published *India: A Study in Profile* while at the Faculty of Research and Doctrinal Studies (FORAD) at the Command and Staff College in Quetta. It is now required reading at the National Defense University as well (National Defense University, n.d.). Among Hassan's other derogatory remarks (181–214), he argues that India is not a nation, characterizes its past as having a "total absence of any popular resistance against foreign domination and rule" (49), describes the Indians as "less Warlike" than Pakistanis (52), and attributes India's military failures to "racial" shortcomings (53).

While most of the military writers proffering varied accounts of Islamic military history focus on unexpected victories in the face of near certain defeat, other writers present a less optimistic set of lessons. Haq (1991) warns that being Muslim itself is not enough to ensure victory against a more numerous, kafir foe: ultimately god gives victory only to good Muslims. To drive home this point he contends that there have been no victorious "Muslim armies in the 20th century," a failure he explains by arguing that "the neglect of faith and abandonment of *Jihad* had led to poor ethics, the creation of an unjust social order, corruption and cultivation of bad habits... If we want to survive, we must understand the conduct of war in Islam" (51). Needless to say, he also devotes an entire subsection to jihad, titled "Motivation for War: The Doctrine of Jihad," which reinforces the previous points about the justness of Pakistan's military cause.

Fourth, the Pakistan Army and the intelligence agency it controls (the ISI) have relied on Islam to legitimize their actions in Afghanistan since the late 1950s, when they introduced JI into the country. Many anti-Soviet commanders—such as Gulbuddin Hekmatyar, Ahmad Shah Masood, and Maulvi Mohammad Yunus Khalis—had JI backgrounds. After the Soviet withdrawal, as Afghanistan succumbed to internecine warfare, Pakistan supported Gulbuddin Hekmatyar (an Islamist Pakhtun) in the hope that he could pacify Afghanistan and ensure it remained aligned with Pakistan. After Hekmatyar repeatedly demonstrated to Army General Headquarters and the ISI that he could not do so, Pakistan began patronizing the Taliban, a Deobandi group (Haqqani 2005). Pakistan has also relied on a bevy of Sunni Islamist militant groups to advance its interests in Indian-administered Kashmir and throughout India. Many of these groups, which come from Ahl-e-Hadith, JI, and Deobandi backgrounds, originated in the anti-Soviet jihad and were later redeployed to India. After 1990, these Islamist militant groups, operating at Pakistan's behest, worked to undermine groups like the Jammu Kashmir Liberation Front, an anti-India group that coalesced around ethnic Kashmiri identity as opposed to Islam (Evans 2000; Jamal 2009).

Not all versions of Islam are treated equally in the history of the military. The secondary literature on the army suggests that the military patronized different sectarian traditions at different times, to the discomfort of Shia, Ahmediyas, Sufis, and non-Muslim minorities (Abou Zahab 2002; Nasr 2002). But the military professional publications and even officer memoirs very rarely discuss sectarian-specific issues. In fact, many writers such as Ayub abjure sectarian cleavages and are wary of the ritualization of Islam in the armed forces. In 1992, Lt. Gen. Jehangir Karamat (who eventually became the chief of army staff during Nawaz Sharif's second term) explained in *The Pakistan Army Green Book 1992: Year of the Senior Field Commander* that "the thrust in our military culture should be towards development of a code of ethics rather than overemphasis on rituals. This code of ethics should be based on our faith in Allah and the senior leader should be seen as a God-fearing person who can be relied upon for fair play and justice... The senior commander must seek to create a command environment in which obsession with rituals or religions does not become a refuge for incompetence" (12).

Implications

Contrary to the conventional wisdom in the United States, the Pakistan Army's embrace of Islam as Pakistan's ideology, and of its own role of defending both ideological and territorial frontiers, is not solely the product of the Zia regime or of the US- and Pakistan-led jihad in Afghanistan. In fact, Pakistan and the army embraced these concepts far earlier. Given the numerous references to jihad and Islamic warfare in Pakistan's professional journals, it would be easy for an untrained reader to assume that the Pakistan Army is a jihadi army. And in fact, this reading is encouraged by Pakistan's long-standing reliance on Islamist militancy as a tool of foreign policy and its insistence that these militants are mujahideen. A more nuanced reading suggests that the army employs Islam for numerous reasons, including forging national unity across ethnic and sectarian cleavages, pushing the public to support sustained praetorianism and war with India, and motivating the troops by boosting morale and denigrating their foe as perfidious, effete Hindus.

The story, however, does not and cannot end there. As noted at the beginning of this chapter, the army has sustained steady infiltration by Islamist militants. Military elites may well have a complex understanding of the multiple purposes Islam serves, but it is far from clear how ordinary officers, much less the enlisted ranks, interpret these incessant references to Islamism, jihad, and perpetual enmity with India, especially when they coexist with some six decades of explicit mobilization of Islamist militants under the banner of Islam.

CHAPTER 5

Pakistan's Quest for Strategic Depth

An enduring component of the Pakistan Army's strategic behavior has been its belief that it requires *strategic depth* in Afghanistan. Despite the ubiquity of the term in the Pakistani national security discourse, there is considerable debate about what it actually means and, more recently, about whether or not the concept retains salience for Pakistan. Many scholars date Pakistan's pursuit of strategic depth to the tenure of Zia ul Haq, during which Pakistan, the United States, and Saudi Arabia backed Islamist guerillas—the so-called mujahideen—against the Soviets. Olivier Roy (2004), for example, describes strategic depth as a "geo-strategic perspective, designed at the time of the Soviet invasion of Afghanistan, with the aim of asserting the regional influence of Pakistan by establishing a kind of control on Afghanistan through a fundamentalist, Pakhtun-dominated movement" (149). Dietrich Reetz (1993), a prominent European scholar of Islam in South Asia, gives a slightly different account, dating Pakistan's pursuit of strategic depth to the loss of East Pakistan in 1971. He agrees, however, that "it was Zia who believed that the 'strategic depth' his country needed in its confrontation with India was best achieved by building an Islamic block [*sic*] between the Arabia Sea and the Urals" (30). Marvin Weinbaum (1991) also suggests that Pakistan's interest in strategic depth dates to the Afghan war, after which, he writes, "Zia felt that by assuming the position of a front-line state, Pakistan had won the right to a regime of its choice in Kabul" (499). In contrast, Rasul Bakhsh Rais (2008), a well-regarded Pakistani political scientist at the prestigious Lahore University of Management Sciences and writer for such military publications as *Hilal*, contends that the policy was not implemented until after the Soviet withdrawal from Afghanistan in 1988, when Pakistan decided to pursue "a policy of 'strategic depth,' meaning that Islamabad would contest the influence of non-friendly states in Afghanistan by retaining some degree of influence" (18).[1]

In addition to the disagreement over when Pakistan began its quest for strategic depth, analysts present different accounts of what Pakistan has tried to achieve through its pursuit of it. Some describe strategic depth as a geographical concept, even though few Pakistani security managers have advocated thinking of Afghanistan in those terms—that is, as a physical space in which Pakistan could safely disperse its personnel and assets during a war with India. Gen. Mirza Aslam Beg, army chief during Benazir Bhutto's first term as prime minister (1988–1991), is the only member of the Pakistani strategic elite to have defined strategic depth in this way (Hussain 2005). Because Beg's concept of territorial depth is anomalous, it should be considered as distinct from the more common understandings of strategic depth that have dominated Pakistani military thinking. The more common understanding of strategic depth requires the cultivation of a "friendly regime, expectedly an Islamist one, in Kabul that would enable Pakistan to avoid traditional insecurity or at least neutralize its western tribal borderlands and avoid future Afghan governments with strong links to New Delhi"; the former emphasizes reducing Pakistan's vulnerability to India's presumably "superior military forces" via "new military assets and capabilities" (Weinbaum 1991, 498–499).

One of the reasons why the army's concept of strategic depth is so poorly understood in the scholarly literature is that the Pakistan Army itself has adopted different definitions of the goal (Beg's territorial strategic depth versus the more typical political strategic depth) and how best to achieve the goal in Afghanistan (e.g., direct intervention, use of proxies, cultivate influence). In this chapter I explain what strategic depth has meant for the army at different points in time and how the army has sought to attain it. While some scholarship maintains that strategic depth is a relatively new addition to the army's evolving inventory of strategic culture components, I agree with Haqqani (2005) that the Pakistan Army's appreciation for strategic depth and concomitant compulsion to develop it is a colonial legacy. There is a high degree of continuity between what Pakistan has sought to do since 1947 and British efforts to conceptualize and manage the various threats coming from the north of the empire. This strategic legacy has shaped Pakistan's relations with Afghanistan but also its policies with respect to its own expansive frontier regions: those areas of Balochistan that abut Iran and Afghanistan, as well as Khyber Pakhtunkhwa (formerly known as the North-West Frontier Provinces, or NWFP), and the Federally Administered Tribal Areas (FATA) on the border with Afghanistan.[2]

Because Pakistan's army inherited much of the British Raj's strategic appraisal of the threats from the western frontier, in this chapter, I first recount Britain's efforts to manage its frontier and the areas beyond in the context of the competition between imperial Britain and, sequentially, Tsarist Russia (1721–1917), post-Revolutionary Russia (1917–1922), and the Soviet Union (from 1921)—usually given the sobriquet The Great Game (Fromkin 1980; McMahon 1993). Next I enumerate the threats inherited by the independent Pakistani state. As I will show in this chapter, the new state of Pakistan, with only a fraction of the empire's resources, faced a threat environment that was in many ways more hostile than that confronted by its colonial predecessor. For the nascent Pakistan Army the compulsions of strategic depth were more or less continuous with those of the Raj, but its resources were a fraction of those possessed by the Raj to manage the same challenges. Subsequently I exposit how Pakistan began its efforts to acquire strategic depth, primarily through manipulating internal affairs in Afghanistan. I then focus upon the complementary internal policies that Pakistan pursued with respect to its frontier populations and the role of the army therein. I conclude this chapter with a reflection on what this enduring feature of Pakistan's strategic culture means for future Pakistani behavior toward Afghanistan.

British Management of the Frontier: The Great Game

The British began to develop the governance and security architecture of the frontier areas (now Balochistan, the Federally Administered Tribal Areas, and Khyber Pakhtunkhwa, or KP) in the 1830s, and at the time of independence this architecture was still evolving (Tripodi 2011, 9). Over the course of some 117 years, British policy changed in response to prevailing strategic concerns (within both Europe and the wider region) and domestic political developments. For much of this period, British security managers focused on Russia's purportedly inexorable expansionism. In 1759, the British Indian and Russian territories were separated by some 4,000 miles. By 1885, the gap had closed to a mere 400 miles (ibid.). It was this imperial rivalry (in the form of the Anglo-Afghan wars) that drew Afghanistan into the international state system (Rubin 2002).

As the Russian and British empires vied for dominance in Central Asia, the areas now known as Afghanistan, Iran, Balochistan, and Khyber Pakhtunkhwa (then known as the NWFP) became sites of contestation and the spaces in which the British sought to develop their concept of strategic depth. Of particular interest were the strategic passes of Balochistan and the Hindu Kush, both of which had long afforded invaders access to the South Asian subcontinent. The British understood that the support or even noninterference of the frontier populations would benefit their interests while their hostility could prove injurious. Thus, these sparsely populated frontier areas became the foci of British efforts to deter an armed invasion of British India via Afghanistan (Hussain 2005; Tripodi 2011). The emphasis on the frontier areas was even greater once the British concluded that Persia was unsuitable as an ally against Russia.[3]

While British Indian leaders typically framed their South Asian policies in terms of the "external threat" from Russia, in some cases they exaggerated the threat to increase the prominence of India within political debates in Great Britain or to justify a particular policy approach. At other times, British threat perception regarding Afghanistan was motivated by enduring concerns over the fundamental stability of the British Raj. During the Indian Rebellion of 1857, for instance, the British feared (without justification, it turned out) that the Afghan government would act to further inflame Indian political sentiments and to undermine British ability to restore order. In the early twentieth century, Afghanistan aided those Indians who demanded independence, increasing Afghanistan's salience for the Raj's leaders.

Throughout the nineteenth and early twentieth centuries, the British moved between an aggressive forward policy toward Afghanistan and a more internally focused, close border policy. The forward policy of the 1830s was the result of British attempts to preempt the Russians from developing a presence in the area. It called for the protection of British Indian interests by extending the authority of the Raj beyond its official borders and by confronting and defeating external threats before they could threaten British Indian territory. This policy aimed to push the boundaries of the empire as far north and west as possible. To do so, the British invaded Afghanistan in an effort to put Shuja-ul-Mulk (Shuja Shah Durrani) back on the Afghan throne.[4] This foray began the first Anglo-Afghan War (1839–1842). Amid growing opposition, in 1842 the British government ordered an ignominious retreat from Kabul during which Afghans massacred the entire British army, with the exception of one soldier. The British returned in the summer of 1842 with an army of retribution and laid waste to Kabul. Dost Mohammad, who had been exiled from Afghanistan since 1839 and was living in India on a British government pension, returned to govern Afghanistan in 1843 (Barfield 2010; Hussain 2005; Rubin 2002; Tripodi 2011).

In the wake of their humiliating defeat in the first Anglo-Afghan war (1839–1842) and evident inability to install a client regime in Kabul, the British changed their approach. From about 1843 to 1875 they pursued a close border policy, also known as a strategy of masterly inactivity. Under this policy the territories west of the Indus were considered to be beyond the administrative remit of British India, and the various tribes were left to order their affairs without British interference. Coming after the defeat of the Sikhs and the subsequent incorporation of the Punjab into British India, the close border policy "envisaged drawing British power—fiscal and material—back across the border into India, crafting an impenetrable defensive system that relied not only on military deterrence but also on a fundamentally secure society that bound together colonial rulers and native subjects and would be able to resist the intrigues of both external and internal enemies alike" (Tripodi 2011, 16; see also Hussain 2005; Rubin 2002).

During this period, the British focused their resources on securing Sindh (which they formally annexed in 1843, after a sustained military campaign) and the Punjab, which they annexed in 1849 (Hussain 2005). The inclusion within British India of the Punjab and other territories formerly under the control of Maharaja Ranjit Singh (such as the frontier town of Peshawar) allowed the British to consolidate their control over the Pakhtun-inhabited areas west of the Indus. Dost Mohammad, for his part, was focused on recovering control of Southern

Afghanistan and retaining control over Herat. The British and Afghans thus established a modus vivendi under which Mohammad incorporated Uzbek, Tajik, and Turkmen territories north of the Hindu Kush but did not disturb the stability of the Pakhtun tribal belt between Kabul and the Indus River (Barfield 2012; Hussain 2005; Rubin 2002).[5]

In 1855, Mohammad formalized relations with British India by signing the Treaty of Peshawar, which obliged both parties to respect the existing borders.[6] In 1857, Mohammad and the British agreed to a second treaty, under the terms of which the British would provide financial support and weapons as assistance in confronting any Persian threat. When the Indian Rebellion of 1857 began in north India, Mohammad refused to declare a jihad against the British in the North-West Frontier and the rest of India, despite pressure from the ulema (Barfield 2012). Britain's investment in Mohammad had resulted in a pliant, if weak, Afghan state. The arrangement suited British interests and lasted until Mohammad died in 1863. After his death, his sons fought to succeed him, with Sher Ali eventually prevailing (ibid.).

Meanwhile, the Russians continued to annex territory north of Afghanistan. While Russia and Britain continued to carry out the Great Game, they also engaged in diplomatic discussions of their respective interests in the region. By 1873, both had conceded in principle that Afghanistan should be a neutral zone, and in that year they agreed that the Amu Darya would form the country's northern boundary (Hussain 2005; Rubin 2002). (This initiated the concept of Afghanistan as a buffer state, which Pakistan's Army later embraced.) In February 1874, Conservative leader Benjamin Disraeli became prime minister. Believing that the Russians were redoubling their efforts in Central Asia, he radically revised Indian security policy by reviving the forward policy for both Balochistan and Afghanistan.[7]

Balochistan, which provided easy access to British India as well as southern Afghanistan, had long been a point of concern for the British. In 1876, the British facilitated an accord between the Khan of Qalat and Balochistan's various lesser rulers in an effort to bring to an end the tribal violence and the predations on British territory.[8] The treaty reiterated the terms of an earlier accord signed in 1854 and emphasized the Khan's obligation to support British interests in exchange for British protection from attack (as well as a robust subsidy). To help consolidate their control over the area and facilitate British movement into Afghanistan, the British built roads, railways, and telegraph facilities around Quetta (Tripodi 2011).[9]

In 1878, in response to Russian attempts to open treaty negotiations with the then-amir of Afghanistan, Sher Ali, the British viceroy Lord Lytton dispatched a mission to Afghanistan to order Sher Ali not to meet with the Russian delegation. Lytton's team was turned away at the Khyber Pass. The British, outraged and humiliated, began the second Anglo-Afghan War (1878–1880) (Hussain 2005;

Mahajan 2002; Tripodi 2011). By early 1879, the British had managed to bring much of southern and eastern Afghanistan under their control. When Sher Ali fled from Kabul to Mazar, the British installed his son Muhammad Yaqub as amir and in May 1879. The British forced him to sign the Treaty of Gandamak, which concluded the first phase of the war. The treaty gave the British complete control of Afghanistan's external affairs, ending the country's status as a buffer state. It reduced Yaqub from an independent ruler to a vassal of the British empire, like the various heads of princely states in British India. It also ceded the districts of Pishin, Sibi, and the Kurram Valley to Britain: the first two areas became part of Balochistan; the third joined the North-West Frontier. In return, Yaqub received an annual subsidy as well as arms and ammunition (Barfield 2010; Hussain 2005; Tripodi 2011).

After the incorporation of Pishin and Sibi, the British developed what would turn out to be an enduring administrative system for Balochistan. (It is often referred to as the Sandeman system, after its architect, Sir Robert G. Sandeman.) This system combined a readiness to use lethal force with a commitment to knowing the various tribes as well as their languages; working through tribal leaders whenever possible, identifying and selectively supporting specific leaders when required, and binding the tribes to the government through reciprocal service and compensation. This system of compensated service, known as the levy system, became the mainstay of tribal administration, and a modified form of it persists even today in Balochistan and the tribal areas (Tripodi 2011).

The British accepted Yakub as the ruler of Afghanistan until mobs attacked Sir Louis Cavagnari, the British head of mission in Kabul. In response, the British dispatched Gen. Frederick Roberts to occupy Kabul. Yaqub was forced to abdicate and flee to India, and after his departure the British ruled Afghanistan directly (Barfield 2010). Viceroy Lord Lytton "concluded that if he could not rule Afghanistan through a compliant amir, he would dismember it" (Barfield 2010, 142). While the British managed to separate Qandahar, in the south, from Kabul, the Pakhtun tribes and the ulema continued to foment unrest. Unable to either pacify Afghanistan or break it up, the British desperately sought a way to retreat without abandoning their interests. They found their solution in the form of Abdur Rahman (a nephew of Sher Ali), who returned to Afghanistan in 1880 (Barfield 2010; Hussain 2005; Rubin 2002). While Rahman was not pleased by British encroachment, he was much more concerned by the prospect of further Russian expansion. Perhaps even more importantly, he feared that should the Russians and the British go to war, Afghanistan would be the site of the conflict. These fears motivated him to back the British against the Russians. Per the terms of the agreement eventually reached between him and the Raj, Rahman received a robust subsidy while Britain retained control over Afghanistan's foreign affairs. In light of the continuing Russian advances, Russian and British authorities became even more interested in delineating the borders of Afghanistan. In a series of protocols signed in the 1880s and 1890s, the two (the Afghans were often not even consulted) finally agreed on Afghanistan's northern borders (Barfield 2010; Hussain 2005; Rubin 2002; Tripodi 2011).

After the numerous challenges of the second Anglo-Afghan war, in 1881 the British reverted to a more conservative policy toward Afghanistan: the masterly inactivity or close border policy. This shift was facilitated by the agreement between the British and Rahman, under which he received a subsidy of some 1.2 million Indian rupees, rising to 1.85 million in 1893, when he agreed to demarcate the boundary between Afghan and British spheres of influence. This boundary, which was drawn with little heed to geography or ethnic distribution, became known as the Durand Line, after its British author, Sir Mortimer Durand, who was a British diplomat and civil servant of British India. The 1,519-mile boundary stretched from the southern tip of Balochistan to the base of the Wakhan corridor at the northernmost point of the North West Frontier.[10] The British and Russians were keen to make the corridor—the mountainous strip that now protrudes from the northeast corner of Afghanistan—a part of Afghanistan because doing so would remove any common border between the Russian and British empires and thus minimize the possibility of any direct clash between the two armies (Rubin 2002). This agreement allowed Rahman to consolidate the Afghan state, focusing on security rather than development (ibid.). As opposition to his practices mounted, Pakhtuns and the ulema mobilized again, creating the conditions for various raids into the tribal areas on the British side of the border (Tripodi 2011).[11]

By the close of the first decade of the nineteenth century, the structure of British Indian administration on the western frontier had taken its current form. The political organization of the frontier was the work of Lord Curzon, who became viceroy of India in 1899. Worried by Kabul's ability to cause trouble on the frontier, skeptical of predictions of Russian aggression, and chary of the increasing military costs of confronting the tribal rebellion, Curzon promulgated a third phase of frontier policy. Known as a modified close border policy, this involved the creation of the NWFP in 1901 and the redeployment of British resources—including the military—back into India to focus on national defense instead of tribal matters.

The NWFP, so named because it was located at the northwestern frontier of the Raj, was composed of five settled districts: Hazara; Peshawar; Bannu; Kohat; and Dera Ismael Khan. The frontier also included British Balochistan and five political agencies in the tribal belt along the North-West Frontier: Khyber Agency (created in 1879); Kurram (created in 1892); and South and North Waziristan and Malakand Agencies (created in 1895) (Barfield 2010; Tripodi 2011). These agencies were renamed the tribal agencies in 1901, and they continued to be treated differently than the settled districts of British India, where the British implemented regular forms of governance and taxation. The agencies, in contrast, were governed by a unique political system, the Frontier Crimes Regulation, which was especially designed for tribal management (Hussain 2005; Tripodi 2009, 2011; White 2008).

The frontier had two distinct kinds of boundaries: one between Afghanistan and British India that was composed of the tribal belt; and another between the tribal belt and the settled areas. Equally important, the establishment of the NWFP also created two distinct kinds of economies. In the settled areas, the state's revenue system created and empowered a few big landlords (often referred to as Khans), who became a Pakhtun bourgeoisie, as well as an increasing population of landless peasants and proletariat. The tribal areas retained the old economic system, but the general scarcity of fertile land led their inhabitants to develop a market economy dependent on smuggling (Khan 2003).

The Frontier Crimes Regulation (FCR)—the legal framework that applied in the tribal areas—differed markedly from the legal architecture that governed the rest of British India. It was promulgated formally in 1901, although it was derived from previous similar arrangements. The various tribes were allowed to govern themselves according to *riwaj*, or customary practices, but each agency was also administered by a Political Agent who was usually a British civil servant or military officer. The agent's decisions were enforced by convening tribal elders (*maliks*) in a traditional deliberative mechanism known as a *jirga*. The British provided these maliks with discretionary funds so that they could reinforce their influence through patronage. The elders maintained security with the assistance of militias made up of local tribesmen, who were compensated for providing basic security duties. These militiamen were ultimately led by the head of the Frontier Constabulary, a British Indian Army officer.

The entire tribal governance framework was placed under the auspices of the NWFP government, so the political agents reported to the governor of the North-West Frontier Province (Hussain 2005; White 2008). When the British introduced governance reforms throughout British India in 1909 and 1920, they did not extend these reforms to NWFP due to their fears of the Pakhtun capacity for unrest.[12] Worse, those in the NWFP who clamored for reforms were punished using civil crime regulation (Khan 2003).

These complicated and carefully considered efforts to indirectly manage Afghanistan and the frontier areas could not prevent violence from erupting throughout the region. In an effort to gain independence from the British, the Afghans initiated the Third Anglo-Afghan War (May–August 1919). Despite experiencing some military success, the British, exhausted by the First World War, agreed to grant Afghanistan complete independence. Britain also ceased all subsidies to the Afghan ruler, Amanullah. This treaty, signed in 1922, marked the formal start of yet another strategic phase: the modified forward policy (Barfield 2010; Hussain 2005; Tripodi 2011). This policy involved returning the army to its pivotal role in South Waziristan (understood to be the epicenter of tribal dissent) while retaining a close border policy toward Afghanistan. Despite persistent

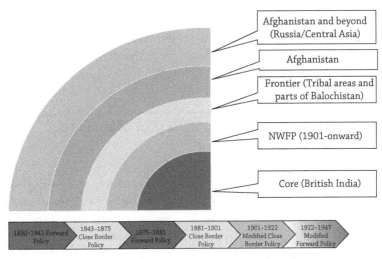

Figure 5.1 Graphical depiction of the security system of South Asia.

and large-scale tribal unrest in 1936–1937, the policy remained in place until Pakistan's independence (Tripodi 2011).[13]

For more than a century, the terrain over which the British played out their concept of strategic depth extended from the border of British India (which moved westward over time) up to the Amu Darya and beyond.[14] This strategic geography can be depicted in several concentric spheres (Figure 5.1). The innermost sphere was British India itself (i.e., the territories east of the Indus), which was to be secured from encroachment at all costs. The outmost arc was defined by imperial Russia, which eventually extended to the northern borders of Afghanistan. The space between these two spheres was negotiated differently at different times. The bulk of modern Afghan territory was variously construed as either a buffer area (the close border policy) or an area of active British power projection (forward policy), depending on the date and the prevailing regional, international, and domestic (British) concerns.

The frontier region (classically known as the Trans-Indus because it generally stretched from the west bank of the Indus River up to southern Afghanistan) was seen as an internal buffer area that provided an additional defense for the British Indian heartland. The British developed a complex arrangement for governing this area, coming over time to outsource security to local tribal structures working in conjunction with British political agents. The British wanted to avoid confrontation and expensive deployments and thus employed military force only when necessary (e.g., when British convoys were attacked in the frontier). Notions of citizenship varied across this space. While those living in the Punjab and Sindh were subjects of British India (with the exception of the citizens of the princely states), different legal regimes existed for inhabitants of the North-West Frontier Province (which was under governor rule), much of Balochistan, and all of the tribal areas. The FATA and parts of Balochistan were governed by the FCR, which, with some modifications, still acts as the legal framework in this region. This is the security concept that Pakistan inherited in 1947 (Ali 1999; Tripodi 2009; White 2008).

Pakistan's Army Seeks Strategic Depth: Managing Pakistan's Frontier and Beyond

At independence, Pakistan's military leaders, all products of the British Indian army, assumed that Pakistan would continue to follow British Afghan policy; Pakistan's geography and neighborhood, however, made this very difficult. Kabul saw the Partition of the Raj as an opportunity to disencumber itself from commitments it had made to the British and reassert its irredentist claims on Pakhtun-majority areas in the North-West Frontier Province, the tribal areas, and even parts of Balochistan. Afghanistan was the only state to oppose Pakistan's inclusion within the United Nations (UN). Even though it eventually relented and withdrew its opposition, relations between the two continued to be uneasy. Afghanistan insisted that the various treaties between Afghanistan and British India became void upon Pakistan's independence, including the treaty that established the Durand Line as the boundary between the two states.[15] Equally discomfiting for Pakistan's civilian and military leadership, Afghanistan also began demanding the creation of an independent Pakhtun state (variously called Pakhtunistan or Pashtunistan) from Pakistan's Pakhtun-dominated areas.[16]

Gen. Ayub Khan (2006), Pakistan's first military ruler, gave an explanation for Afghanistan's behavior that provides considerable insights into how Pakistani military elites viewed Afghanistan from 1947 onward. According to Ayub, Afghanistan initiated these campaigns and gained confidence in its ability to succeed thanks to

> constant Indian propaganda [that] Pakistan could not survive as a separate State. The Afghan rulers believed this to be true and decided to stake a claim to our territory before Pakistan disintegrated.... In this way the idea of an artificial State of Pkhtoonistan [sic] inside our borders was made an issue by the Afghan rulers.... In this claim the Afghans were backed by India whose interests lay in ensuring that in the event of a war with us over Kashmir, the Afghans should open a second front against Pakistan on the North West Frontier. They also reasoned that if they had this understanding with Afghanistan, we would not be able to use the Pathan tribesmen against them. The Indians thought that they would be able to hem us in and embarrass us by a pincer movement (197).

This insight, prevalent among Pakistani defense writers, links Pakistan's problems with Afghanistan inextricably to its security competition with India (see also F.M. Khan 1963) even though India has never supported the Afghan position on the status of the Durand Line. Thus presumed connivance between India and Afghanistan continues to animate the Pakistan army's strategic thinking and will likely do so well into the future.

The early rivalry with Afghanistan complicated Pakistan's already monumental security challenges. Aslam Siddiqi (1958), an official in the Pakistani Bureau of National Reconstruction, explained Pakistan's predicament thusly: it "inherited almost all the burden of the external land defence of undivided India. This mainly meant the defence of the North-West Frontier where about 80 per cent of the Indian Army was normally stationed. But Pakistan soon discovered that the Indo-Pakistan border was still more dangerous and had to post there the bulk of its army" (73). Equally problematic, whereas the British had been able to draw on the revenue of the entire Raj, Pakistan's resources were thin.

In some ways, the newly formed Pakistan faced even greater security problems than the British. The boundary between Afghanistan and the Raj was not actively contested, and Afghan leaders could not credibly challenge British rule except by exploiting internal issues. Pakistan, in contrast, quickly became involved in disputes over a high percentage of its borders: Afghanistan was committed to undoing the territorial status quo vis-à-vis Pakistan, while Pakistan itself sought to revise the territorial status quo with India. Moreover, until 1971 Pakistan's entire eastern wing was surrounded by India. Adding to Pakistan's security challenges was the enduring conviction among its leadership that India sought to undo Partition and that Afghanistan was only a pawn in India's grand designs. Pakistani military leaders thus could not delink their concerns about Afghanistan from their fears regarding India, even though India did not publicly support Afghanistan's revisionist efforts (Haqqani 2005, 162; F.M. Khan 1963).

Part of Pakistan's apprehensions about Afghan interference across its western border can be attributed to political events prior to Partition. As noted in Chapter 3, the Muslim League struggled to garner support for the party, for Jinnah's claim to speak for South Asia's Muslims, and even for the Pakistan movement itself. In fact, many people in the frontier region never signed on to the project of Pakistan. In 1929 the Khudai Khidmatgar (Servants of god), a Pakhtun ethnic movement, emerged under the leadership of Khan Abdul Ghaffar Khan. It was fiercely anticolonial and also uncompromisingly opposed to the Partition of British India and the creation of Pakistan. Viewing the Muslim League as pro-British, Ghaffar allied with the Congress Party. With his help, the party took 15 of 36 seats in the 1937 NWFP provincial elections. (The Muslim League did not win a single seat.) When Ghaffar could no longer ignore the fact that Pakistan was inevitable, he was "completely stunned" and viewed the creation of the new state as an "act of treachery" by the Congress Party (Khan 2003, 77). Ghaffar and his fellow Pakhtun nationalists demanded that the British grant them an independent state as well. The British were unwilling to entertain further division but agreed to hold a plebiscite in the NWFP to decide whether the province would join Pakistan or remain a part of India. The Muslim League, with the support of the British, ran an effective campaign that resulted in an overwhelming vote for joining Pakistan (ibid.).

Nevertheless, given the resistance to Pakistan, overt demands for independence, and even the support for India historically prevalent in the NWFP, Pakistan's security managers viewed the Pakhtuns as "the most potent internal threat to the state" (Khan 2003, 67). This required Pakistan to craft foreign policies to contend with the external challenges emanating from Afghanistan and domestic policies for its own frontier areas. Its solution was to retain much of the security architecture developed by the British. Pakistan, like the British before it, would variously employ a forward policy, a close border policy, or modifications of both, as dictated by the army's security perspectives.

A perusal of Pakistan's several decades of professional military journals attests to the variety of apprehensions Afghanistan provokes within the Pakistan Army. The most prominent concern arises from the direct and indirect security threats posed by the Soviet Union's increasing presence in Afghanistan. For example, Lt. Col. Shamsul Haq Qazi, in 1964, warned that "rapidly increasingly Russian influence in Afghanistan, [has] brought the two mightiest armies [those of China and the Soviet Union] of the world close to our borders" (19). Abdul Sattar (2007), who served as Pakistan's foreign minister under Gen. Pervez Musharraf, made a similar observation when he wrote, "On the Pakistan side, too, inherited and inherent factors prejudiced Pakistan against the Soviet Union. The Pakistani administrative elite, nurtured in the British strategic view, suspected that the Soviet state cherished the czarist aim of carving out a land access to the warm waters of the Arabian Sea, and therefore, posed a danger to Pakistan's security" (34). But while many military authors lamented the growing Soviet influence in Afghanistan, prior to the Soviet invasion of Afghanistan surprisingly few exposited a direct Soviet military threat to Pakistan. This should not be taken to mean, however, that the Soviet Union did not present major problems for Pakistan's foreign policy objectives.

Pakistan's problems with the Soviet Union rose out of Cold War alliances. As will be discussed at greater length in the chapter on US–Pakistan relations, by the mid-1950s Pakistan had become tightly allied with the United States through a series of instruments, including a Mutual Defense Assistance Agreement with the United States (signed in 1954); the Baghdad Pact of 1955, which was renamed the Central Treaty Organization (CENTO) after Iraq's withdrawal; and the Southeast Asian Treaty Organization (SEATO), founded in 1955. Pakistan's military and civilian leadership was keen to secure US assistance to rebuild its weak military, and such alliances afforded Pakistan ample opportunity and resources to do so. Because the formal purpose of these organizations was to limit communist expansion, Pakistan pretended to accede to that objective, even though it was predominantly interested in enhancing its conventional capabilities vis-à-vis India (Haqqani 2005; M.A. Khan 2006; Kux 2001; Sattar 2007). Ayub, Pakistan's first military ruler, described Pakistan's compulsions in this regard in his autobiography, *Friends not Masters:*

> From the day of Independence, Pakistan was involved in a bitter and prolonged struggle for her very existence and survival. By 1954 Pakistan was compelled to align herself with the West in the interests of her security. She became a member of the Baghdad Pact and the South-East Asia Treaty Organization, both of which were suspect in the communist world (M.A. Khan 2006, 136).

In his discussions of Pakistan's foreign policy in *Friends not Masters*, Ayub takes considerable pains to prove that Pakistan joined these alliances out of compulsion rather than shared strategic interests with the United States (ibid.).

Despite the popular belief that Ayub was staunchly anticommunist, and despite the fact that under his watch the Pakistan Army became tightly enmeshed in anticommunist defense pacts with the United States, his autobiography belies this view in some measure. In fact, he argues that it "should be possible to come to an understanding with the Soviet Union by removing her doubts and misgivings" (about Pakistan's participation in US-led treaty alliances to counter the spread of communism) because Pakistan "had never been a party to any design against her and our membership of the Pact was dictated solely by the requirements of our security" (M.A. Khan 2006, 138). Ayub conceded, however, that one of the enduring stumbling blocks to normalization was India's military relationship with the Soviet Union, which was significant despite India's professions of nonalignment.

The Soviet Union also unnerved Pakistan's military leadership by supporting Indian and Afghan efforts to undermine Pakistan's interests in the South Asian region. Siddiqi (1959), making the case for continued US defense assistance, claimed that "Pakistan has faced the full blast of the Soviet warning against "disastrous consequences" [for its military relationship with the United States]" (49). He explained that in December 1955, Soviet leader Nikita Khrushchev "'awarded' Kashmir to India" when he stated "that Kashmir is one of the States of the Republic of India, has already been decided by the people of Kashmir" (ibid.). At the same time, Khrushchev also expressed support for "Afghanistan's policy on the Pushtunistan issue.... [But he also promised that] If Pakistan were to adopt the same independent attitude as for example India, conditions could be provided for the establishment of friendly relations between Pakistan and neighbouring countries" (ibid.). In 1957, the Soviet Union vetoed a UN Security Council Resolution on Kashmir (a move that would become a common feature of

Soviet policy toward India and Pakistan at the United Nations).[17] Even if the Soviet Union did not directly threaten Pakistan's interests, Pakistan's military believed that Moscow's growing support of Kabul emboldened the Afghan government to take a more hostile line on the border dispute and on the status of Pakhtun territories within Pakistan. But despite Pakistan's incessant misgivings about Afghanistan and Afghanistan's own tendency to support anti-state movements in Pakistan, the Afghan government actually supported Pakistan in the 1965 war with India and maintained strict neutrality during the 1971 war between India and Pakistan (Durrani and Khan 2002; Haqqani 2005; Hussain 2005; Sattar 2007).

In December 1971, following the secession of Bangladesh, Pakistan again returned to civilian control under the administration of Zulfiqar Ali Bhutto, whose government believed that the geostrategic environment had become even more inhospitable for Pakistan and that Pakistan must increasingly look to Iran and even Afghanistan for its defense (Calabrese 1997; Malik 2002). After becoming the president and the first civilian martial law administrator of Pakistan, Bhutto went to Afghanistan, ostensibly to thank his neighbor for its neutrality in the 1971 war. He met with King Zahir Shah and raised his concerns about Afghanistan's instigation of Pakhtun nationalist activities in Pakistan, but little came of the meeting. Later in 1973 Sardar Mohammad Daoud overthrew Shah, possibly with Soviet backing. Daoud was a staunch advocate of Pakhtunistan and took every opportunity to harass Pakistan about this issue (Tahir-Kheli 1974–1975). His advocacy may have been a cynical effort to mitigate the growing discontent of the various fractious Pakhtun tribes under his governance, whose members increasingly came to resent his progressive agenda. Upon seizing power, Daoud publicly explained that the resolution of Afghanistan's bilateral disputes with Pakistan depended on a "peaceful and honourable solution to this problem (Pashtunistan) in accordance with the hopes and aspirations of the Pashtun and Baluch people and their leaders" (quoted in Hussain 2005, 78).

Daoud's focus on Balochistan enraged Pakistan in part because Pakistan was experiencing a full-blown Baloch insurgency at that time. The Pakistanis used lethal force to suppress the insurgency, including helicopter gunship strikes using Cobra attack helicopters it had obtained from the United States. Between 1973 and 1975, Daoud's government provided Baloch insurgents with sanctuary as well as arms and munitions, and Afghanistan highlighted Pakistan's use of force in multilateral fora. In November 1974, Daoud wrote to the UN secretary general to criticize Pakistan's treatment of Baloch and Pakhtuns, which he argued violated both the UN Charter and the Universal Declaration of Human Rights. Daoud explicitly sought Indian as well as Soviet assistance for its effort to press Pakistan on the question of Pakhtunistan (Hussain 2005).

Even after the Soviets withdrew from Afghanistan in May 1988, Pakistan continued to harbor suspicions about the threats posed by both Afghanistan and the Soviet Union. Lt. Col. Israr Ahmad Ghumman, writing in the *Pakistan Army*

Journal in March 1990, described Pakistan as a small state that simultaneously confronts "multidirectional threats to her security due to her geostrategic importance, national policies and ideological stance. Pakistan remains sandwiched between an expanding ideology and a hegemonic neighbor forcing it to live in a perpetual state of external conflict" (Ghumman 1990, 26). This is consistent with the views of Siddiqi (1960, 44–45):

> Pakistan inherited almost all the burden of the external land defense of United India. This mainly meant the defense of the north-west frontier where was normally stationed about eighty percent of the Indian Army. But in December 1947, movements of the Indian armed forces became such a menace to its security that Pakistan withdrew all its forces from the northwest frontier and posted them near the Indo-Pakistan border. So the overall burden of defense [that] Pakistan has got to carry is much heavier than that of United India.... Pakistan has to look ahead in the North and watch the trends there. The first line of defense of the Indo-Pakistan subcontinent lies in the Hindu Kush [the mountain range spanning Pakistan and Afghanistan]....

Several persistent themes provide a backdrop for the Pakistan Army's beliefs about Afghanistan and the threats emanating from it. First, while Afghanistan's military may not be able to threaten Pakistan by conventional means, the Pakistan Army has long been convinced that Afghanistan can mobilize the support of hostile international actors—at various times, the Soviet Union, Russia, India, or Iran—to prosecute its hostile policy vis-à-vis Pakistan and that it can directly and indirectly support, or even instigate, antistate activities in Pakistan. Ghumman (1990) captures these sentiments in his 1990 article in the *Pakistan Army Journal*. He argues that while the Afghan Army could not prosecute an all-out offensive against Pakistan on its own, it could still resort to "increasing acts of violation and punitive strike as she had done in the past" (27). He ties Pakistan's domestic stability to these external forces, noting that "the delicate internal balance of Pakistan due to law and order, Pakhtoonistan and refugee problems, have the potential of being exploited by external factors through subversion, terrorism and insurgency.... The dissident elements and miscreants can be exploited by Russia, India and Afghanistan in their nefarious designs" (28).

These concerns continue to animate the Pakistan Army's evaluation of events in Afghanistan since 9/11. Pakistan's military leadership believes that India has expanded its presence in Afghanistan under the US security umbrella following the US ouster of the Taliban in late 2001. Equally important, Pakistan's military believes that India and Afghanistan have played a role in undermining Pakistan's security in Balochistan and in the frontier area, which has been plagued by

Islamist insurgency for much of the past decade. In 2011, Col. Dr. Muhammad Khan (2011), who at the time was a faculty member at the prestigious Lahore University of Management Sciences, wrote in the journal *Hilal*, an official magazine of the Inter Services Public Relations (ISPR):

> Indian growing involvement in Afghanistan is yet another concern both at regional and global level. US is acting as a guarantor to the detrimental role of India in the future set up of Afghanistan. In this regards, Indian role in the reconstruction of Afghanistan is projected more than its true volume. Indeed, US is preparing India as its successor state in Afghanistan, in case it lessens its presence by 2014, under the strong US public pressure. With each passing day, there is an increase in the Indian role in Afghanistan. For countries like Pakistan, this growing Indian influence in Afghanistan is enhancing its security concerns. Already Indian intelligence set up has created internal instability in FATA and Balochistan. The active Indian presence in Afghanistan is pushing Pakistan for a two front war... (19).

In July 2012, Maj. Asif Jehangir Raja (2012), the editor of *Hilal*, claimed that Pakistani terrorists were finding safe havens in Afghanistan. Maj. Raja identified the northeastern Afghan province of Kunar as a place that "was quietly being generated to accommodate the run-away terrorists of Swat who had fled the area due to fear of Pakistan Army" (3). He claims that the terrorists have used these sanctuaries to train recruits, hold planning meetings, and safely conduct raids on the Pakistani military. Raja is incredulous that "a group of hundreds, assemble at some place in Afghanistan, carries out a cross border attack, and goes back without being noticed by Afghan and Allied security forces.... The question arises as why the 'safe havens' are tolerated (or at least not attacked) on the Afghan side of the border?" (ibid.).

Some may quickly dismiss these claims as a fatuous attempt to deflect long-standing American, North Atlantic Treaty Organization (NATO), and Afghan criticisms of Pakistan for providing sanctuary to the Taliban, among other militants active in Afghanistan, but analysts do so at their own peril. The scenario Raja describes is plausible given Afghanistan's past history with Pakistan. Furthermore, it has been my experience that many Pakistanis in uniform share his belief. The fact that the United States has made no genuine inquiry into these issues has prevented it from refuting these serious—if spurious—allegations. Equally important, the belief that India and Afghanistan are both meddling in Pakistani affairs is widely held outside the military as well. Pakistan's media commentators devote significant air time and column inches to the purported mushrooming Indian consulates in Afghanistan, Indian support of militants operating throughout Pakistan, and accounts of anti-Pakistan militants safely ensconced in

Afghan sanctuaries (see, e.g., Ahsan 2006; *Daily Times* 2012b; *Pakistan Express Tribune* 2012; Zahra-Malik 2011). M. Maqbool Khan Wazir (2011), writing in the official publication of IPRI, a government-sponsored think tank, boldly claims:

> The role of foreign players in the ongoing insurgency in FATA, KP and Balochistan would be hard to dismiss given its persistence in the face of the military operation. The investigations made by Pakistani [intelligence] agencies have found evidences [*sic*] of foreign involvement in creating anarchy in Pakistan. These investigations indicate that the Pakistani law enforcing agencies found highly credible evidence proving that the Indians were not only giving comprehensive financial support to terrorists in Pakistan but were also providing them with arms, equipment and technical support. During operation Rah-e-Nijat huge quantity of Indian arms and ammunition, literature, medical equipment and medicines was recovered from Sherawangi area, near Kaniguram in South Waziristan Agency. Rehman Malik, interior minister, has provided evidence to the US of Indian assistance to the militants who are targeting NATO forces and Pakistani troops simultaneously (71).

It would behoove international actors to focus intelligence and other assets on these allegations, if for no other reason than to credibly engage the nature of the claims and their degree of legitimacy. However, given that Pakistanis accept these propositions as statements of fact, I am skeptical that any amount of countervailing evidence can mitigate Pakistani fears and the precarious behaviors they encourage.

The Army Manages the Afghan Threat

In its efforts to contend with the direct and indirect threats flowing from Afghanistan, the Pakistan Army has long used one of its few abundant resources: Islamists. While the major ulema parties did not at first welcome the Partition of South Asia into India and Pakistan (they believed that nationalism was antithetical to the supranational identity politics of Islamism and thought that Partition would weaken the umma, the international Islamic nation, in South Asia), they eventually reconciled themselves to, and even championed, the notion of Pakistan. Key among these parties were the Jamaat-e-Islami (JI) and the Jamiat-ulema-Islami (JUI). They remain so to date. Over time, JI and JUI became the Pakistan Army's partners in developing, promoting, and policing the ideology of Pakistan, first at home and then abroad. By 1960, Pakistan's intelligence agencies, acting under the auspices of the army, encouraged Pakistan's Islamist parties to "pursue a forward policy of seeking ideological allies in Afghanistan"

(Haqqani 2005, 167), and the Pakistani Islamist parties became the principal foes of the Afghan communists (Rubin 2002). During this period, Pakistan was under Ayub's supposedly secular rule, underscoring the fact that even ostensibly secular generals were willing to instrumentalize Islam for domestic and foreign purposes. Some 40 years later, Musharraf, also a professedly secular leader, would do the same. This has been the bedrock of the army's policy to manage Afghanistan.

The principal political party in Afghanistan was the People's Democratic Party of Afghanistan (PDPA), which was founded in 1965. In 1967, the PDPA split into two factions: Khalq (masses) and Parcham (flag). Khalq, under the leadership of Nur Muhammad Taraki and Hafizullah Amin, recruited heavily among Pakhtuns and had a strong base in the Soviet-trained military. Parcham, under the leadership of Babrak Karmal, tended to draw from the bureaucracy and educational establishments. While both were Marxist and pro-Soviet, Khalq preferred more rapid and radical socialist transformation, while Parcham was more gradualist and willing to cooperate with other political organizations (Barfield 2010). Both PDPA factions were small—perhaps in the thousands—and had their base in Kabul's urban population. In fact, the PDPA factions did not have a monopoly even on Marxism in Kabul, much less the rest of Afghanistan. The party appealed to Afghanistan's Pakhtuns because it fervently supported the notion of Pakhtunistan, to Pakistan's unending chagrin. But some non-Pakhtuns, less than pleased by this position, formed their own Marxist groups, which favored autonomy for non-Pakhtuns (Rubin 2002).

While Communist parties competed for power and influence, Islamists were also responding to the spread of leftist ideology. By the mid-1950s, Islamic politics had become firmly entrenched in Kabul, with Islamists gathering at the shariat faculty at Kabul University to debate campus Marxists. These Islamists became Pakistan's early allies, a partnership mediated by Pakistan's own Islamist parties. In 1973, the Islamists formed a leadership shura (council), which held its first meeting in the home of Barhanuddin Rabbani, a junior member of the sharia faculty. Rabbani was subsequently elected leader of the shura, with Ghulam Rasul Sayyaf, one of his colleagues at Kabul University, as deputy leader. Gulbuddin Hekmatyar, a student in the engineering school, was put in charge of political activities, even though at the time of the meeting he was in jail for murdering a Marxist student. The council, which later became known as the Jamiat-i-Islami (Islamic Society) (Rubin 2002), formed the nucleus of the various mujahideen groups that Pakistan began to instrumentalize in its efforts to manipulate Afghanistan's internal affairs.

As Afghanistan's domestic politics continued to churn, with the pro-Pakhtunistan Daoud ousting King Zahir Shah, the insurgency in Balochistan reached a crisis point. Afghanistan's leadership opposed Pakistan's use of force in Balochistan and continued to prosecute its demand for Pakhtunistan. In 1973, the authoritarian civilian leader Zulfiqar Ali Bhutto, unable to resolve his disagreements with Daoud, ordered the ISI to lead covert actions in Afghanistan. According to Gen. Khalid Mahmud Arif (1995), who served as Zia's vice chief of Army Staff:

> An Afghan cell had been created in the Foreign Office in July/August 1973. It met regularly for the next three years, under the chairmanship of either Prime Minister Bhutto or Mr. Aziz Ahmad [the Minister of State for Foreign Affairs under Bhutto], and gave out policy guidelines. The Inspector General Frontier Constabulary and the DGISI [director general Inter-Services Intelligence directorate] worked in concert to conduct intelligence missions inside Afghanistan. The Afghan leaders, Gulbadin [*sic*] Hikmatyar [*sic*] and Rabbani, came into contact with the Pakistani authorities during the period. The Pakistani intelligence agencies also kept communication channels open with the deposed king, Zahir Shah, who was living in exile in Italy. Gradually, the cell became dormant during the final stages of the Bhutto administration. On 2 May 1978, the Afghan Cell was reactivated in the Foreign Office (306–307).

Bhutto's forward policy relied on Islamist elements in Afghanistan who were opposed both to Daoud's liberalizing regime and his efforts to expel them. Rizwan Hussain (2005) emphasizes that Pakistan's decision to aid the Afghan Islamists was driven by strategic considerations rather than sympathy with their ideology: the Afghan Islamists did not support Kabul's territorial claims on Pakistani lands, and they were opposed to friendly relations with India. "Because of this, they made ideal proxies for Pakistan to destabilise Afghanistan. By [supporting them], Islamabad wanted to send a message to Daud [*sic*] that if he persisted in aiding 'secessionists' in Pakistan then he could expect Pakistan to reply in the same vein" (79).

By 1973, several Islamist leaders had fled to Pakistan to escape Daoud. Pakistan established training camps for them in North and South Waziristan agencies (laying the foundation for a larger effort in the 1980s with American, Saudi, and other funders). Not only were these Pakhtun-dominated agencies a virtual black hole in which the press could not operate, they were also conveniently located, bordering Afghanistan's eastern provinces of Paktia, Logar and Paktika. There was already a large Pakistani military garrison at Razmak (in the northern part of South Waziristan, near the southern boundary with North Waziristan), and troops were also stationed in Mohmand Agency, abutting the northeastern, Pakhtun-dominated Afghan provinces of Nangarhar and Kunar. The North-West Frontier Province units of the Frontier Corps (a paramilitary organization whose recruits come from FATA but whose officers are seconded from the Pakistan Army), was ordered to organize and train the Afghans, and the unit's inspector general, Brig. (later Maj. Gen.) Naseerullah Khan Babar, was placed in charge of the overall operation.[18] Gulbuddin Hekmatyar and Ahmad Shah Massoud (who would later become an enemy of Pakistan and a target of the Pakistan-backed Taliban in the mid-1990s) were among the first to receive training.

In summer 1975, Pakistan backed a series of Islamist insurrections in Afghanistan, including one led by Massoud in the Panjshir Valley. While Daoud easily crushed these uprisings, he used them as an excuse to arrest even mainstream Islamists, prompting even more Islamists to flee to Pakistan (Barfield 2012). To ensure that its Afghan project remained covert, Pakistan actually enlisted Afghan Islamists into the Frontier Corps while the ISI and the army's elite Special Services Group trained them. Analysts believe that between 1973 and 1977, Pakistan's armed forces trained some 5,000 militants to fight the Daoud regime (Hussain 2005). But despite their similar goals, the Afghan militants remained divided by ethnicity (Pakhtun vs. non-Pakhtun). Dari speakers (e.g., non-Pakhtuns) tended to support Rabbani, while Pakhtuns tended to support Hekmatyar.

In keeping with Pakistan's past use of nonstate actors (e.g., in the 1947 and 1965 wars), knowledge of the Afghan effort was confined to a small number of persons within Pakistan's military and bureaucratic establishments: Gen. Babur claimed that only Prime Minister Bhutto, Army Chief Tikka Khan, and Minister of State for Defence and Foreign Affairs Aziz Ahmad knew of Pakistan's activities. During their time in Pakistan, Afghan Islamists were able to forge even deeper links with Pakistan's Islamists, in particular members of the JI and the JUI. Both of these parties were closely tied to the military and received funding from Saudi Arabia, among other Arab donors. Hekmatyar would go on to form Hizb-e-Islami-Afghanistan, which had ideological ties to JI leadership in Pakistan (Haqqani 2005; Hussain 2005; Rubin 2002).

Pakistan undertook these initiatives well before the Soviets crossed the Amu Darya and long before the United States became involved. In other words, the basic lineaments of Pakistan's Afghanistan policies were formed long before the Christmas 1979 Soviet invasion of Afghanistan. However, they developed further after the invasion in coordination with the United States and Saudi Arabia and in consideration of Pakistan's own enduring interests. A perusal of these historical facts undermines Pakistan's often-touted narrative that it was "used" by the United States and deployed to service principally American Cold War objectives.

At the same time that he was initiating covert actions in Afghanistan, Bhutto was also requesting additional assistance from the United States. But US–Pakistan relations had cooled after the 1965 Indo-Pakistan war and the ambivalent American response to the secession of Bangladesh, and the United States was not persuaded by Bhutto's arguments for greater military support. In preparation for Bhutto's 1973 visit to Washington, the US Department of State produced talking points cautioning that the United States saw "the resolution of Pakistan's security problems primarily in political/psychological and economic terms and only secondarily in military terms" (Haqqani 2005, 104). In short, at this juncture, the United States was not persuaded that it should provide military support to Pakistan when the solutions to its security problems were not primarily military in nature.

Positive regional political developments temporarily halted Pakistan's first experiments with training Afghan militants. Although the Soviet Union had signed a Friendship Treaty with India even as India was preparing to intervene in East Pakistan, the USSR, which was well-disposed toward Bhutto's leftist politics, also sought to improve its ties with Pakistan. As a part of that effort, Kabul softened its support for the Pakhtunistan agenda. At the same time, Afghanistan was experiencing better relations with Iran, which, like Pakistan, was a CENTO treaty partner. Tehran urged Kabul to reach some accommodation with Pakistan, sweetening the pot with $700 million for development projects. China, another important Pakistani ally, offered Daoud a $55 million loan in the hopes of driving a wedge between Afghanistan and the Soviet Union. A third push came from the United States in the form of Secretary of State Henry Kissinger, who, during a 1974 visit to Kabul, urged Daoud to reach some accord with Pakistan. These efforts bore fruit in 1976, when Bhutto visited Kabul. He and Daoud discussed an array of issues, and even though the two countries did not come to an agreement on the Durand Line, this thaw in relations prompted Pakistan to stop its assistance to the Afghan Islamists in early 1977 (Hussain 2005).

In July 1977, Gen. Zia ul Haq deposed Bhutto and seized power in Operation Fairplay. Daoud, continuing his efforts to reduce tensions with Pakistan, refrained from commenting on what he called an "internal affair," and in return Zia made a number of conciliatory approaches to Kabul, including releasing many of the Pakhtun and Baloch nationalists imprisoned under Bhutto (Arif 1995). Daoud also continued to distance his regime from Moscow. But fast-moving events in Afghanistan soon eviscerated the progress Daoud and Zia made. While Daoud may have espoused some of the PDPA's goals, the party was not happy with his gradualist approach to reform and modernization. Equally problematic for the PDPA, and Moscow, Daoud was essentially a nationalist who wanted to gain greater independence from the Soviets in domestic and foreign affairs (Magnus and Naby 2002; Maley 2002). In April 1978 the PDPA seized power in a coup, in the course of which Daoud was killed. The coup was dubbed the Saur Revolution in reference to the Afghan month in which it took place (Hussain 2005; Maley 2002). Many Pakistani defense analysts remain convinced that the Saur Revolution was backed by the Soviets even though the historical record is less clear on this issue (see, e.g., Chishti 1990).[19]

Within days of the coup, Nur Mohammad Taraki (who led the Khalq faction of the PDPA) was named the president and prime minister, and his rival, Babrak Karmal (who led the Parcham faction), became the deputy prime minister. But the inclusion of both Parcham and Khalq leaders in the new government did not end the hostility between the two factions. Taraki exiled Karmal and other Parcham leaders by sending them to diplomatic postings abroad, and he purged those who remained in the country. His government rapidly imposed socialism on Afghanistan, using extremely brutal methods (including mass executions), which created a strong backlash at nearly every level of society.[20]

Zia and Taraki had a dismal relationship from their very first meeting, which took place in Kabul. When Zia talked about Islam, Taraki took numerous opportunities to mock his professed piety. (For details of their meeting, see Arif 1995, 308). Zia, for his part, believed that the Soviets had instigated the Afghan coup and that the removal of Daoud spelled the end of Afghan–Pakistani cooperation (Hussain 2005; Magnus and Naby 2002; Maley 2002). With no rapprochement possible, Zia focused aggressively on domestic Islamization and on his attempts to undermine many of Bhutto's more leftist policies (e.g., the nationalization of private assets).

In an assessment that clearly reflects the influence of British strategic thought, Zia concluded that the Saur revolution meant that Afghanistan could no longer act as a buffer between the Soviet Union and the rest of the subcontinent, and his military government consequently feared further Soviet moves toward Pakistan. To prevent this, Lt. General Faiz Ali Chishti—an important member of Zia's inner military circle—advocated a forward policy that would counter Soviet influence by "installing a 'favourable government in Kabul, using friendly Pakhtun tribes' as 'defence of Pakistan lay in the defence of Afghanistan'" (Hussain 2005, 97). In May 1978, Pakistan—at the urging of allies such as Iran, the United States, and Saudi Arabia—recognized the newly designated Democratic Republic of Afghanistan. Zia also reactivated the secret Afghan cell that Bhutto had created in 1973 (Haqqani 2005; Hussain 2005).

Throughout summer 1979, the PDPA's policies continued to push Islamists into Pakistan, adding to those who had fled during Daoud's tenure. Zia, taking advantage of the preparatory work done by Bhutto, organized the various Afghan groups into a viable political and military force under his control. The relationship between Zia and the Afghan Islamists was symbiotic: he was able to grant them some degree of international legitimacy, and they bolstered his Islamizing activities within Pakistan. The army recruited numerous Islamist parties, such as the JI and JUI, to strengthen the legitimacy of military rule and also to help organize the Afghan resistance. JI forged particularly tight relations with the two factions of Hizb-i-Islami (Hussain 2005; Rubin 2002).

The Soviet Union observed the increasingly intense violence in Afghanistan with growing alarm. In September 1979, Hafizullah Amin, fearing that Taraki was conspiring with Moscow to have him removed, killed Taraki and appointed himself prime minister. While Taraki had enjoyed the relative confidence of Moscow, under Amin, relations between Moscow and Kabul worsened because he used terror to consolidate his rule. Fearing that it would lose Afghanistan altogether, the Soviet Union invaded on Christmas Day 1979. Soon thereafter, the Soviets killed Amin and installed Babrak Karmal as president (Barfield 2010; Bradsher 1985; Hussain 2005; Magnus and Naby 2002; Maley 2002). The Soviet "intervention provoked a deep sense of alarm in Pakistan. Suddenly the buffer disappeared and the Soviet superpower advanced to Pakistan's borders" (Sattar 2007, 155).

By the time the Soviets had crossed the Amu Darya, Zia's army and the ISI had already created the key Islamist groups that would become the cornerstone of the anti-Soviet jihad. Throughout 1978, Lt. Gen. Fazle Haq worked (under Zia's orders) to reduce the more than 50 Afghan resistance groups to a smaller, more manageable number. The ISI was tasked with deepening the links between Pakistani and Afghan Islamist groups. With the assistance of the Frontier Corps, these efforts resulted in seven major Sunni Afghan Islamist militant groups. (Shia groups that enjoyed Iran's support also operated in Afghanistan.) These groups were developed solely under Pakistan's direction and with Pakistani funds; in fact, American overt assistance to the mujahideen effort did not begin to flow until 1981.[21] Thus, for more than a year after the Soviet invasion, Pakistan "continued to support the Afghan resistance...providing it modest assistance out of its own meager resources" (Sattar 2007, 159).

The reasons for Pakistan's firm support are clear, as Abdul Sattar explains: "the Mujahideen would be fighting also for Pakistan's own security and independence" (Sattar 2007, 157). Arif (1995) echoes this conviction when he writes that "of her own free will, Pakistan adopted the...option to protect her national interest and to uphold a vital principal" by providing "...covert assistance to the *Mujahideen*" (314).

One of the seven Sunni mujahideen groups was the Afghan National Front (Jubha-i-Melli-i-Najat Afghanistan), led by Sibghatullah Mujaddidi, which established an office in Peshawar (in what was then the NWFP) in June 1978. Mujaddidi remained in touch with the ISI until the mid-1990s, when Pakistan stopped supporting his group in favor of more effective organizations. Another group was the Islamic Revolutionary Movement of Afghanistan (Hezb-e-Harakat-e-Inqelab-e-Islami Afghanistan), which was formed in Quetta in late 1978 by Mawlawi Muhammad Navi Muhammadi. This group represented Pakhtun mullahs from the southern Afghan provinces of Helmand, Kandahar, and Zabol and had links to Pakhtun clergy in the eastern provinces of Nangarhar, Logar, Ghazni, and Paktika. Muhammadi had close ties with the JUI. The third and fourth groups were the two factions of the Party of Islam (Hizb-i-Islami): one led by Yunus Khalis and the other by Gulbuddin Hekmatyar. Khalis began operating in Pakistan in summer 1978. (Mullah Omar, the future leader of the Afghan Taliban, was a subcommander in the Khalis' faction.) Hekmatyar came to Pakistan in 1973, and, with Pakistani help, began operations against the PDPA in late 1978. His fiercely anti-Soviet views made him a favorite of Zia, and his militia received more Pakistani support than any of the other groups. Hekmatyar had a close relationship with the JI, but it is important to note that the party, a critical partner of the Zia regime and an influential player in its foreign policy, maintained ties with all the Afghan groups (Hussain 2005; Rubin 2002).

The fifth group was the Islamic Society of Afghanistan (Jamiat-i-Islami-i-Afghanistan), which was one of the largest Islamic parties. Many of its cadres were Dari-speaking Tajiks from Afghanistan's north. While it established an office in Pakistan in 1974, it did not reach its full strength until 1978, when Professor Barhanuddin Rabbani became its leader. Under the famed commander Ahmad Shah Massoud, who was trained by Pakistan's military, the Jamiat-i-Islami had been conducting intermittent guerilla operations in Afghanistan even before the Soviet invasion. Despite the pro-Pakhtun bias of the Pakistani military and intelligence agencies, which prevented the Jamiat-i-Islami from receiving the same resources as Hekmatyar, the Jamiat was perhaps the best organized of the Afghan Islamist parties and was able to put up the most effective resistance to the PDPA (Hussain 2005; Rubin 2002).

A sixth group was the Islamic Unity party (Ittihad-i Islami), led by Abdur Rab Rasul Sayyaf. A former lecturer in theology at Kabul University, Sayyaf formed this group in early 1979. Sayyaf espoused the Salafist interpretative tradition and received substantial support from Saudi Arabia, a fact that likely prompted Pakistan to support his group. The final group was the National Islamic Front of Afghanistan (Mahaz-i-Milli Islami ye Afghanistan), led by Pir Sayed Ahmad Gaylani, which opened its offices in Peshawar in 1978. Gaylani tried to forge an alliance with the Shiite Hazara population of Afghanistan (Hussain 2005; Rubin 2002).

As is well-known, the exiled Islamist parties in Pakistan afforded the United States, Pakistan, and Saudi Arabia, among others, the opportunity to muster an Islamist resistance in the guise of mujahideen. Money from the United States and Saudi Arabia, funneled through Pakistan's intelligence agency and military forces, funded mushrooming madrassahs, burgeoning refugee camps, and other institutions designed to produce mujahideen to fight the Soviets in Afghanistan. In addition to formal financial support from the United States and Saudi Arabia, several Arab individuals began arriving in theatre to support the mujahideen as freelancers. Preeminent among these were Dr. Abdullah Azzam and Osama bin Laden. Because Pakistan sought to minimize Pakhtun nationalist aspirations, it insisted on routing military as well as humanitarian assistance through the seven explicitly Sunni Islamist organizations (Roy 1990). This resulted in disproportionate support to the Pakhtun Islamist militant groups, particularly Gulbuddin Hekmatyar's faction of the Hizb-i-Islami (Magnus and Naby 2002; Maley 2002).

In April 1988, the Soviet Union signed the Geneva Accords, which obligated it to make a complete withdrawal from Afghanistan. The war had resulted in nearly 1 million deaths, physically disabled more than 1.5 million, and created over 6 million refugees. At the time of the Soviet withdrawal, the Afghan state, which was unable to pay its bills on its own, could not function with any degree of autonomy. Afghanistan verged on collapse. Mohammad Najibullah, the president installed by the Russians, faced the daunting challenge of reviving political institutions and restoring their legitimacy. The makeup of the political elite had also changed during the war: on the regime side, traditional authority figures had been supplanted by party cadres, while armed militant activists filled the ranks of the opposition (Goodson 2001; Maley 2002).

Despite these difficult circumstances, Najibullah managed to retain power until 1992. He was able to do so, in part, because the Soviet Union continued economic assistance as well as the provision of equipment and fuel, enabling him to purchase the allegiance of numerous militia commanders. Najibullah sought to make Afghan nationalism the basis for his support and abandon the communist rhetoric of the PDPA. (In 1990 he changed its name to Hizb-e-Watan, Party of the Homeland.) But he was unable to forge a national consensus, and opposition to his rule within communist and resistance circles intensified. Moscow continued to provide assistance until September 1991, when, amid serious turmoil in the USSR, Moscow and Washington agreed to cease all lethal support to Kabul on January 1, 1992. Without Soviet resources, Najibullah succumbed to anti-regime militants in April 1992. He barely escaped assassination and took refuge in the UN compound in Kabul (Maley 2002; Rubin 2002). He spent the rest of his life virtually imprisoned at the compound; he was brutally murdered by the Taliban, who hanged him from a lamppost when they seized Kabul in September 1996.

Various militia factions fought to control the state, with Pakistan supporting Hekmatyar. In April 1992, a temporary political solution (the Peshawar Accord) was forged according to which the major militia commanders would serve as rotating presidents. Sibghatullah Mujaddidi was to serve for two months, followed by Barhanuddin Rabbani for four. While Rabbani clung to power for four years, the various mujahideen parties failed to cohere around a single approach to governing and engaged in sanguinary, protracted civil war that destroyed Kabul. Rabbani's government lasted until 1996 when it fell to the Taliban.

THE RISE AND FALL OF THE TALIBAN

The Taliban first appeared in 1994 in Kandahar, where they gained fame by opposing the local branches of the various armed groups that had become formed during the Afghan jihad. By the mid-1990s, these groups were known as warlords (*jangbazi* in Dari) because of the destruction they wreaked on Kabul in their struggle for control. (The principal *jangbazi* were the Northern Alliance, led by Ahmad Shah Massoud, and Hekmatyar Hizb-e-Islami.) The Taliban, in contrast, attracted considerable popular support, at least in part because they promised security, freedom of movement without harassment, and swift justice.

While the members of the movement, which began in southern Afghanistan, were ethnically Pakhtun and relied on kinship networks in Afghanistan and key madrassahs near Ghazni and Kandahar, perhaps their most significant organizational and ideological connections were to Pakistan. During the 1980s, Pakistan had created hundreds of madrassahs in the NWFP and FATA to produce mujahideen for the anti-Soviet jihad. These schools, particularly those linked to the Deobandi movement, educated a generation of displaced Afghans who were divorced from their tribal structure and therefore less inclined to acknowledge tribal authority.

The Afghan Taliban's first recruits came from this generation of madrassah students. They were led by Mullah Omar, a veteran mujahideen commander who had been running a madrassah in Kandahar. To indicate its madrassah links, the movement named itself the Taliban, the Persian plural of *talib* (student). (*Tuleba*, the plural form in Arabic, is occasionally used as well.) During their time in the madrassahs and refugee camps, where Saudi charities and the Deobandi movement had a significant presence, many members of the Taliban were exposed to and became sympathetic to Salafism, and jihadi Salafism in particular (Johnson and Mason 2007; Rashid 2000; Sinno 2008).

The Taliban first came into contact with the Pakistani political establishment through their ties to a faction of the JUI, the Pakistani Deobandi political party, which at that time was headed by Maulana Fazlur Rehman. Rehman, an important political partner of Benazir Bhutto, facilitated contacts between the Taliban and Maj. Gen. Naseerullah Babar, Bhutto's Minister for the Interior. Babar, who had been in charge of Afghan policy during the tenure of Bhutto's father, Z. A. Bhutto, began providing logistical and other support to the Taliban. The ISI, which had concluded that Hekmatyar could not deliver a stable, pro-Pakistan government in Afghanistan, also welcomed their emergence.

Amid the chaos produced by the warlords' struggles for control of the state, the Taliban were intent on establishing an Islamic government in Afghanistan. Afghans, exhausted by war and the predations of the mujahideen, generally welcomed the Taliban and their promise of security and peace. The Taliban made reestablishing law and order a top priority. Mujahideen commanders had established checkpoints along the highways that collected bribes in return for safe passage, and some of the armed groups even raped women and young boys. The Taliban put an end to these practices and were widely credited as having restored safe passage along Afghanistan's roads. (They particularly enjoyed the support of traders and truckers, who had long been victimized by the warlords.) As they moved out from Kandahar, the Taliban co-opted local warlords and institutions to expand their area of control (Johnson and Mason 2007; Rashid 2000; Sinno 2008).

With the help of massive covert assistance from the ISI and the Pakistan Army and Air Force, the Taliban were able to expel the largely Tajik Northern Alliance regime from Kabul by 1996, and by 1998 they controlled most of Afghanistan. But as the Taliban consolidated their power, Afghans began to fear them. The Taliban used excessive physical punishment to enforce their version of shariat, denied women educational and employment opportunities, and forced men and women alike to abide by their harsh edicts. While the Taliban controlled much of the country, an important pocket of resistance remained in the Panjshir Valley, which was under the control of Ahmad Shah Massoud's Northern Alliance. The Northern Alliance enjoyed the support of India, Russia, and Iran, among other regional actors increasingly concerned about the rise of the Taliban (Fair 2007; Johnson and Mason 2007; Rashid 2000; Sinno 2008). In retrospect, the Taliban did not deliver on Islamabad's most capacious hopes. The Taliban did not settle the international border. The Taliban harbored many of Pakistan's sectarian and criminal elements. They brought disgrace upon Pakistan, which was one of only three states that supported the regime. Yet they did deliver one very important thing for the Pakistan Army: the Taliban managed to keep the Indians away from sensitive parts of Afghanistan. During the Taliban's regime, the presence of the Indians was restricted to the Panjshir Valley, where they aided Massoud.

Massoud remained the Taliban's only serious adversary until September 9, 2001, when al-Qaeda assassinated him in the first suicide attack ever to occur in Afghanistan—a possible preparation for the September 11, 2001 attacks on the United States. After 9/11, Pakistan was forced to formally distance itself from the Taliban. But few, in the US government or elsewhere, believe that Pakistan has abandoned the Taliban, as I discuss in the conclusion of this chapter.

The Army's and the Internal Threat on the "Frontier"

While Pakistan sought to manage direct and indirect threats from Afghanistan, its Pakhtun territories and populations in the KP and the FATA have also received significant attention from Pakistan's military and intelligence agencies. These populations continue to be seen as potential proxies for external actors (India, Russia/the Soviet Union, or even Afghanistan) who seek to destabilize the state. During the colonial period, the frontier served as an internal buffer, separating the core of the Raj (which lay east of the Indus) and Afghanistan (beyond the Durand Line). British management of the frontier "meant dealing with the tribes outside areas of direct rule by paying allowances for good behavior, manipulating intertribal relations, and using punitive expeditions, blockades, and *baramtas* [seizures of animals or other property belonging to a tribe or individual] in response to offenses" (Titus 1998, 660).

After independence, Pakistan largely retained these governing concepts as well as many of the Orientalist characterizations of the Pakhtuns as "unruly," "fiercely independent," and "religiously zealous" and of the Baloch as unruly, dangerous, and even lazy (Titus 1998). While those territories west of the Indus are viewed as troublesome badlands, to be managed at best, Pakistan's heartland is still believed to be the lands that lie east of the Indus—most notably the Punjab but also Sindh. (In contemporary Pakistan the four regular provinces are often referred to as the settled areas, implying that the other areas are not settled.) One consequence of this view was that Pakistan's strategy for defending East Pakistan was "the defense of the east lies in the west." This obsession with Pakistan's strategic core was not lost on the Bengali citizens of East Pakistan: in the 1965 war, the military showed no interest in or capability for defending the east. This was yet another catalyst for the movement for an independent Bangladesh. The enduring nature of this worldview is reflected, in some measure, by the simple fact that until 2010 Pakistan retained the name North-West Frontier Province, suggesting that this heavily populated province was only a frontier for the rest of Pakistan.

Reflecting the continuity in the Pakistani and British views of the frontier populations, at independence Pakistan chose to retain the FCR as the legal code governing the entire frontier (although with some alterations, made in 1947 and after).[22] There are multiple possible reasons for why Pakistan chose to retain this colonial-era legal regime. First, Jinnah had promised to respect the traditions and autonomy of the Pakhtuns in exchange for their agreement to join Pakistan. (Pakhtun consent to accession was necessary because the tribal areas, like the princely states, had a distinct legal status and could have become independent after decolonization.) This bargain required the new government of Pakistan to enter into agreements with the tribal *maliks*, using the political agents, who had been responsible for governing the agencies during the Raj, as intermediaries. The *maliks* affirmed that their agencies were a part of Pakistan, pledged to support the country when needed, and promised "to be peaceful and law abiding and to maintain friendly relations with the people of the settled districts" (Khan 2005, 27). In exchange, the government of Pakistan agreed to continue the benefits paid to the tribal chiefs by the British. On August 15, 1947, Jinnah legally declared the tribal areas to be part of Pakistan (ibid.). These agreements were subsequently revised (in 1951–1952) to provide greater government control over the tribal areas (ibid.).

A second explanation for Pakistan's retention of the colonial governance structure stems from its assimilation of the essentializing colonial narrative that the tribes were "ungovernable." As White (2008) notes, this belief ignored reality, particularly with respect to the Pakhtuns, "millions of [whom] had already been successfully assimilated into a robust system of local governance in the settled areas" (228). A third motivation was the long-standing desire of Pakistan's security managers to use the tribal areas as a buffer between Pakistan's settled areas and the disputed border with Afghanistan, the Durand Line. Finally, the tribal areas, and even the NWFP, were useful to the Pakistani security establishment because they served as sites for training and recruiting the Islamists, and even Islamist militants, whom the state would deploy to achieve its foreign policy objectives in Afghanistan and in India.

At the time of independence, the frontier, including Balochistan, was home to several different kinds of tribal areas, each with their own tribal governance structures (Tripodi 2009). In 1955, the government promulgated the One Unit Scheme, which consolidated all of West Pakistan into a single administrative unit.[23] After sustained protests throughout West Pakistan, in 1970 the government reversed course and reestablished the provinces of the Punjab, Sindh, NWFP (now KP), and Balochistan. The tribal areas of Dir, Swat, Chitral, the Malakand protected areas, and the Hazara territory were incorporated into what was then the NWFP (Khan 2005).

The modern tribal system is laid out in Article 246 ("Tribal Areas") of the current (1973) Constitution of Pakistan. Article 246 defines the tribal areas as including parts of Balochistan and what is now Khyber Pakhtunkhwa as well as the former princely states of Amb, Chitral, Dir, and Swat. These territories are further divided into the Provincially Administered Tribal Areas (PATA) of then-NWFP and Balochistan and the FATA. The PATA include districts of Chitral, Dir, and Swat, parts of Malakand, tribal areas adjoining the district of Mansehra, and the former princely state of Amb. The FATA include the seven agencies of Bajour, Orakzai, Mohmand, Khyber, Kurram, and North and South Waziristan as well as Tribal Areas adjoining Peshawar, Kohat, Bannu, and Dera Ismael Khan.

The system enshrined in the constitution is designed to continue the colonial practice of containing the unruly tribals rather than to extending to them the rights and privileges of Pakistanis living in the settled areas (Ali 1999). Whereas the administration of the PATA of the NWFP (KP) and Balochistan takes place at the provincial level, administration of the FATA remains the responsibility of the federal government acting through the Governor of the NWFP (KP), who is appointed by the president of Pakistan (Khan 2005). The tension, since independence, in Afghanistan–Pakistan relations makes it unlikely that the federal government will relinquish control over the FATA in the foreseeable future.

Until recently, every Pakistani regime has maintained that the FCR has "stood the test of time and pressure of destabilising forces generated by various elements in FATA as a result of having a long unmanned border with Afghanistan" (Ali 1999, 185–186). But Pakistan's judicial system has challenged the FCR on numerous occasions. Supreme Court Justice A. R. Cornelius denounced the FCR as "obnoxious to all recognized modern principles governing the dispensation of justice" in a ruling in the case of *Sumunder v. State* (PLD 1954 FC 228) (Khan 2004). Following the promulgation of the 1956 constitution, the FCR was frequently challenged as repugnant to fundamental rights, with successive superior court judgments declaring provisions of the law inconsistent with fundamental rights and therefore void, such as *Dosso v. State* (PLD 1957 Quetta 9), *Toti Khan v. DM Sibi* (PLD 1957 Quetta 1), *Abdul Akbar Khan v. DM Peshawar* (PLD 1957 Peshawar100), *Abdul Baqi v. Superintendent, Central Prisons, Machh* (PLD 1957 Karachi 694), *Khair Muhammad Khan v. Government of WP* (PLD 1956 Lahore 668), and *Malik Muhammad Usman v. State* (PLD 1965 Lahore 229). But there has been no serious legal challenge to the FCR since the abrogation of the 1956 Constitution, despite the legislation's incompatibility with international human rights principles and Pakistan's current constitution (Khan 2004). The system endures today, even though it is "increasingly out of step with the reformist trends in the country at large" (White 2008, 228).

While analysts often attribute the FCR's endurance to the military's quest for strategic depth, this assessment is not entirely fair. Musharraf did consider integrating the FATA into Pakistan's ordinary governance structures by extending the geographical scope of some version of the Local Governance Ordinance of 2001 as well as of the Political Parties Act of 2002. But these reforms stalled despite the growing consensus that such change was needed (Shah 2012).

In the years since 9/11, Pakistan's security forces have been engaged in various military operations in the FATA as well as in the settled areas of the NWFP. In interviews conducted in August 2010, military personnel in Swat and South and North Waziristan expressed an acute interest in "mainstreaming" the FATA. They feared that without a serious effort to extend the full writ of Pakistani law to the FATA, the area would never be pacified. The army's traditional method of managing its frontier—treating it as a security cordon to establish strategic depth in Afghanistan—has yielded an ironic set of outcomes: Pakistan has become a soft, penetrated state "where aliens of all stripes and colour could enter at will, seek refuge and indulge in unlawful activities" (Haq et al. 2005, 66).

The previous civilian government, led by the beleaguered Pakistan People's Party (PPP), has made important changes to the governance system in the FATA. First, on April 19, 2010, Pakistani president Asif Ali Zardari signed into law a constitutional amendment stipulating that the NWFP would henceforth be known as Khyber Pakhtunkhwa. While this name change signaled a possible shift in how the state viewed the province, the new name also displays Islamabad's wariness of Pakhtun aspirations. After all, Pakhtun nationalists had long called for an independent Pakhtunistan. For this reason, the province could not be named Pakhtunistan; "Khyber" was added to dampen the fears of non-Pakthuns who feared Pakhtun political domination of the province (Adeney 2012). And in August 2011, Zardari signed decrees amending the Frontier Crimes Regulation and extending the Political Parties Order of 2002 to the tribal areas (Shah 2012). The amendments to the FCR granted FATA residents the right to bail and established an appellate tribunal, which is meant to curtail the expansive powers of the political agents by creating a system for appealing judgments.

One of the most interesting aspects of these reforms is that they were sold as a part of Pakistan's military struggle against militants in the region; in fact, it is inconceivable that such changes could go forward without the explicit approval of the Pakistan Army. Maqbool Wazir, writing in *Hilal*, explains that "military operations do not deal with the root causes of the militancy. Fortunately, there is widespread recognition of the need for FATA reforms across the political parties of the country [all have] unanimously agreed that legal and political reforms are the sole solution to the ongoing militancy in FATA. Political reforms should be part of the war strategy" (Wazir 2011, 10). At the time of writing, it remains too early to tell whether these decrees mark the start of meaningful reform or whether Zardari's efforts will go the way of Musharraf's. Either way, it appears that the drive to bring the FATA into the mainstream constitutional order will be driven by the same dictates that for so long kept them out: the demands of security.

Implications: Is the Past Prologue for Afghanistan and the Frontier?

The threat from the western frontier and beyond long concerned British officials during the Raj. In an effort to contend with those threats, the British alternated between aggressive forward policies and indirect management approaches associated with the close border policy. The Pakistan Army adopted this aspect of British strategic culture and adapted British instruments to prosecute these varied policies. Like the British Army in India, the Pakistan Army has pursued aggressive forward policies that have involved direct intervention in Afghanistan as well as policies that more closely resemble that of the close border policy, whereby the army focuses its attention on its own territory. While initially Pakistani apprehensions about Afghanistan were exacerbated by the Soviet Union, over time India displaced the Soviet Union as a source of insecurity. Pakistan has long worried that if India had a base in Afghanistan it could work on its own or with Afghans to disturb Pakistan's western border.

It is important to understand Pakistan's current options in Afghanistan within the historical framework presented here. Since 9/11, it has become apparent that Pakistan, despite its continued denials, long ago resumed its support for Islamist proxies such as Mullah Omar's Afghan Taliban and networks such as that run by Jalaluddin Haqqani (Mullen 2011; Rassler and Brown 2011). Pakistan's continued investment in these proxies ostensibly stems from the army's desire to restrict the ability of India to operate in Afghanistan. However, while Pakistani military personnel are wont to accuse India of any number of nefarious activities, ranging from support for Baloch insurgents and terrorists in FATA to bombing targets deep within Pakistan, they also deny that Pakistan seeks strategic depth.

These denials have persuaded some analysts that Pakistani thinking on this issue has evolved. Most notably, Shuja Nawaz, citing Pakistan's former army chief Kayani, with whom he enjoys close ties, wrote that Kayani "sees Afghanistan offering Pakistan a different kind of 'strategic depth': through its stability rather than as a client state or a haven for Pakistani forces should India successfully invade Pakistan" (Nawaz 2010, 16). Nawaz cites Kayani as saying that "we want to have strategic depth in Afghanistan, but that does not imply controlling it....If we have a peaceful, stable and friendly Afghanistan, automatically we will have our strategic depth because our western border will be secure, and we will not be looking at two fronts" (16). Nawaz believes that Kayani's statement represents a "major shift in strategic thinking inside army headquarters in Pakistan from a view that was born in the minds of [its] military leadership in the late 1980s and has continued to be cited erroneously as a core tenet of Pakistan's military strategy" (ibid.).

Unfortunately, Nawaz's assessment is inconsistent with the various meanings of strategic depth, whether one considers its history since its introduction in the eighteenth century or its modern incarnations in post-Partition Pakistan. Even if one accepts Kayani's claims at face value—despite the abundant evidence to the contrary, including Pakistan's ongoing support for Islamist militants in Afghanistan—what he articulated is not a new notion of strategic depth. In fact, the aforementioned quote is a restatement of the hoary close border policy, which focuses resources inward but which does not involve simply letting Afghanistan pursue its own course free of Pakistani influence. Rather, Kayani is suggesting that Pakistan would prefer to move away from the resource-intensive forward policy it has pursued since 1947 and toward a more conservative approach. Thus, even if Kayani is speaking honestly, his words suggest merely that he endorses different tactics for pursuing strategic depth rather than wishing to abandon that goal.

Furthermore, it is my view that the enduring threats emanating from Afghanistan do not augur well for Pakistan's ability to revert to a close border policy. In fact, it would be hard to argue that Pakistan is not unnerved by the growth of India's influence in Afghanistan over the past 10 years. Moreover, in this same period India has sustained steady economic growth and concomitant defense modernization. Equally important, Pakistan's military and citizenry believe that when the United States leaves Afghanistan it will hand the keys over to India. Brig. (Retd.) Usman Saeed (2012), writing in *Hilal*, captures this view:

> India has largely succeeded in convincing US and allies of her ability
> to fill the power vacuum [in Afghanistan] while Russia and China are
> unlikely to be US choice to fill the space despite the fact that both may be

keen play positive role in rebuilding Afghanistan.... Indian's [*sic*] recent change in posture from confrontation to reconciliation with Pakistan in no way indicates her abandonment of policy of cultural, political and economic domination of the region backed by superior military capability.... Her... infrastructure projects as well as modernisation and indoctrination of Afghan Army to undertake combat operations at the operational and tactical level with assistance of Indian Military Command will become dilemma to our sovereignty (15).

One can question some of Saeed's assertions (e.g., concerning Indian training of the Afghan Army), but, given that his view is more common than the position taken by Kayani, we should be skeptical of Pakistani claims to prefer a closed border policy vis-à-vis Afghanistan.

Where we may expect slow but steady changes—provided that there is not another exogenous shock like the events of 9/11—is in the legal status of FATA and the reform, if not repeal, of the FCR. As noted already, military personnel have long since become averse to the FCR, even if they are at a loss about how to reform it. During my interviews with Pakistani military officials in February 2004, I learned that the army had been attempting, with some success, to undermine the FCR but had no alternative to put in its place. Thus, the worst of all options currently prevails: the FCR no longer serves its original purpose of ensuring law and order, but transitioning to a new system will be a lengthy process. With an active insurgency in the FATA and other Pakhtun areas, there is an appetite for immediate, temporary fixes rather than long-term solutions (Cheema and Nuri 2005; Haq et al. 2005; University of Peshawar, Area Study Centre 2004). Despite growing political and even public support for FCR reform, the army and its equities will dictate the fate of FATA and its second-class citizens.

CHAPTER 6

India under the Pakistan Army's Gaze

India and Pakistan have fought numerous wars (in 1947–1948, 1965, 1971, and 1999) and have endured numerous crises (in 1987, 1990, and 2001–2002, among others) that have brought them to the brink of war (Chari et al. 2001; Ganguly 2001). Both countries accuse the other of supporting terrorist and insurgent movements within their respective states: Pakistan accuses India of supporting Baloch, Pakhtun, and Sindhi nationalists as well as terrorist campaigns throughout Pakistan; India accuses Pakistan of supporting ethno-nationalist and religious-nationalist insurgencies in the Punjab, Kashmir, and the restive northeast as well as many Islamist terrorist attacks throughout India. In this chapter I do not intend to rehearse the scholarly literature on these wars and crises but rather to exposit how Pakistan's defense literature depicts India in the retelling of the two countries' various conflicts. Of course, doing so requires providing at least a thumbnail sketch of these conflicts so that the important points of divergence in Pakistani accounts can be made clear.

Several dominant themes and narrative tropes consistently recur across the decades of defense literature examined during the course of this research, some of which have been hinted at in previous chapters. The first is the persistent claim that India does not accept either Pakistan or the two-nation theory on which Pakistan was founded. Second, and related to the first, is India's supposed aspirations to regional hegemony and the belief that Pakistan alone stands between India and this goal. This is not a new phenomenon: Pakistani defense writers began articulating the idea of an Indian hegemon in the early 1960s, if not earlier. But recent events, such as the US–Indian civilian nuclear deal and other forms of defense and technical cooperation, provide an ex post facto legitimization of this argument. An important and related theme is the assertion that India began every war between India and Pakistan. As I argued in Chapter 4, this claim is important both to sustaining the narrative of Pakistani victimization by Indian aggression and justifying Pakistan's wars with India as defensive jihad. A fourth, and at first blush somewhat perplexing, theme is that India is not the power that it or others increasingly see it to be. Sometimes India's strength is downplayed because it is Hindu; at other times India is denigrated because its causes are not just.

Finally, India is posited as the root of Pakistan's domestic insecurity. This allows Pakistan's military to retain a conventional, India-focused orientation even while it grapples with an array of internal security challenges that would ordinarily be the responsibility of police or other law enforcement organizations.

In this chapter, I provide a brief overview of the numerous crises and wars the two states have weathered. I next provide an exposition of the narrative tropes just detailed, mobilizing the defense literature as its primary evidentiary base. I conclude with a reflection on how the Pakistan Army has constructed India as the enemy and what implications this image of India has for the Pakistan Army's strategic culture and its planning for the Indian threat.

Multiple Crises and Four Wars

India and Pakistan came to brink of war at least three times: during the Brasstacks Crisis of 1986–1987; during the Compound Crisis of 1990; and during the Twin Peaks Crisis of 2001–2002. The Brasstacks Crisis began to unfold with the launch of a yearlong Indian military exercise, named Operation Brasstacks. It was unprecedented in scale and scope and was undertaken against the backdrop of several complicating factors. First, India and Pakistan had been exchanging fire in Siachen since 1984, when India seized undemarcated territory on the high-altitude Himalayan glacier south of the Chinese border. Second, both countries were experiencing domestic unrest at the time of the exercise. India was embroiled in a bloody insurgency waged by Sikh separatists in the Punjab. India accused Pakistan of supporting the insurgents, who were seeking a separate Sikh state to be named either Sikhistan or Khalistan. Pakistan, for its part, accused India of supporting ethnic militants in Sindh. Third, at that time the United States was deeply involved in South Asia, where it was working with Pakistan, Saudi Arabia, and others to eject the Soviet Union from Afghanistan. Pakistan understood the Indian exercise as an expression of the capability to deter Pakistani adventurism in Punjab, if not a prelude to war, and responded with important mobilizations of its own forces in the Pakistani Punjab. Pakistan was no doubt on tenterhooks: in 1982, 1984, and mid-1985, Pakistan had feared that India or Israel was planning to strike its nuclear facilities (Chari et al. 2001). The acute phase of the crisis lasted three months in early 1987.

While the confrontation itself was not overtly nuclear, shortly after its denoue-ment, Abdul Qadeer Khan (a notorious personality in Pakistan's nuclear program who was later linked to an extensive nuclear black market operation) told Kuldip Nayar, a prominent Indian journalist, that Pakistan, if pressed, could develop a nuclear weapon. Because the message was sent after the confrontation ended, it did not directly influence key decisions in India, and officials there claim that they discounted the comments because of the way the message was delivered. India's dismissals are curious, however, since "Pakistan had begun nuclear signaling of one sort or another as early as 1984" (Chari et al. 2001, 67). While it did not escalate to war, Brasstacks "helped accelerate India's and Pakistan's nuclear programs" by convincing both states of the need for a nuclear deterrent (39).

The second major scuffle, which some analysts refer to as the Compound Crisis of 1990, took place amid the breakup of the Soviet Union and America's process of disengagement from South Asia. In the early months of 1990, India and Pakistan seemed to be preparing for war, with each accusing the other of supporting insurgent activity. In August 1989, India had introduced first paramilitary and then military forces into Kashmir and Punjab to counter what India believed to be Pakistan-backed ethnic insurgencies in those states. In December of the same year Pakistan began the largest ever military exercise in the Punjab. Known as Zarb-e-Momin, it was a response to India's Brasstacks Operation. As the number of military forces in the border area mounted, India continued to criticize Pakistan for supporting the militants in Kashmir, while Pakistan expressed its outrage over India's crackdown there, renewed its calls for a plebiscite, and denied that it was providing anything but political and diplomatic support to militants in India. Both Indian and Pakistani forces deployed along the border were on high alert. New Delhi and Islamabad participated in a flurry of diplomatic exchanges in an attempt to defuse the crisis, and the US ambassadors to both capitals became involved in trying to prevent an all-out war. In mid-May, Washington dispatched a high-level delegation led by Deputy National Security Advisor Bob Gates (Chari et al. 2001).

By the first week of June, the crisis had subsided. To this day, historians are divided on whether or not war was indeed likely, whether or not it could have evolved into a nuclear conflict, and what effect foreign intervention had. In the same year, however, the United States concluded that Pakistan had crossed key thresholds in the nuclear weapon production process. Consequently, in October 1990, President George H. W. Bush informed the US Congress, per the requirements of the 1985 Pressler Amendment, that he could not certify that Pakistan did not possess nuclear weapons. Subsequently, the United States terminated all economic and military assistance (including sales of military equipment). A year earlier, in 1989, Bush carefully chose his words in his annual certification letter to the US Congress, writing that Pakistan does not "now possess a nuclear explosive device" but that it "has continued its efforts to develop its unsafeguarded nuclear program" (Gordon 1989). This deliberative process conferred to Pakistan a crude nuclear capability. India, because of its 1974 test and subsequent developments, was also assumed to have some form of nuclear weapons capability (Chari et al. 2001).

The third significant crisis was the Indo-Pakistani crisis of 2001–2002. A few months after 9/11, on December 13, 2001, Pakistan-based and -backed Islamist militants associated with the Jaish-e-Mohammad attacked the Indian Parliament in New Delhi. India quickly placed the blame on Pakistani militants and ordered a full-scale mobilization under the name of Operation Parakram (valor). Despite Pakistani denials of any knowledge of the attack, India insisted that Pakistan cease to support cross-border terrorism and hand over some 20 criminals wanted in India. India stopped all communication between the two countries. By Christmas 2001, it appeared that war was imminent. The prospect was deeply disconcerting to the United States, which was depending on Pakistan to maintain its forces in the west of the country to support US operations in Afghanistan. As India mobilized its largest force since the 1971 war, Pakistan moved its forces from the west to the east. By January, tensions relaxed somewhat, as it became evident to most observers that India would not attack, but forces were not redeployed to their peacetime positions (Nayak and Krepon 2012).

In May 2002, militants associated with the Lashkar-e-Taiba, which like Jaish-e-Mohammad is based in Pakistan and receives Pakistani military and intelligence support, massacred the wives and children of army personnel at Kaluchak in Kashmir. It again seemed that war was imminent, but by the end of June tensions had subsided in the face of significant international pressure on both states: the United States pressed Pakistan to cease its support for cross-border terrorism while encouraging India to avoid further escalation. The crisis formally ended in October 2002. (India wanted to maintain its forces in place until after the October 2002 elections in Kashmir as a deterrent to any Pakistani state or state-sponsored adventurism.)

From India's point of view, it was able to achieve its aims, at least temporarily, by putting pressure on Pakistan via the United States to stop supporting cross-border terrorism. Indian officials that I have interviewed since 2002 concede that Pakistani infiltration has not since reached its pre-2002 levels (although there are numerous explanations for this). While India concluded that its "coercive diplomacy" is what influenced Pakistan, Pakistan surmised that its nuclear arsenal had deterred India from attacking (Chari et al. 2001; Nayak and Krepon 2006). Notably, for reasons that are beyond the scope of this effort, the Lashkar-e-Taiba terror attack in Mumbai in 2008 did not have the military dimensions of the 2001–2002 crisis (Nayak and Krepon 2012).

THE 1947–1948 INDO-PAKISTAN WAR OVER KASHMIR

The 1947–1948 war began in October 1947, when thousands of Pakistani tribal *lashkars* (militia members), with extensive assistance from Pakistan's new civilian government and elements in the military leadership, invaded the princely state of Jammu and Kashmir. Pakistan was growing anxious because the Hindu king, Maharaja Hari Singh, had delayed the decision to join either India or Pakistan and appeared to be holding out for independence. Pakistan believed that the inclusion of Kashmir (which was represented by the letter "k" in the word Pakistan) was essential to fulfilling its destiny as the homeland for South Asia's Muslims, as the two-nation theory demanded. The maharaja's forces were unable to defend against the intruders, and he resorted to asking for Indian assistance. India obliged, but under the condition that Kashmir would accede to India.

Under the terms of the British transfer of power, the maharaja was vested with the full legal power to join India. However, Jawaharlal Nehru was concerned about the legitimacy, as well as the legality, of the accession and requested that Kashmiri nationalist leader Sheikh Abdullah give his consent as well, which he did (Ganguly 2001; Nawaz 2008a, 2008b; Whitehead 2007). India air-lifted troops to defend what was now Indian territory.[1] Indian and Pakistani troops fought pitched battles throughout fall and early winter 1947, and both sides sustained significant losses. The conflict ended on January 1, 1948, with a United Nations (UN)–sponsored ceasefire whose line divided the territory into Indian and Pakistani administrative zones, with India retaining the important Muslim-majority valley of Kashmir.

India was first to take the conflict to the UN, invoking Articles 34 and 35 of its charter, which deal with threats to international peace and security. India's principal complaint concerned Pakistani nationals attacking Jammu and Kashmir. Pakistan denied these claims, questioned the validity of Kashmir's accession, and argued that India was committing atrocities in Kashmir. In January 1948, the UN Security Council (UNSC) passed Resolutions 38 and 39, which called for both states to avoid making the conflict worse and established a commission to help resolve the dispute. The commission's remit was expanded by another resolution (Resolution 47, April 1948), which also laid out three sequential steps essential to implementing a fair and impartial plebiscite on the question of accession. A close examination of this resolution is extremely important to understanding Pakistani and Indian narratives about the nature of the dispute.

First, Pakistan was to "secure the withdrawal from the State of Jammu and Kashmir of tribesmen and Pakistani nationals not normally resident therein who have entered the State for the purpose of fighting" (UNSC 1948). In addition, Pakistan was to "to prevent any intrusion into the State of such elements and any furnishing of material aid to those fighting in the State" (ibid.). Second, when the commission had determined to its satisfaction that "tribesmen are withdrawing and that arrangements for the cessation of the fighting have become effective," India was to "put into operation in consultation with the Commission a plan for with-drawing their own forces from Jammu and Kashmir and reducing them progressively to the minimum strength required for the support of the civil power in the maintenance of law and order" (ibid.). Third, when both of these conditions had been met, the plebiscite would be held under guidelines laid out by the commission (ibid.).

While it is true that for a number of reasons India tried to avoid the plebiscite, it is also the case that Pakistan never fulfilled the first requirement, to demilitarize, on which the rest of this process hinged (Ganguly 2001; Nawaz 2008a, 2008b; Whitehead 2007). Oddly, while many Pakistanis continue to insist today that the plebiscite be held, Pakistan was not enthusiastic about the idea when India first suggested it in 1948 (Wirsing 1998). Equally important, most contemporary Pakistani commentators have either forgotten (or simply choose to ignore) that Pakistan—not India—failed to fulfill the first, necessary (if insufficient) condition for the now much desired plebiscite, making Pakistan unable to blame India alone for its failure to meet subsequent obligations. It should be noted that in my varied interactions with Pakistanis in and out of uniform, I have never met a single individual who can recount what UNSCR 47 actually demanded of both states even though many Pakistanis continue to insist on its implementation.[2]

India has long held that the plebiscite has been made redundant by the ratification of Kashmir's accession to India by Kashmir's provincial constituent assembly and the numerous elections held in the state since then. Pakistan continues to decry Indian excesses in Kashmir and its mismanagement of the state and has generally remained wedded to the plebiscite, raising all of these issues when it deems expedient. In 2003, Pakistan made a historic—if fleeting—change to its position when the Pervez Musharraf government announced that it would no longer insist on the plebiscite. In 2004, however, Musharraf backtracked, again raising the demand for the plebiscite (*Outlook India* 2004). There have been no subsequent indications that Pakistan will relent in its demand for the plebiscite, despite the fact that Pakistan undermined the plebiscite's prospects in the first place.

THE 1965 INDO-PAKISTAN WAR OVER KASHMIR

As discussed in previous chapters, the 1965 war had two components. The first, which lasted from late 1964 into early 1965, was a series of clashes between forward-deployed Pakistani and Indian patrols operating in the Rann of Kutch. Indian and Pakistani accounts of the incident vary, with each inevitably accusing the other of being the aggressor. Undisputed is that India's response was tepid, partly owing to the geography of the area and the seasonal rains that made sustained ground conflict on the marshy terrain difficult. The Pakistanis interpreted India's less than robust response to mean that India did not have the stomach for vigorous combat, thus reinforcing Pakistan's beliefs about the pusillanimity of Hindu Indians. Pakistan was also growing frustrated with Indian efforts to integrate Kashmir into India and by its own inability to bring international pressure to bear on India to grant some concession to Pakistan. Fearing that it would lose the opportunity to redraw the map in Kashmir, Pakistan took advantage of the civil disturbance that arose in Srinagar when a holy relic (a hair of the Prophet Muhammad) disappeared in late 1963. Pakistan believed that the time was ripe to exploit inflamed local sentiments and stoke an insurgency that would free Kashmir from India's grasp. As a result, in spring 1965 Pakistan launched

Operation Gibraltar with the goal of "defreezing" the Kashmir issue (Khan 1993).[3]

As noted briefly in Chapter 4, the plan called for mustering several thousand irregulars, called mujahideen, with training and support by regular Pakistan military officers; estimates of the size of the force range between 3,000 and 30,000 militants (Nawaz 2008a). The fighters were tasked with sabotage activities and initiating a sustained civil war in Kashmir. Operation Gibraltar was to be followed by Operation Grand Slam, in which Pakistani regular forces would cross the ceasefire line and head toward Akhnur to cut Indian forces off from the rest of Kashmir. Pakistan's defense writings tend to assert that the driving forces behind Grand Slam were then foreign minister Zulfiqar Ali Bhutto and his foreign secretary, Aziz Ahmed, who allegedly met strong resistance from the Pakistani military leadership, including Gen. Ayub Khan, who was the chief of army staff at that time. Pakistan's leadership was certainly overconfident in its ability both to control escalation of the conflict and to defeat India, partly because of India's milquetoast response in the Rann of Kutch and partly because of its assessment of India's capabilities and will to fight in the wake of India's devastating defeat in its 1962 war with China (Ganguly 2001; Nawaz 2008a). For a very critical account of the 1965 war fiasco, see Khan (1993) and Ahmed (2002).

Infiltration across the ceasefire line began in August 1965. Not only did the intruders fail to foment a rebellion, but local Kashmiris also alerted the authorities to the intrusion. Despite its loss of the element of surprise, Pakistan continued with the planned operations, launching Grand Slam at the end of August (Nawaz 2008a; Ganguly 2001). But the Indian response surprised Pakistan. First, India was neither unprepared nor unwilling to fight Pakistan: in fact, India's prime minister, Lal Bahadur Shastri, had already approved "military action against Pakistan at a time and place to be chosen by the Army, and General Chaudhuri [the army chief] had indicated that the offensive operations could start by 10 May" (Nawaz 2008a, 209). The Indians decided that Jammu and Kashmir's terrain was not suitable for major offensive operations and instead opened up a new front along the international border, launching their counteroffensive against the key Punjabi cities of Lahore and Sialkot. Most of the subsequent conflict took place in the Punjab, with very little action in East Pakistan. On September 20, 1965, with the war rapidly approaching a stalemate, the UNSC passed a resolution calling for a cessation of hostilities. India conceded, but on political, not military, grounds: it could have sustained the conflict and turned the stalemate into an outright victory (Raghavan 2009). Pakistan was even more willing to settle: military setbacks had cost Ayub his will to continue fighting (Ganguly 2001; Nawaz 2008a).[4] Despite the historical facts that the 1965 war began with Pakistani aggression, Pakistan instituted Defense of Pakistan Day, to be celebrated on September 6 to commemorate the day when "Indian forces sneaked [sic] into the Wagah border and the Pakistan armed forces, when alerted, put up a valiant defence of the motherland and drove them back, thus taking its name as the Defence of Pakistan Day" (*Nation* 2012).

The United States had grown wary of attempting to resolve the Indo-Pakistan conflict and was unwilling to devote further resources to the problem. The Soviet Union stepped into the breach and facilitated the postwar settlement between the two combatants. Under the terms of the agreement, both sides gave up any captured territory, returned to the status quo ante, and agreed to settle future disputes peacefully. Pakistan claimed that it had seized 1,617 square miles of Indian territory and that India had seized 446 square miles of Pakistani territory. India, for its part, claimed that Pakistan seized 210 square miles of Indian territory and that it seized 740 square miles of Pakistani territory (Nawaz 2008a). Whatever the actual figures, Pakistan's actions in Kashmir had precipitated a war in which Pakistan achieved no permanent gains other than to simply keep the conflict alive. Ayub was livid, reportedly proclaiming that never again would Pakistan "risk 100 million Pakistanis for 5 million Kashmiris" (Nawaz 2008a, 240). Worse still, East Pakistanis concluded that Pakistan had no real plans for defending them from Indian aggression. This conviction added to an evolving inventory of grievances that set the stage for the next war.

THE 1971 INDO-PAKISTAN WAR AND THE EMERGENCE OF BANGLADESH FROM EAST PAKISTAN

East Pakistan, unlike West Pakistan, was dominated by a single ethnic group: Bengalis. While most Bengalis in East Pakistan were Muslim, many were Hindus, and after Partition a large Hindu minority of some 12 million remained in East Pakistan, alongside 32 million Muslims (Lambert 1950).[5] At the time of Pakistan's independence, the population of East Pakistan exceeded that of West Pakistan, which was also divided among several ethnic groups (Khan 1960). Under the principle of one man, one vote, the Bengalis of East Pakistan would have been able to dominate the politics of the new state. However, the predominantly Punjabi and Muhajir political elites of West Pakistan were committed to preventing such an outcome.

The West Pakistani political and military elites looked down on the Bengalis for a number of reasons. First, they were not among the so-called martial races and thus were nearly entirely excluded from military service. Second, their mother tongue was Bengali, and they had from the beginning objected to the imposition of Urdu as the national language. Bengalis were aggrieved to find that their language was relegated to second-class status even though they composed the largest portion of Pakistanis. Urdu was not the native tongue of any part of Pakistan; it was the language of the north Indian immigrant population. But both Hindu and Muslim Bengalis used the same Sanskrit-derived script and vocabulary to write their shared language.[6] West Pakistanis thus found the use of

Bengali to be distastefully redolent of Hinduism and sought to discourage it. They tried to persuade Bengali Muslims to use the Perso-Arabic script and to replace Sanskrit-based vocabulary items with Persian or Arabic words. Bengalis, whose nationalism has often been expressed through their language and literature, would not stand for it. Instead, they mobilized to obtain national status for their language (Jaffrelot 2002a).

Third, many West Pakistanis believed that their Bengali compatriots were lesser Muslims on account of their cultural, linguistic, historical, and social proximity to Hindu Bengalis, with whom they had more in common than with the ethnic groups of West Pakistan. In fact, the Muslims of East Pakistan seemed to have only one thing in common with their West Pakistani compatriots: Islam. But many West Pakistanis were convinced that the Islam practiced in Bengal was "contaminated" by its long exposure to Hindu social and cultural practices (Jaffrelot 2002a). Some West Pakistani religious leaders argued for the need to "purify" East Pakistanis citizens of these Hindu recrudescences, if not vestiges that never vanished in the first instance (Haqqani 2005, 62). West Pakistani racism toward their East Pakistani citizens was not even hidden: elites often dismissed Bengalis as "black bastards" (Salik 1997, 29).

While these conflicts emerged over language, the question of the fundamental governance structures of the still-new state was causing other problems. Constitutional debates revealed fundamental disagreements between East and West. The Objectives Resolution of 1949, with its assertion that "sovereignty over the entire Universe belongs to Allah Almighty alone," may have been consistent with the founding logic of the state, but it "destroyed any faint hopes of co-opting East Pakistan's substantial Hindu community into the Pakistan project" (Jones 2003, 154). In addition, representatives from West and East Pakistan clearly disagreed on how power should be shared between the federal and provincial governments. The Awami League, the dominant party in East Pakistan, wanted maximal devolution of power to the provinces, whereas the elites of West Pakistan wanted a strong central state.

The most tendentious constitutional question for the West Pakistani elites was how, given the Bengalis' numerical dominance and greater political coherence, the various states should be represented at the center. The first constituent assembly dodged the question by failing to specify how many representatives each province would send to the national assembly. For Bengalis, this was a clear sign that the West sought to deprive them of their rightful majority. When the constituent assembly revisited the question, it considered a proposal under which both East and West Pakistan would have equal representation. While this was an improvement, it still denied East Pakistan the representation that its population merited. But even this failed to satisfy Punjabi elites, who feared that East Pakistan would form alliances with other provinces in the West to check Punjabi political preferences (Haqqani 2005; Jaffrelot 2002a; Jones 2003).

The 1956 Constitution dealt a serious blow to the power of East Pakistan as well as to the smaller provinces of the West. It enshrined the One Unit Scheme, grouping all of the provinces of the West into one unit to balance the more politically and ethnically homogenous East Pakistan. Both East and West would have equal representation (150 seats each) in a unicameral parliament. The Awami League recognized the move for what it was: an effort to prevent the Bengalis from having a parliamentary majority, despite the fact that Bengalis represented an outright majority of Pakistan's population. But given East Pakistanis' political coherence, it was still certain that any election held under these conditions would nonetheless result in a majority government led by the East Pakistani representatives of the Awami League (Haqqani 2005; Jones 2003).

The efforts of West Pakistani civilian and military elites to deprive Bengalis of political representation further angered Bengalis, who were already underrepresented in the other organs of state power. They were overwhelmingly excluded from the military: by 1963, Bengalis composed a mere 5 percent of the officer corps and 7 percent of other ranks (Jones 2003). This was a particularly vexing issue, not only because East Pakistanis increasingly believed that they were vulnerable to Indian aggression but also because the army had governed Pakistan since Ayub's 1958 coup. East Pakistanis were excluded from the khaki corridors of power and also were also underrepresented in the powerful civil bureaucracy because few Bengalis knew Urdu, a requirement for government service (Jones 2003). Equally important, while West Pakistan continued its path toward praetorianism, East Pakistan's inhabitants had a longer tradition of parliamentary democracy and were more schooled in both the traditions and practice of parliamentary rule of law. In contrast, recall that much of West Pakistan was still under significant degrees of British militarized governance prior to 1947 and had not benefited from the institutionalization of provincial politics to the same degrees as other parts of the erstwhile Raj. East Pakistanis objected to the centralized, military-dominated state that was emerging out of West Pakistan.

Thus, with the single exception of their Muslim faith, the priorities and beliefs of East Bengalis differed in almost every way from those of their fellow citizens in the West (Haqqani 2005). West Pakistani elites responded to East Pakistanis' demurrals and complaints by denouncing them and their political leadership as Indian collaborators. As Haqqani notes, "Almost every leading Bengali political figure after partition was at one time or another accused of working in conjunction with India's intelligence services" (63). In fact, many prominent Awami League leaders were arrested for antistate activities, including former Pakistan prime minister Huseyn Shaheed Suhrawardy (Haqqani 2005; Jaffrelot 2002a; Jones 2003).

Bengali grievances regarding access to power and the constitutional dispensation were in addition to persistent complaints that the West exploited the east, extracting resources while investing very little in return. Bengali political aspirations received their clearest articulation under the leadership of Sheikh Mujibur Rahman of the Awami League. In 1966 he presented his six-point agenda, which demanded a federal structure for Pakistan; separate currencies for the two wings (to curb capital flight from east to west); a militia or paramilitary force for East Pakistan; and restriction of the federal government to defense and foreign affairs, with no central taxation authority and with both wings retaining their own foreign exchange earnings. While these demands had nearly universal support in the east, Pakistanis in the west viewed this agenda as a poorly disguised prelude to secession (Haqqani 2005; Jaffrelot 2002a; Jones 2003).

Ayub was unwilling to relent in his belief that Pakistan needed a strong, central government (controlled by the army), and Bengalis were unwilling to relax their demands for federalism and devolution of powers. Ayub, unwilling and unable to take the needed steps to stem the discontent simmering even within his own regime, ceded power to Gen. Yahya Khan in March 1969. Yahya Khan reimposed martial law and disbanded the assemblies but promised elections would take place in December 1970. The assembly, once elected, would be tasked with producing yet another constitution. Khan reversed the One Unit Scheme and restored individual provincial representation, rejected the parity in representation that his predecessor had imposed on each wing, and even granted universal adult suffrage. These concessions amounted to a de facto acceptance of Bengalis' numerical superiority and political dominance. Despite being delayed a month by a devastating cyclone, the elections took place. The Awami League triumphed, taking 160 of the 162 National Assembly seats allotted to East Pakistan and 288 of 300 in the provincial assembly. According to the principles of parliamentary democracy, Rahman should have been called to head the new government. But this was not to be (Haqqani 2005; Jaffrelot 2002a; Jones 2003).

Bengalis immediately insisted on the implementation of the six points, and in principle the Awami League was in a position to enact its agenda into law if and when parliament convened. But neither Khan nor Bhutto of the Pakistan People's Party (PPP) could countenance such an outcome. Bhutto refused to permit his party to sit in any parliament controlled by Dhaka and declared that "no constitution...could be framed, nor could any government at the centre be run without my party's co-operation" (Jones 2003, 163). Bhutto's claims were simply absurd: the new parliament could make decisions with a simple majority, and the PPP did not even have enough votes for a veto (ibid.). Khan was unwilling to take the course dictated by parliamentary procedures and failed to resolve the impasse between Bhutto and Rahman, both of whom were growing increasingly intransigent. Khan finally lost his nerve and canceled the convening of the National Assembly. This was the final straw: Bengalis, realizing that the West would never allow them to exercise their democratic strength, began demanding complete independence from Pakistan.

On March 26, 1971, Khan announced that negotiations had failed, denounced Rahman as a traitor, and banned the Awami League. By the time he made this announcement, the military had already moved into the east and Operation Searchlight had begun. Operation Searchlight aimed to "decimate the likely sources of political opposition to the military regime in West Pakistan" (Ganguly 2001, 60). Prior to commencing the operation, the military made sure that ethnic Bengali police and military forces were disarmed and dispersed to lessen their ability to resist. Refugees began fleeing into India, creating mounting political and economic problems. India threw its support to the rebels. By April, the Awami League had established an office in Calcutta; later that month, India permitted the declaration of a so-called government in exile, which became known as the Mujibnagar. Once the political leadership was safely in India, India began training and arming the Mukti Bahini (Liberation Force) and provided them with sanctuary. The Mukti Bahini, which was placed under the command of retired East Pakistani army officer Col. M. A. G. Osmani, "played a vital role [by] harrying the Pakistani forces, engaging in acts of espionage and sabotage, and killing collaborators" (62).

On May 1, 1971, India's army chief issued a secret order to begin a war that would end in Pakistan's dismemberment. According to Praveen Swami (2007), an Indian journalist specializing in security affairs who secured restricted and classified documents on the war, India's objectives highly resembled those of Pakistan in the 1965 war. The plan "[envisaged] the use of a covert army as a catalyst for insurrection and a spearhead for regular forces. Its scale and objectives, however, were altogether more ambitious" than those of Pakistan in the 1965 war (118). With Operation Instruction, India's military was formally committed to aid the provisional government of Bangladesh and to motivate the East Pakistani public to support the liberation movement. Most importantly, it committed India to "raise, equip and train East Bengal cadres for guerilla operations for employment in their in their own native land" (ibid.). These cadres were known as the Gano Bahini. India's Eastern Command was tasked with helping the guerillas tie down Pakistan's forces in protective tasks in the east, eroding the Pakistan Army's will to fight, and degrading the Pakistan Army's ability to undertake offensives against the Indian bordering state of Assam and West Bengal. Per the plan, the Indian regular troops would be inducted if Pakistan initiated hostilities against India.

According to Swami (2007), Indian forces set up seven camps for recruiting and training volunteers: two in West Bengal; two in Meghalaya; and one in Bihar, Tripura, and Assam. Awami League officials who fled to India were tasked with screening and recommending recruits for guerilla training. Each camp was designed to handle 1,000 recruits for four weeks of training in sabotage, communications, weapons handling, and field craft. However, some camps were occupied by 3,000 trainees. By September 1971, India dramatically increased the scale of its training, which allowed it to process 20,000 guerillas a month. The training was overseen by Indian soldiers (8 soldiers per 100 trainees). By the end of November 1971, as war was looming, India had trained 83,000 guerillas, of which some 51,000 were operating in East Pakistan at that time (ibid.).

In addition to training scores of guerillas, India employed some 1,800 commandos who operated in the Chittagong Hill Tracts in East Pakistan. These men were part of the Special Frontier Force (SFF), which was established toward the end of India's 1962 war with China, and were Tibetan refugees in India who had fought with the Dalai Llama's Chushi Gandruk irregular forces from the mid-1950s. Members of the SSF were trained not only by Indian military personnel but also by the US Central Intelligence Agency (CIA) at a facility near Denver, Colorado. The SSF men served under Maj. Gen. Surjit Singh Uban, who, according to Indian accounts, operated indirectly under the supervision of Research and Analysis Wing (RAW), India's external intelligence agency. Uban's forces engaged in skirmishes with Pakistani forces and waged an "extraordinary campaign of sabotage and harassment" (Swami 2007, 119).

By the end of March 1971 India's leadership began to see the developments in East Pakistan as an opportunity to weaken Pakistan and were putting pressure upon the Indian army's Eastern Command to move immediately into Eastern Pakistan. In July 1971, K. Subrahmanyam, the now deceased doyen of India's strategic community and who was a government official at the time, called the crisis in East Pakistan an "opportunity of the century" to dismember Pakistan (Chari 2011). However, the chief of staff of Eastern Command, Lt. Gen. J. F. R. Jacob (1977), "protested that this was impractical" (36). He explained to India's army chief Gen. Sam Manekshaw that the army was not prepared. They had only Mountain Divisions, trained for mountain warfare, with little bridging equipment or logistical capabilities. Worse, East Pakistan, with more navigable rivers than roads, would be a challenging battle terrain during the monsoons. Lt. Jacob needed more time to equip and train the force. He assessed that, at the earliest, India's Eastern Command would be ready by November 15. Prime Minister Indira Gandhi was furious but the army leadership held this ground (Jacob 1977; Nawaz 2008a).

India's decision to enter the war was not without risks. India, which was home to several ethnic separatist movements, had little stomach for setting a precedent by backing such a movement in East Pakistan. After all, this could justify similar intervention by outside forces to support Indian separatists. Some Indian leaders also worried that there would be a backlash in the Muslim world if they assisted the breakup of a Muslim country. Equally challenging were the diplomatic, logistical, and military hurdles that had to be cleared before military action could go forward. India was worried about both US and Chinese support to Pakistan. (Pakistan had recently played a vital role in helping the United States to reach a rapprochement with China.) The Soviet Union, however, concerned by the prospect of a US–China alliance, found it expedient to ally more tightly with India.

While the military prepared itself for war, India's political leadership prepared the diplomatic ground for the invasion. In August 1971, India and the Soviet Union signed a Treaty of Peace, Friendship, and Cooperation, which offered India some hope of military assistance if attacked and also assured India the support of the Soviet veto at the Security Council (Ganguly 2001; Jaffrelot 2002a; Jones 2003). In October 1971, Prime Minister Gandhi undertook a tour of global capitals to make her case about the gravity of the situation in East Pakistan, the untenable refugee crisis the conflict had spawned, and the need for Indian military intervention.[7]

The tour was not successful. While the United States wanted to preclude the destruction of Pakistan, President Richard Nixon did not want to "push" Yahya. When Gandhi met Nixon on November 4 in the Oval Office, Nixon refused to exhort Yahya to pursue negotiations with Mujib while Gandhi denounced Pakistan for the genocide in East Pakistan and the concomitant refugee crisis deepening in India. As their meeting concluded, Nixon warned that the United States government would continue providing humanitarian relief and to encourage Yahya to use restraint, but declared that Pakistan's disintegration would benefit no one (Bass, 2013). Astonishingly, the Nixon administration continued to arm Pakistan in complete violation of US law, as Pakistan was still under an arms embargo due to the 1965 war. Nixon persisted in this plan despite receiving numerous admonitions from legal analysts in the Departments of Defense and State and from advisors in his own White House. With little international support other than the Friendship Treaty with the Soviets, India went it alone and began exerting military pressure on Pakistan (Bass 2013).

While India had prepared war plans, the war formally commenced on December 3, 1971, with an "Israeli-style pre-emptive air attack by Pakistan on India's northern air bases.... The attack failed miserably on all counts" (Ganguly 2001, 67). The war was short. On December 15, Gen. A. A. K. Niazi, the commander of the Pakistani forces in the east, sought an unconditional ceasefire, a suggestions his Indian counterpart, Lt. Gen. Jagjit Singh Aurora, rebuffed. The war finally ended on December 17, when Gandhi ordered a unilateral ceasefire; Khan immediately ordered Pakistani forces to reciprocate. The war ended with the emergence of independent Bangladesh (Ganguly 2001; Jaffrelot 2002a; Jones 2003).

After the war, Gandhi and Pakistan's president, Bhutto (Khan had ceded the presidency to Bhutto in December 1971), met in Simla, the former summer capital of the Raj, to reach a postwar settlement. India principally sought to secure Pakistan's commitment to resolve outstanding disputes bilaterally, to repatriate all prisoners of war, and to accept the inviolability of all of India's borders. Pakistan, for its part, had four objectives, which it largely secured. It sought to have its 93,000 prisoners of war released, to stop Bangladesh from holding war crimes trials of captured Pakistani soldiers, to regain some 5,000 square miles of territory that India had seized in the west, and finally to ensure that its position in Kashmir remained fundamentally unchanged. The salient features of the resulting settlement included the restoration of bilateral diplomatic relations, a mutual commitment to avoiding the use of force to resolve the Kashmir dispute, and a change in the name of the 1948 Cease Fire Line to the Line of Control (LOC) (Ganguly 2001; Nawaz 2008a).

After the war, India emerged as the undisputed power in South Asia. The loss of East Pakistan deprived Pakistan of a majority of its populace and half of its territory. Pakistan's inability to bring ethnic Bengalis into the national project had dealt another serious blow to the two-nation theory, which was and remains the ideological basis of Pakistan and its army.

THE 1999 KARGIL WAR

The Kargil War was the first war between India and Pakistan after India's May 1998 nuclear test and Pakistan's reciprocal nuclear tests 17 days later. Some analysts refer to this conflict as a mere skirmish or crisis. I consider it a war, both because battle deaths exceeded 1,000 (the conventional social science standard for coding a conflict as a war; Kapur 2003) and because the forces of both sides crossed a de facto international border after Pakistan made a considerable effort to seize and hold territory (Tellis et al. 2001). Pakistani planning for the conflict began sometime in mid-November 1998, a mere six months after the nuclear tests.

Pakistan's build-up for the Kargil misadventure in fact unfolded simultaneously with negotiations that led to a historical breakthrough in Indo-Pakistan relations. That latter process culminated in a visit to Lahore by Indian Prime Minister Atal Bihari Vajpayee (traveling via the newly opened Delhi-Lahore-Delhi bus service), who addressed Pakistanis at the site of the Minar-e-Pakistan, the revered monument to Pakistani independence. Significantly, Vajpayee was the leader of the Bharatiya Janata Dal/Party (BJP), a Hindu nationalist party that had longed advanced the goal of Akhund Bharat (undivided India). Thus, this gesture showed that even the BJP accepted Pakistan's independent existence.

In addition, on February 21, 1999, Vajpayee and Sharif signed the Lahore Declaration, which acknowledged the nuclear dimension of the two states' security competition and their concomitant responsibility to avoid conflict. The declaration also reaffirmed India and Pakistan's commitment to peaceful coexistence, to full implementation of the Simla Agreement, and to pursuance of universal nuclear disarmament and nonproliferation. Sharif and Vajpayee recognized the importance of confidence-building measures to improve the security environment and referenced a September 1998 agreement in which both sides had acknowledged peace and security to be in the supreme national interest of both states and thus committed themselves to resolving all outstanding disputes, such as that over Jammu and Kashmir (Lahore Declaration Text 1999).

The Kargil operation's origins can be traced back to Lt. Gen. Mahmud Ahmed, the commander of 10 Corps, who in November 1998 asked the chief of general staff, Lt. Gen. Muhammed Aziz, to secure him a meeting with Musharraf. Ahmed was accompanied by Maj. Gen. Javed Hassan, the commander of the Frontier Constabulary of the Northern Areas (FCNA). The two men sought Musharraf's permission to execute a plan to seize and occupy terrain in the Kargil–Dras sectors in Indian-administered Kashmir. Specifically, they proposed seizing several high-altitude Indian outposts, which were normally evacuated during the winter and reoccupied in the spring, with the aim of giving a boost to militant efforts in Kashmir (Lavoy 2009; Qadir 2002). My own interviews with subjects who had insight into Pakistan's planning for Kargil suggest that the army was seeking to redeem itself (and also to punish India) for the 1971 defeat, India's occupation of the Siachen glacier, and India's periodic shelling of the Neelum Valley road and other "provocations" along the LOC. Pakistan also likely sought to exploit its newly confirmed nuclear capabilities to force the lasting political changes in Kashmir that had long eluded Islamabad (Tellis et al. 2001).

The plan remained a tightly held secret among these four principals. In late November or early December, with preparations ongoing, the operation was informally briefed to Sharif. One of his advisors, however, explained to me (and to others in a Kargil study team conducted under the auspices of the Naval Post Graduate School) that the briefing was in English and that Sharif did not seem to understand the possibilities for escalation of the conflict. In fact, "military leadership had not presented a complete analysis of the scale of the operation or its possible outcome" (Qadir 2002, 26). The rest of the army was not notified of the operation until March 1999, by which point it was already under way. The Military Operations Directorate was tasked with evolving a "strategic operational plan, which would have a military aim to fulfill a political objective. Given the fact that they were developing a plan to justify an operation already underway, the response was no less than brilliant" (ibid.). Pakistan, guided by the calculus of this insulated planning cell, believed that India would not respond with an all-out offensive because doing so would result in a stalemate (Tellis et al. 2001). Brig. (Retd.) Shaukat Qadir offers an important insight on the Pakistan Army's view of victory when he notes in his own analysis of Kargil that a stalemate "would be viewed as a victory for Pakistan" (ibid.).

According to Qadir (2002), Pakistan's military goals were to pose a credible military threat to India by seizing territory, presenting it with a fait accompli, and forcing India to the negotiating table from a position of weakness (see also Tellis et al. 2001). The war plan envisioned amassing Pakistan paramilitary forces from the Northern Light Infantry with support from the regular army and some logistical assistance from locals (*razakars*). At the same time, Kashmiri militants (e.g., mujahideen) would pursue a newly energized insurgency, further weakening India's grip on Kashmir. As with Pakistan's calculations in the 1965 war, things did not go as planned. India swiftly moved to repulse the invaders. In retrospect, Qadir's claim that the operation was intended to involve mujahideen is suspect given that the Inter-Services Intelligence (ISI) chief had not been apprised of the mission in advance (Fair 2009b; Lavoy 2009). The involvement of the ISI, the lead agency for dealing with so-called jihadi affairs, was necessary for any success-ful coordination with the militants.

Sharif was not formally briefed until April, well after the operation had begun. The other services were briefed at the same time. The navy's representative (the chief of naval staff was abroad) was apprehensive. The chief of the air staff was skeptical of the army's assessment of the situation and admitted outright that should there be an all-out war, the air force would not be able to provide the kind of assistance the army would likely require. One motivation for this hon-esty was the simple fact that the conflict would be fought at altitudes in excess of 15,000 feet. Aircraft and ordinance behave very differently at such heights than they do at lower levels, and not all fixed-wing (much less rotary) aircraft can operate effectively (or at all) at high altitudes (Lavoy 2009; Qadir 2002; Tellis et al. 2001).

In early May, Indian forces began to detect the intrusion when they attempted to reoccupy the posts they had vacated the previous autumn. At first the Indians thought that the intruders were mujahideen. While it is not clear whether Pakistan had devised that cover story in advance, Pakistan did persist with the mujahideen narrative after India made its erroneous assessments public (Fair 2009b). In fact, to this day there is a lingering belief that the majority of fighters on the Pakistani side in the Kargil War were mujahideen. This is simply not the case. The Northern Light Infantry, a paramilitary organization that recruits in Pakistan's Northern Areas and is officered by Pakistan Army officers, supplied the majority of the fighters. They enjoyed the assistance of the regular Pakistan Army and of locals, who provided minimal logistical and reconnaissance support (Lavoy 2009). Indian official sources assess that between 1,500 and 2,400 intruders occupied roughly a 100-mile segment of the LOC, seizing about 130 outposts to a depth of 5 to 6 miles inside Indian-controlled Kashmir (estimates vary: see Kapur 2003; Lambeth 2012). Indian government officials assess that about 70 percent of these fighters were Pakistan Army forces. Precise troop strength and the ratio of regular army to paramilitary forces remain a subject of debate, but these estimates are commonly accepted (Fair 2009b; Kapur 2003).

Retaking the posts proved a daunting challenge. The Pakistanis had the advan-tage of high terrain and could easily shoot down Indian forces as they advanced. India initially considered expanding the conflict across the international border but ultimately did not. By the end of May, however, it began to use air power. This was a significant escalation, as India had not used air assets against Pakistan since the 1971 war; still, the challenging terrain initially foiled even these efforts. Eventually India mastered the terrain and successfully attacked Pakistani positions. India claims that all of its air strikes were on India's side of the LOC, while Pakistanis claim that India also attacked on Pakistan's side of the LOC, in so-called Azad Kashmir (Ganguly 2001; Lambeth 2012; Tellis et al. 2001). By early June, India had recaptured some 21 positions.

As the conflict unfolded, international opinion was unanimously on the side of India. Even the Chinese told the Pakistanis to withdraw their forces and respect the status quo (Tellis et al. 2001). By mid-June India had managed to retake key positions in Dras and Batalik, overlooking the principal supply route for Indian military positions on the Siachen Glacier, where Indian and Pakistani troops have been fighting since India seized territory there in 1984 (Ganguly 2001). India's slow advance cost the lives of several hundred Indian soldiers as well as at least two of its fixed-wing aircraft (MiGs) and one helicopter (Ganguly 2001; Qadir 2002).

With the conflict showing no sign of abating, Gen. Anthony Zinni, visiting Pakistan in his capacity as the commander of US Central Command, told Sharif to pull back his troops. The US deputy assistant secretary of state for South Asia, Gordon Lanpher, visited India to inform New Delhi of Zinni's mission and to counsel restraint. But the conflict continued into early July, with the tide increasingly turning in India's favor. Sharif, fearing wider escalation and eventual defeat, sought the assistance of the United States in putting an honorable end to Pakistan's war. Ostensibly acting on his own initiative, Sharif traveled to Washington over the Fourth of July weekend to meet with President Bill Clinton. Refusing to accept Sharif's claim that India had started the war, Clinton advised him to withdraw Pakistani troops. In response, on July 12 Sharif announced the withdrawal of the mujahideen. The United States was comfortable allowing Pakistan to maintain this fiction as long as it in fact retreated. But by the end of July 1999, even the Pakistani press began to acknowledge that the mujahideen story was a ruse (Fair 2009b; Lavoy 2009).

Pakistani forces were forced to withdraw amid fears of a catastrophic defeat. Pakistan was marginally successful in its secondary goal of keeping the Kashmir dispute in the international eye. But this came at a high price as evidenced by Clinton's March 2000 admonition to the Pakistani people. He acknowledged Pakistan's purported "convictions that human rights of all [of Kashmir's] people must be respected," but he forthrightly told his audience that they had to come to terms with a stark truth. Namely, "There is no military solution to Kashmir. International sympathy, support and intervention cannot be won by provoking a bigger, bloodier conflict. On the contrary; sympathy and support will be lost" (Clinton 2000). Even if Pakistan partially succeeded in keeping the Kashmir dispute alive, it clearly fell short of its stated political aim of forcing some sort of concession from India.

India: Through the Eyes of the Pakistan Army

While the previous section sought to provide a brief historical account of the various wars and crises that Pakistan and India have weathered in the years since independence, this section employs some six decades of Pakistani defense publications to explore how the Pakistan Army has viewed India during the same period. A thorough perusal of these writings reveals several prominent and intertwined rubrics or narrative tropes. The first of these is that India aspires to the status of hegemon and that only Pakistan can effectively resist India and thus deny it the power it desires. Second, Pakistani defense analysts more often than not seek to understand India as Hindu and to place it in opposition to Muslim Pakistan. The authors first establish that Hindus are dishonorable, meek, pusillanimous, treacherous, and inequitable and then argue that these traits define the country. This absurd essentialism persists despite the fact that India is in fact a multiethnic, multireligious state and that Hinduism itself is not a singular, coherent faith community. At the same time, these writers establish that Muslims are honorable, brave, dedicated to fighting for the umma, steadfastly committed to justice, and fight only when attacked. With equally absurd essentialism, they then aver that these traits define Pakistan.

A third narrative that permeates the defense literature is used to diminish the threat India poses to Pakistan. Although many authors seek to inflate the Indian threat, those employing this trope seek to reveal India as a paper tiger that Pakistan can easily dominate. In many cases, India's Hinduness is used to denigrate its worthiness as an adversary for Pakistan. Finally, India appears in Pakistan's defense literature not only as a perennial source of external conflict but also as the primary source of Pakistan's domestic woes. (In some cases, India is pictured as the puppet or tool of another foe—such as the United States, Israel, or the Soviet Union—and acts as their proxy.) This narrative allows the army to continue to argue that it is the only institution that can protect Pakistan from both external and internal threats, which are seen as essentially isomorphous. Each of these narrative tropes is detailed in the following sections.

INDIA AS A HEGEMON THAT PAKISTAN'S ARMY MUST RESIST

One of the perennial themes of Pakistani defense writing on India is the contention that India rejects the legitimacy of Partition and the emergence of an independent Pakistan and, moreover, that it seeks to either reabsorb Pakistan or merely dominate it. This line of argument is related to a second view: that India aspires to be a regional, if not global, hegemon. Pakistani defense analysts thus pay a great deal of attention to India's supposed hegemonic aspirations and attempts to fulfill them. A final, related, rhetorical line is that Pakistan alone can frustrate India's hegemonic ambitions. Taken together, Pakistan's defense literature casts itself as the noble underdog that must resist New Delhi's unprincipled schemes to undo the Pakistani state. This characterization of India as prosecuting a relentless effort to break up Pakistan gives rise to describing India and its alleged designs in the crudest of ways, replete with obloquy if not contempt. These varied, discomfiting contentions are given full play in Ayub's autobiography *Friends not Masters* (Khan 2006, first published 1967). In that volume, he argues that behind all of the Indo-Pakistan discord is "India's ambition to absorb Pakistan or turn her into a satellite.... From the day of Independence, Pakistan was involved in a bitter and prolonged struggle for her very existence and survival.... Indian efforts in the field of foreign policy were all directed towards one aim, the isolation of Pakistan and its disintegration" (135–137).

Another article detailing India's ostensible hegemonic designs is Maj. M. A. Zuberi's June 1971 piece titled "The Challenge of a Nuclear India." Zuberi likely wrote the article amid the developing crisis in East Pakistan but before full-scale war with India broke out. He opines that "extremists [in India] still harbor a dream of *Akhund Bharat* [an undivided India which includes Burma]. Even moderates would like to see Pakistan in a position of India's satellite" after which "Pakistan would be reduced to a status of an innocuous spectator" (22). Zuberi feared that "a nuclear India would automatically claim the right for leadership of areas in her immediate vicinity if not the entire non-communist Asia and Africa" (23). (While India had not yet tested a nuclear device, its nuclear program was already an open secret.) Zuberi defines Pakistani and Indian security in zero-sum terms when he notes, "It would not be wrong to say that Pakistan's defence is inversely proportional to India's strength" (ibid.).

In Maj. Khalid Mehmud's 1985 essay "India's Posture as a Regional Power," the author describes India's hegemonic aspirations and its desire to dominate not just Pakistan but all of South Asia. As Mehmud explains, "India has its peculiar perception of security for South Asia and wants to impose its security and economic system upon the entire region.... It also wants to restrict the foreign policy choices and options of its neighbours and wants them to make their policies compatible with the Indian foreign policy objectives" (4). In a different piece published later that same year, Mehmud (1985a) notes that, despite these aspirations, "Presently, India does not possess the power and the means to overthrow the structure of power in the international system. However, its aspirations and ambitions for a subject role in the international system are an indication to bring major changes in the existing global power pattern, at an appropriate time" (16). Farhat Khalid, writing in this vein for the *Pakistan Army Journal* in 1988, suggests that "India has ambitions to play a much wider role than just being confined to South Asia. Many in India believe that it is destined to have a global role, and some even visualise it as ranking immediately behind the superpowers and alongside powers like China" (5).

The implications of Indian aspirations (as they appear in Pakistani defense publications) are ominous for Pakistan. Writing in March 1990, as the Cold War was concluding, a few years after the 1986–1987 Brasstacks Crisis, and while the Compound Crisis of 1990 was developing, Lt. Col. Israr Ghumman summarized Pakistan's predicament as a small state confronting "multidirectional threats to her security due to her geostrategic importance, national policies and ideological stance. Pakistan remains sandwiched between an expanding ideology [the Soviet Union] and a hegemonic neighbour [India] forcing it to live in a perpetual state of external conflict" (26). Ghumman believes that India will inevitably become the "dominant regional power," but "she finds Pakistan a much smaller country, as the sole embarrassing stumbling block" (ibid.; see also Bakhtawar 1990; Durrani 1989). While this is of some comfort, he notes that "India is in the process of modernization of her armed forces. Once the Indian military might is developed, it is likely to be unleashed [upon] Pakistan at a time of her choosing" (ibid.). For Ghumman, this conflict is inevitable because India cannot ascend unless she subdues Pakistan. He explains that the "immediate threat to Pakistan emanates from hegemonic designs of hostile India, which considers Pakistan as a stumbling block in her way to achieving a regional power status" (27). Ghumman, like Zuberi before him, believes that the best way for Pakistan to manage the Indian threat is a nuclear deterrent, which would also enable Pakistan to avoid needless investments in conventional forces.

After 1990, when the United States disengaged from South Asia and invoked the sanctions on Pakistan demanded by the Pressler Amendment, Pakistan began to see India not only as a threat on its own terms but also as a proxy for the United States. (This view was also expressed after the 1962 war between China and India, during which the United States provided military assistance to India.) Col. G. Sarwar describes this proxy relationship in a 1995 article titled "Pakistan's Strategic and Security Perspectives." According to Sarwar, Pakistan's insecurity has always stemmed from "the inherent animosity of India against Pakistan" (64). While this alone would be problematic for Pakistan, "America is deliberately conniving at India's belligerent posture... [and] is exerting undue pressure on Pakistan thus endangering its security interests" (ibid.). Sarwar argues presciently that "America is determined to assign an important role to India, ostensibly with the aim of neutralising the strength of [the] Chinese and also decimating all the power potential of Pakistan" (ibid.). He also describes India's 1974 nuclear test as "a part of [India's] design of achieving regional hegemony and the status of a global power" (ibid.). India's test, and its hegemonic aspirations, deeply disquieted Pakistan and prompted it "to acquire nuclear technology for preserving its national integrity" (ibid.).

A perusal of the record of war in South Asia suggests that most of the wars (1947–1948, 1965, 1999) were precipitated by Pakistani actions (although India's position was also occasionally hostile to Pakistan's purported equities in the region). Thus, if one were to rely on the scholarly accounts of the region's history, Pakistan would appear to have initiated all of these wars, with the possible exception of the 1971 war, depending on how one defines the start of the conflict. But Sarwar (1995) uses a technique common in the Pakistani defense literature to paint India as the perennial aggressor. He points to India's "recurrent use of force to impose solutions, i.e. annexation of Junagadh, Hyderabad, Sikkim, Bhutan, use of force in Maldives and Sri Lanka, etc." and explains that "Pakistan is apprehensive of India's long-term objectives of becoming a global power and its hegemonic designs in the region including dismemberment of Pakistan" (64–65).

The use of these themes of Indian hegemonic aspirations and desire to dominate, if not dismember, Pakistan has not abated in recent years. In a 2011 essay in *Hilal*, Col. M. Khan, the head of the international relations department at Pakistan's National Defence University, argues that "at the regional level, the pursuit of domination by one state (India) over its neighbours is the main cause of insecurity and instability of South Asia. Certainly, attempts of regional domination leads [sic] towards a highly dangerous situation" (18–19). To buttress these claims of Indian hegemonic activities, the author claims that India had sponsored the Sri Lankan terrorist group the Liberation Tigers of Tamil Eelam (LTTE, or Tamil Tigers) as well as Maoist insurgents in Nepal. The author notes India's maltreatment of Bangladesh in their ongoing border dispute and its use of the waters of the River Ganges as leverage to coerce Bangladesh to acquiesce to India's designs. While these allegations are certainly hyperbolic, some are not entirely void of merit. In the early 1980s, under Gandhi, India did support Tamil militants operating in Sri Lanka, providing them with military assistance and training and access to Indian territory (Destradi 2012). While there is no robust evidence that India supported the Maoist rebels in Nepal's insurgency, Bangladesh has frequently been disquieted by what it views as India's "big brotherly" approach (Vinayaraj 2009). India's excessive use of force along the Bangladesh border has been detailed by various media reports and human rights organizations alike (Human Rights Watch 2012).

M. Khan (2011) also dilates on the growing "nexus" between India, Israel, and United States, which he believes to be principally aimed at advancing American global domination. ("Nexus" invariably implies something nefarious.) As evidence that India serves US interests, he points to India's "growing involvement in Afghanistan [as] yet another concern both at regional and global level [sic]," and argues that the United States is "acting as a guarantor for detrimental role of India in the future set of Afghanistan" (19). Khan believes, in advance of its planned departure from the country in 2014, the United States is "preparing India as its successor state in Afghanistan" (ibid). India's role in Afghanistan—both real and imagined—is a source of extreme anxiety in Pakistan. Khan hints at this discomfiture when he notes that "for countries like Pakistan, this growing Indian influence in Afghanistan is enhancing its security concerns. Already Indian intelligence set up has created internal instability in FATA and Balochistan" (ibid.). Khan takes some pride in the fact that "Pakistan is the only regional country, which resist [*sic*] the Indian regional domination," even though doing so presents "threats to its security and domestic stability" (ibid.).

In the *Pakistan Army Green Book 2010*, dedicated to information warfare, Brig. U. Durrani (2010) claims that India is employing its own information offensive to influence Pakistan's standing in the international community. India's goals in this regard include ensuring that Pakistan is labeled an "irresponsible, rogue and failing nuclear state whose arsenal is not safe," propagating the notion of Pakistan's tribal areas as "safe havens and epicentre of Islamic terrorists," sustaining the concept that "Pakistan is likely to be overrun [*sic*] by Islamic fundamentalists/terrorists in near future," and "eventually creat[ing] the conditions whereby the international community acts and seizes control of Pakistan's nuclear arsenal or considers Indian aggression against Pakistan as a justified act" (4–5).

Rasul Baksh Rais (2011), one of Pakistan's most well-regarded political scientists who frequently writes for Pakistan's defense publications, offers a similar view. Discussing the October 2011 strategic partnership agreement between India and Afghanistan, which both actors have hailed as a landmark treaty that will ensure India–Afghan cooperation in the coming years, Rais argues that the two states' collaboration on security issues is an ominous sign of their hostile intentions toward Pakistan. He notes with concern that this agreement is "the most comprehensive of all agreements that Afghanistan has signed with any country in the modern history [*sic*]. Under the agreement India will train the Afghan security forces, equip them and the two countries will have sustained high-level consultations on security and political issues" (5). Rais draws the "obvious conclusion … that India is stepping in a big way in Afghanistan as the United States and its allies begin withdrawing from the country. This role fits well into India's regional ambitions of playing a greater role in what its security establishment conceives as a wider and larger neighbourhood" (6). Drawing on Pakistan's experiences with Afghanistan, he concludes that this recent agreement between India and Afghanistan is "historically consistent with [the] conventional Afghan game of seeking powerful external levers to keep Pakistan at bay" (ibid.).

In Rais' (2011) formulation, the Karzai government is behaving irresponsibly by courting India, since doing so poses obvious dangers to Pakistan's interests. Rais goes as far to suggest that this partnership may even provoke another round of the Great Game, noting that Pakistan "will definitely feel insecure with India digging its heels in Afghanistan. In the past, sovereign decisions by Afghan governments have brought in foreign forces through bilateral security arrangements that have caused tremendous damage to Pakistan's national security" (6). This time, he argues, will be no different, because India is Pakistan's historical rival and the source of Pakistan's threat perceptions. Given the realities of the Indo-Pakistan security competition, Rais warns that India's "'security cooperation' with Afghanistan may not be perceived [to be] as innocent as the Afghan authorities might think" (ibid.).

While some US analysts point to the recent improvements in Indo-Pakistan relations, particularly the easing of restrictions on trade and travel, Brig. (Ret.) U. Saeed (2012) is not persuaded that these materially alter the fundamental security competition between the two states. After explaining that "India has largely succeeded in convincing US and allies of her ability to fill the power vacuum" in Afghanistan, he warns that India's "recent change in posture from confrontation to reconciliation with Pakistan in no way indicates her abandonment of [a] policy of cultural, political and economic domination of her region backed by superior military capability" (15). If this is not sufficiently sobering, he warns that Indian contributions to the "modernisation and indoctrination of [*sic*] Afghan Army to undertake combat operations at the operational and tactical level with assistance of [*sic*] Indian Military Command will become [*sic*] dilemma to our sovereignty" (ibid.).

THE PERFIDIOUS INDIAN

Much of Pakistan's defense literature is dedicated to negative depictions of India and Indians, who are almost invariably reduced to their supposed Hindu nature. One prominent element in this approach, painting India as the aggressor in a security competition, was discussed already, in the chapter on the ideology of the Pakistan Army. This rhetoric is critical to supporting the larger argument: that Pakistan's wars with India have been defensive jihads. The arguments proffered by Pakistan's defense publications, which often appear to be at odds with the scholarly literature, merit serious attention. They attest to the durability of this highly stylized history, which is replicated in Pakistan's school curriculum and cultural products aimed at a popular audience, including civilian government officials' accounts (e.g., Hamoodur Rehman Commission 2001; Siddiqi 1964).

Gen. Mohammad Musa, the army chief during the 1965 war, recounts this conflict in his 1983 book *My Version: India-Pakistan 1965*. Musa does not have universal praise for Pakistan: he is extremely critical of the poor intelligence that led Pakistani officials to believe that the agitation surrounding the missing relic had made Kashmir ripe for an uprising. He concedes that in the aftermath of the 1963 Hazratbal crisis, the commander of Pakistan's troops in Azad Kashmir, Maj. Gen. Akhtar Husain Malik, "pressed the Government to take advantage of the disturbed situation in the valley and direct the Army to send raiders in Indian-held Kashmir for conducting guerilla activities there and to help, on a long-term basis, the locals in organizing a movement with a view to eventually starting an uprising against the occupying power" (2). He is very critical of the way the Kashmir Cell developed its various potential strategies for Kashmir and claims that he, like Ayub, was apprehensive about the final strategy and believed that it would indeed devolve into a general war. Finally, while he applauds the efforts of the 7,000 mujahideen, he admits that they generally failed to mobilize a guerilla movement in Kashmir, attributing their failure to poor planning and preparation by army headquarters.

However, despite fully acknowledging the extent to which Pakistan planned Operation Gibraltar and despite his frank admission that India would not tolerate such efforts, Musa (1983) still argues that on September 6, 1965, "India invaded Pakistan" because India chose to operate across the international border instead of restricting its operations to Kashmir (42). Even more surprising is his claim that India did not have any justification for invading Pakistan because "Pakistan had not embarked on the path of aggression. We merely defended our homeland when it was attacked" (96). Despite his extremely candid account of Pakistan's machinations, Musa condemns India's decision to move across the international border as lacking justification (see also Ahmad 1992; Gilani 2003; Majeed 1993–1994).

Pakistani accounts of the 1971 war portraying India as the aggressor are on more solid ground, despite the fact that Pakistan made (what even Pakistani writers admit to be) a preemptive strike on Indian airfields on December 3, 1971 (Rahman 1976). Most Pakistani accounts are generally candid about West Pakistan's malfeasance in the east. Nonetheless, with few, if any, exceptions, they attribute the war and East Pakistan's secession to Indian involvement. Commodore (Ret.) Tariq Majeed, for one, dismisses India's concerns about the millions of refugees who fled into India, arguing that India exaggerated the magnitude of the refugee problem and furthermore that since the refugees were predominantly Hindus they were simply returning to their true homeland. He also contends that India's support to the Bengali insurgents began in 1966, substantially earlier than the scholarly record suggests (Majeed 1993–1994). Brig. C. M. A. K. Zahid (1989) shares Majeed's views, writing that India was involved in the insurgency from the start: "insurgents from the hard core of potential secessionists were trained, equipped and financed by India. A campaign was launched to impair the loyalty of the citizens through brainwashing, temptation and coercion. This was followed by expanding the 'Sympathy Zones' and initiating violence and sabotage to create panic and insecurity" (52). Although Zahid acknowledges that West Pakistan mismanaged Bengali political aspirations, he still attributes the ease with which India fomented insurrection to the inherent Hinduness of the East Pakistani Bengalis.

Lt. Gen. A. A. K. Niazi, who was in charge of the Pakistani armed forces in East Pakistan during the war and who tendered Pakistan's acceptance of defeat, authored his own book about the war in an attempt to redeem himself and the force he commanded. His account of West Pakistan's civilian and political elites is scathing, but at the same time he also displays a fundamental hostility to and distrust of Hindus. In his effort to explain the impasse in East Pakistan, for instance, he explains that whereas most of the Hindus living in West Pakistan had migrated to India, many Hindus living in the east, particularly the "rich and powerful," chose to remain. Thus the "Muslims were in the majority but were mostly subservient to the Hindu landlords and businessmen" (33). Moreover, he contends, "due to the higher incidence of education amongst the Hindus, the vast majority of teachers in schools and colleges were Hindus. The teachers played an important role in moulding the ideas of the youth in their formative years. The West Pakistanis were painted as imperialists, exploiters, and tyrants. The seeds of discontent were sown" (ibid.).

According to Niazi's (2009) account, the Hindu presence in the east frustrated West Pakistan's efforts to integrate its Bengali population. This claim is ironic because even Niazi acknowledges that West Pakistani elites' fears of Bengali dominance set the stage for the political collision. For example, he notes with some criticism the West Pakistani fear that with "twenty per cent of the population being educated Hindus, and given their dominance in all facets of life, who could have stopped them from dictating the national policies? The government would be formed by Bengalis, the iron fist in the velvet glove would be that of the Hindus" (34). In his assessment, the One Unit Scheme introduced in the 1950s was designed to protect "the interests of the West Pakistanis from exploitation by the Hindu-controlled Bengalis" (ibid.).

It should be noted that some writings contradict elements of this general narrative. For example, M. Attiqur Rahman (1976) is extremely critical of Pakistan's planning for the 1965 and 1971 wars. However even he, reflecting on India's decision to keep prisoners of the 1971 war for more than two years, admits that "we have always taken the Indian to be intelligent but wily; however this guile was dishonourable" (58).

INDIA: A PAPER TIGER

While some defense writers set out to construct India and Indians as perfidious and others concentrate on denigrating the strength of Indian armed forces, others still try to do both at the same time. Lt. Col. Mohammad Zaman, for example, wrote in 1992 of "India's False Image," mocking what he saw as India's belief that it is an "equal of China and Japan and an emerging Asia Pacific power." He attributes Indian delusions of grandeur to the influence of the United States and suggests that India is "unnecessarily being pumped like a hollow balloon and made to purchase weapons at colossal cost from the west" (25–26). Commodore Tariq Majeed, in a 1992 essay titled "Weaknesses and Limitations of Indian Naval Capability," argues that India's navy is inferior according to every metric used. One of his reasons for the Indian Navy's ostensible inferiority to that of Pakistan is that it has been forced to induct women.

Hassan (1990) offers one of the most infamous accounts of India's numerous shortcomings in *India: A Study in Profile*. (Recall that he was one of the four authors of the Kargil misadventure.) Hassan researched and wrote the book while he was a member of the Faculty of Research and Doctrinal Studies (FORAD) of the Command and Staff College, Quetta. In the foreword to the volume, Maj. Gen. M. Amin Khan Burki explains that FORAD was set up at Quetta in 1984 as a separate cell "devot[ed]…to the pursuit of research on doctrinal matters and undertake special study projects assigned to the College by the General Headquarters or selected by the [Command and Staff] College" (i). Burki, who laments the paucity of studies about the personality and mind of the Indians, writes that Hassan's book will fill this lacunae and "unfold the mystery and enigma that is India" (ibid.). This foreword indicates the importance of Hassan's work for the Command and Staff College.

Hassan's (1990) book frequently deploys such tropes as the "Hindu psyche" and other patently Orientalist, if not outright racist, concepts. Given Hassan's delight in dated and uncouth stereotypes, it is tempting to dismiss this book as the musings of an eccentric. Yet it continues to be recommended reading at Pakistan's defense educational institutions. I was given my personal copy while visiting what was then called the National Defence College in 2000. Not only is *India: A Study in Profile* widely cited by Pakistani military personnel, but it is also one of only four books on India included by the National Defence University on its "Important Books to Read" list (National Defence University, n.d.).

Hassan (1990) believes that Pakistan has two starkly different, but equally dire, choices as regards India: "Either she acquiesces to the designs of Indian hegemony or she stands up to the challenge; which would mean, as an ultimate, a military conflict provoked by the stronger military power" (xiv). However, he is not fooled by the claims, made by India or others, of India's greatness. "Recorded history bears testimony that whenever assailed by a determined outside power India has been unable to resist the pressure….At the eve of each of these invasions the Indian rulers fielded much larger armies which, if not better, were at least as well-equipped as those of the invading adversaries" (49). Not only has India's military acquitted itself ignominiously, but also another "dismal feature of India's past is the near total absence of any popular resistance against foreign domination or rule" (ibid.).

Hassan (1990) suggests that a contributing factor in these defeats has been the hallmark of Hinduism, which he describes as the non-egalitarian structure of Hindu society and the resultant exploitation of the common man by elite Hindus. This exploited class then becomes the ally of India's invaders. To prove his point he recalls that "history is replete with details of enormous booty that most invaders were able to amass from the vanquished kings and nobles whose people were living under famine like conditions" (51). According to Hassan, India has demonstrated "hopeless performance in protecting its own freedom and sovereignty"— despite the wealth of data to the contrary—and exhibits a "poor track record at projection of power beyond its frontier" (ibid.). To Hassan's credit, he sometimes draws from contemporary Indian sources. However, he also draws from historical events that took place centuries ago to describe modern India as well as from more recent, but ultimately, Orientalist writings from the colonial era to buttress his claims about India and Hindus. For example, he cites a British historian, Sir Halford J. Mackinder, who wrote in 1922 that the Indian people are "less Warlike" (52). Elsewhere he cites Will Durant's 1935 *The Story of Our Civilization—Our Oriental Heritage*: "military ardour and courage (are) not usually associated with India.... By universal admission the Hindus are gentle to the point of timidity, too worshipful and good natured, too long broken upon the wheel of conquest and alien despotisms to be good fighters" (53).

Hassan (1990) also seeks to challenge Indians' purported belief that their state is strong, especially in contrast to Pakistan, which is riven by various kinds of ethnic and sectarian discord. He dedicates an entire chapter to debunking the idea of Indian unity, whether geographical or social. Some of Hassan's claims are strange. For example, he cites as evidence of India's disunity the fact that the Muslims opted out of the Indian project and pursued an independent Pakistan. The problem with this argument is that many Muslims chose to remain in India rather than move to Pakistan. (Today, India has approximately 176 million Muslims compared with that of Pakistan's 160 million. Thus, India is the second largest Muslim country after Indonesia [Pew Research Forum 2012].) Hassan also criticizes the imposition of Hindi as the national language, even though the imposition of Urdu was equally, if not more, problematic in Pakistan. Recall that Urdu had no "homeland" in Pakistan and that, at the time of Partition the majority of Pakistanis spoke Bengali. To buttress his arguments, Hassan mobilizes Indian scholars who are critical of Indian nation building. He is aware that if India were as unstable as he suggests it would have disintegrated long ago. He rationalizes the apparent inconsistency between his vision of a disunified India and the reality of India's stability with the assessment that "the passive nature of the Hindu majority" has precluded the state from rupturing (Hassan 1990, 123).

Drawing on his historical, social, and economic exposition of the Indian malaise, Hassan (1990) lays out what he believes to be India's demands of Pakistan. First and foremost, Hassan believes, India wants Pakistan to renounce the two-nation theory, which would have the effect of "falsify[ing] the partition of India and also contribute to the consolidation of Indian unity" (228). Once this is done, there will be no "*locus standi* for a Pakistani claim to Jammu and Kashmir, rather Pakistan would have to hand over Azad Kashmir to India so as to allow the Kashmiri people to be united" (ibid., emphasis in original). Hassan argues, as have other Pakistani defense writers, that "India wants to be the arbiter of the 'genuine' need of Pakistan's defence. Pakistan would obviously have to renounce its peaceful nuclear programme.... India would also be the arbiter of Pakistan's internal problems 'a la' Nepal earlier and Sri Lanka now" (ibid.). This ultimately reduces to a simple formula: "Pakistan should exercise its sovereignty according to Indian desires" (ibid.). Hassan retains some credibility, however, in that he does cite Indian sources. For example, he quotes Jaswant Singh (a BJP politician who has held several cabinet positions, including Finance, External Affairs, and Defence), who wrote in 1989 that "unless Pakistan accepts India's dominant role in Asia and its readiness to live in [a] friendly neighbourly manner there can be no peace" (ibid.). It is comments such as these that legitimize some of Pakistan's deepest fears regarding Indian intentions.

Hassan (1990) is not alone in reducing Indian actions to mere Hindu behavior. Brig. Jamshed Ali (1990) suggests that one cannot understand "the Indian dream of becoming a super-power" without first comprehending the Hindu psyche, which he believes to be "dominated by four obsessions": "revenge for 1,000 years of enslavement by the Muslims;" "repudiation of the vivisection of Bharat Mata [Mother India];" "claim to the Indian Ocean territories as successors to the British Empire"; and, finally, "world recognition of India's global role keeping with its size, location and performance" (100–101).

Other writers seek to delegitimize India's cause and motivation using the same methods. In 1966, Lt. Col. Mohammad Safdar Iqbal, for example, attempted to explain India's poor performance in the 1965 war despite the "fact" that India had started the war. (Needless to say, this version of events clashes violently with the scholarly account of the 1965 war.) In Iqbal's essay, Indian soldiers are carica-tured as Hindus, in contrast with the Pakistani Muslim soldier:

> Whatever can be gleaned from the coverage given to this short and vio-lent war ... the main cause of failure of the Indian attack was that Indians had no cause to fight for. The Indian soldier had no justification to attack Pakistan. There was nothing that could keep the idea of war aglow in his heart. Nothing could convince his mind that the hardships of battle, the pangs of hunger and thirst, the merciless beating of hostile elemental fury and the extreme rigours and suffering, trials and tribulations and death and decay that had started with it, were worthy of noble ideals of human belief, especially to a people who had been brought up on the lofty ideals of "Ahimsa" ie, non-violence of Mr. Gandhi and neutralism of Mr. Nehru (8).

In contrast, Pakistani soldiers are motivated by their *tarbiyat* (religious instruc-tion), which enabled them to successfully defend themselves against the treach-erous foe with honor and distinction, even though they were outmanned and outgunned by the Hindu forces.

It is important to note that these perceptions of Indians are not restricted to military discourse. The report of the judicial Hamoodur Rehman Commission (2001), established by the Z. A. Bhutto government to investigate the loss of East Pakistan, is replete with similar language.[8] For example, the commission's account grants India a large and nefarious role in the East Pakistan crisis, in part by exerting influence over East Pakistan's Hindu citizens. The report explains that, while the Hindu migration out of West Pakistan was nearly complete (with the exception of Sindh), "over one and a half crores of Hindus had continued to remain behind in East Pakistan. It was felt that this language movement was the outcome of their insidious influence. They were, particularly, exploiting the fact that most of the senior government officers then serving in East Bengal, were either from the Punjab or the United Provinces and most of them did not speak the language of the province [Bengali]" (31). The report acknowledges the intelligence challenges faced by West Pakistani military and civilian officials operating in East Pakistan; in particular it was impossible to recruit "a sufficient number of local agents from whom information could be gathered. In addition to this was the language problem. It is sad to reflect that nearly 25 years after the achievement of Pakistan it should be still possible to have this problem of communication" (89). The report dedicates the entirety of its tenth chapter, titled "Indo-Pakistan Relations," to proving India's malevolent intentions toward Pakistan.

INDIA: THE EXTERNAL AND INTERNAL THREATS CONVERGE

Pakistan has long been beset by an array of internal security threats. Most recently, since 2004 the state has been ravaged by Islamist terrorists who operate under the banner of the Pakistani Taliban (Tehreek-e-Taliban-e-Pakistan, or TTP). But the TTP is only the newest player in Pakistan's violence market; it follows on the heels of the sectarian terrorist groups that have long attacked religious minorities in Pakistan and of the ethnic insurgents who attack rival communities and who are particularly active in Sindh, Balochistan, and Khyber Pakhtunkhwa. Despite these internal security challenges, the Pakistan Army has insisted on retaining a conventional force posture that recognizes India as Pakistan's primary military challenge.

Since the middle of the last decade, the United States has attempted to persuade Pakistan's army to adopt population-centric counterinsurgency, even offering to provide the Pakistan Army with military and paramilitary training as well as weapons systems to enable Pakistan's armed forces to more effectively counter these domestic threats. But the Pakistan Army's leadership has insisted on retaining its conventional orientation against India as well as a conventional approach to internal security operations as embodied by low-intensity conflict (Fair and Jones 2009–2010; Kronstadt 2010). American officials have been bewildered by Pakistan's stubborn retention of its conventional orientation, since even a cursory review of recent South Asian history reveals that, with the possible exception of 1971, Pakistan was the initiator of every war with India. Not only are Americans perplexed by Pakistani belief in the existence of a threat from India, a status quo power, but they are also equally mystified by Pakistani insistence on prioritizing the possibility of a conventional war with India over the enormous internal security threats that have challenged the writ of the state via assaults on military, intelligence, police, civilian leadership, and the general public.

A perusal of Pakistan's defense literature cast some light on the reasons for the Pakistan Army's steadfast commitment to a conventional posture. Pakistan has three arguments for maintaining its current eastward orientation. The first is that Pakistan responds to Indian capabilities and deployments, not India's intentions. Pakistanis, pointing to the large conventional force arrayed on their borders, argue that Pakistan can observe only what India could do rather than what India wants to do. This is a classic security dilemma. India undertakes military preparations to protect itself from a future Chinese as well as an ever-present Pakistani threat. But these defensive preparations unnerve Pakistan and motivate it to take offensive postures in response. India in turn responds accordingly, and the cycle continues. Second, in Pakistan's strategic culture, India always appears as the aggressor, making these capabilities even more deeply worrisome. Third, and most importantly, Pakistan attributes its domestic turmoil to Indian provocation.

Pakistan's defense writings are often straightforward, clear, and even sophisticated in their analysis of the varied fissures that pose innumerable potential threats to Pakistan's coherence. However, most Pakistani writing on the country's internal security challenges holds that these divisions merely have the *potential* for conflict, becoming active only as a result of the actions of "hostile external powers." (This is generally a euphemism for India, although it can also refer to the United States, Israel, or, in the past, the Soviet Union.) By linking Pakistan's internal threats to its external ones, the army justifies retaining its conventional posture, despite the groundswell of domestic security challenges.

In many countries, internal security duties are the remit of domestic police forces. For reasons detailed at length elsewhere, while the army has demonstrated a selective interest in police reform at certain times under specific circumstances, it has resisted professionalization of the police forces, even though these forces are usually the most suitable for internal security duties. This resistance likely stems from the army's professed belief that it alone can defend Pakistan from internal and external threats as well as from its awareness of the fact that civilian elites have heavily politicized the police force (Abbas 2011, 2012).

Pakistani writing about Indian meddling in Pakistan falls into two main genres. The first, which has been covered at length, focuses on India's supposed role in fomenting Bengali unrest in East Pakistan, which culminated in the emergence of an independent Bangladesh. This was a watershed event for the Pakistan Army, one that shaped its understanding of India's destructive power. In fact, prior to the 1971 war, no authors in Pakistan's defense publications blamed India for widespread unrest in Pakistan, with the exception of those who claimed that India encouraged Afghanistan to take provocative positions on the frontier and Pakhtunistan (see Chapter 5). The second genre specifically identifies India as the primary mover behind most, if not all, of Pakistan's internal security menaces. One of the earliest pieces making this connection is a 1978 essay in the *Pakistan Army Journal* titled "The Pakistan Army." The anonymous author of the piece rehearses the challenges of Partition to back his claim that India bears a long-standing hostility toward Pakistan and has attempted from the first years of independence to destroy its neighbor. Like many others, the author concedes that the 1971 war was indigenous in origin but argues that India exploited Bengali unrest to ensure Pakistan's demise. After this debilitating experience, "today the Pakistan Army stands firm with a new confidence in its ranks ready to meet any challenges to the integrity of the nation. However, every Pakistani soldier must search his heart and remain vigilant against internal and external enemies lest we again fall victim to a similar conspiracy" (9).

Despite the importance of the 1971 war and of India's role in breaking up Pakistan, prior to 1989 essays blaming India for Pakistan's internal insecurity were still rare. However, after 1989, they became increasingly commonplace. In 1989, Maj. Gen. Asad Durrani, who served as the ISI chief, wrote, "Pakistan remains a house divided against itself. If Pakistanis are unable to resolve their own domestic troubles, and particularly the fundamental question of national unity, the temptation of outsiders to meddle in the Country's turbulent internal affairs may be uncontrollable." Durrani continues on to argue that Pakistan's internal challenges "are primarily internal weaknesses that are exploited by external aggressors" (11). Ghumman (1990, 28) cautions that "the delicate internal balance of Pakistan due to law and order, Pakhtoonistan and refugee problems, [has] the potential of being exploited by external factors through subversion, terrorism and insurgency.... Chronic political instability is again a matter of concern. The dissident elements and miscreants can be exploited by India and Afghanistan in their nefarious designs."

Many volumes of the *Pakistan Army Green Book* explicate, at length, the links between Pakistan's external and internal threats. For example, Brig. Gul Muhammad, writing in the 2000 issue (concentrating on the role of the Pakistan Army in nation building), admits that Pakistan's internal circumstances are worsening but claims they are "disproportionately exacerbated by external manipulation" (43). He forthrightly identifies the utter failure of "democratic experiments, near collapse of state institutions, rampant corruption, deteriorating law and order situation, ethnic and sectarian polarization" as significant foundational challenges but to this list of internal maladies he adds "the external manipulation which is adversely affecting the security landscape of the country" (ibid.).

The 2002 *Pakistan Army Green Book* is entirely focused on low-intensity conflict.[9] Although the volume went to press after the events of 9/11 brought international attention to al-Qaeda and other Islamist militants based in South Asia, the articles in the volume make only peremptory and passing references to this event. The various articles in this volume use very similar language and memes, suggesting that it was heavily edited for thematic and ideological continuity. One of the volume's persistent themes is the extensive role of India in fomenting low-intensity conflict in Pakistan. This is extraordinary given that production of the volume likely overlapped with the Indo-Pakistani crisis of 2001–2002 following Jaish-e-Mohammad's attack on India's parliament and certainly with mounting US pressure to stem the infiltration of Pakistani Islamist terror groups into India.

The 2002 volume opens with an essay by Maj. Gen. Muhammad Saleem titled "Low Intensity Conflict—Conflictual Framework." Saleem offers the fantastic argument that "LIC looms as the most viable and dangerous option. India, while ensuring that it does not cross a certain threshold to evoke a nuclear response from Pakistan, shall endeavour to wage this kind of warfare by fully exploiting the prevailing socioeconomic conditions" (1).

Other articles offer variations on this bizarre theme. Brig. Muhammad Zia (2002) enumerates the various threats low-intensity conflict poses to Pakistan. He focuses on Pakhtun nationalism in Khyber Pakhtunkhwa, the restless Baloch in Balochistan, and the prolonged political and economic instability in the Saraiki belt in the southern Punjab. While he notes that the Punjab has witnessed several kinds of urban terror, he argues that "most of these groups are foreign funded" and further that "whenever peace and tranquility seems to take root, Indian agents have been known to ignite sectarian tensions through terrorist activities" (34). According to Zia, Karachi, which has long suffered sectarian, ethnic, political, and organized criminal violence, by "virtue of its location enjoys strategic importance [and is] a target of hostile forces, particularly RAW" (ibid.). Zia attributes Indian intervention in Pakistan to the centuries-old philosophy of Chanakaya Kautilya: "peace can only be made with superiors or equals, the inferior must be attacked" (36). He maintains that "this philosophy remains evident behind every Indian overture on national and inter-national level [sic]. Till today, India has not accepted the creation of Pakistan as final and is always on the lookout to exploit any opportunity to undo history" (36). He further explains that India "has enunciated a multi-pronged strategy using Indian media, abetting political subversion, fanning sectarian violence and developing a terrorist network to undermine the logic of our creation and the legitimacy of the state" (36). Zia also sees an American hand in Indian designs. He believes that the United States has sought to develop a strategic relationship with India not only to create a counterweight to China and to exploit potential new markets but also to ensure that "a nuclear (and Muslim) Pakistan [be] kept under control, lest it [lead] the Islamic world towards the formation of a new powerful economic and military block in competition with and or antagonistic to the western alliance" (ibid.).

Writing in the same volume, Brig. Khalid Mehmood Akhtar (2002) echoes the view that India foments sectarianism and funds various sectarian factions to "destroy the very fabric of our unity" (45). Ironically, he excludes Iran and

Saudi Arabia from his assessment, although those states funded Shia and Sunni sectarian militants, respectively. Brig. Asif Murad (2002) agrees with his fellow contributors that Pakistan's internal challenges render the state vulnerable because they "offer India potentially fertile ground for exploitation through dissident groups" (82). Furthermore, he writes that "[India] is already investing heavily in this aspect and engineering bomb blasts and sectarianism covertly through its agencies, the most active being its Research and Analysis Wing (RAW)" (ibid). Murad believes that India's "nefarious designs draw aspirations directly from their continued frustrating attempts to curtail freedom struggle in Kashmir" (ibid.). Lt. Col. Muhammed Nasser Raja (2002) accuses India of being "always ready to initiate steps, which undermine the solidarity and integrity of Pakistan," and alleges that RAW has been "involved in many acts of subversion and terrorism inside Pakistan" (123). He predicts that Indians will seek to foment sectarianism, execute terrorist attacks to provoke communal riots, and provide as much military and financial assistance as possible to separatist elements. He even goes so far as to cast doubt on India's reasons for its military mobilization in late 2001 after the "so called attack on the Indian Parliament" (124; see also M.T. Ahmed 2002; Javed 2002).

The 2006 *Pakistan Army Green Book* was devoted to the subject of terrorism, reflecting the recent increase in terrorist attacks within Pakistan. The essays in this volume are generally of very high quality. Many of them address the current manifestations of internal security issues in Pakistan and recommend counterterrorism or low-intensity conflict approaches to countering these problems. Several stress the importance of using domestic law enforcement agencies in counterterrorism approaches and express concerns about their continued shortcomings and the failure of sequential governments to remedy Pakistan's decrepit law enforcement and judicial institutions. At the same time, many articles rehearse the same flawed narrative, which traces Pakistan's Islamist terrorism problem back to US involvement in the region in the 1980s and the support the United States and Saudi Arabia gave to mujahideen elements via Pakistan's intelligence agency, the ISI. As noted in previous chapters, Islamism and Islamist militancy in Pakistan were fully developed prior to US engagement. Moreover, during the entire period of the 1990s, when the United States disengaged from Pakistan, Pakistan expanded its ties to Islamist militant organizations and redeployed them to help secure its interests in India and Afghanistan. Furthermore, many authors in this volume, although they concede that fissures exist in Pakistani society, focus on India's role in exacerbating them.

For example, Maj. General Athar Abbas (2006), who would later head ISPR, the military's public relations agency, traces the "roots of extremism in Pakistan" to the "Central Investigation [*sic*] Agency sponsored War in the 1980s in Afghanistan against the Soviet occupation" (10). He also argues that "some of what is happening in the country today can be treated as un-resolved outcome of the American-led war and Indian atrocities in Occupied Kashmir" (10). Maj. Gen. Muhammad Asghar (2006) similarly contends that Pakistan inherited "Hindu and Indian hostility right from its inception stage....It lost half the country because of Indian machinations and faces massive Indian covert support to dissident elements in Sindh and Balochistan" (20). According to Asghar, the Pakistan Army, with its nuclear weapons, "now stands as the most visible instrument of ensuring [Pakistan's] physical survival as an independent, sovereign state" (20).

In the same volume, Maj. Gen. Muhammad Farooq (2006) provides a sound account of the factors that contributed to sectarian violence in Pakistan, including different sectarian commitments, the rise of political Islamist parties, the Iranian revolution, and Zia's efforts to Islamize Pakistan as a Sunni state. But he also places considerable blame on the so-called US proxy war in Afghanistan. Disregarding the fact that Pakistan lobbied the United States to support its effort in Afghanistan, Farooq depicts Pakistan as a passive instrument of US actions. As such, he laments, "Pakistan's decision to be conduit and main supporter of the US resulted in influx of the large number of refugees and lethal weapons to Pakistan. While Iran supported mainly Shia Mujahideen groups during [sic] Afghan war, the America-Saudi alliance rendered help to the Sunni groups. This sponsorship had negative fallout on the sectarian harmony in Pakistan" (26).

Farooq (2006) also adds India to the mix, explaining that "India remains the major challenge to Pakistan's national security" because of its presumed "desire to undo Pakistan to establish a hegemonic regime in the region" (26). He believes that "the Indian factor...is the most potent challenge to Pakistan's security" because it is "natural for the Indian intelligence agencies, especially RAW, to take full advantage of sectarian conflict in Pakistan as a revenge to ongoing freedom struggle in Indian Held Kashmir" (26–27). Despite the author's understanding of the varied domestic drivers of violence in Pakistan, he believes that the groups attacking Pakistan have "close links with Indian intelligence agency RAW and other enemies of Pakistan" (30). Not only is this true, he argues, of the ethnic dissidents in Balochistan and Sindh, but also there is even a risk of the "Jihadi organizations falling prey to the nefarious designs of the enemy....Thus sectarian divide, extremism, violence and terrorism presents a favourable playing ground to the enemies of Pakistan to play their nefarious game of making our inner front more vulnerable and exploitable" (ibid.).

While many authors place the blame for Pakistan's domestic ills at the doorsteps of India or the United States, a few authors in this volume stand out. Maj. Gen. Muhammad Ashraf Tabbassam (2006) writes that "a large segment of society especially the religious parties had actively supported Taliban and were sympathizers of Al-Qaeda. A number of Jihadi organizations had also sprouted in the 80s/90s who were encouraged to extend their struggle in the freedom movement in Kashmir" (35). Because "these elements are deeply rooted in all the segments of society," uprooting them will be a "major challenge for the Government"

(35). But Tabbassam, too, ultimately blames outside actors for Pakistan's problem, noting that "sectarianism also flourished due to external support to these organizations which remained unchecked over the years" (36). He also notes the "role being played by Afghanistan," which "on behest of India has adopted totally a negative role vis-à-vis Pakistan. She has…also given free hand to the Indians to use [Afghan] soil for subversive activities inside Pakistan" (37; see also M. Y. Khan 2006).

The 2008 *Pakistan Army Green Book* is dedicated to understanding Pakistan's future conflict environment. The volume opens with an essay by Maj. Gen. Shafqaat Ahmed (2008), the former Pakistani defense attaché to the United States. He shares the view of numerous other Pakistani defense writers that "external forces, including India, have used their proxies from Afghanistan and Iran to create a hostile environment in [Balochistan]" (3). Ahmed, however, believes that India is a surrogate for what he suggests is a US Great Game Plan. In this capacity, India is "financing, training and supporting terrorists in Afghanistan to operate in FATA and border areas of Balochistan. Scores of Indian consulates operating in the near vicinity of Pak-Afghan borders is a clear indication of the same" (4). He further claims that India "continues to encourage centrifugal forces to accentuate/create vulnerability such as ethno-religious polarization, economic disparities and foment dissident groups/forces" and cautions that "India has established ample foothold in Afghanistan and Iran, wherefrom it is supporting centrifugal forces in Balochistan and NWFP…[it] has the potential to support offensive low intensity conflict in Sindh and few other selected areas" (ibid.).

Perhaps the most disturbing allegation in Ahmed's (2008) essay is that the United States is "planning to divide [Pakistan] on ethnic grounds on the lines of Iraq" (4). This was likely influenced by Peters' (2006) article in which he argued for a dramatic redrawing of maps in the Middle East. This caused considerable distress in Pakistan because it was published in the *Armed Forces Journal*, which many in Pakistan believed reflects official US doctrinal and policy preferences. Ahmed contends that the United States, trying to gain access to the "lucrative energy resources of Central Asia," may work to create "an autonomous region between Pakistan and Afghanistan, comprising Pashtun regions of Pakistan and Afghanistan in the north" and a "greater Balochistan, comprising Balochistan Province and part of Iran in the south" (Ahmed 2008, 4; for a similar view, see Khan 2011). It would be tempting to dismiss these claims as the conspiracy theories of an insular paranoiac. But the author derives his authority to speak on American policy issues from his extensive interaction with Americans. What is perhaps most noteworthy about this article is its timing: it was written and published long before the later series of crises that brought the US–Pakistan military-to-military relationship to the brink of collapse.

The 2010 *Pakistan Army Green Book,* which was the most recent volume at the time of writing, dilates upon information warfare.[10] Durrani (2010) writes the lead article, which is dedicated to understanding Indian-backed psychological warfare. He explains that India's efforts are devoted to Pakistan's domestic audiences as well as international audiences, as discussed already. He claims that India's efforts are intended to "disorientate people by attacking Pakistan's cultural identity and the founding principles of Pakistan, i.e. Two Nation Theory" (4). It also aims to "weaken Pakistan's internal cohesion" and thus to create a "lack of trust amongst the people" in the national leadership as well as sow seeds of conflict between the "people and armed forces and brand armed forces as rogue and warmongering" (4). Finally, it aims to break the will of "independent sovereign and defiant" Pakistan (ibid.). The author alleges that India's intelligence agencies have invested widely in print and television media to "wage psychological war against Pakistan" (5).

This belief that India deliberately invests in media instruments to weaken Pakistan is pervasive. Maj. Junaid Khan (2012) devotes an entire essay, titled "Living an Indian Influenced Life," on this subject in *Hilal*. Khan laments that even though Pakistan was liberated from "British slavery and Hindu influenced living" even some 64 years later Pakistanis have been unable to "win freedom from Indian cultural domination" (28). He describes what he calls Gandhi's modus operandi with which India has "no need to occupy Pakistan" because India can "occupy them culturally" (ibid.). Khan complains about how Indian music, movies, and television serials familiarize Pakistanis with the "ways and words of Indian prayers" and how Pakistanis find themselves spontaneously uttering these same "forbidden tunes" (29). Worse yet, these Indian media are a "poisonous capsule targeting our younger generation. In the garb of Hindi translated cartoons, not only our younger generation develops affinity to Hindi language, words, and customs" and become attuned to Indian (read Hindu) traditions, rituals and celebrations (ibid.). He cautions his readers to be mindful of these "Indian shadows" in their lives and notes that he fears "our children may wear 'Sindoor' [the red mark worn on the forehead] and greet each other with 'Namastay' [salutation in Hindi]. It will be a loss of religion, a loss of culture and above all a loss of identity" (ibid.).

Conclusions and Implications

There is considerable variance between scholarly accounts of Pakistan's encounters with India and those offered by Pakistani military publications. Assuming that these publications are reasonably representative of the army's strategic culture and its view of India, we can draw several important conclusions for the Indo-Pakistani security competition. The first is that the Pakistan Army clearly understands concepts like *defeat* and *success* in ways that differ from more mainstream understandings of these concepts. With the exception of the 1971 war, Pakistan does not see itself as ever having been defeated militarily. It is worth noting that some military writers even reject the notion that Pakistan was militarily defeated in that conflict either. For example, Gen. K. M. Arif (2001)—after deriding the performance of the Indian army in 1948 and 1965—boldly asserts that the "events of 1971 in East Pakistan were the result of treachery, not war" (249). For the Pakistan Army, Pakistan will be defeated only if it accepts India's hegemonic position in the region and beyond. Since Pakistan can continue to resist India's efforts to dominate it, despite having lost half of its country and territory in the 1971 war, it remains undefeated.

Returning to Zionts' (2006) concept of (unreasonable) persistent revisionism after a decisive defeat, it is clear that Pakistan does not view itself as defeated since it continues to resist India's hegemony. Pakistan, as the anti–status quo state, wins by denying India the position of uncontested hegemon. This implies an asymmetry in requirements for victory. For India to succeed, it must dominate Pakistan and subject it to its will, but Pakistan will be victorious as long as it has not been defeated and continues to resist India's will. A second insight from this literature is the dogged conviction of Pakistan's defense establishment that India is fundamentally opposed to Pakistan's existence, rejects the two-nation theory, and seeks every opportunity to undo history. Since the Pakistan Army has upheld Islam and the two-nation theory as its institutional ideology, the two states are thus locked in an existential conflict with no obvious resolution. Resolution of their security competition would imply that Pakistan must acquiesce to India's hegemonic position, something the army is unprepared to do. Pakistan takes India's conventional military posture as confirmatory evidence of Indian intent to harm Pakistan. As India increasingly focuses on a possible Chinese threat, and thus maintains a strong conventional force posture, this security dilemma is unlikely to ever disappear.

Third, while many military writings are dedicated to painting India as a threat in perpetuity, much military literature is dedicated to denigrating India as an adversary. The conclusion to be drawn from these seemingly contradictory narratives is that India is an enduring threat because it remains steadfastly committed to subduing Pakistan but also that the threat India poses is ultimately one that Pakistan can successfully resist. Finally, according to these authors, Pakistan's numerous domestic threats are fundamentally reducible to its external foes, principally India, whether it acts on its own initiative or on behalf of another unfriendly state, such as the United States. By linking the external and domestic threats, the Pakistan Army justifies its enduring conventional footing in face of growing domestic problems. This also allows the military to prevent other organs of the state from countering these domestic threats in a way that would erode or challenge the army's primacy in Pakistan's domestic politics. While these narratives are consistent and ubiquitous in Pakistan's defense literature, they also appear in civilian narratives of India as well. This attests the degree to which the military discourse has permeated popular culture and the institutions of civilian governance.

CHAPTER 7

Seeking Security through Alliances

Pakistani commentators—military and civilian alike—agree that Pakistan's security challenges have always been framed with respect to India. Shahid Amin (2000), one of Pakistan's most accomplished diplomats, concedes that the "over-riding motivation in determining Pakistan's foreign policy has been the desire to safeguard the country's independence and territorial integrity [from Indian designs].... The quest for security *vis-à-vis* India has been an unvarying, and almost obsessive, dimension of Pakistan's foreign policy from the beginning" (10). As I sought to show in Chapters 4–6, Pakistan's fear of India is deep and existential. Pakistan's security discourse frames the country's struggle against India in civilizational terms, with India fighting to dominate—if not destroy—Pakistan and extirpate the two-nation theory. Pakistan, in turn, mobilizes its Islamic identity and the two-nation theory both to justify its independent existence and to resist India's hegemonic aspirations.

Pakistan began to seek international assistance, especially in building its military, long before it began its pursuit of nuclear weapons, forging alliances with the United States, China, Saudi Arabia and, intermittently, the Soviet Union (later Russia). Describing Pakistan's three-pronged strategy in a piece in the *Pakistan Army Journal*, Zulfikar Khalid (1989a) wrote, "Pakistan's trilateral strength is based on Islamabad's association with the People's Republic of China, the on-going relationship with the United States and the traditional relationship with the Islamic countries, headed by Saudi Arabia" (2). Pakistan relies on these relationships for general strategic positioning and, more specifically, for extracting civilian aid, military assistance, access to conventional and even nuclear weapons systems, and training for its armed forces. Pakistan has often played one country off another to extract even more benefits.

In this chapter, I attempt to explain how Pakistan's relations with China and the United States fit into its strategic culture.[1] These are the most important partnerships Pakistan has forged, and between them they account for the majority of Pakistani military discourse on alliances. Understanding this chapter's puzzle requires examining two separate historical records. The first recounts the objective actions and transactions comprising the substance of Pakistani relations with both the United States and China. (The facts of these interactions are knowable, even if they are difficult to come by.) The second is the record of how Pakistani military elites describe Pakistan's relations with both of these countries when speaking among themselves or to foreigners. In many cases, there is a yawning gap between the empirical facts of these relationships and what Pakistanis say about them.

Here, I first provide a brief account of Pakistan's relations with the United States and China, drawing largely from the scholarly and peer-reviewed literature. Because very few Pakistanis engage in peer-reviewed scholarship on this subject, this discussion may well be overly influenced by and even biased toward American, or at least non-Pakistani, points of view. Next I dilate upon the narrative tropes in which Pakistan's defense publications describe these same relations. As will become apparent, China and the United States have had similar trajectories and courses of action with respect to Pakistan. Both have been tentative in approaching Pakistan and highly utilitarian in their engagement. However, Pakistan's defense literature treats these important partners in very different ways. Whereas Pakistani defense writers uniformly describe the United States as a perfidious ally, a necessary evil that Pakistan's weaknesses force it to endure, China appears as an all-weather friend, one that has not imposed onerous conditions on its support for Pakistan. On those occasions when China has fallen short of meeting Pakistan's expectations, defense writers are quick to rationalize this failure, omitting the acrimony and antipathy they reserve for the United States. This tendency is both a part of Pakistan's strategy to maximize the benefits of the relationships and a means of sustaining what Ganguly (2001), drawing from the work of Van Evera, calls false optimism among Pakistan's security elites, which in turn conditions Pakistan's risk-seeking behavior with respect to India and other states. In other words, the army's strategic culture requires these understandings of its partnerships to sustain its course of revisionism with respect to India.

Pursuing the Americans: An Alliance for Survival

Both American and Pakistani commentators agree that Pakistan, born during the Cold War, immediately leaned toward the West. In September 1947, Mohammad Ali Jinnah proclaimed during a cabinet meeting that "Pakistan [is] a democracy and communism [does] not flourish in the soil of Islam. It [is] clear therefore that our interests [lie] more with the two democratic countries, namely, the U.K. and the U.S.A., rather than with Russia" (Kux 2001, 20). (India, in contrast, pursued neutrality.) Academic accounts of the postwar period depict the United States as somewhat aloof toward South Asia and as struggling to define its regional interests and, concomitantly, its policies toward the region; the Harry S. Truman Administration was content to let the United Kingdom take the lead in South Asia. Both Britain and the United States sought to develop relationships with

India and Pakistan simultaneously in hopes that the two states would formally or informally align with the West and oppose the Soviet Union. United States planners and their British counterparts tended to view India as the most important diplomatic prize and were wary of antagonizing its prickly leadership (Kux 2001; McMahon 1994; Pande 2011). Ultimately, however, with US attention concentrated upon Western Europe, the Middle East, and East Asia, senior US officials paid scant regard to either India or Pakistan in the initial years after their independence. The US Central Intelligence Agency (CIA) never mentioned India or Pakistan by name or even referenced the region generally in the 1947 and 1948 editions of its annual "Review of the World Situation as it Relates to the Security of the United States."

Academic accounts of this period focus on Pakistan's destitution, mounting refugee problems, eviscerated institutions, and critical human capital shortages. Within just two months of becoming a state, Jinnah "invited the United States to become the principal source of external support" for Pakistan and requested a $2 billion loan over five years (McMahon 1994, 69; see also Kux 2001; Pande 2011). As Jinnah envisioned it, these funds would be used to help Pakistan build up its armed forces and to jump-start various agricultural and industrial projects. While Pakistan's leaders really sought assistance to underwrite its security vis-à-vis India, they were aware that America's principal concern was the Soviet Union and thus couched all requests within strong anticommunist rhetoric.

The magnitude of Pakistan's request revealed how disengaged Karachi (then the capital of Pakistan) was from the realities of American postwar interests. The amount of $2 billion was simply outlandish. By way of comparison, it is useful to recall that the entire US Marshall plan, which was a four-year effort to rebuild war-torn Europe beginning in April 1948, totaled about $13 billion (George F. Marshall Foundation n.d.). The Defense Department budget for 1949 was $14 billion (US Bureau of the Census 1950). Not only was the amount absurd in absolute terms, but it was even more so given that the United States had virtually no interest in South Asia whatsoever when Pakistan made the appeal. Yet Pakistan was unremitting in its efforts to enlist the United States in a quid pro quo, in which Pakistan would align with the United States in exchange for American subsidies. Pakistan's foreign minister, Zafrullah Khan, for example, opined that the "well-known friendship of Pakistan toward the US and Pakistan's obvious antipathy to Russian ideology would seem to justify serious consideration by the US Government of the defense requirements of Pakistan" (Kux 2001, 21). Not only did the United States rebuff these appeals, but in March 1948 (in response to the 1947–1948 Kashmir War) it also imposed an informal arms embargo on both India and Pakistan. The simplest reason for America's lack of interest in the Pakistani proposals was that South Asia was not a priority. Moreover, the US government assessed that any benefits of arming Pakistan would be offset by the animosity and ill will that would inspire in New Delhi (Kux 2001; McMahon 1994; Pande 2011).

In an effort to improve relations with India, the United States hosted Jawaharlal Nehru on a formal state visit in October 1949. Although Nehru did not budge from his stance on nonalignment, Pakistan was horrified by the prospects of closer ties between the United States and India. Pakistani diplomats worked furiously to secure a state visit for Pakistan's prime minister. They succeeded in doing so only by first orchestrating a Russian invitation for Prime Minister Liaquat Ali Khan, naturally causing renewed American attention to Pakistan. Pakistan's ambassador to Washington, M. A. H. Ispahani, wrote to Liaquat that the maneuver had been a "masterpiece in strategy.... Until a few months ago, we were unable to obtain anything except a few sweet words from middling State Department officials" (McMahon 1994, 71). Thanks to this overture, he gushed, the United States began taking heed of Pakistan overnight.

Most US officials believed that Pakistan presented no serious likelihood of communist leanings, and they tended to take Pakistan's Western orientation for granted. But Liaquat Ali Khan's government was vulnerable to persistent domestic criticism that its alignment with the United States had failed to secure a favorable US position on Kashmir, much less financial support, while India, which maintained its nonaligned status, remained the focus of US diplomatic overtures in South Asia. In light of this fact, some within the Truman Administration became more attentive to the relationship with Pakistan. As the decade drew to a close, assistant secretary of state George McGhee began urging the United States to find some way of engaging the Pakistanis in case the United States might "expect aid from them...in time of future need" (McMahon 1994, 73). Despite McGhee's efforts, however, Pakistan was doomed to disappointment. Its continued appeals for aid would receive greater scrutiny after Pakistan refused to contribute troops to the United Nations (UN) force fighting in Korea (Kux 2001; McMahon 1994).

The onset of the Korean War in June 1950 motivated the US government to become more directly involved in security arrangements in the Middle East rather than to continue its previous course of deferring policy initiative to the British. Great Britain had been seeking to establish a Middle East Command as a means of retaining its access to and standing within the region. The Suez Canal was of particular importance to the United Kingdom; however, Egypt vigorously opposed further British meddling. The British, conscious of their diminished clout and financial weakness, turned to the Americans for help, but the United States was wary of any new commitments that would require weapons or troops. In 1953, Secretary of State Allan Dulles went on an extensive tour of the Middle East and North Africa (including Egypt, Iraq, Israel, Jordan, Lebanon, Libya, Saudi Arabia, Syria, and Turkey) as well as Greece, India, and Pakistan. He returned convinced that the British concept was not viable but that a more modest northern tier defense concept could prove valuable in defending the Middle

East from Soviet expansionism. Dulles was particularly impressed with Pakistan and Turkey, both of which were ready to participate in such an alliance (Goktepe 2003; Kux 2001; McMahon 1994).

The final years of the Truman Administration saw growing support for involving Pakistan in the defense of the Middle East. Washington backed the proposal more enthusiastically than Great Britain, which remained concerned as to how a defense pact with Pakistan would affect its relations with India. Ultimately, however, despite Pakistan's willingness to participate, the Truman Administration's plans were derailed by yet another military crisis between India and Pakistan. Reigniting during the summer of 1951, this renewed dispute over Kashmir forced the Truman Administration to abandon any discussion of a defense pact with Pakistan. But the northern tier defense concept would in time provide the framework for engagement with Pakistan under the Dwight D. Eisenhower Administration (Kux 2001; McMahon 1994; Pande 2011).

American accounts of this period described Pakistan's political elites as insistent that the United States substantively engage with Pakistan. The October 1951 assassination of Liaquat, who had sustained scathing domestic criticism for his alliance with the United States, somehow failed to spark American concern over Pakistan's stability or its future orientation. A mere two days after his death, former foreign secretary Mohammad Ikramullah traveled to Washington with the express goal of obtaining "as much military equipment as he could" either "as a gift, under a loan arrangement, or outright purchase" (McMahon 1994, 142). Ikramullah told high-level US officials that Pakistan was eager to participate in the defense of the Middle East and warned that "if Pakistan does not get assistance from the West, the Government's position will be grave. Pakistan may turn away from the West" (143). But Washington's dilemma persisted: its diplomats were appreciative of Pakistan's reliability, especially in contrast to India's abrasive contrarianism, but were unsure of how to proceed given the unpredictable costs and benefits of doing so. Nonetheless, the Truman Administration awarded Pakistan a small percentage of the requested military supplies and offered to provide economic and development assistance.

THE PAKISTAN TILT

The incoming Eisenhower Administration, however, almost immediately signaled that it was more positively disposed toward Pakistan than India. In early 1953, Pakistan, which was enduring a severe food shortage, requested urgent aid from the United States. While the new administration readily agreed to send 1 million tons of grain, the act required congressional approval. Dulles and Eisenhower agreed that Dulles should travel to Pakistan in May 1953 (as part of a larger tour of the Middle East and South Asia) to obtain more information before formally submitting the request to Congress. Dulles, whose trip coincided with the ascendency of the military and bureaucracy in Pakistani politics, was so favorably impressed by Pakistan's potential as an ally that he urged the United States to provide Pakistan with defense assistance even in the absence of a formal arrangement. Upon his return to the United States, Dulles rejected the British proposal for a Middle East Defense Organization, a scaled-down version of the old Middle East Command with Egypt at the center. Instead, he revived the northern tier concept first envisioned by the Truman Administration, proposing a defensive ring composed of Turkey, Pakistan, Iraq, and Iran. In mid-June, Eisenhower requested, and swiftly received, congressional approval for the loan of 1 million tons of wheat; that same summer the administration began to move forward on the northern tier concept despite British reservations and a lack of clear American vision for Pakistan's role in the defense of the Middle East (Kux 2001; McMahon 1994; see also Goktepe 2003).

Pakistan's insistence on a defense guarantee against India had long proved one of the major obstacles to a US–Pakistan defense agreement. This demand remained a deal-breaker for the United States: while it was not pleased with India's nonaligned position, it generally aspired to better relations with the larger South Asian state. Moreover, the United States had no interest in being dragged into the intractable Indo-Pakistan conflict. But although Pakistan's new government under Prime Minister Muhammad Ali Bogra continued to demand a guarantee, Gen. Ayub Khan, now Pakistan's army chief, was anxious to get the alliance moving forward. During a September 1953 visit to the United States, he exclaimed to the assistant secretary of state for Near Eastern Affairs, Henry Byroad, "For Christ's sake... I didn't come here to look at barracks. Our army can be your army if you want us. But let's make a decision" (Kux 2001, 57). Eisenhower, who raised the issue in a January 1954 meeting with Dulles and Defense Secretary Charles E. Wilson, remained concerned that increased closeness to Pakistan would adversely influence American relations with India. His fear was valid: India responded publicly and derisively to the news of the US–Pakistan discussions. Although Washington was not entirely certain as to how Pakistan would fit into defense of the Middle East, the resulting public furor in India made it impossible for the United States to back down. Eisenhower was unwilling to allow India, under the imperious Nehru, to dictate his foreign and defense policies (Kux 2001).

In February 1954, with Washington's encouragement, Turkey and Pakistan negotiated a bilateral treaty for military, economic, and cultural cooperation, the first meaningful step toward the northern tier. Later that month, Iraq and Turkey signed a military agreement; the alliance, now known as the Baghdad Pact, was soon joined by Iran, Pakistan, and the United Kingdom. (In 1959, the new Iraqi regime withdrew, and the pact became known as the Central Treaty Organization, or CENTO.) The Pakistan–Turkey agreement provided the necessary justification for a formal military arrangement between the United States and Pakistan. In May 1954, the United States and Pakistan signed a Mutual Defense Assistance

Agreement (MDA), the first bilateral security agreement between the two states and the legal basis for US aid to Pakistan. Under its terms, the United States would "make available to the Government of Pakistan such equipment, materials, services or other assistance as the Government of the United States may authorize in accordance with such terms and conditions as may be agreed" (Khan and Emmerson 1954, 338). In turn, Pakistan agreed that it would "use this assistance exclusively to maintain its internal security, its legitimate self-defenses, or to permit it to participate in the defense of the area, or in the United Nations collective security arrangements and measures, and Pakistan will not undertake any act of aggression against any other nation" (339).

Pakistan lost no time in following the signing of the agreement with a request for military assistance, which Eisenhower approved (over India's strenuous objections). Yet scholarly accounts make clear that Pakistan continued to be unimpressed by the level of American assistance, even threatening to undo the pact because it considered the initial figure of $30 million inadequate recompense for its new responsibilities. Dulles responded that he was under the impression that "Pakistan had undertaken its anti-communist stand because it was right, not just to make itself eligible for certain sums of dollar aid" (Kux 2001, 68). In the end, Washington offered a $171 million program, a figure that was more to Pakistan's liking (Kux 2001; Pande 2011).

Wary of involving itself in quarrels between the various Arab states, and equally concerned to protect its relationship with Israel, the United States decided not to seek full membership in CENTO. Thus, the United States maintained its "observer" status, allowing the British to shoulder most of the load. Although America's hesitation made Ayub doubtful that CENTO membership offered significant benefits to Pakistan, Turkey's leadership assuaged his fears by assuring him that membership would not add to Pakistan's defense burdens. Pakistan's cabinet approved membership in September 1955, with the proviso that it "implied no commitment that would detract from Pakistan's defense capabilities or involve the country in a military engagement relating to Turkey's membership in NATO" (Kux 2001, 73). (CENTO collapsed in 1979 following the Iranian revolution and Iran's withdrawal from the pact.)

Although US apprehensions about communist expansion in the Middle East prompted the Americans to consider bringing Pakistan into formal defense arrangements against the Soviets, in fact the first anti-communist regional alliance that Pakistan joined was the Southeast Asian Treaty Organization (SEATO), formalized in September 1954, two weeks prior to CENTO. (Pakistan did not formally become a member of what was then the Baghdad Pact until spring 1955.[2]) The US Department of Defense opposed Pakistani membership in SEATO, fearing that its inclusion would drive away other Asian states, and the skeptics were not entirely wrong: the Philippines and Thailand were the only other Asian states to join the pact. Pakistan, however, insisted on participating, perhaps hoping that membership would afford some protection for troublesome East Pakistan.

Pakistan's foreign secretary, Zafrullah Khan, attended the SEATO organizational meeting in Manila in 1954 with the unusual goal of obtaining a security guarantee against all aggression, not simply against threats from communist states. Dulles, who had no interest in allowing the United States or SEATO to become ensnared in the Indo-Pakistan dispute, not only outright refused but also even added explicit language to the treaty declaring that SEATO defense guarantees covered only communist aggression. Khan was supposed to seek further instruction from his ministry if he failed to obtain this guarantee. Instead he signed the treaty without consultation, arguing that backing down after lobbying so hard to be included would do little to help Pakistan. Despite its reservations, the cabinet ratified the treaty in early 1955 (Kux 2001; McMahon 1994; Pande 2011).

American historians do not usually argue that SEATO or CENTO held any military value for Pakistan. But they do contend that Pakistan derived considerable benefit from the treaties and did so without acquiring additional responsibilities. As a result of its memberships in the treaty organizations, Pakistan was able to lay claim not just to American resources but also to a far greater share of US attention. And the Pakistan military was afforded numerous opportunities to interact with other militaries. Still, neither side had many illusions about the basis of the alliance. Americans generally understood that, despite Pakistan's professed rejection of communism, its participation in these arrangements was driven primarily by its fear of India and secondarily by its desire for access to US military equipment, training, and doctrine, all of which had an important impact on Pakistan's military posture and military capabilities. It is less obvious what tangible benefit the United States derived from the relationship before 1959, when, in return for the gift of more than one dozen US-made F-104 fighters, Pakistan agreed to permit the United States to open a communications facility at Badaber airbase some 10 miles outside Peshawar. The United States built a substantial communications facility at Badaber to monitor Soviet plans and activities and used it to fly U-2 spy aircraft into Soviet airspace. The Americans felt that they had finally obtained something "of great importance for US national security" (Kux 2001, 92; see also McMahon 1994).

In May 1960, the Soviets announced that they had shot down a U-2 and its pilot, Gary Powers, near Sverdlovsk (in contemporary Ukraine). Powers had taken off from Pakistan with the intention of flying across Soviet airspace to photograph defense installations. The announcement came as the leadership of the United States, France, Great Britain, and the Soviet Union were assembling in Paris for a much anticipated summit. The incident obviated the summit and put Pakistan in an awkward position. The Soviet Union made clear that if any American plane were "allowed to use Peshawar as a base of operations against the Soviet Union" it would "retaliate immediately" against Pakistan (Kux 2001, 112–113).

The Pakistani response to the incident is telling and bears more than a passing resemblance to its current obfuscating position on US drone strikes

(International Crisis Group 2013). As dictated by the standing agreement, the US State Department claimed that the United States had conducted the U-2 flights without Pakistan's knowledge, much less permission. The Pakistani government followed suit with protests that the flights were not authorized by Pakistan. This episode, perhaps more than any other preceding it, demonstrated to the Pakistanis that the alliance with the United States might entail significant risks. Ayub began to distance himself from the United States, realizing that Pakistan might have cultivated an unhealthy reliance on an unreliable partner. This realization motivated him to try to improve ties with Moscow and provided further impetus to reach out to China (Kux 2001; McMahon 1994).

Tensions between the United States and Pakistan persisted. In 1962, the Americans offered India military assistance in its war with China. Pakistan was dumbfounded that the United States would aid Pakistan's enemy—a country that, furthermore, remained nonaligned. Pakistan was again disappointed in 1965, when the United States cut off all military aid to both India and Pakistan in response to the outbreak of war between the two states. Pakistan was disproportionately affected by the cutoff, as it was more dependent on US weapons systems. Stretching the truth to the breaking point, Ayub "reminded" the Americans of their obligation to help Pakistan, " a victim of naked aggression by armed attack on the part of India" (Pande 2011, 100). Although he did not deny Operation Gibraltar[3] and even conceded that Pakistan had used US-provided weapons in the operation, Ayub still had the temerity to request further assistance. The US ambassador to Pakistan, justifying the US embargo, told then foreign minister Z. A. Bhutto that "it was a fateful decision you took to plan, organize, and support the Mujahid [freedom fighter] operations" (Kux 2001, 162; see also McMahon 2011; Pande 2011).

Pakistan was again doomed to disappointment during the 1971 war with India. Although the treaty language clearly limited defense assistance to communist threats, Pakistan believed that the United States had an obligation to defend its ally against India. Even though Nixon violated US law by continuing to provide Pakistan with defense equipment despite the embargo imposed from the 1965 war, Pakistan did not believe that the United States did enough to protect Pakistan from the inevitable vivisection (Bass, 2013). Following the loss of East Pakistan, Pakistan finally withdrew from SEATO. The relationship between the United States and Pakistan hovered in limbo until the Soviet invasion, when the two once again began to work in concert.

Chasing China: The All-Weather Friend

Compared with the voluminous material on US–Pakistan relations, the literature on Sino-Pakistan relations is relatively sparse. Scholars agree that in 1949

Pakistan warmly welcomed the new communist leadership of China. Pakistan's leaders quickly understood that the communists would hold China's seat on the UN Security Council. Also, given that the Security Council was considering the Kashmir question, Pakistan had far more incentive to cultivate than to antagonize communist China. For China's part, the new government was isolated and embargoed, with most countries following America's lead in refusing to recognize the communist government. With few allies, it welcomed Pakistan's friendly gesture. Curiously, both China and Pakistan successfully avoided any serious confrontation over Pakistan's formal commitments to anticommunist treaties. Both states had their own motivation to downplay this reality. For its part, China did so by characterizing Pakistan as a victimized pawn in US imperial designs, whereas Pakistan did so by arguing that China is not a predatory, imperial regime like the Soviet Union.

In 1949, Pakistan faced a major economic crisis when it refused to devalue its currency at the same time as India. In response, India ceased all trade with Pakistan. In urgent need of an alternative market for its raw cotton and jute, and of a new source of coal, Pakistan finalized a barter agreement with China according to which China would purchase Pakistani cotton in exchange for coal. China thus emerged as an important and powerful ally against India. Aparne Pande (2011, 115) rightly observed of this episode: "Pakistan's rulers and strategists have not forgotten this incident. For them, it was another demonstration of the 'untrustworthiness' of 'Hindu' India and evidence that India and Indian leaders had not accepted Partition and wanted to break up Pakistan" (see also Amin 2000).

But a closer look at the early years of the Pakistan–China relationship suggests that Beijing was less invested than this episode might suggest. From October 1949 until mid-1950, China was in a state of revolutionary militancy. China displayed scant regard for Pakistan during this period: even though Pakistan recognized the communist government on January 4, 1950, and supported its claim to the UN Security Council seat, China did not dispatch an ambassador to Pakistan until September 1951 (Barnds 1975).

China showed particular forbearance when Pakistan joined SEATO and CENTO, two pacts meant to combat the spread of communism, and when Pakistan backed the UN action in Korea and the efforts of UN military forces to unify the peninsula. There are several possible explanations for this unusual tolerance. First, it was clear by this time that China would not have peaceful relations with India. Early attempts at Sino-Indian rapprochement had foundered on the issue of Tibet. India vocally opposed China's occupation of Tibet in late 1950, arguing, among other things, that as a successor state of the British Raj it inherited the Raj's relationship with the territory. Pakistan, in contrast, was indifferent to the situation. Second, while Pakistan was a member of both SEATO and CENTO, it consistently signaled that it had no ill will toward China. Pakistan opposed naming China an aggressor in the Korean War and all trade embargoes on China. It was clear to Chinese leadership that Pakistan's participation in SEATO was directed at India rather than China and that Pakistan "did not go beyond what was necessary to maintain American aid" (Barnds 1975, 469).

Chinese state media used a sympathetic tone when discussing Pakistan's predicament. One editorialist wrote, "It is common knowledge that US war-makers for a long time have been trying to drag Pakistan into planned US Middle East and Southeast Asia aggressive blocs and to convert Pakistan into an important war base for the United States in the region.... The US war-makers want to take advantage of Pakistan's strategic position.... The United States is sparing no effort to use Pakistan to link its aggressive power in the Middle East with that in Southeast Asia" (Pande 2011, 117). China publicly placed the blame on the United States for foisting these alliances on a desperate Pakistan.

Chinese leaders realized that, despite Pakistan's formal association with SEATO and CENTO, China could achieve greater benefits by not forcing Pakistan to choose between China and the West. China's support of Pakistan made it nearly impossible for either the United States or the Soviet Union to entrench itself across the length and width of the subcontinent as long as the Indo-Pakistan rivalry persisted. Equally important, China could forge a "close working relationship with a Pakistan hostile to India in order to keep New Delhi as preoccupied as possible within the subcontinent and thus reduce its ability to challenge China" (Barnds 1975, 466). Moreover, just as its ties with India put Soviet Russia in a better position to affect the balance of power in Asia, "China's ability to frustrate Soviet designs is furthered by keeping Pakistan—which stands astride the overland route between the U.S.S.R. and India—outside anything resembling a Soviet sphere of influence" (ibid.). Given Pakistan's willingness to support other Chinese goals, and the fact that it provided China with political and physical entrée into the Middle East, China found it best to endure Pakistan and its anticommunist commitments (Kux 2001; McMahon 1994; Pande 2011).

The nature of the understanding between the two states was encapsulated in remarks delivered by Chinese Premier Zhou Enlai at the April 1955 Afro-Asia Summit in Bandung (Indonesia), following at least two private meetings with Bogra. Zhou told the conference political committee "that he and the Pakistani prime minister had reached an understanding on matters of 'collective peace and cooperation.' He had received the assurance that Pakistan would not support any aggressive action that the United States might launch against China under the SEATO treaty and that she neither opposed China nor apprehended aggression from her" (Syed 1974, 61–62). According to another account, Zhou added, "we achieved a mutual understanding although we are still against military treaties" (Arif 1984, 9).

Bogra, addressing the same summit, took the opportunity to distinguish between the Soviets and the Chinese. He argued that China must be viewed as distinct from the Soviet Union: the former was an imperialist power, whereas the latter had never brought other nations "under its heel" or made them into satellite states (Syed 1969, 109). Bogra insisted that Pakistan "wanted good relations with Beijing, notwithstanding the security arrangement with the United States" (Kux 2001, 71). In 1956, Zhou and Bogra exchanged state visits, at the conclusion of which they issued a joint statement explaining that neither their countries' differing political systems nor their divergent views on many problems should "prevent the strengthening of friendship between [them]." Both reaffirmed their commitment to expanding cultural and commercial ties and placed "on record that there is no real conflict of interests between the two countries" (Joint Statement Signed by the Prime Minister of Pakistan and China, 1956).

Sino-Pakistan ties came under some strain when Ayub seized the reins of power in 1958. This was partly the result of Chinese domestic politics. In 1958, the Communist government announced the Great Leap Forward, which the Communist Party boasted would "propel China to surpass Great Britain in industrial production in 15 years and the United States in 20 or 30 years" (Li and Yang 2005, 841). The plan ended in ruin. Bad central planning and weather catastrophes contributed to a famine, among the worst in recorded history, that caused the premature death of some 16.5 to 30 million people (ibid.).

The second reason for the frost was Ayub himself: he was personally more inclined toward the United States and was sensitive to US anticommunist commitment. Pakistan's position on China's membership in the United Nations also shifted as it moved closer to the United States: for several years Pakistan voted against seating communist China (Barnds 1975). Pakistan jointly sponsored a UN General Assembly resolution criticizing China's suppression of the 1959 Tibetan uprising. And in 1959, Ayub offered India a joint defense agreement that would protect them both against Chinese or Soviet aggression. India immediately rejected the proposal, and Pakistan turned towards China once again (Pande 2011; Raghavan 2009).

China did not completely ignore these mood swings. When Pakistan changed its position on the Chinese seat at the United Nations, Beijing labeled it an unfriendly act. Chinese papers accused Pakistan of playing imperialist propaganda tunes and conniving in anti-Chinese activities. One Chinese paper oddly cautioned Pakistan to "pull up the horse before [the] precipice" (Barnds 1975, 469–470). Yet seen in the grand scheme of things, China's criticism was still relatively muted. China, like Pakistan, had few options: Sino-Indian tensions were mounting, and its détente with the Soviet Union was disintegrating. The United States and India were drawing closer, signing an agreement covering defense assistance prompted in large part by India's 1962 conflict with China. Russia's continued alignment with India further discomfited China (Amin 2009; Pande 2011).

In 1961, after several turbulent years, China and Pakistan began once again to attempt to improve their relationship. Several events galvanized this warming. China sought to exploit the growing Pakistani anger with US assistance to India, despite the latter state's persistently nonaligned position. Closer ties to Pakistan would serve as a lesson to the Soviet Union that its strategy of using India to counter China was not without consequences. What is more, such an approach would be relatively inexpensive for China as it would "not require [Beijing] to assume the burden of supplying Pakistan's external needs as long as Pakistan's links with the US were not completely cut—something [Beijing] never demanded" and likely never wanted (Barnds 1975, 470–471). For Pakistan's part, Ayub's realization that conflict between India and Pakistan would continue and that the United States would help India against China forced him to reassess China's value.

The most important impediment to increased Sino-Pakistani engagement and cooperation was their outstanding territorial dispute. In September 1959, Pakistani authorities noticed that Chinese maps were labeling parts of Hunza, claimed by Pakistan, as Chinese territory (Anwar 1969). In October 1959, the two countries began negotiations on the border in what appeared to be a mutually beneficial transaction (ibid.). China was willing to settle the border dispute in exchange for Pakistan's support of communist China's admission to the UN. In 1962, the two countries came to a provisional agreement, with final disposition pending resolution of the Kashmir dispute. India was discomfited by this development, as the border negotiations between Pakistan and China were taking place against the backdrop of mounting Sino-Indian tensions in the run up to the 1962 Sino-Indian war.

The Chinese–Pakistan border agreement was signed in 1963, a few months after the conclusion of the Sino-Indian war. India dismissed the border agreement as illegal; for its part, China refused to discuss border demarcation with India and adhered to its policy of not recognizing Kashmir's accession to India (Amin 2000; Pande 2011). Syed (1969, 111) dismisses the "impression in certain quarters abroad" that the border agreement was related to the 1962 Sino-Indian War. Anwar claims that China ceded 750 square kilometers to Pakistan "beyond the main watershed of the Karakoram range" while Pakistan "surrendered no part of the territory under its control." While the new territory offered few economic or other advantages, the agreement brought Pakistan manifold political benefits. First and foremost, it removed an irritant in Sino-Pakistan ties. Second, it gave Pakistan secure possession of key parts of the Indus River watershed. It also provided China with an opportunity to reject India's claim that Kashmir was entirely Indian. Finally, it both gave substance to and justification for the increasingly friendly ties between Pakistan and China (ibid.).

Once the border question was settled, Pakistan and China quickly sought to deepen their relationship. Because the lack of air routes connecting the two countries limited commercial and other traffic, in 1963 they signed a civil aviation accord. The United States vociferously objected, calling the accord "an unfortunate breach of free world solidarity" (Kux 2001, 143). For the first time, the US government imposed consequential penalties on Pakistan: the John F. Kennedy

Administration indefinitely postponed a $4.3 million US Agency for International Development loan to build a new airport in Dhaka (the planned departure point for the flights to China). All things considered, this was a relatively mild sanction given the importance countering China held for US foreign policy of the time. Perhaps more problematic for the United States, Pakistan ceased negotiations regarding an expansion of the "communications intercept facility" in Badaber (ibid.). In the same year, Pakistan and China granted each other Most Favored Nation Status and opened up trade and shipping facilities. Pakistan began importing metal and steel products from China as well as cement, coal, machinery, chemicals, cotton and jute products, sporting goods, leather, and surgical instruments. In July 1964, China offered Pakistan a $60 million loan, to be used to purchase Chinese goods (Pande 2011).

While China's economic and cultural engagements with Pakistan were important, Pakistan's real interest was military assistance against India. It is perhaps impossible to overstate the degree to which America's 1962 decision to send military aid to India shook Pakistani confidence in the United States. This theme recurs during discussions with Pakistan military personnel as well as with ordinary Pakistanis. Pakistan, "convinced that its only hope was to secure political and military support from China[,] . . . . tried to push the pace of developments in this area" (Barnds 1975, 472).

It appears that Pakistan more or less deftly managed its complex relations with both the United States and China throughout this period. There is little evidence that the United States punished Pakistan for refusing to provide military assistance in Vietnam or Korea despite being a member of SEATO.[4] (This is in contrast to Pakistan's persistent, if factually shaky, criticism of the United States for its refusal to assist Pakistan in its wars with India in 1965 and 1971, citing both SEATO and CENTO commitments.) However, this does not mean that Americans suffered these irritations in silence. Both the United States and Great Britain groused that Pakistan had weakened its commitment to SEATO by signing various agreements with Communist China. Pakistan responded that it was in fact furthering SEATO's peaceful mission by settling its boundary dispute with China, thus removing any friction between the two states (Pande 2011).

Harsh words were exchanged in 1963, when Pakistan's ambassador to the United States, Aziz Ahmed, made a farewell call on Kennedy before returning to Pakistan to become Ayub's foreign secretary. Ahmed complained bitterly over the long-term military aid the United States was offering India. After all, India remained staunchly nonaligned, and the Chinese military threat had receded, while the Kashmir dispute remained very much alive and a perennial potential flashpoint for the next Indo-Pakistan crisis. This decision to help arm India, Ahmed claimed, fundamentally threatened Pakistan's security. Kennedy responded that the United States was taking Pakistan's concerns into consideration and in fact was providing India with far less assistance than it had requested. He reminded Ahmed that America had little influence over Indian actions in Kashmir or Pakistani actions in Afghanistan. He spoke frankly about Pakistan's dalliances with China and the inflammatory anti-American commentary in Pakistan's press, explaining that "[the] Pak[istanis] display little appreciation of this primary concern of ours and instead apparently feel impelled to move towards [Communist China] and away from us because [of] Pak[istani] concerns about India. In [the] last few months [the] Pak[istani] press has exceeded all but [Communist China] in its attacks on us. One would gather from [the] Pak[istani] press, which is closer [to the government of Pakistan] than [the American press is] to [the US government], that [the] US was enemy number one" (Kux 2001, 142–143). Kennedy took the opportunity to remind Ahmed "that [the] US has one basic interest—prevention of control over Europe by [the] USSR or Asia by [Communist China]. Pakistan should understand this outlook since it accepted [the] responsibilities of [an] alliance with us" (143).

Nevertheless, Pakistan continued to develop its ties to China, even as it tried to minimally satisfy its commitments to the Americans. By 1963, Bhutto reposed sufficient confidence in Beijing to declare in a debate in the National Assembly that any "attack by India on Pakistan would involve "the largest state in Asia" (Kux 2001, 143). Such hints gave rise to a general presumption that Bhutto had some sort of defense arrangement with China in hand. But, as Barnds (1975, 472) suspects, this speech may have been an attempt by Bhutto to "frighten India and commit China" to Pakistan's defense.

The Strains of War

The 1965 Indo-Pakistan war further strained Pakistani relations with SEATO and helped to strengthen ties between Pakistan and China. China applied "strong military pressure on India to stop the war" (Amin 2000, 161), including a public declaration that it was enhancing its defense preparations and alertness along the Sino-Indian border. On September 16, China ordered India to "dismantle all of its military works on the Chinese side of the border and return all captive Chinese nationals and livestock, within three days" or bear sole responsibility for the consequences of refusal (ibid.). This move brought the conflict before the UN Security Council, which demanded an immediate ceasefire. China (through the offices of the US Embassy in Poland) also warned India against attacking East Pakistan. The Chinese identified India as the aggressor in the war with Pakistan, continued to support Kashmiri self-determination, and accused the UN of acting to the detriment of Pakistan (Barnds 1975; Syed 1969). China would not provide such direct assistance in any subsequent Indo-Pakistan conflict.

In contrast, the United States refused to come to Pakistan's assistance, both because the defense agreement addressed only communist aggression and because Pakistan had used American weapons to start the conflict. Gen. Musa, in a November 1965 conversation with Maj. Gen. Robert Burns, the chief of the US military assistance mission in Pakistan, condemned the US for giving military aid to India in 1962. Musa exclaimed that Pakistan had "'burned her bridges' in accepting US military assistance and was now paying the price" for its decision (Kux 2001, 161). While Pakistan could not understand America's actions, Americans were flabbergasted by the audacity of Pakistan's request. The United States cut off military aid to both India and Pakistan.

China's gamble on Pakistan paid off because Pakistan became China's window to the Western world. US–Pakistan relations improved in the late 1960s after the US election of Richard Nixon, whose disposition toward Pakistan was positive. Nixon and his chief foreign policy adviser Henry Kissinger were interested in a rapprochement with China, but the Vietnam War and the status of Taiwan remained impediments. Against the backdrop of worsening problems in East Pakistan, in 1970 Gen. Yahya Khan facilitated a secret meeting between Nixon and Enlai, which marked the start of the entente between the two nations (Amin 2000; Kux 2001; Pande 2011). But the relationship would again be tested in 1971. As Pakistan's crisis in East Pakistan deepened, it beseeched China for more economic assistance and diplomatic support. However, while China continued to provide Pakistan with weapons, it carefully crafted its position on the issue to avoid being dragged into the conflict: it stated its support as only for Pakistan's "state sovereignty and national independence...not its territorial integrity" (Barnds 1975, 483). By spring 1971, while Pakistan was still playing an important role in facilitating US–China détente, China was less dependent on Pakistan. China may also have come to understand that if East Pakistan became independent, China could simultaneously "support a conservative West Pakistan and radicalism in Bangladesh" (484). Decades later, China's responses to the 1999 Kargil War and the 2001–2002 crisis were similar to those of the United States and even India.

But although China has never again matched the support it provided Pakistan in the 1965 war (a point usually glossed over by Pakistani commentators), Pakistan has to a considerable extent obtained the support it hoped the bilateral relationship would provide. Until recent decades, "at regular intervals China has vetoed proposals harmful to Pakistan or lobbied against bringing a proposal to the UNSC which would hurt Pakistan's interests" (Pande 2011, 118). Military assistance has been substantial, including the 60 MiG-19 fighters, 100 tanks, and small arms that China provided Pakistan in June 1972. Between 1971 and 1974, China provided Pakistan with $300 million worth of military equipment, in addition to helping Pakistan establish ammunitions and arms factories and later licensing the production of a light tank. China provided extensive assistance in setting up an aeronautics complex in Kamra. After India's 1974 nuclear tests, China promised Pakistan that it would continue to support Pakistan's sovereignty and international independence "in the face of foreign aggression and even nuclear blackmail" (125). China sustained its economic support during Gen. Zia ul Haq's rule (ibid.).

In addition, until 2009 China used its veto power at the UN Security Council to ensure that key jihadi assets like the Lashkar-e-Taiba, operating under the name of Jamaat-ud-Dawa (JuD), would not be declared a terrorist organization. China ceased its resistance only after the November 2008 terror attacks in Mumbai (Fair 2011a; Pande 2011). Unlike the United States, which has often intervened publicly in Pakistan's domestic affairs, China has generally avoided doing so (at least publicly).

One important exception to this general rule took place in 2007 during the so-called Lal Masjid (Red Mosque) debacle. In early 2006, Islamist militants seized this mosque and an adjacent madrasa, both of which are located in the middle of Islamabad and a short distance from the Inter-Services Intelligence (ISI) headquarters. Until July 2007, the militants engaged in arson, extortion, kidnapping, and violent demonstrations, among other illegal activities, in their effort to bring down the government and assert shariat in the country. The Pakistani government dithered while a serious security threat challenged the writ of law in the capital city. Finally, after militants there kidnapped several alleged Chinese prostitutes, China exerted considerable influence on Pervez Musharraf to take control of the situation in late June 2007. Within days of the June 27 meeting between China's minister of public security Zhou Yongkang Zhou, and Pakistan's minister of interior, Aftab Ahmed Khan Sherpao, in Beijing, Musharraf ordered Operation Silence (renamed Operation Sunrise) to commence on the mosque. The operation lasted about a week, at the end of which the Pakistan military finally had control of the mosque (Pardesi 2008; *Shanghai Daily* 2007).

Most important, China has been a valuable benefactor in Pakistan's quest for a deployable nuclear deterrent (discussed in Chapter 8). The available evidence suggests that Sino-Pakistan nuclear cooperation began early in the 1980s. In 1983, American intelligence discovered that China had provided Pakistan with an entire nuclear weapon design, along with sufficient weapons-grade uranium for up to two weapons. In 1986, Pakistan and China forged a comprehensive nuclear cooperation agreement; later that same year Chinese scientists began guiding Pakistanis on how to enrich weapons-grade uranium. China is even believed to have involved Pakistan scientists in its 1989 nuclear tests at Lop Nor (Center for Nonproliferation Studies 1999; Pande 2011, 126).

Pakistan's Relations with the United States and China through the Eyes of the Army

As the previous sections demonstrate, Pakistan's relations with both the United States and China were dictated solely by the players' national security interests. This should not be surprising. Unexpected, however, is the way Pakistan's defense literature recasts the facts of Pakistan's foreign relations, even creating new facts as the occasion warrants. This section focuses on Pakistani defense literature's narratives of its relations with the United States and China. The literature devotes less space to Pakistani relations with China than to those with the United States, and this section reflects that discrepancy. Demonstrating the degree to which the military's strategic culture has permeated that of civilian institutions, few differences can be found between military and civilian accounts of these relationships.

NARRATING AMERICAN DUPLICITY

Several narrative tropes cut through both Pakistani military and diplomatic histories. First, whereas the previously discussed Western accounts suggest that the United States was indifferent toward South Asia in the early years after independence, Pakistani military and civilian writers insist that the United States immediately, and feverishly, sought to drag Pakistan into its orbit. Brig. (Ret.) Tughral Yamin, writing in *Hilal* in 2011, explains that Pakistan's early "decision to move into the American camp was basically premised on the national security threat from India.... The Americans *exploited* Pakistan's geo-strategic position by integrating it within their overarching strategy to contain the rising tide of communism" (Yamin 2011, 9, emphasis added).

One of the most important and enduring tenets of Pakistani military accounts of US–Pakistan relations is that the United States connived to draw Pakistan into an anticommunist alliance yet, having done so, repeatedly failed to defend Pakistan in its various misadventures with India. The same essay affords a typical and recent example. In addition to "exploiting Pakistan's geostrategic position," Yamin alleges that the United States took cunning advantage of Pakistan's security predicaments. He opines that "naturally, [the Americans] were aware of Pakistani threat perceptions from India, but as long as it suited their convenience, they were willing to turn a blind eye" (9). Yamin even claims that the Americans "relentlessly pursued the Pakistani leadership and literally seduced it into submission" (ibid.). In his assessment, Pakistan bears no responsibility for undertaking commitments not to attack India while at the same time seeking to obtain military aid to do just that.

In another essay for *Hilal*, Yamin (2012) rehearses Pakistan's disappointment with the supposed American failure to honor its defense commitments to Pakistan in the 1965 and 1971 war. Drawing on Pakistan's ostensible experience of American perfidy, he cautions against entering into such "one-sided relationships" and avers that "never again should we allow our young men to become cannon fodder in somebody else's war" (9). He adds, "At least four times in the past, Pakistan has allowed itself to become part of the American scheme of things. Each time it ended up as the loser from this lopsided equation" (9–10). A. Z. Hilali, in a 1990 essay in the *Pakistan Defence Review*, makes a similar claim: "Americans didn't help Pakistan in [the] 1965 and 1971 Indo-Pakistan wars, in which India was regarded as an aggressor by many Americans and Western Partners but Pakistan could not invoke much support in American circles" (58).

Other Pakistani defense writers seek to downplay the value of Pakistan's various western alliances while exaggerating the costs to Pakistan of such agreements. For example, Zia's associate Gen. Khalid Mahmud Arif (2001) describes Pakistan's relationship with the United States as an unequal friendship, with Pakistan desperate to address its security concerns vis-à-vis India. Arif emphasizes, if not outright exaggerates, the burdens that Pakistan took on as a result of this relationship but minimizes the political, diplomatic, and military aid that Pakistan received. He contends that the United States convinced Pakistan to aid its efforts to oust the Soviets from Afghanistan; however, as this volume has already shown, Pakistan's Afghan policies in Afghanistan predated the Soviet invasion, and it sought and received highly lucrative US support for these policies.

Pakistan's defense writers occasionally suggest that Pakistan's leadership did not adequately appreciate the onerous burdens it was accepting when it entered into these various commitments. Ayub himself employed this strategy in his 1967 autobiography *Friends not Masters* (2006), in which he explains that his interest in CENTO was "exclusively in terms of the defense of the country. I was anxious to take maximum advantage of this arrangement to build up the defence forces of Pakistan" (136). In joining CENTO as well as SEATO, he opined, Pakistan alienated the Soviet Union and "lost her sympathy.... Since we had never been a party to any design against her and our membership of the Pacts was dictated solely by the requirements of our security, it should be possible to come to an understanding with the Soviet Union by removing her doubts and misgivings" (138). This set of statements is telling because it demonstrates the extent to which Pakistan wanted to have the benefits of alliances against the Soviet Union without incurring the costs of its choice. These statements also stand in sharp contrast to American narratives in which successive Pakistani officials—including Ayub himself—persistently offered Pakistan's cooperation should the United States wish to form an alliance against the Soviet Union.

Ayub similarly disavowed SEATO. He claims that "we soldiers were not consulted; I think we learnt of it in the General Headquarters after the Foreign Minister had already signed the Pact" (M.A. Khan 2006, 179). Since he was the army chief at the time the treaty was signed, it is inconceivable that his input was not solicited, particularly given that power was already shifting from the politicians to the bureaucratic-military complex and that the US–Pakistan relations had historically been the responsibility of the army. Despite the evidence that Pakistan lobbied to be included in SEATO, Ayub writes, "Even at that time I thought that Pakistan had no reason to join SEATO at all. Perhaps the main consideration was to oblige the United States, who had been giving us considerable economic help. Beyond that, I really did not see any purpose to our being a member" (ibid.).

Other authors focus on how Pakistan's alliances with the United States undermined its relations with other countries, including key Arab states. Zulfikar Khalid (1989a), writing in the *Pakistan Army Journal*, argues that Pakistan broke the ranks of Arab solidarity on Palestine by joining CENTO. His logic is based on CENTO's inclusion of Turkey, which Khalid explains felt "honoured by cooperating with the Jewish state" (4). Khalid laments that Saudi Arabia, held in high regard in Pakistan, retaliated by feting Nehru in September 1956. To Pakistan's horror, Saudi Arabia's leadership declared its belief that Indian Muslims are safe in India and welcomed Nehru with slogans such as "prophet of peace" (5). Even Egypt retaliated against Pakistan by declaring that the "Suez is as dear to Egypt as Kashmir to India" (ibid.). Pakistan was able to restore its relations with Saudi Arabia by "assert[ing] the Islamic roots that were the underpinnings of Pakistani ideology and the rationale for its separation from India in 1947" (8). Saudi Arabia eventually became a major source of aid to Pakistan.

Another, more recent, rhetorical strategy is to distort the history of US nuclear sanctions against Pakistan. Pakistani accounts continually focus on the unfairness of US laws, arguing that India escaped punishment for its 1974 test. But India's test (which did not violate US laws in place when it occurred) did prompt the American government to begin erecting an elaborate nonproliferation regime, using domestic law and international accords to prevent further Indian proliferation as well as proliferation by others, including Pakistan. Pakistanis also tend to emphasize the final invocation of Pressler Amendment sanctions against Pakistan in 1990. Pakistani defense narratives suggest that the sanctions were punitive and Pakistan-specific and were invoked only when the United States felt it could safely discard Pakistan. However, as I explain in Chapter 8, the Pakistan-specific nature of the sanctions was actually an attempt to resolve the interagency discord that arose when US knowledge of Pakistan's nuclear program conflicted with the need to work with and through Pakistan during the anti-Soviet Afghan campaign. Indeed, Pakistan's Foreign Ministry was a part of the negotiations leading to the amendment's passage and the Foreign Ministry even viewed the legislation as a victory for Pakistan. As I argue in Chapter 8, Pakistan was given ample warning that the Pressler sanctions would be imposed if Pakistan refused to roll back its program or crossed very clear red lines. Ultimately, Pakistan's defense literature does not hold Pakistani civilian and military leadership accountable for their decisions.

Pakistani accounts of US–Pakistan relations devote considerable space to the 1980s, when the United States, Saudi Arabia, and Pakistan worked to eject the Russians from Afghanistan. Pakistani military authors writing about this period typically minimize the benefits Pakistan obtained through its alliance with the United States and at the same time exaggerate the costs this relationship forced

Pakistan to bear. These narratives depict Pakistan as a passive pawn of US strategy and often—but not always—omit Saudi Arabia's massive contributions to the jihad against the Soviets. Most importantly, they leave out any mention of Pakistani involvement in Afghanistan prior to the Soviet invasion and ignore Pakistani attempts to get America involved in Afghanistan even before the Soviets crossed the Amu Darya. These narratives also tend to conflate the Taliban with the mujahideen who fought the Soviets. This allows Pakistani interlocutors to lay a whole host of problems at Washington's door including typical claims that the Americans created the Taliban and al-Qaeda; that America abandoned Pakistan to a drug, gun, and jihad culture; and that America created Pakistan's purported madrasa problem. This narrative is most pernicious because it blames the United States for Pakistan's current Islamist insurgency and turns a blind eye to the role played by decades of Pakistani government support for Islamist proxies.

Col. Muhammad Khan's 2009 essay for the *Pakistan Army Journal* provides both a representative sample of this argument and also displays the complex revisionism such narratives may propose. According to Khan, Pakistan's dalliance with Islamist militancy began with the anti-Soviet jihad. Khan also claims— contrary to a growing body of evidence—that the roots of terrorism and extremism in Pakistan also reach back only to the Afghan war: "the reality is that the roots of the extremism and terrorism in the country are linked with the Western sponsored Jihad against the invasion of former Soviet Union in Afghanistan from 1979–1989" (40–41). This statement not only ignores Bhutto's aggressive use of militant elements in Afghanistan but also absolves the Saudis, themselves vigorous supporters of the jihad. Khan similarly discounts the possibility that Pakistan solicited American involvement, noting that the "United States needed Pakistan and its soil for launching a proxy war against its rival Communist Soviet Union. Through the consent of Pakistan, [the] US then encouraged feelings of Islamic War" (41). The historical record is quite clear on this point: using jihadist rhetoric was not an American innovation, as the term "mujahideen" had long been used to describe the militant proxies Pakistan deployed in Afghanistan and India.

According to Khan (2009), after the United States had succeeded in ousting the Soviet Union the "US and west left the region in haste leaving behind a jihadists culture" (41). Even more egregiously, Khan informs his readership that the United States not only remained in contact with the Taliban but also was funding the movement (ibid.). Although the United States did have contact with the Taliban, the claims that it made payments to the group are absurd. Yet Khan makes no mention of Pakistan's extensive contact with and support for the movement. He reluctantly concedes that "misguided Jihadists, Taliban and even so-called Al-Qaeda persons took refuge in FATA of Pakistan" (ibid.). But he makes the bizarre claim that, over the years, the Taliban "were strengthened by acquisition of latest weaponry and equipments and an unending financial support by forces operating from outside the Pakistani borders, having historical rancor against us"

(44). (Khan does not need to name India since his meaning would be clear to his audience.) Even more audaciously, he intimates that the militants may not be actual Muslims; rather, "all tangible evidences [sic] and analysis are indeed leading to the coherent conclusions that camouflaged like Muslims, these militants are operating against Islam…indubitably none is follower of Islam or well wisher of Muslims, in general, and Pakistan, in particular" (45).

This article not only absolves Pakistan of any responsibility for the current internal security situation but also externalizes the entire problem of Islamist militancy against the Pakistani state. Khan (2009) claims that the enmity that these militants have toward Pakistan has been

> fully exploited by RAW and some other intelligence agencies of the anti-Pakistan forces. These anti-state spying agencies are reinforcing the militants through trained manpower both foreigners and locals by equipping them with the latest and sophisticated weaponry to fight against Pakistani security forces in the attire of religion. They are being trained in Afghanistan and then harboured into Pakistani soil through the abetment of Afghan Government. In order to support the terrorist activities in Pakistan, India has established six consulates and over 50 offices in close proximity of Pakistani frontiers in Afghanistan. Afghan puppet regime and some major powers are said to be assisting Indian activities through the provisioning of finance, training and sophisticated arms and ammunition (48).

To be clear, I do not claim that India is completely innocent of any interference in Pakistan. But Khan's version of history is dangerous because it excuses Pakistan from any and all responsibility for the problems it faces and perpetuates the belief that an anti-Pakistan alliance seeks to destroy the state. Khan insists that Pakistan, now a battlefield, was once a country at peace with itself and with its neighbors. "It is beyond doubt that Pakistan is suffering, mainly because of its historical alliance with [sic] US and West whose policies and actions against Muslims have created the so-called Islamic militants in Pakistan and elsewhere in the Muslim world" (45).

In recent years, writers in Pakistan's defense publications have begun to contend that the United States is deliberately seeking to destroy Pakistan or is even aiding and abetting the Pakistani Taliban in its operations against Pakistan's armed forces, police, political leadership, and ordinary civilians. For example, Maj. Gen. A. S. Bajwa (2012) argues that attackers under the command of Maulana Fazlullah (a wanted terrorist of Swat) regularly raid Pakistan from safe havens in Kunar, Afghanistan. He claims that "it is not believable that a group of hundreds, assemble at some place in Afghanistan, carries out a cross border attacks, and goes back without being noticed by Afghan and Allied security forces. The Americans' claim and complain that there are 'safe havens' for terrorist groups here in Pakistan, but the same can also be claimed about those who attack Pakistani territory from Afghanistan and then return to their sanctuaries" (3).

Pakistani defense commentators who fear that the United States is seeking to harm Pakistan and its interests were galvanized by the American/North Atlantic Treaty Organization (NATO) attack on a Pakistani outpost in Salala in November 2011. United States and NATO forces made a series of deadly mistakes that resulted in the deaths of nearly two dozen Pakistan military personnel. The United States refused to apologize, inflaming Pakistani sensibilities and inadvertently providing support for the claim that the United States had attacked the Pakistanis in retaliation for Pakistan's supposed assistance to the Afghan Taliban. In February 2012, Ahmad Rashid Malik, writing in *Hilal*, cited Pakistan's director general of military operations, Maj. Gen. Ashfaq Nadeem, who told Pakistan's Senate Standing Committee on Defense that the attack was "deliberate and *pre-planned* and was conducted by US Special Forces, over which NATO has no control inside Afghanistan" (11, emphasis in original). The Salala check post incident became a rallying cry for many in Pakistan. Malik, for example, called it "the most critical outcome of the decade-long US war in Afghanistan. During this war, over 30,000 [Pakistani] civilians have sacrificed their lives in drone attacks, suicidal bombings, and sabotage activities. Over 3,000 Pakistani soldiers have embraced martyrdom and thousands more have been injured during the war on terror. The financial losses have been estimated [to be] over US $80 billion in addition to the total ruining of road infrastructure by NATO logistic supply from Karachi to Chaman and Torkham" (11–12). These arguments are adduced to counter American claims that Pakistan has been amply rewarded for its selective cooperation with the United States and growing anti-Pakistan feeling within the US government.

MAKING EXCUSES FOR CHINA

In its early years the *Pakistan Army Journal*, which began publishing in 1958, carried a few articles expressing skepticism of Communist China (a sentiment shared by then army chief Ayub). In the journal's first volume, for instance, Maj. Wasiuddin Ahmad (1958) warned of the dangerous spread of Chinese communism, which "not only laid the foundations of a new Chinese empire in Southeast Asia but also led to the introduction of the powerful ideology of Communism, in its most vicious form.... The vacuum, thus created by the withdrawal of Western influence, is being filled by limitless Communism" (55).

But Ahmad's (1958) perspective would prove exceedingly rare over the course of the decades of literature read during the course of this research. Since the 1960s, Pakistani military authors are far more likely to treat China as a more reliable partner than the United States. Maj. Muhammad Aslam Zuberi's (1971) article for the *Pakistan Army Journal* offers more typical fare. Reflecting the growing concerns over India's nuclear aspirations and the possibility that a nuclear India would "claim the right for leadership" throughout South Asia and the rest of noncommunist Asia and Africa, Zuberi calls for Pakistan to develop a independent nuclear deterrence (23). He takes care to note that he does not suggest "matching India bomb for bomb or missile for missile" and instead advocates for the "concept of minimum deterrent [that] has been successfully preached by Britain and France" (ibid.). Because Pakistan will not soon be able to afford a minimum deterrent on its own, Pakistan should pursue nuclear collaboration, most likely with China. China, he argues, is anxious for friends and may want to "retain its friendship with Pakistan and help it" (25). By way of contrast, Zuberi raises another alternative: pursuing a security guarantee from the United States. He immediately rejects this option, rehearsing the "failure of the United States to aid Pakistan in her war with India during 1965 in spite of a Mutual Defence Aid Pact" (26). He considers requesting the Soviet Union for help but acknowledges that it has no reason to extend its nuclear umbrella, especially given its ties to India. Zuberi concludes that a nuclear guarantee from China or some other form of nuclear assistance from China is the safest course for Pakistan.

For many authors, China and Pakistan are the twinned victims of American machinations. As early as 1995, Pakistani defense writers fret that the United States is "determined to assign an important role to India, ostensibly with the aim of neutralising the strength of Chinese and also decimating all the power potential of Pakistan..." (Sarwar 1995, 64). What's more, "America is deliberately conniving at India's belligerent posture... [and] exerting undue pressure on Pakistan thus endangering its security interests" (ibid.). In light of India's nuclear explosion in 1974 and India's "recurrent use of force to impose solutions," Pakistan has had no choice but to seek a nuclear weapons capability, relying on all available sources of help (64–65).

Sarwar (1995) acknowledges that China has at times worked with the United States and against Pakistan's interests, especially with regards to Kashmir, where both China and the United States support a bilateral settlement that would avoid referring the matter to the United Nations (Pakistan's preferred outcome). Yet he insists that a Chinese–Indian rapprochement does not come at the expense of Islamabad. In other words, while US engagement of India is seen as zero-sum with respect to Pakistan, and Pakistani officials do not hesitate to denounce US–India engagement, China's rapprochement with India is treated as relatively benign. Increased Chinese (and Iranian) ties to India do not worry Sarwar since both remain supportive of Pakistan's position vis-à-vis India—even if they muffle their sentiments out of deference to Indian equities. While Sarwar concedes that both China and Iran refrain from "mentioning the UN resolutions on Kashmir or the right of self-determination of the Kashmiri people" (73), this discussion of China's policies lacks the rancorous tone and invective that Pakistan's defense writers reserve for the United States. Whereas Pakistan's defense writers go to great lengths to emphasize American deceit, they go to equal lengths to either ignore or downplay China's own shortcomings. Oddly, Pakistanis have even taken in stride China's admonition about the presence of Islamist Uighers who have received military training in Pakistan. According to *China Daily,* these militants learned how to make explosives and use firearms in training camps in Pakistan run by the East Turkistan Islamic Movement (Wei et al. 2011). Whereas Pakistan routinely bristles at American demands to do more against the Taliban and al-Qaeda, Pakistan typically responds with alacrity in operating against the Uighers (Perlez 2011).

Conclusions and Implications

At first blush, the narratives repeated in Pakistani defense writings on its alleg-edly sordid mistreatment by the United States appear to be a curious strategy for managing domestic perceptions of the army. After all, the tales of American schemes to exploit the vulnerable army makes the military appear to be little more than a puppet of the United States. And this is indeed how the army's domestic constituents sometimes view it. When public opinion turns against it, the army works assiduously to rehabilitate its image, not infrequently by accentuating its own weakness and cultivating sympathy for the institution. In the aftermath of the unilateral US raid on a Pakistani cantonment town that resulted in the death of Osama bin Laden, the army's strategy was to play up the enormous technologi-cal gaps between the hegemonic, bullying American army and Pakistan's force. This approach was successful: Pakistanis generally blamed the Americans for the fiasco and set aside public demands to understand why bin Laden was in a canton-ment town for so many years and why Pakistan's security and intelligence agen-cies had failed to find him first.

Because the Pakistan Army is a political force, it cares about maintaining a positive image among Pakistanis, and it has evolved numerous methods of manipulating its country's varied media to achieve this goal. In the past, pres-sure was exerted through the Ministry of Information, but in recent years ISI has established its own media cell tasked not only with monitoring international and domestic reporting about Pakistan but also with reaching out to and actively managing reporters. The military's Inter Services Public Relations (ISPR) works to ensure that "right wing polemicists and preachers" who promote the army's preferred narratives are invited on talk shows to discuss Pakistan's "national secu-rity, its foreign policy and the prevailing ideology of the state and the society" (Farooq 2012a, 40). In addition, the army has long influenced Pakistan's text-books, in which the army appears as the institution best able to handle any crisis (Farooq 2012a, 2012b; Kohari 2012; Sabri 2012). These tools ensure not only that the army can control its image at home but also that its preferred narratives about its partners are shared by institutions well beyond the military.[5]

Perhaps the most important implication of these highly stylized narratives of Pakistan's relations with the United States and China is the rent seeking they enable. By leveraging distorted narratives of the past, aggrandizing the relevance of Pakistan to US national security interests, and threatening to supplicate China or more unscrupulous partners should the United States demure, Pakistan successfully wrests expansive military, economic, and other assistance from the United States. The United States does usually get something from these transactions (e.g., ability to launch U-2 flights or more recently drones, logistical support for operations in Afghanistan), but it is far from obvious that the benefits have been worth the costs paid, particularly when the transactions permit Pakistan to further invest in programs that undermine US interests (nuclear proliferation, sustained support for Islamist proxies).

Such rent seeking has been a fundamental and enduring component of the army's strategy in engaging with the United States. As Schaffer and Schaffer (2011) note, these selectively structured narratives have permeated Pakistan's political and bureaucratic organs, and there are virtually no differences among the ways these different state organs utilize them, particularly when engaging with the United States. Fundamentally, information asymmetries allow Pakistan's strategy to succeed. Whereas Pakistani officials—in and out of uniform—know their brief, their American counterparts are more often than not ingénues lacking even a rudimentary understanding of Pakistan's history or that of US–Pakistan relations. In contrast to poorly prepared Americans who engage Pakistanis, Pakistani negotiating partners are able to call on a rich and extensive, though selective, narrative of American perfidy to bamboozle their American interlocutors, many of whom have been dealing with Pakistan for only a brief time.

Schaffer and Schaffer (2011) describe this process as the perfected art of the guilt trip. The authors, both diplomats with unusual depth and experience in South Asia, offer a concise description of this strategy: "in important negotiations, Pakistan usually tries to create a sense of obligation on the part of the United States, or to nurture and intensify the fear that failure to honor Pakistan's requests will lead to disastrous consequences for US interests" (3). They observe that Pakistani military officers are particularly likely to paint a picture of American betrayal, highlighting past cessations of US military aid, the arming of India in 1962, and repeated US failures to help Pakistan in its time of need. "[Pakistan] Army officers tend to assume that the Americans they are dealing with know little about Pakistan. More than any other Pakistan government representatives, military officers start their presentations to US officials with a textbook brief on India-Pakistan and, in some cases, Pakistan–Afghanistan relations. They do not deviate from their cleared script, which in any case is probably close to their personal convictions" (65). Pakistan's general "institutional culture of avoiding blame or self-criticism shows up at the negotiating tables as a strong tendency to blame the army's problems on the United States, and to try to make their American counterparts feel guilty about Pakistan's difficulties" (ibid.).

In other words, Pakistanis in and out of uniform use this revisionist history to convince the United States that it owes Pakistan for its past failures. This approach is obviously most efficacious during times when the United States believes it needs Pakistani help to pursue its interests in the region, notably during the anti–Soviet War and the so-called Global War on Terror. It is imperative that the Pakistani military—and civilian—personnel who deal with the United States believe this history. This is one of the reasons the military has invented so many tools for controlling key narratives both within and beyond the barracks.

Without extensive research on how Chinese leaders contend with Pakistan's strategic culture, an effort that is beyond the scope of this volume, it is difficult to say whether the Pakistanis are equally successful at convincing the Chinese that they "owe" Pakistan. This is doubtful, however. In recent years, Pakistan's military and civilian officials have busily obscured China's repeated failures to act as the all-weather friend— a reliable alternative source of aid and support should the United States abandon Pakistan—that Pakistani defense publications claim it to be. Aparna Pande (2011) observes that when it comes to China's failures Pakistani officials constantly devise various rationales for China's inability (as opposed to unwillingness) to assist Pakistan. During the Cold War, Pakistanis forgave China's shortcomings because it was also threatened by the Soviet Union. Other analysts seek to diminish the scope of China's commitments in the first place; for example, some observers suggest that Yahya and Bhutto misinterpreted China's pledge of "support for Pakistan's independence and state sovereignty," which they argue did not convey some sweeping security guarantee for all of Pakistan but rather simply meant that China supported a strong and independent West Pakistan (124).

Pakistan's military authors seem unable to contemplate the possibility that China will not strongly support Pakistan in a future Indo-Pakistani conflict. As Pande (2011) notes, the reason for this refusal is obvious: should Pakistan's military establishment admit this possibility, it would have to accept that China, like the United States, engages Pakistan on terms that advance its national interests. But the depiction of China as Pakistan's all-weather friend has allowed Pakistan to wrest greater resources from the United States.

It is unlikely that the United States will call Pakistan's bluff and deprive it of this essential bargaining tool. Doing so would require American diplomats who are as thoroughly knowledgeable as their Pakistani counterparts (Evans 2012). Even if more American negotiators were able to counter the narrative presented by their Pakistani counterparts and prevent them from employing their preferred strategy of playing on American desire to make restitutions for past failures, it is not obvious that they would do so. American policymaking—toward Pakistan generally and the army in particular—is always aimed at quickly completing transactions to meet short-term needs. Finally, as we will discuss in Chapter 8, the introduction of nuclear weapons provides further insurance that the United States will not walk away from South Asia.

CHAPTER 8

Seeking Security under a Nuclear Umbrella

While Pakistan's nuclear weapons program is generally associated with its army, it was actually initiated by a civilian, Zulfiqar Ali Bhutto, in the late 1960s. In fact, while Bhutto tried to build a constituency around nuclear weapons, Pakistan's army leadership opposed them: Gen. Ayub Khan was convinced that they would be a costly boondoggle and would alienate Pakistan's Western partners. Moreover, he naively believed that, should India acquire a nuclear bomb, Pakistan could simply buy one "off the shelf" from one of its allies (Bhutto 1979; Khan 2012a). With the army opposed, the nuclear weapons program did not gain momentum until after the loss of East Pakistan in the 1971 war and Bhutto's subsequent ascendance. India's (risibly named) Peaceful Nuclear Explosion of 1974 gave a further impetus to Pakistan's quest for a nuclear deterrent. After Bhutto was deposed in 1977, the program fell into the hands of the army, where it has remained ever since.

While India and Pakistan did not become overtly nuclear until their reciprocal tests in May 1998, Pakistani and Indian analysts alike concede that their mutual possession of nuclear weapons technology and later weapons had long influenced Pakistani and Indian behavior during crises. Nuclear proliferation pessimists (Kapur 2008; Krepon and Gagne 2001; Tellis et al. 2001) argue that the nuclearization of the subcontinent has enabled low-intensity conflict, whereas proliferation optimists such as Ganguly (2008) attribute the lack of any major conflicts in the region to the nuclear deterrent. In many ways this debate offers a faux binary. As the evidence I present here demonstrates, nuclear weapons do encourage risk-taking behavior (especially by Pakistan but also by India, e.g., during the Brasstacks crisis), which precipitates conflict. However, they also ensure that these conflicts do not escalate to a general war where nuclear use becomes possible.

In this chapter, I argue that Pakistan's army sees nuclear weapons as a way of enabling risk-taking vis-à-vis India in two key, interrelated ways. First, Pakistani defense writers cited here agree that it is not an objective assessment of

Pakistan's capabilities that deters India but rather ambiguity about what Pakistan can or would do in a crisis. This allows Pakistan to engage in risk-seeking behavior (or to support terrorist elements that engage in such behavior) as part of its effort to change the status quo: the Pakistan Army believes that India is likely to put up with such "minor" trespasses for the sake of preventing a crisis that could go nuclear. In other words, Pakistan's nuclear deterrent increases the cost of Indian action.

Second, Pakistan's nuclear weapons ensure that the United States, among others, will become involved in efforts to prevent any regional crisis from becoming a full-fledged conflict. The United States is motivated to intervene for two reasons. First, it remains a preeminent US interest to prevent a nuclear exchange in South Asia. Second, the United States understands that when weapons are assembled, mated to their delivery vehicles, and forward deployed they become vulnerable to theft. In recent years, Pakistan has publicly claimed that it is pursuing tactical nuclear weapons in response to defense and civilian cooperation between the United States and India and Indian efforts to develop a doctrine of limited war (Hoyt 2001; Smith 2013). American concerns about preventing a nuclear war and precluding theft during dispersal are even more acute when tactical nuclear weapons enter the picture. Nuclear weapons thus confer a degree of immunity, shielding the army from bearing the full costs of its adventurism; in fact, in the army's eyes this is the main benefit of Pakistan's nuclear program.

In this chapter, I first present a brief historical overview of Pakistan's nuclear program. Next, I examine the concerns about proliferation that arose in response to Abdul Qadeer Khan's nuclear black market and detail Pakistan's doctrines of nuclear development, deployment, and employment. Then, I review the ongoing debate over the role nuclear weapons play in the region's frequent crises. Employing a modified version of Kapur's (2007) analytical approach, I offer an assessment of nuclear weapons' effects on the crisis-proneness of the Indo-Pakistan security competition. I conclude with a discussion of the implications of the nuclear program for Pakistan's strategic culture and the army's revisionist agenda as regards India.

Origins of Pakistan's Nuclear Program

Pakistani writers correctly note that, relative to India, Pakistan was late to develop nuclear weapons. Pakistan's nuclear program was founded in the mid-1950s under the Atoms for Peace Initiative begun by US president Dwight D. Eisenhower. The Pakistan Atomic Energy Commission (PAEC) was founded in 1956, but its chair reported to a "relatively junior officer in the Ministry of Industries and had no direct access to the chief executive," and the civilian bureaucracy "had an apathetic attitude" toward the endeavor from the start (Khan 2012b, 8; see also

Khan 2012a). The effort received some impetus in 1958, when Bhutto became the minister of fuel, power, and natural resources. During his term in office, which lasted until 1962, he lobbied for Pakistan to develop a robust civilian nuclear program and established the Pakistan Institute of Nuclear Science and Technology (PINSTECH) (IISS 2007; Khan 2012a, 2012b). Under Khan, Pakistan's military leadership was opposed to pursuing a nuclear weapon, viewing it as a costly misadventure that would estrange Western allies. He also believed that if India were to develop a nuclear bomb Pakistan could simply procure one from the United States or another ally (Cohen 2004; Khan 2012a, 2012b; Salik 2009).

In 1963, Bhutto began pushing for Pakistan to develop a nuclear weapons capability in his capacity as minister for foreign affairs. When China tested at Lop Nor in 1964, he was certain that India would follow suit (IISS 2007). He was not alone in this view. Maj. Muhammad Aslam Zuberi, writing in the *Pakistan Army Journal* in 1971 (three years before India tested its first nuclear device), expressed the fear that once India, with its conventional advantages, acquired a nuclear weapon, "Pakistan would be reduced to a status of an innocuous spectator....A nuclear India would automatically claim the right for leadership of areas in her immediate vicinity if not the entire non-communist Asia and Africa" (22–23).

Lt. Gen. (Ret.) Kamal Matinuddin (2002) argues that Bhutto's unwavering contention that Pakistan required nuclear weapons was confirmed by the 1965 war with India, which proved to Bhutto that Pakistan could not defeat India and also that Pakistan's international partners would not necessarily come to its aid. According to Matinuddin, Bhutto also learned an important lesson from Operation Gibraltar, which he initiated during his time as foreign minister. Bhutto concluded that it would be dangerous for Pakistan not to plan for a nuclear deterrent; this conviction was "reinforced by the fact that the United States had imposed an arms embargo on Pakistan after the Indo-Pakistan War of 1965" (83). In 1965, Bhutto declared that "Pakistan will eat grass or leaves, even go hungry" to acquire a nuclear weapon (IISS 2007, 15). Bhutto grew increasingly alarmed as India appeared to be "on the threshold of becoming nuclear as early as 1966" and wanted to signal to the Indians that "aggression against Pakistan would be a very dangerous affair. What he had in mind was an effective deterrent" (Matinuddin 2002, 83).

But Bhutto's vision did not bear fruit until after the 1971 war. Following the loss of East Pakistan, on December 20, 1971, Gen. Yahya Khan resigned in disgrace, transferring power to Bhutto, whose party had won the most West Pakistani seats in the 1970 elections. Bhutto, who became Pakistan's president, commander in chief, and first civilian chief martial law administrator, made it a top priority to energize Pakistan's lethargic nuclear weapons program. In January 1972, a few weeks after assuming power, he convened a meeting of several dozen of Pakistan's nuclear scientists in Multan. He requested the assembled scientists to produce a nuclear bomb within five years and placed Munir Ahmad Khan in charge of the PAEC, who reported directly to Bhutto (IISS 2007; Khan 2012a, 2012b; Salik 2009).

Following a similar path as India's scientific enclave, the PAEC initially opted to produce weapons-grade plutonium. This route was the obvious choice, both because M. A. Khan was a plutonium expert and because Pakistan would need only a reprocessing plant to recover the plutonium produced by its civilian reactor (IISS 2007). But Pakistan's reactor, the Karachi Nuclear Power Plant (KANUPP), was inefficient and was monitored by the International Atomic Energy Agency (IAEA). Furthermore, as Pakistan came to be seen as a proliferation risk, western states began to restrict its access to reprocessing technology.

Given the uncertainty of the plutonium option, Pakistan also began to pursue a "less technically efficient, but more discreet, highly enriched uranium (HEU) route as early as 1974" (IISS 2007, 17). This shift was facilitated by two events. The first, which took place in 1974, was India's Peaceful Nuclear Explosion in the Pokhran Desert in Rajasthan. The second was the appearance on the scene of Abdul Qadeer Khan, often referred to as A. Q. Khan. He received a PhD in metallurgy from a Belgian university and was employed by a Dutch member of the Urenco enrichment consortium, where, among his other responsibilities, he translated a German report on centrifuge technology. In September 1974, he wrote to Bhutto and offered his services to help Pakistan acquire a nuclear weapon. Bhutto apparently requested that Khan stay in the Netherlands a while longer so that he could acquire more technical knowledge. In 1975, however, having attracted the suspicion of the Dutch government, Khan fled to Pakistan with stolen centrifuge designs. Given Bhutto's dissatisfaction with PAEC's progress, Khan persuaded Bhutto to grant him direct control of the centrifuge project (IISS 2007; Khan 2012a, 2012b; Matinuddin 2002).

By this time, a number of trends that began in the mid-1960s had converged, rendering the nuclear option irresistible to Pakistan. First, "the asymmetry in power with India prompted Pakistan to search for potential counterweights other than the conventional sources" (Hilali 2011). Second, during Pakistan's wars with India, the United States had avoided providing robust support to Pakistan. This led Pakistani military writers to question the credibility of conventional, much less nuclear, security guarantees (Zuberi 1971). Third and fourth, "the creation of Bangladesh in 1971 and India's nuclear explosion in 1974 once again brought to the surface Pakistan's fears of India's hegemonic designs" (Hilali 2011, 200; see also Anwari 1988; Durrani 1989; Sarwar 1995). Bhutto shared the army's fundamental threat assessment: the worst threat to Pakistan's sovereign existence was India, either acting alone or in alliance with external actors, such as the United States (which Bhutto viewed with suspicion). Bhutto believed that a nuclear weapons program would allow him to manage two problems simultaneously: it could counter India's military might while also providing a counterweight to Pakistan's overly powerful military, which justified its expansive claims to resources and to interfering in affairs of governance with reference to the ever-present Indian threat. By pursuing a nuclear weapons program, Bhutto could both "reduce the army's role and could face India on an equal footing" (Cohen 2004, 80). Bhutto worked assiduously to keep the military far from the program to ensure civilian control over national security and domestic politics in general and the nuclear program in particular. The military, however, did provide the resources the nuclear program required (Khan 2012a, 2012b).

In 1979, during the imprisonment that ended with his execution, Bhutto wrote *If I Am Assassinated*, an autobiography-cum-manifesto defending his actions and policies. He explains that he—not the military—achieved Pakistan's nuclear weapons capability, reminding Pakistanis that he sent hundreds of young men to North America and Europe for training in nuclear science and that he success-fully negotiated the purchase of a five-megawatt reactor from France. He bitterly decries the United States for prevailing on France to cancel the sale, a success that Bhutto attributes to the untrustworthiness of the military's regime and to American perfidy. Bhutto even argues that the United States (for the sole purpose of preventing Pakistan from acquiring a reprocessing capability) facilitated the coup that overthrew him by backing his political rivals and encouraging the army. Bhutto further insinuates that his opponents, in and out of uniform, sold him, and Pakistan's nuclear future, to the Americans.

Consistent with Bhutto's claim that it was he, and not the army, who had tire-lessly sought to secure Pakistan's future vis-à-vis India by developing nuclear weapons, he asserts that at the time he became president, Pakistan lagged behind India by some 20 years but that by the time he was deposed in 1977, Pakistan was on the threshold of possessing a nuclear capability. He brags that even though Christian, Jewish, and Hindu civilizations as well as the Communist powers had acquired a nuclear weapons capability, it was he who delivered this capability to all of Islamic civilization (Bhutto 1979; Khan 2012a).[1]

The Jimmy Carter Administration was disquieted by nuclear developments in Pakistan. In late 1978, European intelligence had obtained evidence that Pakistan was constructing a uranium enrichment plant, a claim confirmed by the US Central Intelligence Agency (CIA). In April 1979, Carter found Pakistan to be in violation of the Symington Amendment, which prohibits most forms of US assistance to any country that traffics in nuclear enrichment technology or equip-ment outside of international safeguards (Hathaway 2000; Salik 2009).[2] After the 1979 Soviet invasion of Afghanistan, however, Carter's national security advi-sor, Zbigniew Brzezinski, told him that the United States would need to secure Pakistan's support to oust the Soviets and that this would "require...more guar-antees to [Pakistan], more arms aid, and, alas, a decision that our security policy cannot be dictated by our nonproliferation policy" (Coll 2004, 51). The Carter Administration held its proliferation concerns in abeyance, offering Gen. Zia ul Haq a $400 million aid package which would be equally divided between economic and military assistance. Shrewdly, Zia rejected it and denounced it as "peanuts." As Brig. (Ret.) Naeem Salik (2009) notes, Zia "patiently waited for over a year after the Soviet military intervention in Afghanistan, and so was able to obtain a more substantive deal than the 'peanuts' offered by Carter. Zia and his advisors had correctly appreciated the outcome of the US Presidential elections and were willing to bide their time to see off the last few months of the Carter presidency" (97).

Zia's gambit paid off. President Ronald Reagan, who took office in January 1981, pledged $3.2 billion dollars in economic and military assistance over five years (Salik 2009). Aid began to flow to Pakistan in 1982. But before Zia agreed to the terms of the US aid package, he asked the United States to clarify its position on Pakistan's nuclear program, which Zia defended as a sovereign right. Secretary of State Alexander Haig "made it clear that the nuclear issue would not be the 'centerpiece' of [the] US-Pakistan relationship. He did, however, strike a note of caution, that in case Pakistan were to conduct a nuclear test, the Congress would not allow the Reagan administration to cooperate with Pakistan in the manner in which it intended" (98). A tacit agreement was thus established between the Zia and Reagan governments: "the Reagan administration could live with Pakistan's nuclear programme as long as Islamabad did not explode a bomb" (ibid.).

This understanding was even codified in US law: while the US Congress passed Reagan's assistance plan and even agreed to a six-year waiver of the Symington Amendment sanctions that had been in force since 1979, it also strengthened legislation banning all economic and military assistance to any country that exploded a nuclear device (Hathaway 2000; Peterson Institute for International Economics 2012; Salik 2009). However, US discomfiture with Pakistan's nuclear progress did not disappear. Nonproliferation elements within the US Congress, US Department of Defense, and intelligence agencies continued to worry about Pakistan's intentions and capabilities (Kux 2001). In December 1982, a *Newsweek* article alleged that Pakistan was covertly procuring technology for nuclear reprocessing from around the world. The report also claimed that a Pakistani scientist had stolen enrichment technology from Holland and that China had supplied Pakistan not only with uranium but also with blueprints for a nuclear bomb. While Pakistan denied those charges, the State Department instructed its personnel in Pakistan to offer "no comment" on the article (Salik 2009; US Department of State 1982). By June 1983, the US Department of State reported, "There is unambiguous evidence that Pakistan is actively pursuing a nuclear weapons development program" and expressed confidence that Pakistan's considerable progress was due in part to extensive Chinese assistance. Adding to the growing anxiety, in April 1984 A. Q. Khan told the Urdu-language newspaper *Nawai-i-Waqt* that Pakistan could successfully enrich uranium to weapons grade. In June of that year, US Senator Alan Cranston claimed that Pakistan would be able to produce "several nuclear weapons per year" and chastised the State Department for downplaying the danger posed by Pakistan's program (Kux 2001, 275).

But despite the mounting concerns of American nonproliferation advocates, in Congress and beyond, Pakistan remained critical to the fight to repel the Soviet Union from Afghanistan. Thus, the Reagan Administration had to forge a new understanding with Zia. Vice President George W. Bush traveled to Pakistan in May 1984 to secure Zia's assurance that Pakistan would not acquire a nuclear device as long as he remained the head of state. Bush emphasized that " 'exploding a device, violating safeguards, or reprocessing plutonium would pose a very diffi-cult problem for the Reagan administration' and that the nuclear issue continued to be a very sensitive topic in the United States" (Salik 2009, 106). Salik concludes from these interactions that the "Americans knew about Pakistan's enrichment effort, and were prepared to live with it, as long as Pakistan did not detonate a nuclear explosive device" (Salik 2009, 106). But reports in the media contin-ued to insinuate that Pakistan was pursuing a bomb. In 1984, for example, A. Q. Khan told the *London Times* that "Pakistan has broken the western countries' monopoly on the enrichment of uranium" (107). In September 1984, President Reagan warned Zia of serious consequences if Pakistan were to enrich beyond 5 percent (Kux 2001, 276). This was perhaps the first time that the United States had presented Pakistan with a clear red line rather than simply repeating bland statements that Pakistan should not detonate a device. But Zia's response was noncommittal (Kux 2001; Salik 2009).

In the fall of 1984, the Reagan Administration again sought congressional approval for an aid package that promised Pakistan $4 billion over six years. But many members of the US Congress believed that Zia was dissembling regard-ing his country's nuclear aspirations (Kux 2001), and nonproliferation propo-nents such as Senator John Glenn criticized the administration for its soft line on Pakistan's nuclear program. Zia, for his part, insisted that Pakistan had the right to continue its program (Cronin et al. 2005). To resolve this impasse, in July 1985 the US Congress passed the Pressler Amendment (Kux 2001). While many Pakistani and even American commentators believe that the legislation was meant to pun-ish Pakistan, it was actually written in consultation with the Pakistani Ministry of Foreign Affairs, and its passage was welcomed by Pakistani leadership as a vic-tory for Pakistan (Haqqani 2007). Under the terms of the Pressler Amendment, prior to the United States providing assistance to Pakistan, the US president had to certify both that Pakistan did not possess a nuclear weapon and that provision of the assistance would materially diminish the likelihood that Pakistan would develop such a weapon (Schaffer and Schaffer 2011). The legislation essentially moved the US red line from an enrichment threshold—which Pakistan had likely already surpassed—to possession of an actual nuclear weapon. This was indeed a major—if temporary—victory for Pakistan.

As the anti-Soviet jihad in Afghanistan began to wind down with the sign-ing of the Geneva Accords in spring 1988, it became increasingly difficult for the US administration to make the annual certification, which would allow aid to continue flowing to Pakistan. In November 1988, Reagan certified that Pakistan did not possess a nuclear weapon. However, he warned Congress that "as Pakistan's nuclear capabilities grow, and if evidence about its activities continue to accumulate, this process of annual certification will require the President to reach judgments about the status of Pakistani nuclear activities that may be difficult or impossible to make with any degree of certainty" (Gordon 1989). A year later, in a letter to the US Congress, then president Bush wrote that he had "concluded that Pakistan does not now possess a nuclear explosive device" but also that "Pakistan has continued its efforts to develop its unsafeguarded nuclear program" (ibid.). In October 1990, Bush refused to make this annual certification, and the sanctions that had been deferred since April 1979 were once again imposed—to Pakistan's utter astonishment (Schaffer and Schaffer 2011).

Throughout the 1990s, Pakistan continued to make progress in its nuclear weapons program and in developing delivery vehicles. In May 1998, India conducted a set of nuclear explosions in the Pokhran Desert, and shortly thereafter Pakistan reciprocated. Some commentators believe that the Indian tests afforded Pakistan an opportunity to decisively demonstrate its own nuclear capabilities and neutralize India's conventional advantage (Salik 2009; Tellis et al. 2001). Pakistan is currently believed to have some 90–110 nuclear weapons, but this could well be an underestimate, since it continues to produce highly enriched uranium (HEU) at a rate of 100 kilograms per year and its HEU-based warheads require between 15 and 20 kg of HEU each (DeYoung 2011; Kerr and Nikitin 2012; Norris and Kristensen 2007; Sanger and Schmitt 2011). Pakistan is also producing plutonium for plutonium-based warheads (Kerr and Nikitin 2012).

Pakistan's delivery vehicles include aircraft (including modified F-16s and Mirage Vs) under the control of its air force as well as several surface-to-surface missile systems controlled by the army. Pakistan has roughly three ballistic missiles that are thought to be nuclear capable, including the solid-fuel Hatf-III (Ghaznavi) with a range of 300–400 km, the solid-fuel Hatf-IV (Shaheen) with a range in excess of 450 km, and the liquid-fuel Hatf-V (Ghauri) with an approximate range of 1,300 km (Kerr and Nikitin 2012). Pakistan is also developing the Hatf-VI (Shaheen-II), which will have a range of 2,000 km, and, as discussed herein, is working to build tactical nuclear weapons that can neutralize Indian doctrinal evolution toward limited war. Consistent with this objective, in 2011 the Inter Services Public Relations (ISPR) announced that Pakistan had successfully developed and tested a "Short Range Surface to Surface Multi Tube Ballistic Missile Hatf IX (NASR)." According to the press release, the NASR will "add deterrence value to Pakistan's Strategic Weapons Development programme at shorter ranges. NASR, with a range of 60 km, carries nuclear warheads of appropriate yield with high accuracy, shoot and scoot attributes. This quick response system addresses the need to deter evolving threats" (ibid.).

Proliferation under the Eye of the State

The Pakistan Army's control over Pakistan's nuclear program engenders considerable alarm. Given Pakistan's track record of proliferation under the auspices of A. Q. Khan, some analysts fear that nonstate actors may acquire Pakistan's nuclear technology, materials, or knowledge. Others worry that the army may split, with one faction providing nonstate actors with nuclear technology, materials, or know-how. And given the army's long history of sponsoring Islamist terrorists, observers of the Pakistan Army incessantly fret that these weapons may fall into the hands of terrorists. Of equal concern is the prospect that the state will deliberately choose to proliferate for strategic reasons. Given the gravity of these fears, it is useful to address them briefly here.

It is well-known that A. Q. Khan's nuclear black-market activities were initially focused on importing technology and materials into Pakistan, but at some point these networks were mobilized for export. From the 1980s (and possibly earlier) through 2002, Khan exported nuclear technologies and materials from Pakistan to North Korea, Iran, and Libya (Kerr and Nikitin 2012). Considerable controversy persists over whether Khan operated as a rogue actor or with state sponsorship. On one hand, Pakistani military commentators like Feroz Hassan Khan (2012a, 2012b)—a retired brigadier in Pakistan's Strategic Plans Division (SPD), now at the Naval Postgraduate School—maintain that A. Q. Khan exploited bureaucratic fissures and that in the absence of a single nuclear command authority he was able to conduct his illicit nuclear commerce without state approval. Salik (2009), his successor at SPD, further alleges that Khan's supposed misdeeds have been exaggerated, presumably by Indian and American analysts, as part of a cynical attempt to "malign the Pakistani nuclear programme and the country itself" (9).

Others reject these exculpatory accounts. Matthew Kroenig (2010) at Georgetown University, for example, concludes that A. Q. Khan's nuclear exports were "state-sponsored by any reasonable definition of the term" (135). The Government of Pakistan entered into formal agreements with North Korea, Libya, and Iran and facilitated the export of the nuclear materials by providing help with advertising, shipping, security, and other logistical details. Either the Pakistan Air Force provided military air assets to make the deliveries or the Government of Pakistan chartered aircraft for this purpose (Kroenig 2010; see also IISS 2007).

Given the "indisputable evidence that the Pakistani state actively supported and authorized the sensitive nuclear transactions" (Kroenig 2010, 136), the question arises as to why the state would sponsor such transfers. The reason is strikingly simple. All of the states to which Pakistan made such transfers were foes of the United States and all were threatened by American power projection. Gen. Aslam Beg, who served as Benazir Bhutto's army chief, feared that with the collapse of the Soviet Union, the United States—now the unrivaled power in South Asia and the Middle East—would be able to threaten Pakistan's interests. Beg believed that the "increased global diffusion of nuclear weapons could lead to a multipolar world that would better suit Pakistan's interests" and thus that by exporting nuclear technology and materials to America's foes, Pakistan could constrain American military power (142).

Pakistan has undertaken significant efforts to fortify its nuclear command, control, and security arrangements since the revelation of A. Q. Khan's activities. In perhaps one of the best descriptions of Pakistan's peacetime security arrangements, Christopher Clary (2010) details why popularly rehearsed doomsday scenarios generally do not reflect the important progress Pakistan has made in securing its nuclear arsenal. Pakistan's efforts to improve its command and control arrangements began in 1998 (prior to the May nuclear tests) when Army Chief Jahangir Karamat appointed Maj. Gen. Khalid Kidwai to head the newly formed Evaluation and Research Cell. This group offered several recommendations for improving nuclear command and control arrangements, foremost among them the creation of a National Command Authority (NCA), composed of military and civilian leadership, a secretariat to support the NCA, and specialized strategic forces. Later that year, Prime Minister Nawaz Sharif abruptly dismissed Karamat, appointing General Pervez Musharraf in his place. It was Musharraf who brought the NCA into being in 2000, along with the SPD, the NCA's secretariat, and the specialized strategic forces (Clary 2010; Khan 2012a, 2012b).

The SPD is tasked with protecting Pakistan's strategic assets both from internal and external threats; after all, if Islamist terrorists could infiltrate Pakistan's program, so could Indian, American, or even Israeli intelligence agencies. SPD provides a three-tiered security perimeter for nuclear facilities, which includes investigating and monitoring personnel, physical countermeasures, and counterintelligence teams tasked with identifying potential threats (Clary 2010; Khan 2012a, 2012b). Despite these improvements, however, the challenge remains daunting. It should be recalled that in August 2007 the United States Air Force lost track of half a dozen nuclear warheads for 36 hours, despite decades of work on command, control, and security arrangements (Weitz 2007). Kidwai, now retired from the army but still the head of SPD, estimated that some 70,000 people work in Pakistan's nuclear complexes. This figure includes some 7,000 to 8,000 scientists, of whom perhaps 2,000 possess critical knowledge. As Clary notes, Pakistan has also adopted measures, such as the equivalent of a two-man rule and some crude but functional versions of permissive action links, to protect against accidental use of weapons (Clary 2010).[3]

As Clary (2010) notes, most of these improvements have the greatest impact during peacetime when the weapons are not mated to their delivery systems and when the bombs themselves may not be assembled. Recent, but hotly contested, accounts of Pakistani security measures have caused alarm among analysts of Pakistan. SPD routinely moves its nuclear weapons among the 15 or more facilities where they are maintained. Such movement is regular and is done for several reasons. On occasion, they require maintenance. However, Pakistan also moves these assets around to make it more difficult for American or Indian intelligence agencies to discern their locations. Sometimes components are moved via helicopter or road. According to Jeffrey Goldberg and Marc Ambinder (2011), Pakistan does not use armored or well-defended convoys to transport these assets; rather, SPD prefers to "move material by subterfuge, in civilian-style vehicles without noticeable defenses, in the regular flow of traffic. According to both Pakistani and American sources, vans with a modest security profile are sometimes the preferred conveyance." If this were not hair-raising enough given the prevailing insecurity in Pakistan and looming fears about the potential for jihadists to seize the assets, the authors further report the assessment of a senior US intelligence official, who said that SPD has also "begun using this low-security method to transfer not merely the 'de-mated' component nuclear parts but 'mated' nuclear weapons" (ibid.).

In addition to these persistent concerns about command and control and quotidian movements of the components if not warheads during peacetime, during periods of heightened escalation a whole new set of apprehensions emerge. During escalation, Pakistan (and probably India as well) begins to assemble the warheads and mate them with their delivery systems. As the conflict continues to intensify, these assembled and mated weapons may be forward deployed, both to prepare for employment and to ensure a retaliatory capacity. At this point, concerns about theft or other unauthorized transfer become far more plausible than when the weapons are in their peacetime posture. Furthermore, as Clary (2010) cautions, when the assembled and mated nuclear weapons are forward deployed, the "two-man" rule may be insufficient to prevent accidental or unauthorized launch amidst the heightened strain of emergency. Finally, as part of its deterrence strategy Pakistan deliberately cultivates ambiguity as to the precise redlines that would precipitate nuclear escalation.

In fact, the risks that accompany its nuclear program are part of Pakistan's calculations about the utility of the weapons in the first place. As I describe in Chapter 9, Pakistan relies on nuclear weapons to restrain India, both by raising the costs of Indian action against Pakistan and by bringing in the United States and other actors to manage the conflict once it starts. The United States and other international actors are motivated to intervene for two reasons. First, preventing an Indo-Pakistan conflict that could potentially escalate to a nuclear confrontation remains an important US objective. The resulting devastation would be unprecedented, and few countries other than the United States would be in a position to help manage the humanitarian disaster that would follow. Pakistan also knows that analysts in US intelligence agencies, as well as those working in nonproliferation billets in other US organizations, understand this problem. Consequently, Pakistan expects the United States to intervene early in a crisis to preempt assembly, mating, and forward deployment of nuclear weapons in an effort to diminish the potential for theft or misappropriation. American fears of command and control failures have intensified as Pakistan has continued its pursuit of tactical nuclear weapons. Surely, inciting such anxieties was one of Pakistan's objectives in doing so in the first instance.

Nuclear Doctrine and Use

Pakistan's nuclear weapons are India-specific. Pakistan's army has long believed that only an "openly deployed rudimentary nuclear system would adequately compensate for India's superiority in conventional military power," and thus the army views the acquisition of nuclear weapons not only "as an urgent response to equalize the disturbing balance of power in South Asia but [also] as a long-term option for the stable security of the country" (Hilali 2011, 203; see also Cheema 2000). There were some debates about timing. Maj. Gen. Asad Durrani (1989), who served as the head of Pakistan's Inter-Services Intelligence (ISI) from 1990 to 1992, argued in 1989 that Pakistan should defer overt nuclearization: if Pakistan nuclearized first, it would legitimize India's making similar moves. He explained that "under these circumstances [including a fallout with the US], perhaps the best policy is the one that the others believe Pakistan is following: the policy of deterrence through nuclear ambiguity, in the footsteps of Israel and South Africa" (21). But he concedes that "ultimately, Pakistan will have to acquire a credible nuclear capability, if Pakistanis wish to achieve an honorable relationship with India" (22). Ultimately, Pakistan followed this course, becoming an overt nuclear power only after India had taken that step.

While India insists that it will adhere to a rigorous "no first-use policy," Pakistan has refused to give up its "right of first-use of nuclear weapons" both because it has no confidence in India's no first-use declaration and because doing so would undermine the deterrent value of its weapons (Cheema 2011). Rather than pursuing a massive and unaffordable nuclear arms race, Pakistani defense writers argue that Pakistan should have a minimal, credible deterrent (Anwari 1988). Zuberi (1971) explains that the concept of a nuclear deterrent does not mean "matching India bomb for bomb or missile for missile" and advocated following in the footsteps of France or Great Britain (23). Lt. Col. Israr Ahmad Ghumman (1990), after detailing the varied weaknesses in Pakistan's military system, argued that with a nuclear deterrent, "Pakistan can cut down her large conventional forces and cut down the defence expenditures while ensuring her safety" (34). Speaking more recently and with greater authority, Kidwai, in an address at the US Naval Postgraduate School, explained that Pakistan's nuclear policy has four key features: deterring all forms of external aggression; deterring a counterstrike against strategic assets; stabilizing strategic deterrence in South Asia; and investing in conventional and strategic deterrence methods (Cheema 2011, 60).

Peter Lavoy (2008), a longtime observer of Pakistan's nuclear weapons program who served as the principal deputy assistant secretary of defense for Asian and Pacific Security Affairs and now as the acting assistant secretary of defense for Asian and Pacific Security Affairs, observes that Pakistan's strategic deterrence strategy has five major components. The first is an effective conventional fighting force capable of confronting a wide array of subconventional and conventional threats. Pakistan's armed forces believe that its conventional military capabilities are the "first line of defense against Indian conventional military attack and the backbone of the country's overall deterrence posture" (131).

Pakistan has consistently employed this logic, with considerable effect, to secure conventional military assistance from the United States. Not only was this an important argument during the rule of Ayub and Zia, but also it was used during the Musharraf era and even into the most recent period of civilian governance. According to leaked US cables, the US effort in 2006 to provide Pakistan with F-16s was motivated by arguments of "symbolic, and perhaps emotional, salience" but were "directly tied to the existential threat Pakistan perceives from India. India maintains a substantial, and growing, conventional military advantage over Pakistan; Islamabad's nuclear and missile programs reflect its need to counterbalance this advantage. An enhanced F-16 program also has deterrence value by giving Pakistan time and space to employ a conventional, rather than nuclear, reaction in the event of a future conflict with India" (*Hindu* 2011). Perhaps counterintuitively, as the weaker power in the India–Pakistan dyad Pakistan believes that it must have "escalation dominance at all rungs of the military ladder—from low-intensity conflict to conventional war and all the way to nuclear war" to ensure survivability (Lavoy 2008, 133–134). Pakistan's defense planners believe as an article of faith that if "they allow India to seize the advantage at any level of violence—from subconventional through conventional to nuclear warfare—then India is sure to exploit it," endangering the security of the Pakistani state (134; see also Anwari 1988; Sarwar 1995; Zuberi 1971).

The second component is a minimum nuclear deterrence doctrine and force posture. Zafar Iqbal Cheema (2000) notes that Pakistan "did not have a nuclear declaratory, deployment, or employment doctrine" prior to the May 1998 nuclear tests (159). Although Pakistan has since disclosed significant features of its command and control arrangements and has laid out crude redlines, it has deliberately kept these aspects of is deployment and employment doctrine opaque. Even though Pakistan has not formally declared its doctrine for nuclear employment, it does have "operational plans and requirements for nuclear use integrated within its military war-fighting plan" (Lavoy 2008, 134). The army's principal task is to deter an Indian conventional military attack, first through conventional military preparedness and ultimately—if necessary to prevent the loss or occupation of Pakistani territory or the decimation of Pakistan's military forces—through the use of nuclear weapons (Lavoy 2005, 283).

Bhutto laid out the basic lineaments of Pakistan's nuclear employment doctrine in December 1974, explaining that "ultimately, if our backs are to the wall and we have absolutely no option, in that event, this decision about going nuclear will have to be taken" (Lavoy 2008, 135). In April 2002, at the height of the 2001–2002 standoff with India, Musharraf made a similar statement. Although he called nuclear weapons a "last resort" and asserted that he was "optimistic and confident that we can defend ourselves with conventional means," he conceded that nuclear weapons could be used. "If Pakistan is threatened with extinction, then the pressure of our countrymen would be so big that this option, too, would have to be considered" (Lavoy 2005, 283).

Kidwai, in an extraordinarily rare exposition of Pakistan's nuclear doctrine, explained that Pakistan's nuclear weapons are India-specific and that Pakistan would resort to nuclear use "if the very existence of Pakistan is at stake" (Lavoy 2005, 283). In the event that deterrence should fail, he identified four conditions under which Pakistan would employ nuclear weapons: "a) India attacks Pakistan and conquers a large part of its territory (space threshold); b) India destroys a large part either of its land or air forces (military threshold); c) India proceeds to the economic strangling of Pakistan (economic strangling); d) India pushes Pakistan into political destabilization or creates a large-scale internal subversion in Pakistan (domestic destabilization)" (ibid.).

While it is well-known that Pakistan's military understands preventing India from either destroying or overwhelming Pakistan as the primary purpose of Pakistan's nuclear weapons, the precise activities that would meet these criteria are kept purposefully ambiguous to buttress their deterrent force. After all, if Pakistan were to articulate these red lines more clearly, India could simply modify its strategic plans and operations accordingly. Pakistan's refusal to articulate the Indian actions that would prompt it to employ nuclear weapons increases the uncertainty in the "minds of Indian policymakers as to how far they can press Pakistan on the battlefield" (Lavoy 2008, 137). Zia himself explained this in the late 1980s, when he said "that ambiguity is the essence of deterrence. The present programs of India and Pakistan have a lot of ambiguities, and therefore in the eyes of each other, they have reached a particular level, and that level is good enough to create an impression of deterrence" (Giles and Doyle 1996, 147). Beg similarly explained that a "state of uncertainty and ambiguity...serves as a meaningful deterrence" (Documentation: General Mirza Aslam Beg's Major Presentations 1991, 41). Cultivating this ambiguity, and thus strategic instability, is a central element of what Kapur (2007) describes as the instability–instability paradox that characterizes Indo-Pakistan security competition.

The third component of Pakistan's deterrence, in Lavoy's (2008) inventory, is a sufficient stockpile of nuclear weapons and delivery systems to assure a second strike capability (131). Although Pakistan does not publicize its force requirements, it asserts that it wants only the minimum necessary deterrent (based on Pakistani assessments of India's own capabilities and assumptions about the nature of future contingencies). Pakistan aims to have a stockpile large enough to permit dispersal to multiple launch sites and thus ensure a second-strike capability (ibid.).

Pakistani calculations about the necessary size and nature of its deterrent have changed in recent years, due to post-2005 developments in the US–India relationship. Pakistani defense officials frequently note with alarm that the 2005 Indo-US civilian nuclear deal as well as other defense-related aspects of the Indo-US strategic partnership have "put Pakistan's policy of a 'minimum credible deterrence' under an intense pressure" (Khan 2011, 1). Specifically, the nuclear deal and the concomitant India-specific amendments to the Nuclear Suppliers Group will afford India access to new "vistas of dual-use technology and other scientific avenues between India, US, and other members of the [nuclear suppliers] cartel" (ibid.). Cheema (2011), then with Pakistan's National Defence University, maintains that "the most fundamental international developments affecting the minimum credible deterrence posture of Pakistan" include "the Indo-US Nuclear Agreement" and the "Nuclear Suppliers Groups' unconditional exemption," which allows India to purchase certain nuclear material that was formerly prohibited (44–45). Cheema's principal fear is that the agreement will allow India to purchase uranium on the international markets for its civilian nuclear program, freeing up its own supply of uranium for exclusive use in its weapons program (ibid.).

These developments, along with India's search for ways to punish Pakistan for, and compel it to abandon, its terrorist misadventures in India while still avoiding escalation, has prompted senior Ministry of Defense analysts like Khan (2011) to argue that Pakistan should "reinvigorate its present nuclear doctrine of a 'minimum credible deterrence,' to an offensive-deterrence posture" (1). Khan also believes that Pakistan could "bolster its limited conventional capability and accord it a confidence by inducting a whole series of tactical nuclear weapons into its strategic calculus and, to deploy them along its borders with India" (ibid., 2). Such "doctrinal restructuring by Pakistan would induce 'restraining effects that are based on the fear of nuclear war'" (ibid., 3, citing Art 1985). Inducting such tactical nuclear weapons would allow Pakistan to have escalation dominance in a crisis with India, perhaps to deter a crisis in the first place, and—if necessary—wage and win a conflict with India. Given the conventional forces Pakistan confronts, Khan argues that "Pakistan should focus on maintaining the balance of terror with appropriate strategy against its adversary—India, instead of indulging in conventional forces number game" (7). He argues that "any transparency [in Pakistan's nuclear doctrine]…would only undermine Pakistan's ability to deter India's calibration of 'Cold Start Strategy' or limited conflict thinking, to its peril" (25).

A fourth component of Pakistan's deterrence posture is the survivability of its strategic forces, including the ability to withstand conventional military attacks, sabotage, and at least one Indian nuclear attack (Lavoy 2008, 131). Since the beginning of Pakistan's nuclear weapons program, Pakistan has feared that the United States, India, or even Israel may act to eliminate or degrade Pakistan's strategic capabilities. (As noted already, Bhutto [1979] believed that the United States deliberately undermined his government because of his insistence on acquiring a nuclear weapons capability.)

These general suspicions crystallized into specific fears on at least four occasions in the 1980s. In 1982, in the wake of Israel's 1981 attack on Iraq's Osirak reactor, Pakistani press reports suggested that India might seek to attack Pakistan's nuclear facilities. Chari et al. (2001) conclude that while "there is no evidence…of plans for such an attack….Indian officials certainly discussed it and Pakistan definitely raised it with the Americans" (24). Two years later, Pakistani officials, citing Canadian and European intelligence reports, concluded that Israel was planning a strike on the nuclear facility at Kahuta and that Indian or Soviet help would be necessary for such an attack. Zia even made a speech before Pakistan's legislature in which he announced that India might launch an Osirak-like attack on Pakistan. US officials also believed that an Indo-Pakistan war, or at least an Indian attack, was imminent and took immediate steps to prevent such a crisis. This same drama played out again in mid-1985, when Pakistani officials again came to believe that India was preparing a strike against Kahuta (ibid.). In 1986, a démarche from Moscow indicating that it would take "retaliatory steps if Pakistan were to acquire a military nuclear capability" caused Pakistan once again to fear an attack (26).

Pakistan registered similar concerns about potential attacks in the early 1990s, as the Pakistan-supported Kashmir uprising intensified, and again after India's May 1998 nuclear tests. On this latter occasion Pakistan cited both the provocative statements of the Indian ruling party (the Hindu nationalist Bharatiya Janata Dal/Party, or BJP) and ISI reports that an Israeli aircraft had been identified in India while Pakistan was preparing for its own tests (Cheema 2000). Pakistan's assessment that its strategic assets would come under attack was a major factor in Musharraf's 2001 decision to work with the United States, as he explained during his September 19, 2001 speech. The most recent spasms of nuclear fears were set off by the December 13, 2001 attack on India's parliament, which spawned the 2001–2002 crisis, and by the November 2008 Lashkar-e-Taiba attack in Mumbai (Lavoy 2008). As noted already, Pakistani analysts such as Salik also suspect that the A. Q. Khan affair has been exploited to make Pakistan's program appear illegitimate and thus to legitimize an attack on Pakistan's nuclear capabilities.

Chari et al. (2001), however, note that many of these alleged threats to Pakistan's nuclear program actually had the effect of encouraging the United States to support Pakistan during a period (the 1980s) when Washington was growing increasingly alarmed by the Pakistani nuclear program. They suggest that this behavior fits "into a larger Pakistani strategy... of linking its own nuclear program (at the highest policy level) with an American commitment to defend Islamabad" (27). This judgment likely extends to the post-2001 crises as well. Both periods were marked by an American dependence on Pakistan that out-weighed even its deep concerns about Pakistan's nuclear program.

Given these concerns about the vulnerability of its program, which date back to the 1970s, Pakistan has prioritized the "survivability of all nuclear production facilities, weapons and missile storage complexes, and potential launch facilities" (Lavoy 2008, 148). While Pakistan does not publicly disclose the various efforts it has taken to ensure survivability, Lavoy suspects that they likely include "an emphasis on mobile systems; camouflage; hardened and deeply buried facilities; and strict compartmentalization of information about the plans, locations, and standard operating procedures governing the movement, deployment, and pos-sible employment of strategic forces" (149).

The fifth and final component of Pakistan's deterrence strategy is a responsive strategic command and control system. Whereas India has tended to be more open about operational and doctrinal concerns and reticent about command and control systems, Pakistan has sought to portray itself as being open about the latter while avoiding significant disclosures about the former. Important land-marks in the development of Pakistan's command and control system include Musharraf's 2000 formation of a National Command Authority, located at the Joint Services Headquarters, with the SPD serving as its secretariat. In the same year, Musharraf established related bodies such as the Employment Control Committee, which provides policy direction and exercises authority over strate-gic forces, and the Developmental Control Committee, which is responsible for optimizing the "technical and financial efficiency of the entire program to imple-ment the strategic force goals set up by the Employment Control Committee" (Lavoy 2008, 150; see also Clary 2010; Khan 2012a, 2012b). As discussed already, the A. Q. Khan imbroglio motivated Pakistan to seriously reconsider its command and control arrangements (Clary 2010; Khan 2012a, 2012b; Lavoy 2008; Salik 2009).

Risk-Taking under an Expanding Nuclear Umbrella

Pakistan's pursuit of nuclear weapons was motivated by the shift in the conven-tional military balance and the loss of half of Pakistan's population and territory that followed the 1971 war. India's 1974 test of a nuclear device further motivated

Pakistani efforts (Cheema 2000). While the deterrent value of nuclear weapons is clear, they play several other strategic roles that may be less evident.

At one level, Pakistan's nuclear weapons are political tools. Pakistan has used its nuclear weapons and the threat of nuclearized conflict to draw international attention to the Kashmir dispute. By most accounts, this strategy has worked. Following the 1999 Kargil War—the first conventional conflict after the overt nuclearization of the subcontinent—President Bill Clinton remarked that Kashmir was the most dangerous place on earth (Iype 2000). In the wake of the 9/11 terror attacks and the subsequent 2001–2002 Indo-Pakistan crisis, US Secretary of State Colin Powell expressed concern about the role the Kashmir dispute played in preventing a lasting peace in the region (Ahmed 2002). Barack Obama focused on Kashmir and the importance of resolving the dispute during his 2008 presidential campaign. Upon winning the presidency, he appointed senior US diplomat Richard Holbrooke as a special envoy to the region. After swift, skilled Indian protest, Kashmir was removed from Holbrooke's portfolio, and he became known as the special representative to Afghanistan and Pakistan without any reference to India or Kashmir (Wax 2009).

With the Obama Administration's increased focus on the US-led war in Afghanistan, scholarly and analytical attention returned to the problem of Kashmir, with prominent analysts such as Barnett Rubin and Ahmed Rashid (2008) arguing that Pakistan will not stand down its jihadi proxies in Afghanistan until the Kashmir question is resolved to its satisfaction. Rubin and Rashid argue that the United States should pursue a regional grand bargain that would bring a wave of peace from Afghanistan into Pakistan and Indian-administered Kashmir. (Notably, Rubin became an adviser to Richard Holbrooke.)

Pakistan continues to raise the issue of Kashmir at every opportunity. For example, in November 2012 Pakistan's foreign minister, Hina Rabbani Khar, explained to the 39th Session of the Organization of Islam Countries Council of Foreign Ministers that Kashmir remains a constant source of conflict between India and Pakistan (*Dawn* 2012). A few months earlier, Pakistan's president Asif Ali Zardari gave a similar speech before the UN General Assembly (*Rediff* 2012). By constantly raising the specter of a nuclear war for the Himalayan territory, Pakistan continues to draw international attention to this matter (despite the fact that any such war would likely be begun by Pakistan).

Nuclear weapons clearly have also facilitated Pakistan's use of low-intensity conflict. Stephen Cohen (1984) observed that a Pakistani nuclear bomb, "besides neutralizing an assumed Indian nuclear force, would provide the umbrella under which Pakistan could reopen the Kashmir issue" (153). Pakistan's nuclear deterrent facilitates low-intensity conflict and proxy war in two important ways. First, by cultivating ambiguity as to its employment and deployment doctrine and the redlines that would precipitate Pakistan's use of nuclear weapons, Pakistan hopes to deter any militarized Indian response either to territorial incursions by regular or irregular Pakistani troops or significant activity against Indian interests by Pakistan-supported or Pakistan-based terrorists. Pakistan assumes that given its possession of nuclear weapons and, increasingly, tactical nuclear weapons, India is simply likely to "tolerate" these nuisances rather than risk a full-scale war (Khan 2011).

Second, nuclear weapons facilitate Pakistan's ability to wage low-intensity conflict by drawing in international actors who work to limit a conflict once it begins (Lavoy 2005; Tellis et al. 2001). The United States is the most important target audience for the maneuvers. For example, during the 2001–2002 crisis Washington pressured New Delhi not to escalate, thus shielding Pakistan from direct military threat, either as a deterrent to future terrorist attacks or a punishment for the December 2001 attack that sparked the crisis. Musharraf explained in April 1999 that while the likelihood of a conventional war was virtually zero, due to the presence of nuclear weapons, proxy wars were not only possible but in fact very likely (Kargil Review Committee 2000). The Pakistan military seems to have concluded that nuclear weapons have "reduced the prospect that India will use force to solve regional problems" and "enhance[d] Pakistan's foreign policy leverage vis-à-vis India and its other neighbors" (Cheema 2000, 180).

Equally important, Pakistan's nuclear weapons make it virtually impossible for the United States to simply abandon Pakistan to suffer the consequences of its own vices. Lt. Col. Masood Navid Anwari (1988) admits that the warnings (issued by the United States and others) against Pakistan developing a nuclear weapon appear "menacing at the moment." However, "once we do develop the capability it would be very difficult for the major powers to execute these threats." He explains that in "international politics, it is easy for a major power to abandon a weak partner but very difficult to abandon a strong one. Pakistan as a 'free lance nuclear power' will be far more important to the interests of these major powers, and contrary to what they may be saying, they would rather keep nuclear Pakistan in their fold than abandon her" (47). Anwari's predictions have been proven by time. No matter how vexed Washington may be with Islamabad, it will be loath to simply abandon Pakistan, both from fear of a nuclearized Indo-Pakistan crisis but also the ever-lingering threat of proliferation to either states or nonstate actors.

In many ways, its possession of nuclear weapons has "warped judgments about Pakistan's real strengths and weaknesses.... Strategically, it enabled Pakistan to put off the day of reckoning with India, by providing the appearance of equality between the two states" (Cohen 2004, 80–81). It has also fostered a false belief that Pakistan is a "technologically advanced country" (ibid.) that can stand up to India and the West. In contrast to Pakistan's narrative of self-reliance, sacrifice, and honed expertise, the historical record suggests that Pakistan's program was "a triumph of espionage and assistance from a friendly power, not the product of a technologically advanced state" (80).

There is also evidence suggesting that Pakistan has drawn unjustified conclusions about the efficacy of its nuclear program. Whereas many analysts believe that Pakistan had an actual bomb by the early 1990s (Cheema 2000; Cohen 2004; Lavoy 2005, 2008), prominent Pakistani writers such as former foreign minister Abdul Sattar (2007) insist that Pakistan had a nuclear device as early as 1983 (148). Khan (2012a) claims that Pakistan had "large bombs that could be delivered...by a C-130" as early as 1984 (189).

Equally important, the Pakistan Army believes that it had a deterrent capability long before even 1990. The Pakistan Army believes that Pakistan's nuclear capabilities were critical in deterring Indian attacks in 1984–1985 (during India's Punjab crisis), 1986–87 (during the Brasstacks crisis), 1990 (during the Indo-Pakistan Crisis of 1990), 1999 (during the Kargil War), and 2001–2002, implying that Pakistan believed in the deterrent power of its nuclear program before India or the United States (Cheema 2000; Lavoy 2005; Sarwar 1995). This suggests a perhaps unique dimension of the deterrent relationship between India and Pakistan: it is the presence of ambiguity about capability rather than an actual capability that may matter more to the cost–benefit analysis of both states. Pakistani military writers believe that as long as India cannot rule out a Pakistani nuclear attack with certitude it will be deterred from initiating a conflict. To some degree, this also implies that the Pakistan Army views India as being fairly pusillanimous. Indeed, the various essays discussed in this volume provide ample evidence that this is the case.

Until the nuclear tests of 1998, many analysts described the deterrence between India and Pakistan as *existential deterrence*, using the term introduced by McGeorge Bundy. Under the various conditions of opacity and uncertainty, the mutual deterrence calculation of India and Pakistan did not rest on "relative capabilities and strategic doctrines, but on the shared realization that each side is nuclear-capable, and thus any outbreak of conflict might lead to a nuclear war" (Kumar 2007, 240–241). Scholars of South Asia have coined other expressions that slightly modify this concept, including George Perkovich's notion of *nonweaponized deterrence* and Jasjit Singh's *recessed deterrence* (ibid.). Varun Sahni (2009) describes Pakistan's beliefs that its capabilities deterred crises in the 1980s and refers to the lingering but indecisive role of nuclear weapons as "nuclear overhang" (22). According to Sahni, "The notion of nuclear overhang is certainly more expansive than the concept of existential deterrence—i.e. we could conceive of a degree of nuclear overhang even without existential deterrence" (23).

Paul Kapur (2007), mobilizing Correlates of War (COW) Militarized Interstate Disputes (MID) data, concludes that nuclear weapons have made South Asia more conflict prone. His analysis can be situated within the body of scholarship proffered by deterrence pessimists (Krepon and Gagne 2001), who focus on the destabilizing effects of nuclear weapons in South Asia. Proliferation pessimists contend that nuclear weapons enable low-intensity conflict; in contrast, proliferation optimists point out that full-scale war has not broken out between India and Pakistan (Ganguly and Kapur 2010; Joeck 1997). For a debate about nuclear weapons and stability beyond the specific context of South Asia, see Sagan and Waltz (2002). In many ways, these positions offer a false binary. A perusal of the history of the region and of the literature suggests that both positions have merit: while nuclear weapons facilitate subconventional and low-intensity conflict, they do operate to prevent either side from escalating to a full-scale war.

Kapur (2007) explains Indian and Pakistan behavior using what he calls the instability–instability paradox. He correctly notes that the literature on deterrence in South Asia frequently uses the stability–instability paradox to explain the way nuclear weapons enable conflict at the low end of the spectrum (Jervis 1989; Krepon and Gagne 2001; Snyder 1965) and also that this application of the paradox is inapt. First, the stability–instability paradox was born in the context of US–Soviet Union deterrence: having achieved strategic *stability* by making very clear which actions would elicit a nuclear response, the two states were encouraged to pursue low-intensity conflict in other theatres. The United States was particularly motivated to establish strategic stability because the Soviet Union was the revisionist state and was also conventionally superior in Europe. The Soviets would not logically expect the United States to risk a nuclear war if the Soviets invaded Europe. Thus, the United States posted American troops and nuclear weapons in Europe to signal to the Soviet Union that it would indeed respond with nuclear weapons should the Soviet Union seek to disrupt the status quo there.

Kapur (2007) sagaciously identifies two problems with scholars' widespread application of this concept to South Asia. First, while the Soviet Union was the revisionist and conventionally superior state, in South Asia Pakistan is revisionist but conventionally inferior to India. Second, Pakistan is able to perpetrate low-intensity and subconventional conflict precisely because of the strategic instability it deliberately fosters by obscuring its redlines. Using COW MID data, Kapur concludes that it is in fact strategic *instability* that fosters conventional instability in the subcontinent.

As Bad as It Gets?

I replicated Kapur's analytical methods with a few important modifications derived from my engagement with Pakistan's defense literature. Upon doing so, I found that nuclear weapons have been even more destabilizing than Kapur's analysis suggests. Like Kapur, I included all international disputes between India and Pakistan between 1972 and 2002 that appear in the COW militarized interstate disputes database to evaluate the impact of nuclear weapons upon all conflict proneness.[4] (It makes little sense to use data prior to the 1971 war and the loss of East Pakistan.) I employ the same recoding as implemented by

Kapur: I updated the COW data to include both of the 2001–2002 crisis by adding an observation for this conflict, which lasted from December 2001 to October 2002; amended the dataset's information on the 1986–1987 Brasstacks crisis by adding an observation that spans from December 1986 to March 1987; and remedied the dataset's failure to handle the Kargil War appropriately by separating it from the earlier Kashmir dispute and adding an observation for a three-month dispute in 1999 (Kapur 2007). I also used Kapur's definition of a *dispute month* as "each month in which a militarized dispute" took place between India and Pakistan (19).[5]

Where my analytical methodology diverges from that of Kapur is in the periodization of nuclearization in South Asia.[6] I define the nonnuclear period as the period from 1972 to April 1979. I suggest that April 1979 (when the United States applied Symington Amendment sanctions) should be taken as the starting point for Pakistan's nuclearization.[7] Taking this as the start date accounts for the extensive Pakistani interference in the Sikh insurgency beginning in the early 1980s and the Pakistan Army's enduring belief that its latent nuclear capability deterred Indian aggression throughout the 1980s as well as during later crises. (Recall that India tested a rudimentary device in 1974.) Second, I define the incipient nuclear period as May 1979 (when sanctions were first applied) to August 1990 (when the Pressler sanctions came into effect). I define the de facto (or covert) nuclear period as September 1990 to May 1998. Finally, I define the overt nuclear period as June 1998 onward.

I cross-tabulate the conflict months by nuclear status (Table 8.1) to demonstrate that peace was far less likely in the de facto and overt nuclear periods than in the nonnuclear period and that conflict was more likely (by two orders of magnitude) in all three nuclear phases. In Table 8.2, I calculate the conflict rates for these four periods. In the nonnuclear period (1972–1979), I find a conflict rate of 0.011 (compared with 0.139 for Kapur's nonnuclear period, 1972 to 1989). The conflict rate steadily increases: rising from 0.011 to 0.265 as one moves from the nonnuclear period toward the incipient period, then again to 0.710 as one moves to the de facto period, and finally to 0.818 in the overt nuclear period.[8]

Other factors, quite apart from the expanding nuclear umbrella in both India and Pakistan, likely have contributed to the conflict proneness of the region. Looking at the period from 1972, what is most striking is that during two of the nuclear periods (per my coding scheme), the United States and Pakistan were closely allied, with the United States using a variety of military and economic assistance packages to encourage Pakistan to support US strategic goals. For much—but not all—of what I have coded as the incipient nuclear period, the United States provided considerable military and economic support to Pakistan to reward it for helping the United States (along with Saudi Arabia, among others) to repel the Soviets from Afghanistan. Similarly, for some of the overt nuclear period (i.e., after September 2001) Pakistan was again the beneficiary

Table 8.1 **Cross-Tabulations of Conflict Months by Nuclear Status**

Hostility Status		Nuclear Status				Total
		Nonnuclear Period	Incipient Nuclear Period	De Facto Nuclear Period	Overt Nuclear period	
Peace	Months	87	100	27	10	224
	% of Peace Months	38.84%	44.64%	12.05%	4.46%	100%
Dispute	Months	1	36	66	45	148
	% of Dispute Months	0.68%	24.32%	44.59%	30.41%	100%
Total	Months	88	136	93	55	372
	% of Total Months	23.66%	36.56%	25%	14.78%	100%

Notes: Pearson chi-squared = 143.2426, chi-square < 0.000.

Source: In-house data tabulations of the Correlates of War Militarized Interstate Disputes data employing the same database modification as Kapur (2007), using new coding scheme.

Table 8.2 **Conflict Rate by Nuclear Period**

Nuclear Level	Time Period	Number of Conflict Months per Period	Total Number of Conflict Months in Period	Conflict rate = (Number of Conflict Months/All Months in Period)
Nonnuclear period	Jan. 1972–April 1979	1	88	0.011
Incipient nuclear period	May 1979–August 1990	36	136	0.265
De facto nuclear period	September 1990–May 1998	66	93	0.710
Nuclear period	June 1998–onward	45	55	0.818

Source: In-house data tabulations of the Correlates of War Militarized Interstate Disputes data employing the same database modification as Kapur (2007), using a revised coding scheme.

of substantial US military and economic aid meant to induce Pakistan to assist the United States in Afghanistan. Given that Pakistanis easily appreciated how much the United States relied on Pakistan during these two periods, Pakistan no doubt assumed that it had greater leeway to engage in adventurism in India, fully expecting that the United States would pressure India to back down in any crisis. Thus, US involvement is a compounding factor that may have encouraged Pakistan to ever more boldly pursue revisionist behavior.

Conclusions and Implications

Nuclear weapons have figured in the Pakistan Army's strategic culture since the 1970s, even though Bhutto prioritized them much earlier. Once the army endorsed nuclear weapons, Pakistan could further innovate at the lower ends of the conflict spectrum, as I discuss in Chapter 9. In the army's vision, nuclear weapons can neutralize its larger conventional foe, render Pakistan immune from Indian punishment for its use of low-intensity and subconventional conflict, and ensure that the United States cannot walk away from Pakistan despite the former's disquiet with the latter's outrages. In this chapter, I present strong evidence that Pakistan's nuclear weapons program encourages risk-seeking behavior, which has often led to crises, be it interstate war or militarized disputes short of war. Pakistan's nuclear weapons have distorted Pakistan's perception of its own capabilities, encouraged it to think of itself as India's peer competitor on equal terms, and afforded a degree of impunity for its risk-seeking behavior.

In this chapter, I focus mostly on the history and empirical data about nuclear weapons and conflict in South Asia. The data I present here suggests important correlations between crisis proneness in the region and the expanding nuclear umbrella. In Chapter 9, I provide evidence from Pakistan's defense literature that strongly suggests not only a correlation but also a causal relationship between nuclearization and conflict. In Chapter 9, I also exposit the ways Pakistan Army writers have explicitly imagined subconventional conflict as a military tool for changing the status quo. Many defense writers explicitly concede that Pakistan's nuclear umbrella enables Pakistan to engage in this risky behavior. After all, as we have seen, defeat for Pakistan is not defined using the terms of game theory. For the Pakistan Army, defeat is defined as succumbing to India and accepting its hegemonic position, in South Asia and beyond. As long as Pakistan can continue challenging India, it has not been defeated. Pakistan's nuclear weapons play a critical role in enabling Pakistan to continue denying and retarding India's rise.

CHAPTER 9

Jihad under the Nuclear Umbrella

Scholars and policy analysts alike generally agree that Pakistan first began employing Islamist militants as a tool to prosecute its foreign policy objectives during the anti-Soviet jihad. Under Zia ul Haq, Pakistan, working with the United States, Saudi Arabia, and others, built a massive system for producing Islamist insurgents, generally known as mujahideen, to fight the Soviets in Afghanistan. According to this narrative, when the Soviets formally withdrew from Afghanistan, Pakistan redeployed its battle-hardened operatives to Kashmir. Even prominent intelligence officials repeat this truncated version of Pakistan's jihad history. For example, Bruce Riedel (2008), who spent nearly three decades at the US Central Intelligence Agency (CIA) and who has advised four presidents on Middle East and South Asian affairs, wrote, "The contemporary jihadist terrorist movement has its origins in the war against the Soviet occupation of Afghanistan in the 1980s" (Riedel 2008, 32; see also, e.g., Coll 2004; Evans 2000; Markey 2007; Nasr 2004; Stern 2000).

Despite this narrative's staying power, it is simply inaccurate. Most important, it understates the duration of Pakistan's involvement with nonstate actors generally and Islamist militants in particular. Pakistan has relied on nonstate actors to prosecute its policies in Kashmir since its birth in 1947. In that year, the nascent state mobilized numerous lashkars, or tribal militias, from Pakistan's Pakhtun areas to invade and seize Kashmir, while the maharaja of Jammu and Kashmir vacillated on whether to join India or Pakistan (Nawaz 2008a, 2008b). Furthermore, Pakistan's efforts to employ political Islamists, and later Islamist militants in Afghanistan, began as early as the late 1950s. State-supported Islamist militants fought Bangladeshi insurgents in East Pakistan during the crackdown that spawned the 1971 war (Haqqani 2005). By the early 1990s, Islamist militants had seized the lead in Kashmir from ethnic Kashmiri insurgents. And while Pakistan is most known for instrumentalizing Islamist militants, in the late 1970s and early 1980s it also supported Sikh insurgents in India as well as other ethnic insurgencies in the northeast of India.

This chapter examines Pakistan's use of proxy fighters in India, Afghanistan, and, in some cases, within Pakistan itself. The first section draws on the Pakistan

Army's professional publications to map the history of that organization's conception of asymmetric conflict, variously described as *jihad, guerrilla war, people's war, infiltration*, and the like. The second section gives a brief overview of the militant milieu in Pakistan, presenting evidence that as Pakistan unfurled its nuclear umbrella in the late 1970s, it ever more boldly supported militants in India and elsewhere. Finally, while most studies of Pakistan's proxies focus on their utility in external operations, the third section presents a case study of one organization, Lashkar-e-Taiba (LeT), to show how it serves not only external but also domestic goals.

Origins of Pakistan's Use of Nonstate Actors

Cohen was the first to observe that Pakistan's interest in proxy war may have been piqued by the training in counterinsurgency it received from the United States during the 1950s, when the two countries were formally allied against the communist threat (Cohen 1984, 2004). Although the defense pacts also applied to China, for reasons described in Chapter 7, Pakistan was largely exempted from participating in any US effort to contain Chinese communism. Pakistani defense writing of the 1950s suggests that engagement with the US military led the Pakistan Army to adopt important doctrinal shifts toward guerrilla warfare. Ironically, while the purpose of this training was to enable Pakistan to suppress and defeat insurgencies, Pakistani officers increasingly concluded that the army could successfully wage a people's war, perfect the art of infiltration, or even develop its own people's army as a second line of defense against India (Cohen 2004).

The Pakistan Army General Headquarters began publishing the *Pakistan Army Journal* in 1957. In its early years, the journal frequently augmented the indigenous contributions with articles from foreign military journals, especially those of the Commonwealth of Nations and the United States. In its first volume, the *Pakistan Army Journal* republished an article by Maj. C. H. A. East (1958) titled "Guerrilla Warfare," which had originally appeared in the *Australian Army Journal*. East writes that "the aim of guerrilla warfare is to reduce the effectiveness of the opponent's regular forces. It is achieved best when conducted behind enemy lines to further specific large-scale operations by regular forces" (58). He argues that three concepts must be carefully appreciated to prosecute guerrilla warfare successfully: terrain; political situation; and national conditions. The ideal terrain, according to East, includes mountains, especially with jungles and forests, or a flat area covered by swamp, jungle, or forest. Politically, guerrilla forces must enjoy the full backing of either their own or an allied government. This is necessary to ensure the requisite logistical support. They must also attract the political sympathies of the local civilian population, thus motivating the locals to provide them with loyal support. East explains that the civilian population in question should "possess a strong national desire for independence and a hatred of the enemy... [that] can be stimulated by propaganda, although this characteristic should be strong in areas which have been occupied by an aggressor" (ibid.). Finally, he suggests that the surest method of exerting control over guerrilla forces is to "provide the trained personnel and organization from the regular army to establish a formal guerrilla organization" (ibid.).

Since East (1958) was writing for an Australian military journal, his conclusions were meant to be relevant to his readership in Australia and perhaps other Commonwealth of Nations countries (of which Pakistan was one). But any reader familiar with the Kashmir dispute and Pakistan's precipitation of the 1947–1948 war would immediately understand the applicability of this article to Pakistan's Kashmir dilemma and thus its appropriateness for the pages of the *Pakistan Army Journal*. After all, Kashmir's mountainous and jungle-covered terrain matched East's ideal insurgent environment. Politically, guerrilla forces in Kashmir would enjoy the full support of the Pakistani state, including the military. Pakistan also believed that Kashmiri civilians would provide the fighters with moral and physical support and also that they were seething with hatred and resentment of their "occupier." Finally, the Pakistan Army could provide the kind of training, organization, and oversight of guerrillas that East recommends.

One year later, the *Pakistan Army Journal* reprinted an article written by E. Downey (1959) for an American publication, *Military Review*. Downey, reflecting conventional military wisdom at the time, fears that "most Americans will think this discussion [of guerrilla warfare] boringly academic since, as everyone knows, we have a Strategic Air Force equipped with nuclear weapons capable of wiping out an enemy in a few short hours" (26). But he argues that the possession of nuclear weapons and the ability to wipe out an adversary does not preclude the need to plan for guerrilla war. After all, "no matter how destructive the war, conventional or nuclear, chances are something will be left after it is over" (27). Having justified the case for American defense planners to prepare for a "day-after" scenario, when the country may need to pull itself together and sustain a guerrilla war, the author presents the foe in stark ideological terms: the communist for whom "absolute brutality, or use of any means, is in accord with the grandiosity, even the unreality of Communist aims" (29).

Downey (1959) describes several aspects of the day-after guerrilla war Americans may need to wage to secure their sovereignty. First, American war planners must accept the possibility that such a war will be necessary and thus the need for a planned resistance. After all, "any society which has lost a war to protect its social values should have devised some means of continuing its culture in the face of an organized social change. The answer is a resistance movement: guerrilla warfare" (30). In Downey's vision, the guerrilla organization is not only a military force but also a "transmitter of culture" (ibid.). He draws on the experiences of Communist China to derive lessons that will enable the United States to wage a protracted resistance without any outside help. In fact, only "guerrillas can operate in a country that is conquered by the enemy. Unlike a national army, they are not dependent upon supply bases and fixed communications" (33). Moreover, because they "choose the time and place of attack, they always hold the initiative. Melting into the countryside after an attack, they demoralize the enemy who faces a shadow army" (ibid.). Downey concludes with a call to develop a comprehensive theory of guerrilla warfare and to require training in guerrilla operations at US military institutions.

Downey's (1959) article offers many insights into Pakistan's security situation in the late 1950s. First, Pakistan faced (as it continues to face) a much larger Indian conventional army—thus, a day-after scenario, nuclear or no, could certainly have appeared relevant. Second, while overt nuclearization of the Indo-Pakistan dispute occurred decades after his article was published, Pakistan's defense writing of the period demonstrated an interest in nuclear war, even if the contexts of that conflict were theoretical or vague. Third, it should be recalled that India's nuclear program began much earlier than Pakistan's. Prior to independence, and with Jawaharlal Nehru's support, India's key nuclear scientist, Homi Bhaba, sought to "master the atom" because doing so "represented modernity, potential prosperity, transcendence of the colonial past, individual and national prowess, and international leverage" (Perkovich 1999, 13). Nehru's official position was that the program would have only peaceful uses. He told the Lok Sabha (India's lower house of parliament) in 1957, "We have declared quite clearly that we are not interested in and we will not make these bombs, even if we have the capacity to do so" (ibid.). While Nehru viewed military uses of nuclear technology with contempt, Bhaba had a different view and by the late 1950s was stating privately that he believed that India should build a nuclear weapon (ibid.).

Even though the Pakistan Atomic Energy Commission (PAEC) was founded in 1956, it was for many years a ramshackle operation. In contrast, by 1959, the Atomic Energy Commission of India in Trombay had over 1,000 scientists working on civilian nuclear technology (e.g., nuclear energy to power India's economic development). But India's nuclear policy began to change in the mid-1960s following the Sino-Indian war in 1962 and China's 1964 nuclear test. Nizamani (2000) describes this transition as a shift from a stance of "nuclear celibacy," marked by the general absence of public discussion of nuclear weapons, toward one of "nuclear ambiguity," in which the taboo surrounding weaponization "gave way to discussions about the potential deterrence value of nuclear weapons" (31).

Given that India's scientists were speaking privately about the need to develop a nuclear bomb while its leaders publicly sought a civilian nuclear capacity, it is not improbable that rumors of these discussions reached the Pakistan military or the intelligence agencies. Thus, a conventional day-after contingency was relevant to Pakistan's military planners, and also by the late 1950s Pakistan's defense planners may even have been considering a nuclear day-after scenario. In either case,

Downey's (1958) vision of a war in which (as Pakistanis would have imagined it) Pakistani partisans would fight an Indian occupier both to secure Pakistan's freedom and to ensure that its cultural values survived the period of occupation would have appealed to the army. Downey also offers thoughts on how a nation such as Pakistan could sustain a people's war in Kashmir, in Pakistan's view an occupied territory whose inhabitants must fight off the Hindu Indian occupier while retaining and transmitting Kashmiri cultural values (i.e., Islam and Muslim identity).

Throughout the 1960s, the *Pakistan Army Journal* presented the musings of Pakistani authors on topics such as the importance of infiltration, the need to develop a people's army for both defensive and offensive operations against India, and, increasingly, the utility of people's war. Several authors expand on the idea of infiltration as a "form of attack" (Akram 1964; El-Edroos 1961; Niazi 1964; Parker 1964). El-Edroos (1961), in the same way as the other authors, sees attack through infiltration as ideal for Pakistan because of Pakistan's presumed conventional inferiority to India. Not only is infiltration a "form of attack [that] is the most superior as it achieves the maximum results with the minimum of casualties," but also a "critical analysis of infiltration will indicate a technique of attack best suited to the native genius of our peasant-soldier and to our severely limited material resources" (3, 5). El-Edroos, in particular, places infiltration within the context of operations led by historical Muslim warriors, notably Zahir-ud-din Muhammad Babur Beg, also known as Babur.

Babur holds an important place in Pakistani history; he was a Central Asian conqueror and descendent of Genghis Khan and founded the Mughal Empire in South Asia. Although his tenure was short (1526–1530), Babur laid the foundations of a dynasty that persisted until 1857, when the British absorbed the remnants of the empire and overthrew the last Mughal ruler (Bahadur Shah II) because he supported the Indian partisans in the Indian Rebellion of 1857. Babur is associated with consolidating an enduring Muslim political system in South Asia. For proponents of Hindutva (Hindu nationalists), the tenure of the Mughals (and that of the various Muslim dynasties that pre-dated Babur) "is at the root of the myth of a continuous thousand-year old struggle of Hindus against Muslims.... The myth of the Muslim invader and Hindu resistance has also been deployed to prove that Hindutva represents the true, native, nationalism" (Basu et al. 1993, 2–4). In contrast, Pakistani textbooks date the origins of the Pakistani state to this same period, and invoking Babur in this context would be particularly meaningful to a Pakistani reader. It is worth noting that the Pakistan Army has even named its Babur cruise missile after him—the Babur is also known at the Hatf (ISPR 2012).

In 1964, Brig. A. A. K. Niazi offered his own exposition of infiltration. As he notes in his autobiographical account of the 1971 war, Niazi was commissioned in 1937 and served with distinction as a lieutenant during World War II, commanding a platoon that fought the Imperial Japanese Army on the Burma front (Niazi

2009). Niazi rose to the rank of lieutenant general and served as the last governor
and martial law administrator of East Pakistan. He was also the last unified commander of the Eastern Military High Command of Pakistan's armed forces, and
it was he who signed the instrument of surrender in December 1971, formally
concluding the 1971 war and finalizing Pakistan's loss of East Pakistan (ibid.).

Given Niazi's time in the China-Burma-India theater during World War II,
his 1964 discussion of infiltration reflects the effective use of the tactic by the
Japanese and Germans, Italians, Chinese, and North Koreans (Niazi 1964). He
explains that "infiltration implies by-passing of enemy posts by relatively small
parties which penetrate deep and unseen into the defences and converge at a
pre-designated objective" (3). He argues that when a military employs trained
troops for infiltration, with careful planning and in optimal terrain, weather,
and political conditions, it "will achieve much better results with far lesser
casualties than any other form of attack" (4). Niazi describes the "battlefields
of the future," where infiltration will be most useful, as fluid and characterized
by extended engagements. Units will be widely dispersed and not necessarily
in contact with one another. This battle space will be "a heaven for infiltrating
forces" (ibid.). In Niazi's system, strategic infiltration entails identifying weak
spots in the enemy's defenses, breaking through enemy lines deep into the rear,
and creating chaos among the opponent's forces. Both regular forces and elite air
troops can effectively infiltrate the foe in this way, and hilly, heavily wooded terrain (as in Kashmir) is well suited for such efforts. Tactical infiltration, like strategic infiltration, aims to cause maximum disorder among enemy forces while
minimizing casualties, but it involves fewer troops and a shallower penetration
of enemy lines.

Niazi (1964) expects that "small parties could infiltrate and lie down in the
enemy area and remain there for extended periods if required... [and] could send
or bring back valuable information about the enemy" (6). If large groups infiltrate
enemy defenses, they should ideally "create another flank or... cover an existing
flank" (ibid.). The infiltrating force can be used to contain or divert the enemy's
counterattack or even to deceive the enemy about the infiltrating army's intentions. Alternatively, he proposes that the "infiltrating force may be the main effort
and the deliberate attack merely a deceptive measure" (ibid.). Infiltration parties are ideally situated to conduct "harassing tasks," which include blowing up
targets (e.g., munitions dumps, bridges), changing sign posts, intercepting tele-
phone lines and providing fabricated orders, killing senior commanders, creating panic in the population (even creating a refugee problem which complicates
enemy operations), and attacking administrative headquarters and installations
(ibid.). Niazi argues that Pakistani troops should train for counterinfiltration as
well, since Indian planners may have similar expectations for the future battle
space. He concludes his essay with a final appeal: while "more advanced nations"
may not require an infiltration doctrine, "the adoption of these tactics by the

lesser developed nations like ours is a compelling necessity. It should resolve the dilemma that we face to-day" (9).

While Niazi (1964) does not specify the dilemma to which he alludes, it is quite likely that he is referring to India's moves to consolidate its control over Kashmir. Niazi served in the 1965 war, which took place less than a year after his article was published, as a colonel and commanding officer of the 5th Paratrooper, Punjab regiment, and was promoted to brigadier general during the conflict. As discussed elsewhere, the 1965 war began when Pakistan infiltrated irregular and regular troops into Kashmir in hopes of igniting an insurgency there and loosening India's grip on the territory. That ill-planned effort failed to bring about a wider insurgency, although it did spark the second Indo-Pakistan War. Niazi also offers many salient insights into the troubles brewing in East Pakistan, where the Indians did indeed infiltrate Indian forces as well as infiltrating and exfiltrating Bengali partisans whom they trained to fight the West Pakistanis.

In the same year that Niazi (1964) published his article, then colonel A. I. Akram offered his own views on the values and merits of infiltration. Akram retired from the Pakistan Army in 1978 as lieutenant general and became a military historian and founder of the Institute of Regional Studies (funded by Pakistan's Ministry of Information), serving as its president until his death in 1989 (Tikekar 2004, 34). His argument is similar to Niazi's, in that he agrees that infiltration is a form of offensive maneuver, is most appropriate when enemy forces are dispersed, and is ideal for Pakistan because the enemy—always India—is superior to Pakistan in terms of manpower and war materiel. He adds, however, what he calls a "moral dimension" to this tactic, arguing that irrespective of how cleverly the Pakistan Army maneuvers, the "objective [e.g., enemy defensive location] must have so much physical and *moral* strength applied against it before it will collapse" (Akram 1964, 1–2, emphasis added). Furthermore, because of the inordinate risk posed to the partisans who have infiltrated enemy lines, "infiltration is an operation for one who has the courage of a lion and the cunning of a fox" (2). Later he stresses that the operation should be sufficiently robust to "make the moral crisis, created in the enemy's rear, more effective" (4).

Akram (1964) never articulates what he means by moral strength. But given what we have already learned about Pakistan's strategic culture and the ways the army has historically viewed the conflict in Kashmir, we can assume that with *moral* he is referring to the rectitude of Pakistan's cause: liberating Kashmir from Indian occupation, seen as "immoral" in Pakistan's defense literature. Indeed, this view played an important role in Pakistan's decision to launch Operation Gibraltar in 1965.

A second set of concepts that figures strongly in Pakistani defense writing of the 1960s is the notion of a *citizens' army* and the concomitant *people's war* that such an army would wage. Defense writers argue for a critical study of these concepts and of those who have effectively employed them, in hopes that Pakistan will be able to develop doctrines that will allow it to "beat the enemy in conventional and unconventional warfare or in both" (El-Edroos 1962, 40; see also Adram 1971; El-Edroos 1964a, 1964b; Qazi 1964; Shafi 1964; Siddiqi 1964). Perusal of these writings underscores the relevance of Cohen's 2004 observation: while the United States was training the Pakistan Army to combat a people's war, Pakistan's defense writers were equally interested in understanding how Pakistan could wage one.

In 1964, for example, El-Edroos published a study of General Vo Nguyen Giap of the Vietnam People's Army, a principal commander in the fight against both the French, during the Indo-China war (1946–1954) and the United States during the Vietnam War (1960–1974). Giap commanded the North Vietnamese in significant battles during both of those conflicts, including Dien Bien Phu (1954) and the Tet Offensive (1968). Both the timing and subject matter of El-Edroos' article are interesting. Recall that in 1954, Pakistan and the United States signed the Mutual Defense Assistance Agreement. Pakistan joined the Southeast Asian Treaty Organization (SEATO) in the same year and the Central Treaty Organization (CENTO) in 1955. Pakistan withdrew from SEATO in 1971, after it concluded that membership (which could not prevent the loss of half of Pakistan's territory) offered few benefits. Pakistan remained a CENTO member until 1979, when the organization dissolved following the Iranian Revolution. While Pakistan has long complained that the United States did not support it in its 1965 war with India and even aided India in its 1962 war with China, the United States had no treaty obligation to defend Pakistan in 1965. Pakistan, however, did have an obligation under SEATO to participate in the Vietnam War, an obligation that it deftly dodged (see Pande 2011). Thus, El-Edroos' fawning treatment of the Vietnam People's Army is at odds with Pakistan's own treaty commitments.

El-Edroos (1964a) provides a flattering biographical sketch of Vo Nguyen Giap's early childhood and describes his "revolutionary zeal" as a "family characteristic" (10). He describes, in heroic terms, Giap's various victories against the French in several campaigns in the early 1950s, culminating in the French defeat at the Battle of Dien Bien Phu (March 13–May 7, 1954). The essay reads more like a biographical sketch of Giap than a thoughtful analysis of his strategies. Nonetheless, the author makes the case that the "entire concept and application of a Revolutionary People's War needs to be thoroughly studied and analysed, as this form of war could be effectively used by any weak country against a vastly superior and sophisticated enemy" (16). Later the same year, El-Edroos (1964b) published a similar study of Mao Tse-Tung and the Chinese People's Liberation Army. The implications of El Edroos' thesis are obvious: a people's war could be used effectively by Pakistan against India. But the author stops short of direct application, leaving it unclear whether he is envisioning a people's war to fend off a future Indian occupation of Pakistan or to dislodge the Indian "occupiers" of Kashmir.

In the same issue of the *Pakistan Army Journal,* Lt. Col. Shamsul Haq Qazi (1964) makes the case for what he calls a citizens' army. Qazi is concerned that even though Pakistan has few economic resources, it "enjoys the distinction of being one of the very few nations who spend the major portion of their public revenue on national security... spending 50 to 60 per cent of [its] budget on defence, whereas some very rich countries devote only 3 to 15 percent" (18). A poor country like Pakistan must divert funds needed for development to defend itself against India, which has been overtly hostile from the moment of Pakistan's inception. In addition to the threat from India, which he calls a second-class military power, Qazi also identifies the expanding Russian presence in Afghanistan as another source of concern. He acknowledges that in light of Pakistan's evolving threat environment it must revise its defense policies. But he wisely cautions that "even a policy of over-mobilization cannot keep pace with such monstrous armies as our northern neighbors possess" (19). Given Pakistan's current economic circumstances and prevailing threat environment, he argues, "there is a case for organising a strong citizen army for the effective defence of Pakistan" (ibid.).

In terms reminiscent of writers (discussed in Chapter 4) who argue that every Pakistani must be prepared to wage jihad, Qazi (1964) maintains that the Pakistan Army should prepare its defense plans on the assumption that "every Pakistani is a soldier"(20). This would allow Pakistan to avoid needless expenditures on a large peacetime force. In fact, the size of Pakistan's "standing regular army should be just enough to absorb the initial shock of attack and to provide the necessary leadership and training facilities for the citizen army" (ibid.). To prepare Pakistan for a defensive war against superior forces, citizens must become "soldiers in plain clothes, and the soldiers become citizens in uniform" (22). Qazi notes that in some measure this system already operates successfully in "districts close to tribal areas where villagers are given public arms for their collective defence" (ibid.). He concludes that the "terrain conditions in both East and West Pakistan are ideally suited for unconventional fighting" and that "unorthodox fighting behind the enemy lines can make this enemy build-up very expensive. Once our unconventional forces effectively cut the enemy's rear it would be comparatively an easy job for our reserve echelons to destroy the entrapped enemy" (23).

Qazi (1964) also discusses the utility of a citizens' army under nuclear conditions: "ground action by smaller combat teams would be a normality rather than an exception" and citizen armed forces would be ideal for such employment (24). In short, he concludes that although the shape and size of Pakistan's standing army are dictated by a "second rate military power, because of [Pakistan's] limited resources she is already suffering from the evils of over-mobilization" (ibid.). Moreover, even Pakistan's "presently over-mobilized standing army would be a mere drop in the ocean if ever a threat is posed from any of her powerful neighbours [Russia and China]" (ibid.). The most feasible way forward is thus a citizens' army that can provide more comprehensive protection against external aggression.

Maj. Mohammad Shafi (1964) offers the most detailed exposition of guerrilla warfare and its utility to Pakistan. Like other writers in Pakistan's defense journals, he extols the virtues of the guerrilla who can successfully "demoralize the regular army by inflicting steadily mounting losses on it, thus bleeding it white slowly but inexorably. Meanwhile, guerilla forces gather the necessary strength to give the exhausted army the finishing blow" (5). Shafi also notes that because guerrillas live off the land they are not plagued by the resupply issues that bedevil regular armies. He is so persuaded of the value of subconventional conflict that he believes it should actually take precedence over regular warfare, "especially in countries which lack the means of equipping and maintaining the costly and sophisticated regular forces of modern times" (7). (In this sense he tends to agree with Qazi's assessment.)

Shafi (1964) presents a list of "Essential Ingredients of Guerilla Success." The first is a worthy cause; mere wrath or indignation is inadequate. This echoes the "moral dimension" identified by Lt. Col. Muhammad Akram (1971). Second, Shafi thinks that difficult terrain, such as mountains, jungles, or even deserts, is best for such warfare. Third and fourth, guerrilla warfare requires a warlike people and a sympathetic population; fifth, it requires outside assistance. High-quality leadership and strict discipline are also prerequisites. While "in the secure environments of a regular army...a mediocre leader may fill the bill...in a guerilla force, only dedicated, self-sacrificing, and outstanding leadership can hold the mixed crowd together" (Shafi 1964, 10). Curiously, and perhaps recalling the experiences of the so-called tribal marauders of 1947–1948, he writes that the guerrilla leader must "reckon with a number of shady characters who may drift into his command not out of high idealism, but to satisfy base motives of loot and plunder" (ibid.). He recognizes that such characters may be "good fighters, but their rapacity must be held in check by the leader as otherwise they can antagonize the local population and weaken the popular goodwill on which a guerrilla movement leans so much for its survival and success" (ibid.). Finally, the subconventional combatant must learn proper guerrilla tactics.

As with other writers, Shafi (1964), too, stops short of specifying where or how Pakistan should employ guerrilla warfare. But Pakistan's past dalliance with guerrilla warfare in 1947–1948 and its similar misadventure in 1965 provide abundant clues to the theater Shafi had in mind: Indian-administered Kashmir. As has been discussed throughout, Pakistan's army, and even its general population, believes that Pakistan's position on Kashmir is moral and, moreover, that Kashmiris living under Indian occupation share this view. Second, the terrain of Indian-administered Kashmir is both mountainous and covered in jungle. Pakistan can augment the faltering Kashmiri rebels with its own warlike populations, who enjoy the support of Pakistan and supposedly of the Kashmiris themselves; Pakistan clearly can provide outside assistance as well as the necessary leadership and discipline to ensure that the subconventional combatant stays the course; and the Pakistan Army can provide training in the appropriate guerrilla maneuvers. In some measure, this is exactly what Pakistan sought to do in 1965.

It should be noted that the focus on infiltration and a people's war during this period was not exclusive to the military. After all, Z. A. Bhutto strongly supported the Operation Gibraltar misadventure, which escalated to a general war. And Aslam Siddiqi, a civilian bureaucrat in Ayub Khan's National Reconstruction Bureau, devoted a significant portion of his 1964 book *A Path for Pakistan* to a discussion of the utility of people's war. In fact, Siddiqi goes even further than the military writers by explicitly invoking the language of jihad to describe this people's war. *A Path For Pakistan* contains an entire chapter on jihad. Although it begins with three paragraphs on nonviolent jihad, the chapter spends far more time (some 15 pages) on militarized jihad (98–113).

Echoing the military writers' call for a citizens' army, Siddiqi (1964) demands a jihad in which "every able-bodied person is expected to participate. The penalty is rejection by God and replacement by another folk" (113). He chastises Carl von Clausewitz for allegedly failing to recognize the virtues of such a war and explains that had Clausewitz "studied the warfare conducted by the Prophet and his immediate successors, he might have changed his opinion. The prophet organized his 'people's war' which did consume the enemy totally" (113–114). Siddiqi, who suspects that Clausewitz "was perhaps unmindful of the power of faith" (114), situates irregular warfare within the prophet's own military history and claims (without evidence) that "in the Prophet's strategy of war, three elements, namely political, regular and irregular war techniques, were present in descending order" (ibid.). Siddiqi also believes that historians have generally downplayed the prophet's reliance on irregular warfare. After all, the prophet's base in Medina was a known soft target. Given that the Muslims were few in number and thus could not be dispersed, the prophet was "driven to adopt the technique of irregular warfare" (ibid.).

Siddiqi (1964) agrees with his military counterparts that, given Pakistan's weakness vis-à-vis India, "the best defence" requires "every able-bodied national" to participate, eliminating "the difference between a civilian and a soldier" (133). Conveniently for Siddiqi, "*jihad* envisages this arrangement" (ibid.). Also like his officer contemporaries, Siddiqi examines various historical instances of irregular warfare: Chinese resistance to the Japanese; Mao Tse-tung's fight against Chiang Kai-shek; Korean militias; Yugoslavia's war of liberation; and even Chinese operations during the 1962 war with India. He draws several lessons for Pakistan from this review. First and foremost, he concludes that a weak country must train "irregular fighters, intensely devoted to the national cause" (132). Second, Pakistan needs "armaments which the people at large should be able to make or procure. Inferior armaments have to be compensated by superior skill in their use [*sic*]" (ibid.). Third, Pakistan needs to exploit space. Irregular fighters under Pakistan's command and control should "be able to disperse widely and thus force dispersion on the enemy" (132–133).

Siddiqi argues that the civil–military divide is fundamentally a Western concept. Islam does not bifurcate the umma into military and nonmilitary spheres. On the contrary, Islam "obliges all Muslims to stand together in defence.....The military is an instrument to carry out political tasks when other means fail. Politics is no more than the application of ideology of day-to-day affairs. Soldiering should, therefore, be raised from the status of a profession to service of the ideology.... Only on the basis of ideology can the military hope to lead the entire people during a crisis. Soldiers should in fact become the warriors of the faith" (134). Siddiqi supports his military contemporaries in calling for a "new wing to prepare the people for war.... Their primary duty should be able to teach the people how to resist internal subversion and also to conduct generalized guerrilla warfare in case the enemy occupies the territory.... The doctrine of *Jihad* provides the background to the entire activity" (135).

Siddiqi (1964) argues that guerrilla warfare, despite its numerous advantages, also has some limitations and that it should only be attempted when the enemy is so superior in number or in equipment that Pakistan is unlikely to prevail in a positional war. Successful guerrilla warfare-cum-jihad, in Siddiqi's view, has several nonnegotiable requirements (many of which overlap with Shafi's [1964] list of prerequisites). Most notably, it requires political preparation. This is perhaps the most important step because it is "the people who pay for the successes of the guerrilla fighter. They should be identified with the cause so much that they can face suffering and still continue supporting the fighters. [Political preparation] aims at informing the fighters and the people of the stakes involved in the war. This will build morale and inspire them to fight the enemy most vigorously" (136). Second, such guerrilla warfare requires large numbers of trained guerrilla and regular fighters (138). Siddiqi even proposes a similar strategy for naval defense, as atomic submarines have "rendered almost all surface ships useless;" thus he suggests training "fishermen" as "potential sea warriors" (139, 142). Last but not least, ideology must be used to motivate the mujahideen to fight.

Siddiqi (1964) presciently anticipates a problem with harnessing the power of ideology: "emphasis on ideology creates ideological minorities which tend to become stones in the stomach....It is, therefore, necessary to find ways to win over the minorities" (170). After all, "in guerrilla warfare, the stake is not so much the territory as the people. Minorities with counterfeit loyalties must severely restrict fighting, subvert and even defeat it" (ibid.). Pakistan's use of Islam, and of Sunni Islam in particular, has indeed resulted in such ideological minorities. This approach alienated the Hindus and eventually the Muslim Bengalis in East Pakistan, and, as described later in this chapter, it has fanned the flames of a violent sectarianism that continues to claim lives.

As a new decade dawned, articles on these issues ceased to appear in Pakistani defense publications. The last notable effort was Akram's (1971) article. However, he took a tack different from his 1950s and 1960s predecessors. His article uses the battle of Dien Bien Phu to explain how the Vietnamese defeated the French. At Dien Bien Phu, "a weak nation...defeated a powerful and arrogant colonial power equipped to the teeth with an arsenal of sophisticated weapons" (29). He thus concludes that ultimately "it is the determination of a nation, reighteousness [sic] of its cause, dynamic faith, skill, courage, discipline and training which determine the outcome of any war" (36). This conclusion is not without irony. After all, Akram's article appeared amid the insurgency in East Pakistan, which would eventually grow into the 1971 Indo-Pakistan war. One cannot help but wonder whether the piece was intended as a deliberate criticism of Pakistan's military and civilian approach to the looming East Pakistan problem. As Akram writes (with considerable relevance to Pakistan's coming defeat in the east), "The French were out-witted and defeated in the battle of Dien Bien Phu because of poor leadership, lack of motivation, inadequate preparation of defences, faulty intelligence, unrealistic reliance on the air...and above all, the blunder of occupying a remote basin, unmindful of the heights around—an unsound proposition, both strategically and tactically" (ibid.).

From People's War to Low-Intensity Conflict under a Nuclear Umbrella

In the mid-1970s, following the 1971 war and India's 1974 explosion of a nuclear device, Pakistan's defense writers moved away from the themes of infiltration and people's war to focus on deterrence and low-intensity conflict (LIC). A number of authors explicitly identified the link between LIC and the nuclear environment. Anwari (1988, 47), who argued that Pakistan should develop nuclear weapons and means of delivery to "avoid being presented with a *fait accompli*," also believed that guerrilla warfare should be part of Pakistan's deterrence package and that India must be aware of this capability. But while Anwari retained some delicacy in his handling of this issue, Maj. Gen. Asif Duraiz Akhtar sought to leave nothing in doubt. Writing in the 2000 edition of the *Pakistan Army Green Book*, he explains that the "nuclear explosions of 1998 have brought a semblance of equilibrium in the region...[and have] put the conventional all out war scenario on the back burner" (1). But, as he makes clear, "This situation leaves the room open for low intensity conflict (proxy war) or the war with limited aims restricted to confines of disputed areas e.g. Indian-held Kashmir and Siachin" (1).

The entire 2002 edition of the *Pakistan Army Green Book* is dedicated to the subject of LIC. Many of the volume's authors agree that it is the most likely form of militarized dispute between India and Pakistan. Maj. Gen. Muhammad Saleem (2002) proclaims in the volume's lead essay that LIC "looms as the most viable and dangerous option" (1). As mentioned already, the 2002 *Green Book* went to press in the midst of the 2001–2002 dispute between India and Pakistan, which was sparked by the December 2001 attack on the Indian Parliament carried out by Pakistani-backed and -trained terrorists. Yet most of the authors in this volume, astonishingly, discuss LIC only in the context of Indian actions. Saleem, for example, argues that "India, while ensuring that it does not cross a certain threshold to evoke a nuclear response from Pakistan, shall endeavour to wage this kind of warfare by fully exploiting the prevailing socioeconomic conditions" (1).

In the same volume, Brig. Muneer Mahmud (2002) suggests, with greater honesty, that even though conventional war between India and Pakistan is unlikely, the prevailing environment is conducive to LIC. Important vulnerabilities exist in "the internal dynamics of India and Pakistan. Social dissent, economic disparities, political instability and ethnic polarization are some of the most vulnerable areas. These vulnerabilities provide sufficient grounds for LIC scenario" (21). Mahmud predicts that "due to the economic constraints and emerging trends, maintaining huge armies may not be a viable option for India and Pakistan" (ibid.). It should be noted that no evidence existed in 2002 that India was unable or unwilling to bear the costs of sustaining one of the world's largest armies. It is even doubtful that Pakistan's security managers had such concerns at that time since Pakistan had just embarked on another round of close military cooperation with the United States and was beginning to enjoy the financial benefits of its decision. Nonetheless, using economics perhaps as an excuse, Mahmud argues that "both countries will, however, continue to be engaged in confrontation due to [the] un-settled core issue [of Kashmir]. This situation favours LIC as the most appropriate form [of conflict] in future" (ibid.).

Other authors in the same volume address the likelihood of LIC between India and Pakistan in nearly identical language, suggesting that the publisher exercised editorial control to ensure uniformity. Brig. Muhammad Nazar Tiwana (2002), for example, identifies several structural factors that dispose the two countries to such conflicts, namely: "The history of the Indo-Pak rivalry, the adverse psychological mindset, the three dilapidating military confrontations between two countries, Indian hegemonistic designs and nuclearisation of South Asia" (26). He echoes Mahmud when he writes that "social dissent, economic disparities, political instability and ethnic polarization and religious extremism are some of the most vulnerable areas [that]…provide sufficient grounds for low intensity conflict scenario." Most importantly, nuclearization "reduces chances of an open all-out war between both the countries but also indicates low-intensity conflict as the most likely option" (ibid.). Tiwana, reflecting on these varied considerations, concludes that LIC is the most appropriate form of future warfare.

In 2004, the Pakistan Army dedicated the *Green Book* to the topic of limited war. Writing in its pages, Brig. Muhammad Ifzal makes a clear statement of Pakistan's conception of limited war: "While retaining the capability to undertake large scale limited conventional operations both defensive and offensive, Pakistan's army concept for Limited war will fundamentally hinge on asymmetric warfare and nuclear deterrence against India" (17). Ifzal argues that India also values low-intensity conflict for its own reasons: India believes that Pakistan is exploiting its nuclear umbrella to engage in LIC (most importantly by deploying mujahideen) and to annex all of Indian-administered Kashmir "without resorting to conventional war" (ibid.). While acknowledging the utility of LIC to India, Ifzal believes that Pakistan's policy of ambiguity regarding its nuclear threshold will curtail India's freedom of operations, particularly with respect to the military objectives of a limited war (ibid.). But Ifzal, understanding that India has redlines as well, suggests that Pakistan should prosecute LIC with care so as not to exceed the "tolerance threshold of the Indians" while "at the same time, disallowing Indians to reach the patience threshold of the Kashmiris" (ibid.). This is an important recognition of the trade-offs for Pakistan of its policy in Kashmir. On one hand, Pakistan cannot antagonize India to a point of escalation (as happened in 1965). On the other hand, Ifzal acknowledges that Pakistan's center of gravity in Kashmir is the Kashmiri population and thus that Pakistan needs to be mindful of how Indian countermeasures affect Kashmiris' attitudes toward the conflict and Pakistan's role in it.

As with other military writers, Ifzal (2004) supports a short conflict as most appropriate for Pakistan's "war stamina as compared to the Indians," especially if Pakistan can "achieve significant gains in early stages of the war" (17). In contrast, he notes that "a long drawn limited conventional war would be in India['s] interest," as it would allow India to exploit its advantages (ibid.). His view of nuclear weapons is similar to that of many other Pakistani writers: Pakistan values nuclear weapons because they essentially "deny [the] enemy the option of an all-out conventional war due to the nuclear deterrent and denial of limited War option to India by threatening all-out war" (18). Because both India and Pakistan recognize that limited war is the only option after May 1998, and given that they remain locked in a dispute over Kashmir, Ifzal anticipates that Kashmir will remain a flashpoint. He cautions that there is a "chance that freedom struggle in IHK [Indian-held Kashmir] goes beyond the Indian tolerance limits at a stage, which forces her to react for limited objectives in Kashmir" (ibid.). Reflecting on Pakistan's experience in the 1965 war, he anticipates that India may believe that it has the freedom of action to launch punitive operations across the Line of Control (LOC) or even the international border to punish Pakistan for the "precarious situation in Kashmir" because it thinks that choosing a "shallow depth of targets [is not likely to] provoke any nuclear response [from Pakistan]" (ibid.).

Other authors in the 2004 volume of the *Pakistan Army Green Book* share Ifzal's (2004) assessment. For example, Maj. General Shahid Iqbal (2004) writes that "nuclearisation of the Subcontinent has given a shot in the arm to this erst-while concept of limited war" (83). Like other authors in this volume, he antici-pates that limited war between the two states will be "intricately intertwined with [the] freedom struggle in Kashmir, the impact of exterior manoeuvre by respective countries, the global interests in the region, the consequent world opinion and the makeup of political forces in the two states" (ibid.). Although Iqbal believes that the "freedom movement in Kashmir will be the catalyst for any conflagration in foreseeable future, the initiative to cross the Rubicon stays with India" (ibid.). And while India retains the option of responding accord-ingly, it is Pakistan that gets to wield "leverage/influence on the tempo of free-dom struggle." Furthermore, India's options are limited by Pakistan's nuclear deterrent: as Iqbal notes, "during [the] Kargil conflict, India had its freedom of action drastically curtailed due to [Pakistan's] extant nuclear deterrence" (ibid.). Pakistan, in contrast, faces different constraints. Iqbal suggests that "Pakistan had to restrain itself due to international pressure, and [an] unfavour-able correlation of conventional forces" (ibid.). But, as he notes that with respect to India's mobilization in 2001–2002, India's "aggressive posturing was check-mated due to Pakistan's firm resolve coupled with utterly unfavourable regional and international climate" (ibid.).

This argument is worth scrutinizing in detail. Not only does Iqbal (2004) explicitly state that Pakistan can calibrate the violence in Kashmir with impu-nity, thanks to its nuclear deterrent, he also acknowledges what I described in the previous chapter: Pakistan's nuclear weapons also attract the attention of international actors who seek to constrain India, Pakistan, or both. For example, the "unfavorable regional and international climate" he mentions in his discussion of the 2001–2002 crisis refers to the US military presence in Afghanistan and Pakistan and the American goal of keeping Pakistani forces concentrated in the west to hunt al-Qaeda and Taliban fugitives crossing the Durand Line. Any Indian mobilization, much less outright war, would have seriously compromised American war objectives by drawing Pakistan's forces away from its western border and toward its border with India in the east. Iqbal correctly notes that the United States exerted diplomatic pressure on India not to escalate and at the same time tried to persuade Pakistan's leadership to make at least a minimal commitment to ceasing support for terrorism to enable India to deescalate.

Iqbal (2004) also identifies a key similarity of the Kargil and 2001–2002 con-flicts: Kashmir was a central issue for Pakistan in both conflicts, and India's con-ventional superiority did not deter Pakistan from acting. Both conflicts validated Pakistan's assumptions about the role of international influence as well as its belief that nuclear deterrence "restrained India from crossing the Line of Control

(LOC)/international borders, even in air and sea, despite manifest desire/posturing to escalate" (83). Astonishingly, Iqbal boldly states that Pakistan's importance to the US-led global war on terror and "Indian naivety in understanding the nuances of balance of power in the region" enabled Pakistan's course of action (ibid.). This article is perhaps the clearest explication of Pakistan's use of nuclear weapons to deter Indian escalation and convince international actors to restrain India's response to its actions in Kashmir.[1]

In 2008, the Pakistan Army dedicated the *Pakistan Army Green Book* to the future conflict environment. Reflecting the changed nature of US–Pakistan relations, in this volume the United States appears, along with India, as a possible future foe. Unsurprisingly, nuclear weapons play a role in enabling Pakistan to manage the perceived threat from the United States as well as India. Brig. Shaukat Iqbal's (2008) essay, which is typical of the volume, begins with an insinuation that the Americans are "creating [an] environment to handle Pakistan. [The c]ase of nuclear proliferation of Dr. Abdul Qadeer Khan is like a hanging sword....It may be used against Pakistan, as and when situation arises [*sic*]" (43). But Iqbal imagines not only an American threat, but an Indian one as well. The author is disconcerted that "India has become bride-groom of both West and the East. China, forgetting its border disputes, intends winning over India, Russia is using its leverage of past relations, The USA and the West is attempting to develop India as a strategic partner" (ibid.). Iqbal cautions that "through focused propaganda, prevailing perception will be strengthened that Pakistan intelligence and security forces are supporting Talibans [*sic*] in war against Western Coalition [*sic*]; Pakistan is Talibanized and extremist forces are posing threat to Pakistan's nuclear weapons" (46). Moreover, such a disinformation campaign will be used by Pakistan's enemies to "destabilize it internally before launching of military blitz" (ibid.). The author intimates that India, which has secured the trust of the United States, may act against Pakistan as a US proxy. Incredibly, Iqbal argues further that the Pakistan Army is "perceived to be Centre of Gravity...of Pakistan which is back [*sic*] by irregular forces (like Mujahideens [*sic*]) and is reinforced by nuclear weapons. It has ability to create synergetic effects in asymmetric environment by employing Mujahideens [*sic*] and nuclear doctrine" (ibid.).

To contend with this complicated future threat environment, Iqbal (2008) recommends, among other actions, that the army employ the intelligence agencies to "train, prepare and organize the 'guerrillas in combat units to fight a guerrilla warfare' to bleed the enemy forces and disrupt its supply line (48)." Necessarily, this will require the "highest level of training to fight defensive battle in conjunction with employment of 'guerrillas'... [that] may demand...retention of potential to prepare, train and employ Mujahideens [*sic*] as guerrillas" (ibid.). Most importantly, he contends that this strategy "requires retention of credible nuclear deterrence throughout" (ibid.). Iqbal doesn't make clear in which theatre these irregular forces would be used. He could conceivably be contemplating the deployment of mujahideen (or even Taliban) against coalition forces in Afghanistan, in India, or even within Pakistan itself, in the event that Pakistan is attacked on its own territory. Nonetheless, he is very clear that Pakistan can use these nonconventional assets only as long as it possesses a robust nuclear deterrent.

As I have shown in Chapter 8, there is a positive correlation between nuclearization of the subcontinent and militarized disputes between India and Pakistan. The present chapter provides further evidence that nuclearization has encouraged Pakistani adventurism—by both deterring India and forcing the international community to restrain India, to act to resolve the crisis by encouraging both sides to take palliative steps, or to punish one or both sides, among other measures. My examination of Pakistan's literature demonstrates that early concepts of infiltration and guerrilla war continued to evolve along with Pakistan's (and India's) nuclearization. By the twenty-first century, Pakistan Army authors were writing explicitly about Pakistan's ability to prosecute subconventional conflict under its nuclear umbrella. In the next section, I present a brief overview of the various Islamist militant groups that the state has groomed to prosecute these varied efforts. I focus on this set of proxy actors both because it is currently the most destabilizing ensemble of militants in the region—whether we look at Afghanistan, India, or Pakistan itself—and because these groups have been the mainstay of Pakistan's proxy war initiatives. While Pakistan aided and abetted Sikh insurgents in the Indian Punjab from the late 1970s until the insurgency ended in the early 1990s, Pakistan did not create the insurgents but rather made use of them when possible. In contrast, Pakistan, from the beginning of its existence, has created, nurtured, supported, trained, financed, and deployed Islamist proxies.

Pakistan's Militant Assets

Prior to Pervez Musharraf's acquiescence to Washington's demand that Pakistan join the US-led global war on terrorism after September 2001, one could parse Pakistan's militant[2] landscape according to sectarian orientation, primary theater of operation, ethnic constitution, and even preferred attack techniques. One array of militant groups (*askari tanzeems*) traditionally focused on Kashmir; this cluster included the Deobandi groups of Jaish-e-Mohammad (JeM) and Harkat-ul-Ansar/Harkat-ul-Mujahideen (HuA/HuM); Ahl-e-Hadith organizations such as the Punjab-based LeT; and the Jamaat-e-Islami influenced groups such as Hizbul Mujahideen and Al-Badr.[3] Analysts typically call these militant organizations Kashmiri groups; this is a misnomer, however, because these organizations include few ethnic Kashmiris among their ranks and most do not operate exclusively in Kashmir. LeT and JeM, for example, have long operated throughout India. In recent years, splinters of JeM and other Deobandi groups have begun operating in Pakistan as part of their war on the Pakistani state. LeT, as well as several Deobandi militant groups, also operate in Afghanistan against US, North Atlantic Treaty Organization (NATO)/International Security Assistance Force (ISAF), and Afghan civilian and military personnel alike. In contrast, Al-Badr and Hizbul Mujahideen tend to be composed mostly of ethnic Kashmiris and have retained their focus on Kashmir.

A second group of *askari tanzeems* is traditionally sectarian in nature, in that they target Pakistan's Shia community, among other religious minorities. Two of the most important anti-Shia sectarian groups are Lashkar-e-Jhangvi (LeJ) and Sipah-e-Sahaba Pakistan (SSP), both of which are under the sway of the Deobandi ulema political party the Jamiat-ulema-Islami (JUI) and are funded by wealthy Arab individuals and organizations. Notably, these sectarian *tanzeems* have overlapping membership with other Deobandi militant groups, including the Afghan and Pakistani Taliban, all of which have strong connections to the JUI (Abou Zahab and Roy 2004; Fair 2011b). In the past, Shia sectarian groups have also been lethally active. These groups, which have now largely disappeared, targeted Sunni Muslims and received funding from Iran (Fair 2011b).

Since 2004, if not before, Pakistan has witnessed the development of a cluster of militant groups whose commanders and partisans call themselves the Pakistani Taliban. These groups have successfully established an archipelago of shariat (Islamic law) stretching across the Pakhtun belt in the Federally Administered Tribal Areas (FATA) and Kyber Pakhtunkhwa (KP). The Tehreek-e-Taliban-e-Pakistan (TTP) often appears in popular media as a monolithic entity, the umbrella organization for nearly all anti-Pakistan Islamist militants in the seven tribal agencies of South and North Waziristan, Orakzai, Kurram, Khyber, Mohmand, and Bajaur; and in the Frontier Regions of Peshawar, Kohat, Bannu, Lakki Marwat, Tank and Dera Ismael Khan; as well as in the settled districts of Swat, Buner, Upper Dir, Lower Dir, Bannu, Lakki Marwat, Tank, Peshawar, Dera Ismail Khan, Mardan, and Kohat. Militants from these areas do claim to be affiliated with the TTP. But serious analysts of the movement do not believe that the TTP has a coherent command and control structure.[4] Rahimullah Yusufzai, for instance, a leading Pakistani journalist and expert on the TTP and other Islamist groups, argues that the organization is neither coherent nor disciplined (Yusufzai 2008). Seth Jones and I made a similar argument in a volume that we coauthored in 2010 (Jones and Fair 2010). Drawing on the work of John Arquilla and David Ronfeldt (1997), we describe the TTP's constituent groups as forming a system of loose networks. These networks vary in size and tend to be dispersed. However, the various "nodes" (e.g., overlapping militant commanders or other shared personalities or organizational functions) can communicate with each other and may even coordinate their campaigns.

Analysts generally cite 2007 as the year that the TTP formally coalesced. In November of that year, several Pakistani militant commanders, rallying under the leadership of Baitullah Mehsud, announced that they would henceforth oper-ate under the banner of the Pakistani Taliban (TTP). Mehsud (who was killed by a US drone strike in August 2009) claimed many allies, most of them Deobandi militants seeking to establish shariat within their personal areas of operations throughout the Pakhtun belt. But it should be noted that many commanders who call themselves Pakistani Taliban were not a part of this alliance. In late February 2008, two important dissident commanders, Mullah Nazir and Hafiz Gul Bahadur, temporarily set aside their differences with Mehsud to forge the Shura Ittehad-ul-Mujahideen. But the short-lived alliance collapsed almost as soon as it was announced because the commanders had serious differences of opinion about the suitability or prioritization of fighting the Pakistan military versus assisting the Afghan Taliban to oust the foreign occupiers and the Karzai regime they installed and support (Abbas 2009).

Following Baitullah Mehsud's death, TTP leaders announced that Hakimullah Mehsud would take over the leadership role. Under him, the TTP became more coherent and intensified its campaign of suicide bombings of Pakistani security and intelligence agencies (*New York Times* 2010; Pakistan Institute for Peace Studies 2009; PBS 2010). Under the leadership of Hakimullah, TTP campaigns against civilian targets became more vicious, singling out Shia and Ahmedis (also spelled *Ahmediyyas* by some), who are considered *munafiqin* (Muslims who spread discord in the community) and *murtad* (apostate), respectively. Nor has the TTP spared important Sufi shrines: since 2005, militants have launched more than 70 suicide attacks on such sites, killing hundreds. Attacks have intensified in recent years. For example, Lahore's prominent Datta Ganj Bakhsh—perhaps the most important Sufi shrine in the Punjab—was attacked in late June 2010 (Tavernise 2010; Tohid 2010), and in April 2011, suicide bombers assaulted a shrine dedicated to a Punjabi saint, Sakhi Sarvar, in Dera Ghazi Khan (Masood and Gillani 2011). This focus on sectarian violence no doubt reflects Hakimullah's long-time association with the sectarian terrorist group Sipah-e-Sahaba-e-Pakistan. The United States killed Hakimullah on 1 November 2013 in a drone strike. He has been replaced Mullah Fazlullah. At the time of writing it is too early to discern how the TTP will fare under his leadership (Golovnina and Tanveer, 2013).

But the Mehsuds are far from the first, or only, highly visible Pakistani militant commanders. Several individual militant commanders had risen to prominence prior to the official consolidation of the TTP in November 2007. For example, Nek Mohammad Wazir (from the Ahmadzai Wazir tribe in Wana, South Waziristan) was perhaps the first Pakistani militant to acquire some degree of infamy. During the Pakistan Army's spring 2004 offensive in South Waziristan, Mohammad fought the army to a standstill, compelling it to ratify its own defeat in a peace deal known as the Shakai Accord, the terms of which were dictated by Mohammad. The signing ceremony for the accord was held in

Shakai, his own stronghold, and during the ceremony he was publicly garlanded by the 11th Corps Commander, Lieutenant General Safdar Hussain. This event was heavily covered by Pakistan's media, helping Mohammad gain widespread legitimacy (Yusufzai 2006). Baitullah rose to prominence in the same way, forcing the Pakistan Army to concede and ratify defeat in the Sararogha Agreement of February 2005.

Hafiz Gul Bahadur, another prominent mujahideen leader, became the amir (commander) of the Pakistani militants of North Waziristan. Bahadur quickly distanced himself from the TTP and its leadership. During the winter of 2007–2008, Bahadur refused to come to Baitullah's assistance when the latter was under attack by the Pakistan Army and warned him against fighting the Pakistan security forces in North Waziristan. Bahadur subsequently signed a peace accord with the Pakistan security forces. He remained opposed to the TTP's now-deceased leader, Hakimullah, as well as the TTP's targeting of Pakistani civilians and defense and intelligence personnel. Bahadur focuses exclusively on US and NATO forces in Afghanistan. For this reason, the United States has sought to kill him through armed drone strikes, although thus far without success (Gopal et al. 2010; Khan 2007).

Furthermore, several militant groups had begun challenging the writ of the Pakistani state long before the TTP formally announced its existence. These groups arguably began to gain prominence coincident with—or even as a result of—Pakistani military operations in the FATA undertaken at the urging of the United States. Several Pakistani analysts contend that the onset of US air strikes in the FATA—first via conventional air platforms and later by unmanned aerial vehicles, or drones—catalyzed the insurgency. They point in particular to US drone strikes in October 2006 against an al-Qaeda–affiliated madrasa in a Chingai village, Bajaur, as the most important catalyst of suicide attacks against security forces in the FATA and North-West Frontier Province (NWFP) (Gul 2009; Kronstadt 2006; *Radio Free Europe* 2006). (The strikes were targeting top al-Qaeda leader Ayman al-Zawahiri.)

The Chingai madrasa was run by the Tehreek-e-Nafaz-e-Shariat-e-Mohammadi (TNSM), a Sunni militant group founded by Sufi Mohammad. (Mohammad achieved some notoriety in 2001 when he sent 8,000 volunteers to Afghanistan to support the Taliban's war against the United States and the Northern Alliance.) Sufi Mohammad's deputy, Maulvi Liaquat, was killed in the Chingai strike. Following that attack, Inayatur Rahman, a local pro-Taliban elder, announced that he had prepared a squad of suicide bombers to target Pakistani security forces, using tactics similar to those employed against Americans in Afghanistan and Iraq, and that the squad would carry out these suicide attacks soon (Ansari and Khan 2006; Roggio 2006). When Sufi Mohammad was imprisoned, his son-in-law, Mullah Fazlullah, took over the organization.

Although the so-called Talibanization of the tribal areas was initially limited to North and South Waziristan, the phenomenon spread rapidly. Pakistani Taliban surfaced in areas that had previously been free of such activity, including Bajaur, Mohmand, Orakzai, and Kurram agencies. In 2008, aid workers with whom I spoke expressed surprise that Kurram had become so dangerous. But the agency has long been the site of sectarian violence due to its large Shia population. Given the intensifying sectarian agenda of the TTP, these developments in Kurram should not have been surprising (Abou Zahab 2002). The Pakistan Taliban also undertook activities in the frontier regions of Bannu, Tank, Kohat, Lakki Marwat, Dera Ismail Khan, and in the settled area of Swat. Throughout the summer of 2007, the Frontier Corps and the Frontier Constabulary battled Pakistani militants associated with the TNSM, which had seized the Swat Valley in late October 2006 (Fair 2011b).

The local leaders of these various TTP-affiliated militant groups effectively exploited socioeconomic grievances (e.g., the state's failure to provide services, including access to rule of law and justice) and frustration with the corrupt colonial-era governance structures in place in the FATA. The Pakistani Taliban in Swat reportedly pursued a system of redistributive justice, seizing the land of wealthy landowners and awarding it to landless peasants who supported the group (Khan 2009; Perlez 2009a; for an opposing view see Taj 2008). Similarly, militant commanders in the FATA have pressured political agents to provide services without demanding bribes and have established a functional, albeit draconian, police system and process of dispute resolution. The much maligned *qazi* courts (courts run by *qazis*, or Islamist jurists) to be established in Swat were required to add new *qazis* if the caseload of the existing bench exceeded 150 cases. No such provision exists for the mainstream courts. The TTP also established procedures for solemnizing love marriages; this measure appealed to youth who resent forced marriages and lowered the economic barrier to marriage for young men who would otherwise have to pay high bride prices (author fieldwork in Pakistan in February and April 2009 and August 2010).

In April 2009, news reports announced the arrival of the Punjabi Taliban, referring to the various militant groups ensconced in the Punjab, the most populous province in Pakistan (Abbas 2009; Tavernise et al. 2009). Despite its ostensibly recent coinage, the term *Punjabi Taliban* has a long and complex history. Since 2009, however, it has acquired significant political importance (Yusufzai 2010). Many Pakhtuns support the use of the term to emphasize that Pakistan's insurgency is not solely Pakhtun, but many non-Pakhtuns reject the term for the same reason. The latter prefer to attribute the threat against Pakistan to the Pakhtun other, often stereotypically characterized as uncivilized, warlike, and violent (author fieldwork in summer 2010; see also Sana 2010).

Pakistan's political class has also sought to exploit the controversy over the term. Leaders of the Punjab-based Pakistan Muslim League Nawaz (PML-N) object to the term, likely in part because of the PML-N's ongoing support for groups such as SSP and LeJ, which is largely driven by electoral considerations. Shahbaz Sharif, the chief minister of Punjab and a member of the PML-N, accused Interior Minister Rehman Malik of using the terms *Punjabi Taliban* and *Punjabi terrorist* to foment conflict between provinces—a tactic, he argued, that is tantamount to a condemnation of the people of Punjab (Yusufzai 2010).

While it is tempting to view Punjab as a new theater of Talibanization, sites of militancy across Pakistan are interrelated. Punjab-based groups such as the Deobandi LeJ and JeM are components of the TTP and conduct attacks in its name. In fact, the so-called Punjabi Taliban groups form the backbone of the TTP and have played an important role in attacking Sufi, Shia, Ahmedi, and other civilian targets throughout Pakistan and in the Punjab in particular (Roggio 2010).

In addition to the Pakistani groups, Pakistan also hosts elements of the Afghan Taliban, with shuras in Quetta, Peshawar, and Karachi (Levin 2009). The Afghan Taliban remain focused on ousting foreign forces in Afghanistan, over-throwing the Karzai regime, and reclaiming a role in governing Afghanistan. Pakistani territory is also used by al-Qaeda, whose operatives are known to reside in North and South Waziristan and in Bajaur, among other parts of the Pakhtun belt. Moreover, many al-Qaeda operatives(e.g., Abu Zubaidah, Khalid Sheikh Mohammed) have been arrested in Pakistani cities with the help of Pakistani authorities (BBC 2007). The Americans, working unilaterally, eventually found and killed Osama bin Laden in his refuge near the Pakistan Military Academy (PMA) at Kakul.

The Pakistani people were slow to countenance the government's counter-terrorism and counterinsurgency efforts. Public opinion surveys conducted in Pakistan in 2007, and even later, demonstrated that Pakistanis overwhelmingly supported government efforts to reach peace deals with militants and believed that such efforts would secure peace, despite consistent evidence to the contrary. Equally important, Pakistanis remained opposed to the army undertaking offensives against Pakistan's own militants. These trends remained more or less constant until April 2009, when public opinion dramatically changed course after the Taliban reneged on the sharia-for-peace deal and overran Buner. Survey results in May 2009 and July 2009 suggest that the public was increasingly opposed to peace deals and supportive of military action (Fair 2009c). The Pew Research Center has monitored Pakistani support of and opposition to the Pakistan government's fight against terrorism since that important event in 2009. While opposition to the government counterterrorism efforts remained relatively stable (between 20 and 25 percent) from 2009 to 2011, it jumped to 35 percent in 2012. Over the same period, support for the effort plummeted,

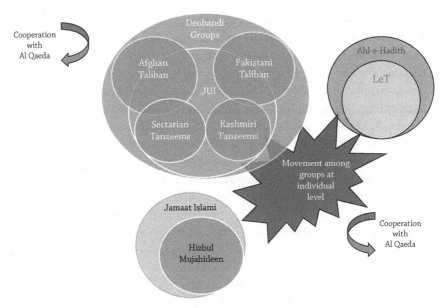

Figure 9.1 Graphic depicting the relationships among the various Pakistani militant groups.

from 53 percent in 2009 to 32 percent in 2012. The remainder of respondents (33 percent in 2012) refused to answer the question (Pew Global Attitudes Project 2012).

Figure 9.1 attempts to graphically depict the relationships between the myriad militant groups and allied Islamist political parties that operate in and from Pakistan. To the left is a large cluster of groups commonly associated with the Deobandi interpretive tradition. This cluster includes not only the Deobandi ulema political party, the JUI, but also the various Deobandi sectarian militant groups, the so-called Kashmiri tanzeems, the Pakistan Taliban, and the Afghan Taliban. To the left of that cluster is an arrow indicating that these groups have historically maintained close ties with al-Qaeda through their association with the Taliban and the constellation of Deobandi madrasas and mosques that link the various Deobandi militant groups and political factions of the JUI.

To the right is a smaller cluster representing the Ahl-e-Hadith interpretive tradition and the primary militant group it has spawned, the Lashkar-e-Taiba. This organization, which never shared training camps and other infrastructure in Afghanistan with the Taliban, is not organizationally linked to al-Qaeda— although some analysts (e.g., Raman 2002; Riedel 2012) have tried to prove a connection. Contrary to conventional belief, LeT did not sign Osama bin Laden's fatwa, or declaration of jihad against the West in 1998 (Federation of American Scientists n.d.). While LeT has disavowed the TTP, individual LeT fighters have

joined the ranks of Deobandi militant groups, and some members have even provided assistance to al-Qaeda. However, LeT currently has no need to form an
alliance with al-Qaeda. It is the preeminent terrorist group in South Asia, enjoys
massive support from the Pakistani state as well from key sectors of its citizens,
and maintains extensive sanctuaries in Pakistan. Joining al-Qaeda would jeopar-
dize all of these amenities. Thus, one could argue that (at least in the context of
South Asia) al-Qaeda has greater need for LeT than LeT has for al-Qaeda.

The bottom of Figure 9.1 depicts the group mostly tightly associated with the
Islamist political party, the Jamaat-e-Islami, namely the Hizbul Mujahideen (and
related splinters thereof). This group remains focused on Indian-administered
Kashmir and has not provided assistance to the TTP (Fair 2011b).

While Pakistan has a long history of using Islamist militants as proxies,
Washington's 1979 determination that the country had crossed nuclear red
lines enabled Islamabad to expand the scale, scope, territorial range, and intensity of its use of asymmetric proxies (Tellis et al. 2001). Recognition as an overt
nuclear power allowed Pakistan to support irregular militant groups with
increasing impunity, confident that New Delhi would find conventional punitive measures too risky. Thus, it is not a coincidence that Pakistani jihadi groups
spread in increased numbers to Kashmir in the immediate aftermath of the US
decision to apply proliferation-related sanctions to Pakistan.

Throughout the 1980s, Pakistan became even more aggressive in its use of
such actors. But it was the reciprocal nuclear tests in 1998 that allowed Islamabad
to really push the envelope of its asymmetric strategy. In May 1999 Pakistan
launched a limited incursion into Indian-administered Kashmir with the objective of seizing a small amount of territory in the Kargil–Dras sectors. Though
Pakistan's territorial aims were limited, the use of mujahideen as a cover for the
military incursion was part of a denial and deception strategy that marked a
watershed in Pakistan's use of low-intensity conflict. Many analysts have argued
that such a brazen incursion would have been unlikely before Pakistan became an
overt nuclear weapons state following the nuclear tests of May 1998 (Kapur 2007;
Tellis et al. 2001).

Kargil was the first conventional conflict under the nuclear umbrella (albeit
with a mujahideen cover story), but Pakistan has also used proxy warfare and
irregular fighters more brazenly since 1998, underscoring the fact that nuclearization has both enabled and emboldened its use of militancy. Subconventional
attacks since 1998 include the 1999 LeT attack on a security establishment
near a New Delhi tourist attraction, the Red Fort; the 2001 JeM attack on the
Indian Parliament; the LeT massacre of army wives and children in Kaluchak
in May 2002; and various strikes by LeT and affiliated groups throughout India,
including the 2006 and 2008 attacks in Mumbai. The development of first a
covert and then an overt nuclear capability (and the concomitant means of
delivery) appears to have enabled Pakistan to pursue the boldest aspects of its

proxy strategy with confidence that doing so will have few, if any, important consequences.

Pakistani Support for the Militants?

Implicit in various US attempts to compel Pakistan to cease its support for militant groups is the assumption that the country could do so if it mustered the requisite will. The truth of this supposition is far from obvious. Islamabad's ability, or lack thereof, to fight these groups will arguably condition its readiness to cease active and passive support, much less take aggressive action to eliminate these groups.

This section advances several propositions about the degree of Pakistani state support for various groups and assesses the state's ability to control or counter them. This assessment overwhelmingly draws on my fieldwork in Pakistan (including discussions with military, intelligence, and civilian officials as well as with journalists and analysts) over several visits beginning in 2000, fieldwork throughout Afghanistan since 2007, and extensive interactions with US officials about Pakistan and Afghanistan over the same period.

Pakistan's army and intelligence agencies tend to segment the country's militants into a range of groups over which the state exercises varying degrees of control. Pakistan is widely assumed to wield significant influence over the Afghan Taliban (including Jalaludin Haqqani's North Waziristan–based network), even holding Taliban families hostage in Pakistan to ensure compliance. Since 2001, however, the Afghan Taliban have experienced regular turnover of midlevel commanders (Giustozzi 2008). The new commanders are less beholden to Pakistan, in part because of their age: they were children in the mid-1990s, when the Inter-Services Intelligence (ISI) began nurturing the Taliban. What's more, the tribal foundations of the Afghan Taliban are also changing. Thus, Pakistan is struggling to cultivate influence among the emerging Afghan Taliban factions even while it seeks to control elements of Mullah Omar's Quetta Shura, the organization's top leadership council. Islamabad worries that members of the Quetta Shura may forge a separate peace with Afghan president Karzai, one that does not recognize Pakistan's equities. Exemplifying its efforts to counter such moves, in February 2010, Pakistan arrested Taliban leader Mullah Baradar because he was negotiating with Karzai independently (Nelson and Farmer 2010).

US analysts tend to believe that the Pakistani security services maintain reasonably tight control over LeT through providing resources, monitoring group activity, and most importantly continuing to provide LeT the most important asset it enjoys: virtually unfettered access to operate (e.g., recruit, raise funds, train, plan missions) in and from Pakistan. That said, LeT has established proxies in India, principally among them, the Indian mujahideen and its predecessor, the Students Islamic Movement of India (Fair 2010a). It has also developed logistical bases in Bangladesh, Sri Lanka, the Maldives, and Nepal, among other countries. Some LeT cells within India are at least partly independent of its headquarters in Muridke (Fair 2010a; Roul 2010). One highly suggestive piece of evidence is the significant signals traffic between the ISI and JeM recorded after JeM's 2001 attack on the Indian parliament, indicating the ISI's anger with JeM for that attack. In contrast, significantly less traffic was detected after the November 2008 terrorist attacks on Mumbai. This spike in traffic could have been an attempt by Pakistan to defuse the former crisis, but if so it is puzzling that such a strategy was not used in 2008.[5] After the 2008 Mumbai attacks the United States granted Indian officials access to David Headley, an American citizen, after he had been arrested and charged with involvement in the attacks. According to Indian officials, Headley conceded ISI involvement (Burke 2010; Perlez et al. 2010). Bob Woodward (2010) reported that the previous director general of the ISI, Shuja Pasha, acknowledged that persons connected to the ISI were involved in the attacks but insisted that the operation was rogue. US officials have declined to endorse this claim.

At the other end of the spectrum is the aforementioned array of Deobandi groups. Pakistan's ability to control these groups appears variable, perhaps even tentative at best. Masood Azhar's Bahawalpur-based JeM network is perhaps the most tightly controlled of all the Deobandi groups; as Pakistani analysts explained to me in July 2010, the army is keen to continue supporting Azhar because he has remained adamantly pro-Pakistan and has refrained from attacking the state. Azhar demonstrated his pro-state bona fides as early as 2001, when he opposed calls from within his organization to attack western targets in Pakistan as well as the Pakistani government. Azhar informed the ISI of these conspiracies (Howenstein 2008). Pakistani analysts argue that as long as Azhar can maintain the coherence of his following in the Punjab, members of his group are less likely to join the TTP. But it is well-known that elements of JeM have split from Azhar and launched attacks against foreign and domestic targets in Pakistan in association with its sectarian counterpart, the Lashkar-e-Jhangvi. JeM for example, was responsible for the 2002 suicide attack on the US consulate in Karachi, and the organization has been implicated in the 2006 plot to blow up planes leaving from Great Britain (Carsen 2006; *Dawn* 2006).

Other, albeit intimately interrelated, Deobandi groups, such as the network of commanders under the umbrella of the TTP, are beyond the grasp of the state, as evidenced by their persistent attacks within Pakistan. The military and the ISI have tried to manage this complex web of allied foes by provoking or exacerbating disagreements among commanders. For example, Pakistan cultivated Mullah Bahadur and Maulvi Nazir in an attempt to counter the antistate elements of the TTP generally and Baitullah and Hakimullah Mehsud in particular (Wadhams and Cookman 2009; Yusufzai 2007, 2008). Pakistan has at times tried to placate the militants by making peace deals; at other times it has sought to defeat them militarily, with varying degrees of success (Jones and Fair 2010).

Unfortunately, it is unlikely that Islamabad will have the ability—much less political will—to degrade these groups in any significant way. Despite its seeming dedication to combating those elements of the TTP that target the state, Pakistan will likely remain unable or unwilling to eliminate even those groups, owing to the overlapping membership between the vehemently antistate components of the TTP and Deobandi groups that Pakistan still views as assets as well as to Islamabad's fear that its militant proxies will be crucial allies in any future war against India.

The Internal Jihad: A Case Study of Lashkar-e-Taiba

Until now I have primarily discussed Pakistan's militant groups in the context of Pakistan's external goals.[6] But Pakistan itself is a critical theater of state-supported militancy. I use a case study of LeT to explore this phenomenon. As discussed already, LeT has not joined the Pakistani Taliban, and it has never attacked any target within the state of Pakistan (Fair 2011a). But the organization is actually very active within Pakistan. First, although LeT trains many recruits, only a small percentage actually see combat (ibid.). Of all the recruits that LeT sends to its basic training course (Daura-e-Aam), fewer than 1 in 10 will be selected for its advanced training course, Daura-e-Khas. Fewer still progress beyond Daura-e-Khas to higher-level courses such as intelligence, driving, and swimming. And even fewer are ultimately sent out on missions in India or elsewhere.[7]

Working with West Point's Combating Terrorism Center, my research team assembled a database of 708 slain LeT activists using published biographies of the fighters. From this body of evidence, it is clear that individuals are accepted for a mission only after significant lobbying of the organization's leadership, particularly Hafez Saeed, its top commander, and Zia-Ur-Rehman Lakhvi, its supreme commander for Kashmir and chief of operations in India. (Lakhvi was the mastermind of the 2008 Mumbai attacks. While he is technically currently being held in a Pakistani prison, he continues to guide the organization.) The biographies also suggest that Lakhvi and Saeed are intimately involved in assessing the candidates' reliability, dedication, and intellectual and physical fitness for the mission (Rassler et al. 2013).

The available evidence suggests that the vast majority of persons who receive some degree of LeT training are ultimately sent back to their home districts, where they are expected to engage in proselytization and propagation of the group's theological message and to recruit other candidates for the same cycle of training (again with low odds of ever being deployed for combat operations). At first glance, this is a strange use of organizational resources given the costs of training and the operational risks involved in returning so many potential operatives to their home villages with little to no supervision. The riskiness of this venture has increased since 9/11, as the international community has grown ever more concerned about LeT. Any weakness in operational security could compromise parts of the organization, critical facilities, planned operations, or important personnel. Moreover, although LeT has sought to lower its profile by operating under the thin cover of ostensible philanthropic organizations, first as the Jamaat-ud-Dawa and more recently as the Falah-e-Insaniat Foundation, the highly public appearances of LeT members in public demonstrations remain a perpetual irritant to Pakistan's neighbors and international partners. (The organization routinely uses English-language banners during these protests, likely to ensure that international observers are aware of its involvement.)

Assuming LeT rationally employs its organizational resources, the organization (and in turn the state) must derive some benefit from this heavy investment in persons who will never carry out operations in India or Afghanistan. The value of these domestic investments made by LeT lies in its *domestic politics*. The utility of the group's domestic focus becomes apparent only when one appreciates the ways it differs from the other groups operating in Pakistan, in particular as regards its theological basis. Unfortunately, this aspect of the group has been neglected by previous analyses, with the exception of Fair (2011a).

All of the groups that have turned on the state are Deobandi, whereas LeT is affiliated with the Ahl-e-Hadis interpretative tradition. This theological distinction is exceedingly important and equally underappreciated. First, the Deobandi groups are deeply sectarian and have long targeted Pakistan's Shia and Ahmediyya populations. (In 1974 Z. A. Bhutto declared the Ahmediyyas non-Muslim as a sop to Islamist opposition groups.) The groups also began attacking Sufi shrines in Pakistan, as discussed already. Worshippers at the shrines follow the Barelvi school of Islam, whose adherents believe in mysticism, revere saints, and frequent shrines where their spiritual guide, the saint's descendent, may intercede on their behalf. Many, if not most, Pakistanis are believed to be Barelvi, although there are no reliable data on this point. Pakistanis generally hold these shrines in high esteem, as these Sufi saints brought Islam to South Asia (Kamran 2008; Metcalf 2002; Talbot 2007). Deobandis, however, denounce these mystical practices and beliefs as un-Islamic accretions derived from Hinduism (Waraich 2011). Deobandi militant groups also attack Pakistan's non-Muslim minorities, such as Christians (Minority Rights Group International 2010).

In short, Barelvis, Shia, and Ahmediyyas all espouse religious practices that Deobandis find anathema because these practices are what Deobandis deem *munafiqit*, or actions that spread disunity within the global body of Muslim believers (umma). The term *munafaqit* is sometimes translated as the state of hypocrisy or the state of doing things that are hypocritical. One who perpetrates *munafiqit* is called *munafiq* (plural *munafiqin*). Thus, *munafiq* is sometimes translated as a "hypocrite," implying that members of these religious groups are not truthful to themselves or others. Deobandi militant groups, which include the Pakistani Taliban and its constituent subgroupings, such as JeM, SSP, and LeJ, have concluded that anyone who does not espouse their beliefs is *munafiq*. This includes Pakistani security personnel as well as political leaders and any citizens who oppose these groups and their violent agenda. Under this pretext, Deobandi groups have launched a sustained campaign of violence, first in the FATA and then expanding into the settled parts of the frontier in Khyber Pakhtunkhwa and well into the Punjab.

This campaign has had lethal effects. Using data available from the University of Maryland's Global Terrorism Database, between January 1, 2000, and December 31, 2011 (the last date for which information is available for Pakistan), Pakistan has experienced 3,209 terror attacks in which some 7,334 persons died and another 14,652 were injured. (Yearly breakdowns of incidents and victims are given in Figure 9.2.) The Global Terrorism Database is almost certainly biased downward in that it accounts for fewer terror attacks than actually occur. Recall that these figures are a full order of magnitude lower than Pakistani reported fatalities, which indicate that tens of thousands of Pakistanis have been killed.

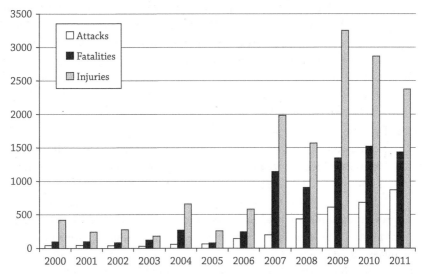

Figure 9.2 Islamist terrorist attacks and victims: January 1, 2000–December 31, 2011. Source: University of Maryland, Global Terrorism Database, online. Available http://www.start.umd.edu/gtd/. Note that we included all incidents between January 1, 2001 and December 31, 2011, that met Criteria #1 (crit1 = 1) and for which there was no doubt that the incident was terrorism (doubtterr = 0). Per the GTP Codebook, this criterion is defined thusly: "The violent act must be aimed at attaining a political, economic, religious, or social goal. This criterion is not satisfied in those cases where the perpetrator(s) acted out of a pure profit motive or from an idiosyncratic personal motive unconnected with broader societal change."

The value of these data is not in any given number of events in any given year but rather in the trends over time. One important observation is that the frequency of attacks increased markedly after 2005, when the Pakistani state began engaging in vigorous antiterrorism efforts against these groups, and these attacks became more lethal whether lethality is measured in fatalities or injuries.

Understanding the violence perpetrated by these Deobandi groups is critical to understanding LeT's domestic utility (Fair 2011a). LeT does not fight in Pakistan and does not target Pakistanis. In the LeT manifesto *Hum Kyon Jihad Kar Rahen Hain?* (Why Are We Waging Jihad) the anonymous author explains why LeT "does not wage jihad in Pakistan instead of Kashmir" and other parts of the Muslim world where Muslims are oppressed (Jamaat-ud-Dawa 2004, 42–45).[8] This section makes clear the domestic importance of the organization: in contrast to the Deobandi groups that attack the state and its citizens, the manifesto reveals LeT's fundamentally nonsectarian nature and its commitment to the integrity of the Pakistani state and its diverse polity.

The manifesto is structured around a series of questions posed by an imaginary reader. These are cleverly framed to address an array of important messages, including the virtues of jihad *outside* of Pakistan and the reasons LeT does not fight *within* Pakistan. For instance, one question asks, "People ask why are you not waging jihad in Pakistan? ... The government of Pakistan is cooperating with you [e.g., LeT]. Yet the government of Pakistan is an oppressive, imperial power. It supports the kafirs and has spread disbelief and disunity [*munafiqit*] throughout the country" (Jamaat-ud-Dawa 2004, 42). Thus, the manifesto forthrightly addresses the primary Deobandi critique of the government. This critique has particular salience in the post-9/11 era, during which the government of Pakistan has been collaborating with the United States and has seen the subsequent emergence of a domestic insurgency.

The manifesto's author argues that, while the state is indeed guilty of these things, Pakistani Muslims, whatever their creed, have read the Kalma, a series of statements attesting to the speaker's belief that there is no one worthy of worship except Allah and that Muhammad is the prophet or messenger of Allah. Because he has read the Kalma, such a Muslim is a brother, the author explains, and LeT will not fight him as long as "he doesn't raise a hand against us. We will see him as being confused or wrong. We will also tell him that he is guilty of disbelief and not accepting the unity of God. But we will not fight him. If we fight those who have read the Kalma, then we cannot fight those who refuse to do so" (Jamaat-ud-Dawa 2004, 42). The author continues to elaborate that even "grave worshippers" (Barelvis or Sufis) or "those who are hostile to the companions of the prophet" (Shia) still accept the Koran and must not be attacked (43).

This section of the manifesto performs two important tasks. It concedes, but defends, LeT's contacts with the Pakistan government, and it undermines the Deobandi arguments for attacking Pakistanis on the basis that they are *munafiqin*.

What's more, the author proceeds to dismantle the claim these persons are *munafiqin* in the first place. This is a bold effort to undermine the theological underpinnings of the Deobandis' violent sectarian position. The manifesto contends that those who follow interpretative traditions of Islam other than Deobandism are not *munafiqin* because they are not hypocrites. Instead, the author argues that these people are in fact *kufar* (unbelievers, singular *kafir*). While disbelief may seem even worse than hypocrisy, Pakistani *kufar* are in fact less problematic in the Deobandi worldview than are *munafiqin* because, as the author contends, they are not at war with the Muslims in Pakistan. If *kufar* are not at war with Muslims, they cannot be attacked.

In contrast, the author argues that *kufar* outside Pakistan (e.g., Hindus, Jews, Christians, atheists) are at war with Muslims and are thus legitimate targets. The author writes, "As long as kufar have power anywhere in the world, then one can be tormented [by them] for no other reason than being a Muslim. Should anyone want to convert [to Islam], he/she will hesitate out of fear of doing so.... You are required to fight until the time when there are no obstacles to becoming a Muslim.... God has commanded this" (Jamaat-ud-Dawa 2004, 6). The author adds, "As long as Islam is not supreme throughout the world and as long as the laws of Allah are not enforced, fighting kufar is a duty.... I have been commanded to keep fighting them until the kufar have given proof that there is no other worthy of worship but Allah and that Mohammad is the prophet [e.g., read the Kalma and become brothers], that they do *namaz* [pray as a Muslim], and they give *zakat* [Islamic tithe]" (6–7). The balance of the volume is made up of a series of arguments, derived from the Quran, Sunnah, and Hadith,[9] that jihad against the external *kufar* is a compulsory obligation (*farz-e-ein*).[10]

The author disparages those who accept the Deobandi claim that Pakistan is as suitable for jihad as India. He laments, "When I hear some Muslim brother who considers India and Pakistan equal for jihad, I feel pity [for him]. I clearly see the Hindus' preferred thinking in his mind and the Hindus' favorite language in his mouth" (Jamaat-ud-Dawa 2004, 35). This crucial passage suggests that those who want to conduct violence in Pakistan are doing the Hindus' bidding and furthering India's ostensible goal of destroying independent Pakistan. The author extends this argument in response to another imagined question: "if we protect the building of Islam from the outside through jihad [e.g., protect the *ummah* outside of Pakistan] and it remains weak from inside [e.g., in Pakistan], then what is the point? Please explain." In response, he argues that "the internal strength of this building will also come through jihad against enemies" (ibid.). He makes clear that external jihad also serves the state's supreme interest: its integrity. The author argues that there is only one way to end the domestic violence that has riven Pakistan: fight the external *kufar*. He predicts that when Pakistanis stop fighting this foe Pakistan will devolve into violence and chaos.

These passages explain both LeT's domestic policies and the state's lasting support for the group. Lashkar-e-Taiba is the only militant organization to actively challenge the Deobandi orthodoxy that has imperiled Pakistan's internal security. It is also the only such group to present an easily understood argument about the legitimate targets of jihad and the utility of external jihad. Thus, LeT's doctrine helps to maintain the integrity of the Pakistani state, even as it complicates Pakistan's external relations. Knowing this, Pakistan's support for this organization seems less puzzling. Given the enormous domestic importance of LeT and also Pakistan's continued belief that it can use its nuclear deterrent to control fallout from the organization's external operations, Pakistan is making a sophisticated cost–benefit assessment of the utility of the organization.

Not only does this understanding of Lashkar-e-Taiba explain Pakistan's reliance upon the group, but it also helps to illuminate LeT's use of its own resources. Given LeT's large role in domestic politics, it makes perfect sense that the group actually sends only a small percentage of its trainees on external missions. But members who are never deployed outside of Pakistan are not wasted investments: they further LeT's domestic mission by countering the Deobandi message of sectarian violence, promoting the group's pro-state agenda of external jihad, and cultivating ever more recruits who will continue the same cycle of training and domestic deployment.

This pattern is crucial to LeT's continued viability. The group does not primarily recruit from among adherents of the theological tradition from which it derives (Ahl-e-Hadith) (Fair 2004b, 2008; Rassler et al. 2013). There are two reasons for this: first, because many of the Ahl-e-Hadith ulema have rejected violent jihad, LeT has drifted from its theological roots. Given its differences of opinion with the ulema, it should not expect many strict Ahl-e-Hadith adherents to join (Rana 2004). Another reason is that the Pakistani Ahl-e-Hadith community is quite small, perhaps less than 10 percent of Pakistan's population of 180 million.[11] Thus, LeT overwhelmingly recruits Deobandis and Barelvis, who together comprise the majority of Pakistan's population. In Daur-e-Aam (basic training), recruits undergo rigorous religious indoctrination. This is an important opportunity to attract those with a taste for violence to a pro-state militant organization rather than a Deobandi group. It also provides LeT the opportunity to dissuade Deobandis (or others) from attacking Pakistani political leaders, security forces, or civilians.

Pakistan's support of LeT's expansion into providing social services after 2002 (particularly in its guise as Jamaat-ud-Dawa) comports well with this understanding of the organization's increasingly important domestic utility. By 2004 LeT was building schools (not madrasas) and clinics and providing other social services throughout Pakistan, including Sindh, Balochistan, and beyond. The group contributed large quantities of money and relief supplies to the victims of the 2004 tsunami in Southeast Asia; organized relief and medical assistance after the 2005 Kashmir earthquake; provided social services to internally displaced persons fleeing the military offensive in Swat in 2009; and helped the victims of the 2010 monsoon-related flooding.[12]

Pakistan has endured serious criticism for its continued patronage of Lashkar-e-Taiba/Jamaat-ud-Daawa or its latest incarnation, Filah-i-Insaniat Foundation (US Department of State 2010). But when one appreciates LeT's importance in countering the violent agendas of the rival militant groups savaging Pakistan, it is clear that the state has an enormous incentive to encourage and facilitate LeT's expansion throughout Pakistan. By bolstering the organization's domestic legitimacy through the provision of social services, Jamaat-ud-Dawa makes LeT ever more effective at countering the competing narrative offered by Deobandi groups. Those who doubt Pakistan's ongoing support for the organization should note that after the Mumbai attack of 2008 the Punjab provincial government began managing the organization's substantial assets in the Punjab and has even placed many Lashkar-e-Taiba/Jamaat-ud-Dawa members involved in various ostensibly charitable activities on its official payroll. In addition, the Punjabi government has made substantial grants to the organization (*Dawn* 2010; Geo TV 2009).

Given the important domestic role that LeT plays in helping to counter the Deobandi violence that has ravaged Pakistan, the organization will become more important as Pakistan's domestic security situation degrades. This suggests that no matter what may happen vis-à-vis India, Pakistan's military and intelligence agencies will resist cutting ties with the group. Unfortunately, there is little cause to be optimistic that Pakistan's civilian institutions will see this issue very differently; after all, it was Bhutto who first instrumentalized Islamist groups in Afghanistan in the early 1970s, laying the foundation for what would become Gen. Muhammad Zia's Afghanistan strategy after the Soviet invasion. Bhutto's daughter, Benazir Bhutto, continued to support Islamist militants in Afghanistan, including the Taliban, during her time as prime minister, and both she and her main political rival, Nawaz Sharif, have long histories of supporting the so-called Kashmiri groups operating in Kashmir and India. Sharif also maintained Bhutto's support for the Taliban.

Conclusions and Implications

In this chapter, I sought to explain the strong positive statistical correlation between the increasingly overt nuclearization of the subcontinent and the level of conflict between India and Pakistan. As a first step, I have demonstrated that the Pakistani doctrine of proxy warfare and low-intensity conflict has undergone a systemic evolution since the earliest years of the state's existence. From the 1970s onward, Pakistani military planners increasingly saw irregular warfare as enabled by Pakistan's expanding nuclear umbrella. As Pakistan's militant groups continued to proliferate and as its nuclear deterrent evolved from covert to overt, Pakistan's brazenness as regards these proxies increased as well. As a result of the events that followed 9/11 and Pakistan's decision to support some aspects of the US War on Terror, many of these militant groups have forged an antistate alliance. The Pakistan Army has sought to manage this threat, preferably by brokering peace deals but using military force when necessary (Jones and Fair 2010).

While much ink has been spilled over the external utility of these actors, analysts of South Asia have not considered the domestic utility of such groups. LeT should be seen as serving two functions simultaneously: prosecuting Pakistan's external policies while also undermining Deobandi groups that advocate attacking within Pakistan. (It is possible that similar arguments could be made concerning other militant groups, including the sectarian groups and Hizbul mujahideen, but making such a case is beyond the scope of this volume.) Without understanding the domestic and foreign functions of these militant groups, one cannot fully comprehend how they align with the strategic goals of the Pakistan Army: to preserve and protect not just the state but also the state's ideology. Lashkar-e-Taiba has long served both purposes.

10

Is the Past Prologue?

It is difficult to imagine what sort of defeat would compel Pakistan to abandon its persistent revisionism and its reliance upon the use of Islamist proxies under its expanding nuclear embrella to pursue its revisionist agenda. Despite losing half of its territory and population in the 1971 war with India, Pakistan redoubled its commitment to overturning the territorial status quo and undermining India's ascent. Given the increasing international commitment to intervening in any Indo-Pakistan military crisis to prevent escalation to a full-scale war, it is doubtful that any crisis would evolve to such a point where India would be able to inflict a devastating defeat on Pakistan. This necessarily assumes that India would have the capability and will to do so (Joshi 2013; Ladwig 2008). It is useful to consider other means by which Pakistan's strategic commitments could evolve. After all, strategic cultures do change despite their conservative qualities. A number of plausible scenarios could bring about a slow reshaping of the Pakistan Army's strategic culture and the behaviors it facilitates. This chapter proposes and evaluates several endogenous (internal) and exogenous (external) shocks that could galvanize change within the Pakistan Army's strategic culture and place the country, over time, on a different course. This list is certainly not exhaustive, but it does include the most probable sources of change.

Endogenous Game Changers

Several plausible endogenous developments could influence the way the Pakistan Army as well as Pakistan's citizens understand the army's role in society and the capacious freedom the army has seized to shape domestic and foreign policy per its preferences. One such endogenous change is a fundamental evolution away from army-dominated governance. A second is that Pakistani civil society will force the army to alter its policies. A third possibility is the further erosion of Pakistan's economy, which may drive the Pakistan Army to acquiesce to some degree of economic liberalization as regards India. Fourth, change may come from within the army itself as a result of changing patterns of recruitment its policies has precipitated.

DEMOCRATIC TRANSITION?

One possible source of change in the way the army understands the world and the ways it can behave is a genuine democratic transition. While this may have seemed far-fetched a few years ago, observers are now willing to cautiously consider the possibility that Pakistan is on the verge of such a transition away from praetorianism (Grare 2013; Mallet and Bokhari 2012). The government led by the Pakistan People's Party (PPP) that was ousted in the May 2013 elections was the second consecutive government to serve out its term since the restoration of democracy in 1988, albeit with some important caveats, and the first since the 5th National Assembly (1972–1977) to do so under an entirely civilian dispensation. (The first government to serve out its complete term since 1988 was the 12th National Assembly, which was elected in October 2002 and served until 2008. However, it did so under the auspices of President Pervez Musharraf's military-dominated government.) The March 2008 elections marked Pakistan's first constitutional change of government under a fully civilian dispensation, and those of May 2013 heralded the second.

While the previous PPP-led government was distinguished mainly for its corruption, it did take several important steps toward consolidating democratic processes and institutions. The 13th National Assembly (2008–2013) passed more legislation than any other in Pakistan's recent history (National Assembly of Pakistan Official Website n.d.). Only the 5th National Assembly, which promulgated the current 1973 Constitution of Pakistan, passed more bills than did the 13th National Assembly. The Pakistan Institute of Legislative Development and Transparency (PILDAT), an independent organization that monitors legislative affairs in Pakistan, observed that "while the outgoing Government deserves appreciation as it did not bulldoze legislation through the House, the opposition should also be applauded for playing a positive and constructive role in bringing major changes in the 1973 constitution and for positively contributing to key legislation" (PILDAT 2013a, 7).

The PPP-led government made considerable strides in institutionalizing democracy. Perhaps the most surprising was the government's efforts to take greater responsibility for foreign and defense policymaking, which have been traditionally the exclusive bailiwicks of the powerful army. The parliament set up the Parliamentary Committee on National Security (PCNS) in November 2008 through a Joint Resolution of the House. According to PILDAT (2013a), the PCNS has been "one of the effective Committees during the past five years. The unanimous passage of the 14-point recommendations of the Parliamentary Committee on National Security by the Parliament marked the beginning of an oft-demanded Parliamentary overview and ownership of Pakistan's foreign policy" (7). It is likely that the PCNS garnered support from the popular outrage over events such as the unilateral US raid in May 2011 to kill Osama bin

Laden in his Abbottabad safe house (Schiffrin et al. 2013); the Raymond Davis affair in which Davis, a US Central Intelligence Agency (CIA) contractor, shot and killed two suspected Inter-Services Intelligence (ISI) contractors whom he claimed attempted to rob him at gunpoint (Waraich 2011); and the accidental US/North Atlantic Treaty Organization (NATO) assault on Salala, a Pakistani military post near the Afghan border, which killed 24 Pakistani troops (Masood and Schmitt 2011).

US officials were ambivalent about the PCNS in part because several of the PCNS recommendations undermined US interests, particularly the closure of the ground lines of supply to the war in Afghanistan between November 2011 and July 2012 (CNN 2012) and the denial of drone operations from the Shamsi airbase (Masood 2012). In the long run, the PCNS' activism ultimately advanced US long-term interests in having Pakistan's civilian institutions of governance assume a more prominent role in providing security governance in the country. To the dismay of many Pakistanis, the government did not rigorously adhere to the entirety of the PCNS framework to restructure the US–Pakistan relationship. This road map to restructuring bilateral relations with Washington was the cornerstone of the Parliamentary resolution that came out of the PCNS review. PILDAT (2013a) observed of this process that "the facilitation of this review and the unanimous approval of these recommendations indicated the Government's maturity and due regard to the institution of Parliament" (7). The PCNS review also helped establish some semblance of parliamentary oversight of governmental policies in the realms of defense and foreign policy, which have long been the exclusive bailiwick of the army. Even though the government did not execute the PCNS guidelines with fidelity and while the parliament and the PCNS carefully managed this process to avoid fundamentally challenging the preferences of the army, Pakistan's peoples have become more accustomed to seeing politicians weighing in on foreign and defense policy issues. Attesting to the importance accorded to politicians engaging in these hefty affairs, all of the major political parties featured civil–military relations in their various party manifestos in the run-up to the 2013 elections (PILDAT 2013b).

Although the 13th parliament made important strides in asserting itself in national security affairs and security governance, with the passage of the 18th Amendment in April 2010 President Asif Ali Zardari became the first sitting Pakistani president to devolve his extensive presidential powers voluntarily to the prime minister. This is no small accomplishment in a country where the president has often enjoyed more power than the prime minister or parliament. The 18th Amendment modified some 97 of 280 articles of the 1973 Pakistani constitution. This amendment denuded the president of the powers to circumvent the legislative function of the parliament and decreased the period of time that the president can consider bills that have been passed by the parliament before approving them. It also removed the deeply problematic Article 58-2(b) that was promulgated first under the military dictator Zia ul Haq and then revived under Musharraf. This provision permitted the president to unilaterally dismiss the government. It also required the appointment of a caretaker government, with appointments to the same deriving from consultations of the outgoing prime minister and opposition leader. It also removed the term limits that precluded prime ministers from serving more than two terms.

With the 18th Amendment, Pakistan formally returned to a parliamentary democracy with the prime minister and his ministers composing the "federal government." It reinstated the prime minister as the chief executive of the nation rather than the president. However, despite this important constitutional change, for all intents and purposes Zardari retained his hold over those aspects of the state in which civilians might have been able to engage meaningfully until Zardari was ousted in the July 2013 presidential elections. Equally important, the international community continued to engage Zardari as well as the army chief in its interactions with Pakistan after the promulgation of the 18th amendment. Despite the important reallocation of power from the presidency to the prime minister, the prime minister remained largely irrelevant. A testament to the irrelevance of this post is the ubiquitous celebratory contention that this current government served out its terms even though the 18th Amendment clearly defines the government as the prime minister. Since Prime Minister Yousaf Raza Gillani was ousted in June 2012, the claim that this government has served out its term would be suspect in any country with a more robust tradition of parliamentary democracy.

Another important contribution of the 18th Amendment is that it was the first serious effort to devolve power to the provinces. It eliminated the so-called Concurrent List, which enumerates state function for which federal and provincial governments may legislate but provides supremacy to the federal law. As a part of devolution of power from the center to the provinces, the amendment also altered the way the National Finance Commission establishes the distribution of national revenue to the provinces. Unfortunately, this remains a likely source of increased friction between the central government and provinces. Significant devolution of power to the provinces may be an important means of tempering the significant concerns of ethnic groups who feel dominated by the Punjabi state. While the 18th Amendment draws most of the attention, the 13th National Assembly also passed the 19th Amendment, which changed the way judges are appointed to the superior judiciary, and the 20th Amendment, which established a new procedure to handle government transitions through the consensual appointment of a caretaker government.

This impressive slate of legislative initiatives represents an important and unprecedented step in ensconcing civilian institutions—perhaps modestly—in the security governance of the state (Malik 2009). This does not mean, of course, that Pakistan's democracy is in the free and clear. There are numerous and daunting tasks ahead for the next government. The Nawaz Sharif government must consolidate democratic institutionalization, strengthen civilian control over the military, forge consensus among the various political parties at the level of the federal government and in the provincial governments, resist political infighting, preempt military interference, and bravely seek economic reforms against the wishes of the party's constituents and the party's own economic interests. This may prove too herculean an agenda.

While the government has moved forward by leaps and bounds in the last few years, progress might be slower in the ones ahead despite the sweeping electoral mandate that Pakistan's current prime minister, Sharif, secured in the May 2013 election. While much of the durability of the 13th National Assembly can be attributed to Sharif's maturity and commitment to ousting the PPP through constitutional elections rather than conspiring with the military to pro-rogue the government, it is not obvious that the PPP will have such forbearance while it is in the opposition. The early signs are not positive. Both the PPP and the Awami National Party boycotted the July 2013 presidential elections, which foisted Mamnoon Hussain of the Pakistan Muslim League Nawaz (PML-N) to the now largely ceremonial post.[1] Not only is the forbearance and patience of the opposition parties a looming question, but it is also far from obvious that the army will make a quiet retreat to its barracks to permit democracy to take deeper root.

Even if Pakistan were to undergo a permanent democratic transition in which civilians shape foreign and domestic policies, as discussed in Chapter 2, it does not obviously follow that the civilians would abandon the policy of persistent revisionism with respect to India. This is because of the deep presence of the army's strategic culture, based on the ideology of Islam and the two-nation theory, within Pakistan's civil society, political culture, and bureaucracies. It is certainly reasonable to posit that such a democratic transition is a necessary but insufficient condition for Pakistan to move away from its persistent revisionism, but a democratic transition is unlikely to lead to a change in the preferred policies of the state without a fundamental evolution in the ideology of Pakistan. Under what conditions are the Pakistani state and its citizens willing to jettison a national ideology, rooted in religious and civilizational terms that would permit any meaningful accommodation with India, which is also defined in religious and civilizational terms?

CIVIL AND UNCIVIL SOCIETY: IMPETUS FOR CHANGE?

A second possibility is that Pakistani civil society will force the army to alter its strategic culture and the policies it motivates. However, this is not terribly likely because many components of the army's strategic culture are deeply assimilated in Pakistan's civil society and sustained through the public and private media, through public education, and in the country's bureaucratic and political institutions. Such change is not entirely impossible over a longer time horizon. Pakistan's media, while compromised, is vibrant and diverse. Some observers even argue that the "army's hegemony of the intellectual discourse has weakened, if not completely disappeared" (Farooq 2012a, 40). While I do not share this view, it is certainly true that although right-wing, army-backed ideologues dominate Pakistan's media landscape, there is also an increasing number of media personalities champion "the cause of unqualified liberalism and unconditional secularism" (ibid.). Although illiberal forces have shown themselves past masters of social media and Pakistani liberal civil society remains in disarray, events of recent years prove that civil society, while weak, is not dead (Cohen 2011).

Perhaps the most important demonstration of the complexity of Pakistan's civil society is the so-called lawyers' movement, which first crystallized in 2007. The country's lawyers, exhausted with Pervez Musharraf's authoritarianism, staged national protests to secure the reinstatement of Iftikhar Muhammad Chaudhry, a popular Supreme Court justice who had been ousted by Musharraf. International media reported with great excitement that Pakistan's civil society was standing up to praetorianism. This exuberance was short-lived. In January 2011, the governor of Punjab, a noted opponent of Pakistan's blasphemy laws, was assassinated by his bodyguard. The same international media that had been so impressed with the lawyers' movement was repelled when this ostensibly "liberal" movement mobilized to defend the killer (author fieldwork in Pakistan during the assassination). The movement's tight association with the Islamist political party, the Jamaat-e-Islami, and controversial figures such as Lt. Gen. (Ret.) Hamid Gul, a well-known Taliban apologist and supporter of Pakistan's varied Islamist militant groups, further undermined any semblance of the movement's liberal credentials. Siddiqa (2012), in an analysis of the lawyer's movement, remarked shrewdly that "it can be concluded from the socio-political nature of the legal community and its behavior after the end of the 2007–2009 protest that a strengthening of the system of justice for the benefit of the common man was certainly not the core purpose." Instead, she suggests that the movement was really a means to increase the legal community's "nuisance value and membership as a secondary partner of the powerful [military-dominated] establishment" (ibid.). Siddiqa was surely correct.

Part of the problem with Western hopes that "civil society" will rescue Pakistan is that most Westerners seriously misunderstand what civil society means in Pakistan. Whereas in the West civil society conjures up images of liberals and others challenging the state, in Pakistan civil society is populated by a diverse set of actors and includes those who want more authoritarianism or even theocracy as well as those who want greater separation of mosque and state, liberalism, and robust democracy. Zaidi (2006) notes that whereas Western literature on civil society suggests some inherent opposition to the state this is not the case in Pakistan. Rather,

> for civil society in Pakistan, whether of the westernising/modernising kind or of the more fundamentalist Islamic kind, the question has not been one of democracy versus non-democratic norms, but of "liberalism" against the perceived and variously interpreted Islamic symbols and values. Unlike in the traditional (western?) notion of civil society, the pursuit of democratic ideals is not a necessary and defining condition. Not only is this a fundamental difference, but so too is the necessary distinction of the autonomy from the state, so integral to the meaning of civil society, in theory. If sections of civil society are expected to challenge the state, in Pakistan many of them are the state's partners, acquiring mutual benefits of some kind or the other (3556–3557).

There is as much—if not more—opposition among the varied elements of Pakistan's civil society as there is between these civil society organizations and the government, whether civilian or military. It is simply too early to say how this conflict will be resolved and whether the proponents of democracy and liberalism will prevail over those who want more autocracy, a more pronounced role of the military, or even a greater role for Islam and Islamism in Pakistan's governance.

ECONOMIC SHOCKS—FOR BETTER AND FOR WORSE

A third plausible endogenous shock is the further erosion of Pakistan's ramshackle economy. This may drive the Pakistan Army to acquiesce to some degree of economic liberalization as regards India. Over time an economic rapprochement could transform the nature of the relationship from conflict to cooperation. Since 2011, Pakistan and India have steadily deepened their economic ties, a development that has given rise to optimism about a potential resolution of the enduring rivalry. In 2011, Pakistan gave India "most favored nation status," finally reciprocating a move India had made in 1996 (Ahmed 2011; Lal 2012). Despite the initial enthusiasm about this initiative, as of early 2014 there has been very little progress in implementing this status. In late 2012, Pakistan and India also signed an unprecedented visa liberalization agreement (Pattanaik 2012). Some authors have mused that given the "massive economic challenges, a burgeoning population, energy and water shortages, and huge and growing numbers of unemployed workers, especially youth, Pakistan needs to look for ways to move itself out of the economic hole into which it has fallen. Greater trade with India offers an immediate and rich possibility of economic growth for both Pakistan and India" (Hussain 2011, 1).

But even this guarded optimism assumes that the Pakistan Army approves of such developments. After all, the Pakistan Army, not the Ministry of Foreign Affairs, currently sets the limits of what is possible in Pakistan's relations with India. And in fact, it appears that Rawalpindi has given its tacit but tentative approval to this course. Some analysts attribute the army's willingness to consider this to the fact that "the Pakistani army has watched, with some concern, as Pakistan's macro-economic indicators have dropped and India has managed to sustain its economic performance despite a worldwide recession.... The Generals in the Army can see that if this goes on for much longer, the disparity between India and Pakistan will be unbridgeable" (Malhotra 2011). Numerous author interviews with US Department of State and UK Foreign Office personnel show that this optimism is widely shared in Washington and London. But the observable trends do not warrant unbridled enthusiasm. Any serious rapprochement with India would weaken the army's political position within Pakistan. Thus, the army will seek to limit the relationship, achieving economic gains while ensuring that the rivalry remains intact.

In the past, the army has acted to sabotage the peace process, either through army actions (e.g., the Kargil War) or the deployment of jihadi proxies who undertake attacks in India. In January 2013, just as both sides were moving forward to enact a landmark visa regime, a scuffle took place on the Line of Control. While both sides dispute the other's narrative of who trespassed first, what is clear is that Pakistani armed forces killed two Indian soldiers, one of whom was beheaded. This sent the relationship into a tailspin. India predictably "decided to 'pause' the implementation of the liberal visa regime on 'technical' grounds" (Pattanaik 2013). This has left many Indians wondering—again—whether an India–Pakistan peace process is sustainable; whether it can be delinked from ongoing conflict, especially in Kashmir; and whether, given the army's opposition, Pakistan's struggling democracy can be a partner in forging a path to peace (ibid.).

The materials examined in this volume suggest that three changes must take place before the Pakistan Army will accept normalization with India. First, the army would have to abandon its practice of describing the rivalry with India in civilizational terms. This would likely require the Pakistan Army to revise its ideological commitment to the two-nation theory. Second, the army would have to accept a less privileged, even subordinate, position with Pakistan's governance institutions. Peace with India would deprive the army of its status as the single institution capable of protecting Pakistan from India's destructive designs and consequently its claims to political and financial resources and to the right to take control of the government when it deems necessary. Finally, peace would require that the civilian bureaucratic and political elites develop preferences that diverge starkly from those of the army. There is no evidence to suggest that this is likely to occur anytime soon. Given the degree to which the army's understanding of

India as an existential threat permeates government institutions and the popular imagination, it is difficult to imagine what endogenous events could bring about these changes. For purposes of fairness, it is important to also consider that far less likely possibility that Pakistan's economy can be rectified through sagacious political leadership with or without varying degrees of international support. Should this occur, it would be unlikely to change the preferences of the Pakistan Army in a way that would diminish its conflict proneness and persistent revisionism. If anything, the additional revenue would strengthen the army's hand by expanding the resources it may use for conventional and nuclear investments while decreasing its vulnerability to international actors who consider the army's revisionism to be a serious obstacle to peace in South Asia.

CHANGE FROM WITHIN THE ARMY?

Perhaps the most important sources of endogenous change may be the military itself.[2] As Fair and Nawaz (2011) show, the Pakistan Army has struggled since independence to expand its recruitment base. Given that the army has long dominated the political process and has also established a robust system of perquisites for its members and their families, it has become increasingly important that the majority of Pakistanis feel that they can access this system. The army has relaxed its recruiting standards in Sindh and Balochistan, hoping that increased recruitment of Pakistan's more reluctant ethnic groups will entice them to support the national project and diminish their resistance to the state.

Analysis of district-level recruitment data for the officer corps between 1971 and 2005 (Fair and Nawaz 2011) demonstrates the dramatic success the army has had in changing the geographic distribution of new recruits. Figure 10.1 converts district-level recruiting data into shares of total recruits by dividing the number of officers recruited in a given district by the total of all officers recruited that year. In 1972, the figure shows, recruitment was concentrated in a few districts in the Punjab and Khyber Pakhtunkhwa (KP); in fact, most of Pakistan's districts produced no officers. But by 2005 most of Pakistan's districts were producing officers. Of course these data show only geographical diffusion and cannot confirm the ethnicity of the new recruits. While the army claims that it has made strides in recruiting ethnic Baloch and Sindhis, it is possible that the army is recruiting Punjabis, for example, from Balochistan and Sindh.

Survey data suggest that even if the army's geographic expansion does not translate directly into ethnic diversity, greater regional diversity in the officer corps may have important implications for the attitudes of incoming officers. In 2009, the author (along with Jacob N. Shapiro and Neil Malhotra) fielded a 6,000-person survey among a nationally representative sample of Pakistanis (Blair et al. 2013). The survey queried respondents about their views on Islamist militancy, beliefs about governance structures (including civil–military relations), preference for

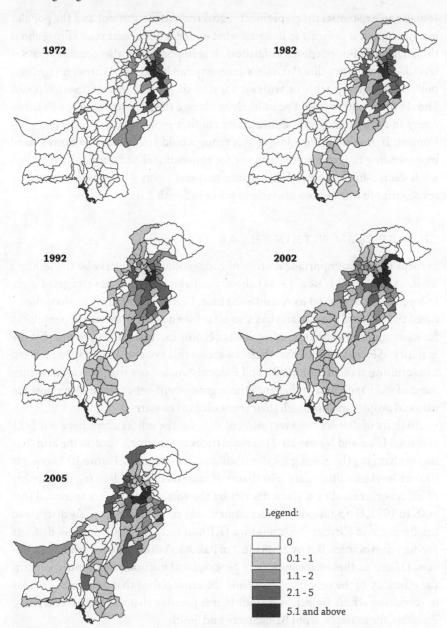

Figure 10.1 Share of officer recruits by district: 1972, 1982, 1992, 2002, and 2005.
Source: In-house manipulations of army officer recruitment data.

shariat, and opinions about the aspirations of India's Kashmiri Muslims. The size of this sample and the fact that it was drawn to permit robust province-level analysis means that it provides important insights into how the evolving recruitment base may result in a corps of officers with different views on key issues facing Pakistan. The sample includes 2,508 respondents from the Punjab, 1,488 from Sindh, 1,128 from KP, and 876 from Balochistan. The data also include information about the ethnicity of the respondent (proxied by the respondent's mother tongue).

For purposes of this discussion, I focus on seven key questions that cast light on a respondent's views on jihad, Islamism, governance, and civil–military affairs. These questions and their response categories are given in Table 10.1. Using these data, I compare Punjabis living in the Punjab to Punjabis elsewhere in Pakistan.

Table 10.1 **Survey Items Analyzed**

Q50. Some people say jihad is a personal struggle for righteousness. Others say jihad is protecting the Muslim umma through war. What do you think? A) Jihad is solely a personal struggle for righteousness; B) Jihad is both a personal struggle for righteousness and protecting the Muslim umma through war; C) Jihad is solely protecting the Muslim umma through war.
Q60. How much do you think Pakistan is governed according to Islamic principles (shariat)? A) Completely; B) A lot; C) A moderate amount; D) A little; E) Not at all.
Q150. Seeing the current situation in Pakistan, do you think that shariat should play a A) Much larger role; B) Somewhat larger role; C) About the same role; D) Somewhat smaller role; E) Much smaller role.
Q180. If shariat were given a greater role in Pakistani law, how much more or less corruption would there be? A) A lot more; B) A little more; C) No change; D) A little less; E) A lot less.
Q310. How much do you think Pakistan is governed by representatives elected by the people? A) Completely; B) A lot; C) A moderate amount; D) A little; E) Not at all.
Q370. The 1973 Constitution of Pakistan says civilians should control the military. This means the military cannot take action without orders from civilian leaders. In your opinion, how much control should civilians have over the military? A) Complete control; B) A lot of control; C) A moderate amount of control; D) A little control; E) No control at all.
Q400. Thinking about the political preferences of Muslims in occupied Kashmir, please tell us which statement you agree with the most: A) In occupied Kashmir the majority of Muslims want to be part of India; B) In occupied Kashmir the majority of Muslims want an independent state; C) In occupied Kashmir the majority of Muslims want to be part of Pakistan.

Source: For additional information about this survey, see Blair et al. (2013).

(Punjabis are the largest ethnic group in the army, and most of the army's infrastructure is located in the Punjab.) I examine differences in responses to the questions listed in Table 10.1 using the Pearson chi-square test to determine whether the distribution of responses is statistically significant for the groups of people compared. (Not all response categories and only relevant sample sizes are presented in the tables.)

First, I examine differences between Punjabis living within (2,015) or outside (136) the Punjab. As Table 10.2 shows, Punjabis in and beyond the Punjab differ markedly in their responses to several questions. For example, Punjabis living outside of the Punjab are less likely than those in the Punjab to view jihad as a militarized struggle and more likely to see it as a struggle for righteousness. They are also somewhat less likely to say that Pakistan is "not at all governed" by Islamic principles, much less likely to want shariat to play a larger role in governance, and are less confident that there would be "a lot less corruption" were the role of shariat increased. Punjabis outside of the Punjab are also less likely to share the belief

Table 10.2 **Punjabis in the Punjab versus Elsewhere**

Question	Punjabis in the Punjab N = 2015	Punjabis Beyond the Punjab N = 136	X2 Test p-Value
Q50 (A) Jihad is a personal struggle for righteousness.**	15%	47%	104.1***
Q50 (C) Jihad is a militarized struggle.	28%	12%	104.1***
Q60 (D) The government is "not at all" governed by Islamic principles (shariat).	26%	15%	51.7***
Q150 (A) Want shariat to "play a much larger role than present" in the state.	49*	15%	138.0***
Q180 (D) There will be "a lot less" corruption in Pakistan under shariat.	47%	24%	41.6***
Q310 (A) Believe that their government is governed "completely" by elected representatives.	41%	14%	68.7***
Q370 (A) Civilians should have "complete control" over the military.	41%	24%	118.9***
Q400 (C) Kashmiris living under India's rule would prefer to join Pakistan.	58%	42%	33.6***

Notes: *** indicates Pearson chi-square is significant at the 0.001 level; ** at the 0.05 level; * at the 0.1 level. All percentages are weighted.

that the government is controlled by elected representatives than are Punjabis living in the Punjab; however, Punjabis outside of the Punjab are also less supportive of complete civilian control over the army. Finally, Punjabis beyond the Punjab are less likely to believe that Muslim Kashmiris living in Indian Kashmir would prefer to join Pakistan. These data suggest that ethnicity is not the single most important predictor of views on these issues.

Table 10.3 focuses on the views of two groups of residents of the Punjab: those who are ethnically Punjabi (2,015); and those who are not (493).[3] Table 10.4 demonstrates that ethnicity is not the best predictor of a person's views on these issues; Table 10.5 explores whether ethnicity matters at all (at least as far as the Punjab is concerned). While the differences in the distribution of answers given by Punjabis and non-Punjabis are often statistically significant, the magnitude of these differences is not large for most items. One results stands out: Punjabis in the Punjab are much more likely than their non-Punjabi neighbors to believe that their government is governed by elected representatives and that the government is not at all governed by Islamic principles.

Table 10.3 **Punjabis versus Non-Punjabis in Punjab**

Question	Punjabis in the Punjab N = 2015	Non-Punjabis in the Punjab N = 493	X2 test p-Value
Q50 (A) Jihad is a personal struggle for righteousness.**	15%	19%	10.6*
Q50 (C) Jihad is a militarized struggle.	28%	23%	10.6*
Q60 (D) The government is "not at all" governed by Islamic principles (shariat).	26%	24%	39.4***
Q150 (A) Want shariat to "play a much larger role than present" in the state.	49%	50%	10.6*
Q180 (D) There will be "a lot less" corruption in Pakistan under shariat.	47%	50%	20.8**
Q310 (A) Believe that their government is governed "completely" by elected representatives.	41%	26%	55.6***
Q370 (A) Civilians should have "complete control" over the military.	41%	40%	19.3**
Q400 (C) Kashmiris living under India's rule would prefer to join Pakistan.	58%	57%	4.4

Notes: *** indicates Pearson chi-square is significant at the 0.001 level; ** at the 0.05 level; * at the 0.1 level. All percentages are weighted.

Table 10.4 **Punjabis versus Sindhis in Sindh**

Question	Punjabis in the SindhN = 94	Sindhis in SindhN = 737	X2 test p-Value
Q50 (A) Jihad is a personal struggle for righteousness.**	54%	41%	14.3**
Q50 (C) Jihad is a militarized struggle.	5%	18%	14.3**
Q60 (D) The government is "not at all" governed by Islamic principles (shariat).	13%	14%	22.5***
Q150 (A) Want shariat to "play a much larger role than present" in the state.	12%	20%	37.2***
Q180 (D) There will be "a lot less" corruption in Pakistan under shariat.	22%	23%	11.7*
Q310 (A) Believe that their government is governed "completely" by elected representatives.	10%	21%	30.8***
Q370 (A) Civilians should have "complete control" over the military.	15%	96%	184.4***
Q400 (C) Kashmiris living under India's rule would prefer to join Pakistan.	45%	36%	6.8

Notes: *** indicates Pearson Chi-Square is significant at the 0.001 level; ** at the 0.05 level; * at the 0.1 level. All percentages are weighted.

Similar analyses of Punjabis versus Sindhis in Sindh (Table 10.4) and Punjabis versus Baloch in Balochistan (Table 10.5) demonstrate that Punjabis respond very differently from either Sindhis (in Sindh) or Baloch (in Balochistan), yet the Punjabis of Balochistan and Sindh also differ from Punjabis in the Punjab. (An analysis comparing Punjabis and Pakhtuns in KP found no statistically significant differences.) Taken together, these data demonstrate that the Pakistan Army, simply by changing its recruitment policies, is bringing in recruits whose views differ from those of their predecessors in an army dominated by recruits from Punjab Province. This is true even if the new recruits from Balochistan are not, in fact, ethnically Baloch. Still, it is difficult to predict how and whether these incoming cohorts will change the values and ideology of the Pakistan Army.

Exogenous Sources of Change?

In addition to these internally derived sources of potential changes, what are the prospects for exogenous sources of change—that is, sources of change that

Table 10.5 **Punjabis versus Baloch in Balochistan**

Question	Punjabis N = 30	Baloch N = 225	X2 test p-Value
Q50 (A) Jihad is a personal struggle for righteousness.**	37%	54%	11.1**
Q50 (C) Jihad is a militarized struggle.	20%	9%	11.1**
Q60 (D) The government is "not at all" governed by Islamic principles (shariat).	20%	11%	22.1***
Q150 (A) Want shariat to "play a much larger role than present" in the state.	27%	17%	5.1*
Q180 (D) There will be "a lot less" corruption in Pakistan under shariat.	17%	17%	4.3
Q310 (A) Believe that their government is governed "completely" by elected representatives.	20%	8%	15.8**
Q370 (A) Civilians should have "complete control" over the military.	47%	34%	5.9
Q400 (C) Kashmiris living under India's rule would prefer to join Pakistan.	37%	32%	9.3**

Notes: *** indicates Pearson chi-square is significant at the 0.001 level; ** at the 0.05 level; * at the 0.1 level. All percentages are weighted.

Pakistan cannot directly control? A number of potential scenarios could bring meaningful change to the strategic culture of the Pakistan Army and would motivate the army to attenuate or even abandon its revisionism.

First and foremost, it is possible that Pakistan will so provoke the international community that the United States, perhaps in concert with India or another ally, retaliates with military force—even degrading, if not destroying, Pakistan's nuclear assets. (This is the scenario that Pakistan's army most fears.) This may seem difficult to imagine, given America's tolerance for Pakistan's provocations. A US-led military strike is not unthinkable should a Pakistan-based or -backed terrorist group attack against the United States or its allies, or should any terrorist launch such an attack by employing nuclear materials with Pakistan's nuclear signature (e.g., with nuclear materials associated with Pakistan's program). The United States will certainly consider such retaliation even if there is no evidence that the Pakistani state sanctioned the attack or facilitated the transfer of nuclear material. It is difficult to imagine that any lesser outrages would provoke such actions by the United States. It is also possible that India may, in response to a devastating terror attack by one of Pakistan's erstwhile proxies, call Pakistan's nuclear bluff and proceed to deliver it a decisive defeat. However, if 1971 is a guide, a military defeat short of nuclear emasculation is not likely to convince the Pakistan Army that its goals are unreasonable. Moreover, the international community will work assiduously to dampen any conflict to prevent precisely such a scenario.

A second possibility is a natural disaster of such magnitude that the Pakistan Army is unable to respond effectively, undermining its claims to be the guarantor of Pakistan's security. This is even less likely than the first scenario. The 2005 earthquake and the massive monsoon-related flooding in 2010 both wreaked unimaginable destruction. Many Pakistan watchers were convinced that Pakistan would rise up in outrage after the 2010 floods. But nothing of the sort took place; in fact, the army came out well in both instances, burnishing its image as the most competent institution in Pakistan. And should Pakistan fall victim to a disaster so severe that it renders the army helpless, it is highly unlikely that the other state institutions will perform any better.

A third possibility is that the United States and its partners will forge a coherent plan to invest in Pakistan's civilian institutions with the explicit goal of slowly undermining the strength of the army. The United States took the first steps on this road with the 2009 Kerry-Lugar-Berman legislation, which was designed to encourage investment in Pakistan's civilian institutions while placing strong conditions on security assistance. The legislation proved a failure, both because the Pakistan Army worked to undermine it and because the United States could not sacrifice its short-term goals in Afghanistan to the long-term goal of a democratic Pakistan at peace with itself and with its neighbors. Thus, endogenous sources of change seem more likely than exogenous ones.

Conclusions: Prospects for Change from Within and Without?

Most prospects for internally or externally driven change in the strategic culture of the Pakistan Army and the behavior it encourages appear rather dim. Should the changes observed in the officer corps recruitment base produce any meaningful change, it will likely do so in future decades. Should a democratic transition occur as some suggest, it will have to be accompanied by profound changes across Pakistani society, which tends to embrace the Pakistan Army's strategic culture and preferences. Other possible shocks, should they occur at all, could have more precipitous effects on the army's strategic culture but are themselves even more unlikely precisely because of the presumed calamitous effects they would have on Pakistan. Even a cursory review of Pakistan's history suggests that it is surprisingly capable of surviving economic crises and natural disasters as well as internal political strife with surprising endurance. Pakistan, it seems, is a very stable instability. With few prospects for substantive change in Pakistan's strategic culture, in the assessments this culture encourages, or in the behavior it incentivizes, the world should prepare for a Pakistan that is ever more dangerous and ever more committed to its suite of dangerous policies.

CHAPTER 11

The Army's Strategic Culture and Implications for International Security

Several components of the army's strategic culture, some of which predate Partition and the emergence of Pakistan, condition the army's decision-making calculus. Perhaps the most important of these is the two-nation theory, which forms the basis of Pakistan's ideology. The Pakistan movement's definition of Muslims as a "nation," which is distinct from and in opposition to Hindus, caused problems for Pakistan from its first days and continues to pose challenges today. Ironically, Pakistan's rejection of any separation between mosque and state has been accompanied by an erosion of tolerance towards Pakistan's diversity: militant groups, many of them the army's erstwhile clients, have led the call for violence against Ahmediyas, Shias, and even Barelvis, in addition to Christian and Hindus. The state has evidenced no appetite for eliminating these organizations, at least in part because their membership overlaps with groups that still serve the army's purposes in India and Afghanistan. To abandon the two-nation theory would undermine Pakistan's claim to Kashmir, something the army is unwilling to do.

Partition, and the bloodshed that ensued, bequeathed to the newly independent Pakistan an incomplete state apparatus, a disproportionate refugee crisis, and a fraction of the resources necessary to manage the enormous challenges the nascent state faced. The process of Partition confirmed the Pakistan movement's description of India as a begrudging Hindu nation that could not reconcile itself to an independent and strong Muslim neighbor. Despite the passage of time, this xenophobic and outright flawed image of India has not faded.

The army's arrogation of the responsibility for defending the ideology of Pakistan means that it defines the threat from India in ideational and civilizational as well as military terms. For the army, acquiescing to India is tantamount to accepting that the two-nation theory is illegitimate or defunct, thus undermining the founding logic of Pakistan itself. No military, political, or diplomatic defeat Pakistan has yet suffered has been adequate to persuade the army to revise its anti–status quo position (not only its claims to Kashmir but also its resistance to India's hegemonic aspirations in the region and beyond). Pakistan's defense writers take pride in Pakistan's role as the sole country with the courage to deny India the hegemonic status it ostensibly craves.

Zionts' (2006) discussion of unreasonably revisionist states is crucial to understanding Pakistan's behavior. He defines *unreasonable revisionism* as failing to revise an anti–status quo position after suffering a clear and devastating defeat. If Pakistan were reasonably revisionist in Zionts' parlance, Pakistan should have come to an agreement with India in 1971, if not earlier. But this assessment depends on a misapprehension of the Pakistan Army's understanding of defeat itself. Even after the 1971 war, Pakistan did not view itself as defeated; rather, it saw itself as emerging from the wreckage still capable of challenging India. In the army's view, Pakistan will be defeated only when it can no longer actively work to deny India's claims—on Kashmir specifically and on regional ascendancy in general. This is a startling realization, prompting us to ask what sort of defeat it would take for Pakistan to relinquish its revisionism? Would the world stand by as such a defeat was meted out to Pakistan, given the numerous risks for asymmetric retaliation as well as nuclear proliferation? As I discussed in Chapter 10, this is simply an unreasonable expectation.

Equally old and enduring is the army's compulsion to view Afghanistan through the lens of strategic depth. As discussed in Chapter 5, this concept is not new or even rooted solely in the twenty-first-century state system. In fact, it first appears as early as the eighteenth century, in British discussions of the threats beyond the northwest frontier of British India. That frontier looms perhaps even larger in the mind of Pakistani strategists, since Pakistan inherited the entire border but only a fraction of the resources with which to manage it. India's refusal, postpartition, to follow through on its commitment to provide Pakistan with a fair share of the assets of the Raj only buttressed Pakistan's belief that India seeks to undo it, either independently or in collusion with Afghanistan or, in the past, with Russia. Whereas in earlier decades Pakistan feared an Indian and Russian plot, with the collusion of Afghanistan, to destabilize its western territories, in recent decades its fears center on Indian and Afghan subversion, perhaps with Washington's tacit approval. This threat perception has mobilized Pakistan to pursue various courses of behavior, alternating between an aggressive forward policy that actively seeks to insert proxies (with Pakistani advisors) into Afghanistan and a close border policy under which Pakistan merely seeks to persuade Afghanistan's leadership to pursue policies favorable to Pakistan. And it has shaped the army's belief that the restive populations of Pakistan's west, such as the Baloch and the Pakhtuns, are ripe for Indian—or, increasingly, American—manipulation.

Pakistan's army has refined its unsavory images of India through its narratives of India's behavior in peace and war. It is difficult to believe how many Pakistanis continue to believe that India started every war with Pakistan and that Pakistan outright won each conflict or heroically fought India to a draw (with the exception of the 1971 war), forcing it to concede. But it is dangerous to fail to recognize the popularity of this version of Pakistan's military history. Collective perceptions of the two nations' history animate popular support for the army and help to sustain widespread willingness to continue funding the army and its adventurism, even while Pakistan's economy and democracy wither on the vine.

The army has fashioned equally specific narratives of its relations with China and the United States. Whereas Pakistan Army mouthpieces routinely rehearse a steady stream of—often exaggerated—American failures, they engage in rhetorical contortions in an attempt to explain away China's shortcomings as an ally. These stylized retellings of its history are an important part of Pakistan's strategic culture and negotiation strategy: it seeks to build an ever accumulating and ever ossifying wall of perfidies, real and imagined, so that it can extract greater rents from the United States. It augments this strategy with the threat of a reversion to China. The army propagates its fictionalized retelling of its relations with the United States and China not only to make this bargaining strategy more effective but also to manage domestic expectations for its relations with both.

Another consequence of the Pakistan Army's view of India is its resistance to accepting that Pakistan's internal security problems may present a greater existential threat than the external challenge posed by India. The army will occasionally acknowledge the severity of the internal threat, and in January 2013 Pakistan watchers were surprised to read news reports claiming that the Pakistan Army had made a much anticipated change in doctrine, for the first time making internal security its top priority. In what should have been a sign that the news was unlikely to be true, the journalists who broke the story cited the *Pakistan Army Green Book* as their source; the reports were indeed nonsense (Ehsan 2013; for a view discrediting such reports, see Swami 2013).

As demonstrated throughout, the Pakistan Army has long conceded the severity of the internal threats confronting Pakistan. There is no dearth of professional military analysis of the numerous cleavages in Pakistan's social fabric, whether they be socioeconomic, ethnic, communal, or sectarian. But the literature generally portrays these cleavages as potential rather than active and makes clear that it is India—with other enemies of Pakistan—that exploits dormant tensions and brings them to the surface. By insisting that these cleavages would not otherwise pose a problem, the Pakistan Army is able to retain its conventional focus against India while seemingly attending to the domestic threat.

This is not simply a rhetorical approach but an institutional survival strategy for the Pakistan Army. A core tenet of the army's strategic culture is that the army, out of all Pakistan's institutions, is best suited to protect Pakistan's ideological as well as territorial frontiers. Should relations with India improve, the army would find it more difficult to justify its claim on national resources. Thus, the army is itself the single most likely spoiler of any rapprochement. But the army has also ensured the diffusion of its strategic culture throughout civilian institutions as well as the popular imagination. This too makes an enduring rapprochement with India less probable—but not impossible.

Alas, this exercise will not satisfy those who insist on isolating the effect of strategic culture, the independent variable, from behavior, the dependent variable. In most cases, Pakistan's strategic culture translates into a series of behaviors that it encourages and even requires. But the interaction between strategic culture and behavior sometimes makes it difficult to distinguish the two. For example, Pakistan continues to develop its views of India through its engagement in wars and skirmishes, entry into which is driven by these same perceptions. Similarly, Pakistan's negotiations with the United States both shape and vindicate Pakistan's core beliefs about its partner. The failure to distinguish cause and effect may be the fault of the current effort or of the ways scholars try to define this dynamic or both.

My research suggests that it would be unwise to expect that the army will move away from these discourses and the behaviors that they not only enable but also encourage. The Pakistan Army is unlikely to give up its attempts to manipulate events in Afghanistan, and it will work to ensure that Pakistan's civilians do not undermine its interests there. Similarly, the army views India as an existential threat that it must resist; failure to do this is the only defeat the army cannot accept—even if its victory comes at the cost of a hollow state. The army's tools for pursuing these objectives will likely remain its alliances with the United States and China as well as asymmetric warfare under Pakistan's ever expanding nuclear umbrella.

Living with Pakistan's Persistent Revisionism?

My research detailed in this volume makes the case that Pakistan's revisionism is not likely to disappear within any policy-relevant time horizon. The elements of Pakistan's strategic culture that motivate it to be risk-acceptant, if not actively risk-seeking, in pursuing its revisionist agenda are enduring and are rooted in Pakistan's history and its social development. This suggests that the United States and others should stop attempting to transform the Pakistan Army, or Pakistan for that matter. It is unlikely that the United States can offer Pakistan any incentive that would be so valuable to Pakistan and its security interests that the army would abandon the varied tools it has developed to manage its security competition with India, much less consider a durable rapprochement. As the past history of US–Pakistan engagement attests amply, conventional weaponry and military training cannot address Pakistan's neuralgic existential fear of India and its resistance to the prospect of Indian hegemony. Given the army's narrative of its history with the United States, security guarantees are also unlikely to persuade Pakistan to accept the status quo.

In recent years, some analysts and policymakers have suggested that should the United States offer Pakistan a conditions-based civilian nuclear deal for Pakistan, the United States could at least position itself to see whether change is possible in Pakistan (Cohen 2013; Fair 2010b; Kimball 2010; Riedel 2012). Is it possible that Pakistan would abandon its nuclear jihad for such a deal? It is difficult to say. Given Pakistan's performance in the global War on Terror, there would be little appetite among American policymakers for such an innovation, and it would face stiff opposition from entrenched interest groups opposed to nuclear proliferation generally and Pakistan in particular. Former Pakistani ambassador to the United States Husain Haqqani agrees. In April 2013, he wrote to me and explained that he pursued a political solution whereby Pakistan secured nuclear legitimacy in return for shutting down jihad. However, Haqqani found no interest in the Pakistan Army, the Inter-Services Intelligence (ISI), or the American administration.[1]

What if Pakistan represents that rare case of a purely greedy state (Glaser 2010), which is revisionist because it wants to increase its prestige or spread its political ideology or religion, even when doing so is not, strictly speaking, needed to preserve the state's security or, worse, when doing so puts at risk the integrity or even viability of the state? The current and past US policy approaches to Pakistan have assumed that Pakistan is a state that is motivated largely by security concerns that can be satisfied with some territorial concession and thus capable of abandoning its revisionism with the appropriate allurements. But what if Pakistan is a purely greedy state as the evidence I present intimates? If so, then any policy of appeasement may in fact aggravate the problems that Pakistan poses to regional and international security. If Pakistan is a purely greedy state, driven by ideological motives, then appeasement is in fact the more dangerous course of policy prescription.

This is exactly the conclusion that I hope readers will draw from my work here. Pakistan may have legitimate security concerns, but at the root of its revisionism is not security but rather deep ideological commitments that predate the independence of the state. This suggests that those who are interested in Pakistan and its destabilizing impact on regional and international security must thus adopt an attitude of sober realism about the possible futures for Pakistan and the region it threatens. In the absence of evidence that any existing approach can persuade Pakistan to abandon its most dangerous policies, it is time to accept the likely fact that Pakistan will continue to pursue policies that undermine American interests in the region. For India, the implications of this conclusion are stark: the Pakistan Army will continue to seek to weaken India by any means possible, even though such means are inherently risky. In the army's eyes, any other course would spell true defeat. The United States and its partners should seriously consider what it means to contain the threats that emanate from Pakistan, if not Pakistan itself. And no matter which choices the United States considers, Pakistan will no doubt deliberate its options as it comes into increasing conflict with the international community.

APPENDIX

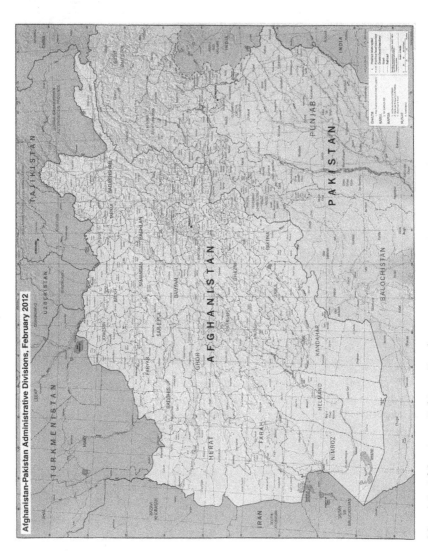

Map A.1 Afghanistan-Pakistan Border. *Source:* Used with permission from the Perry-Castañeda Library Map Collection, http://www.lib.utexas.edu/maps/afghanistan.html

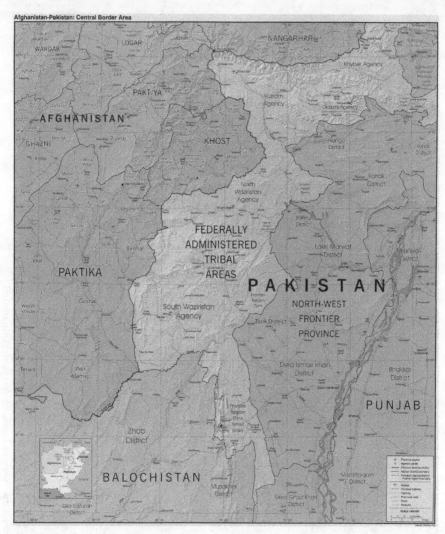

Map A.2 Afghanistan-Pakistan: Central Border Area. *Source:* Used with permission from the Perry-Castañeda Library Map Collection, http://www.lib.utexas.edu/maps/middle_east_and_asia/txu-oclc-308991615-afghan_pakistan_2008.jpg

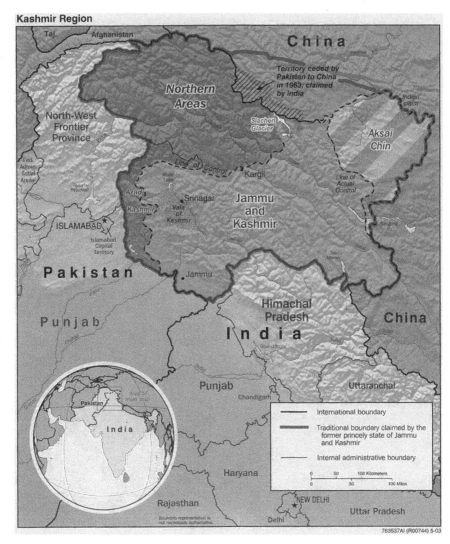

Map A.3 Kashmir region. *Source:* Used with permission from the Perry-Castañeda Library Map Collection, http://www.lib.utexas.edu/maps/middle_east_and_asia/kashmir_disputed_2003.jpg

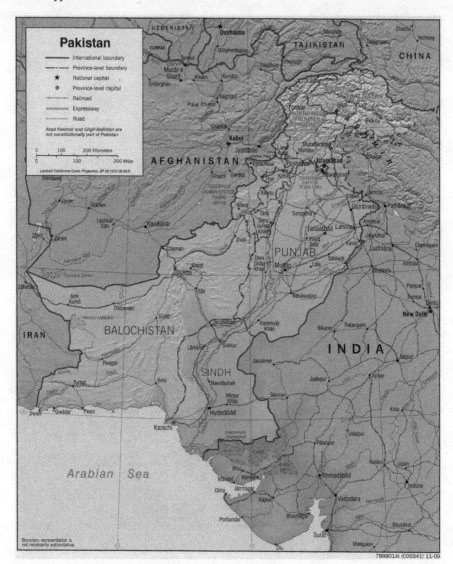

Map A.4 Pakistan, showing border areas with Afghanistan and India. *Source:* Used with permission from the Perry-Castañeda Library Map Collection, http://www.lib.utexas.edu/maps/middle_east_and_asia/txu-pclmaps-oclc-607860461-pakistan_rel-2009.jpg

Map A.5 Afghanistan administrative divisions. *Source:* Used with permission from the Perry-Castañeda Library Map Collection, http://www.lib.utexas.edu/maps/middle_east_and_asia/txu-oclc-309296021-afghanistan_admin_2008.jpg

NOTES

Chapter 1

1. Whereas some scholars may use the term *revisionist* with respect to the territorial status quo, I use it in a more general sense to denote a state's desire not only to change borders but also to alter political orders.

2. For a more nuanced comparison of India and Pakistan's conventional military balance and capabilities, see Tellis (1997) and Gill (2005). India's conventional superiority would begin to confer advantages only as the length of the conflict stretched out into weeks. In a short war along the Indo-Pakistan border, India and Pakistan would be relatively well-matched–one more reason why Pakistan is keen to ensure that any war between the two countries remains limited. As India continues to modernize, however, it may well disturb this relative balance of forces.

3. Like many databases, the Pakistan Institute for Peace Studies is not always clear about what sorts of attacks are tallied and what criteria are used to code different kinds of violence. These numbers are taken from two of their annual reports from 2008 and 2011. In 2011, they reported 7,107 killed; in 2010, 10,003; in 2009, 12,632; in 2008, 7,997; in 2007, 3,448; in 2006, 907; and in 2005, 216, for a total of 42,310. The University of Maryland's (2012) Global Terrorism Database (GTD) provides a far lower figure: it records 6,443 deaths between 2001 and 2010 caused by violent acts that were "aimed at attaining a political, economic, religious, or social goal." GTD surely undercounts given the sources from which it codes its incidents, and thus this number represents a low estimate of actual fatalities due to political violence (National Consortium for the Study of Terrorism and Responses to Terrorism 2012).

4. Pakistan's army chief, Gen. Ashfaq Parvez Kayani, began emphasizing water as a source of conflict between India and Pakistan only as recently as 2010 (see, e.g., Almeida 2010). For the most part, Pakistan has not framed its dispute with India over Kashmir in terms of water security even though scholars of hydro-politics fear that the dispute may well evolve as such in the future. Pakistan may not have done so because the Indus Water Treaty of 1960 has more or less functioned to resolve conflicts over the Indus waters. However, that treaty has come under considerable strain in recent years (Uprety and Salmon 2011; Wirsing 2007).

5. Pakistan may well exemplify what political scientist Charles L. Glaser (2010, 5) calls "a greedy state," which he defines as "fundamentally dissatisfied with the status quo, desiring additional territory even when it is not required for security. These nonsecurity goals result in a fundamental conflict of interests that makes competition the only strategy with which a greedy state can achieve its goals." In the case of Pakistan, it seeks not only

to change the territorial status quo but also to deny India's rise in South Asia and beyond and insists upon being treated as India's equal.

6. The terms *Pashtun, Pakhtun,* and *Pathan* generally refer to the same ethnic group of Pashto-speaking peoples.

7. Islamism refers to movements and ideologies that draw on "Islamic referents—terms, symbols and events taken from the Islamic tradition—in order to articulate a distinctly political agenda (hence the expression 'political Islam,' which is usually seen as synony- mous with Islamism)....Islamism....is a form of instrumentalization of Islam by indi- viduals, groups and organizations that pursue political objectives" (Denoeux 2002, 61).

8. Nasr (2001, 3) articulates the process of Islamization as ensconcing "Islamic norms, sym- bols and rhetoric in the public sphere, and in the process, it has had a notable impact on politics, policy making, law and social relations."

Chapter 2

1. This chapter draws from and synthesizes my previously published work (Fair 2004a, 2004b, 2004c, 2009a, 2011a, 2011b).

2. I want to emphasize at the outset that I approach this puzzle principally as a scholar of South Asian languages and civilizations who is trained to take texts as objects of study as well as the contexts of their production and consumption. I am aware that this project may be germane to ongoing debates among scholars of international relations; however, it is not my intent to inveigh upon these arguments directly. In undertaking this effort, I expect that my scholarly contribution will be largely empirical and aimed narrowly at explaining why Pakistan's army behaves as it does.

3. Whereas some scholars may use the term *revisionist* with respect to the territorial status quo, I use this term in a more general sense to denote a state's desire not only to change borders but also to alter political orders.

4. An enduring rivalry is characterized as "conflicts between two or more states [that] last more than two decades with several militarized inter-state disputes punctuating the rela- tionship" (Paul 2005, 3).

5. The first nonproliferation provision to affect Pakistan was Section 101 of the Arms Export Control Act, which was itself an expanded version of Section 669 of the Foreign Assistance Act of 1961. "This provision forbids aid to countries that acquire nuclear enrichment facilities that are not under the inspection and safeguards system of the International Atomic Energy Agency (IAEA). The Carter Administration, in April 1979, invoked Section 669 and suspended aid to Pakistan after intelligence information confirmed that Pakistan was building a secret uranium enrichment facility" (Cronin 1996, n.p.).

6. This concept is detailed in Chapter 8. *Existential deterrence* was introduced by McGeorge Bundy and implies that under the conditions of opacity and uncertainty Pakistan and India make their mutual deterrence calculation not upon "relative capabilities and strate- gic doctrines" but rather "on the shared realization that each side is nuclear-capable, and thus any outbreak of conflict might lead to a nuclear war" (Kumar 2007, 240–241).

7. Game rationality derives from the work of Thomas Schelling (1960) and posits that there is an ahistorical and acultural, universal strategic calculus that guides a rational player's decision-making based on available information. Game rationality implies that multiple actors would make the same decision using this universal cost-benefit calculus and the same information to attain a stated objective.

8. A debate is ongoing over which theory of international relations—realism, classical real- ism, neoclassical realism, modern realism, and so on—best addresses the question of why revisionist states are revisionist. However, much of this debate is fought on epistemologi- cal and methodological grounds. Curiously, scholars in this literature generally do not

attempt to explain why a state remains revisionist (see different arguments advanced by Glaser 2010; Jervis 1999; Mearsheimer 2001; Rynning and Ringsmose 2008; Schweller 1994; Taliaferro 2000–01; Waltz 1979).

9. Zionts (2006) notes that some scholars such as Davidson (2002) attempt to identify the preferences of domestic and external factors as necessary but insufficient conditions for revisionism, which ultimately materialize when international opportunity structures arise. However, he also notes that neoclassical realism lacks "an explanation of revisionisms' persistence. Though this may seem unnecessary under the intuition that revisionism ends simply when the conditions for its origins disappear, the world is not so symmetrical" (632).

10. One anonymous reviewer objected to the use of the terms *reasonable* and *unreasonable* revisionism because the reviewer thought that it implied some normative judgment. Zionts (2006) is making this assessment based not on a normative evaluation of the goal to be achieved but rather on the feasibility of achieving this goal within a threshold of acceptable costs.

11. Between October 1999 and August 2008, Musharraf served first as the chief executive and later as the president of Pakistan. Under political pressure, he retired his uniform when he resigned as the chief of army staff in November 2007. However, he remained president until fresh presidential elections were held in August 2008. It was constitutionally illegal for Musharraf to hold both posts of president and army chief, and doing so was a violation of the oath he took when he became an officer in the army.

12. Johnston (1995b) is adamant that strategic culture must offer up an ordered set of preferences rather than simply a menu of options for two reasons. First, it is possible that there would be enough variation in a state's menu of preferences that they would overlap with those of other states. Second, he believes that insisting upon a ranked order of preference should more easily give way to explicit predictions about state behavior than simply a menu of unranked options (Johnston 1995b, 47–48).

13. There have been several unsuccessful coups, however. The first was the so-called Rawalpindi Conspiracy of 1949 led by Maj. Gen. Akbar Khan and left-wing activists against the government of Liaqat Ali Khan. (Khan conceived of the tribal invasion of Kashmir which precipitated by the 1947–48 war.) The second occurred in 1980, when Maj. Gen. Tajammul Hussain Malik led a plot to assassinate Zia-ul-Haq. The third occurred in 1995, when Maj. Gen. Zahirul Islam Abassi (an Islamist) led an unsuccessful coup against Benazir Bhutto along with several Islamist militants.

14. This section draws from Fair (2014).

15. Cohen (1984) reported that at the time of his research in the late 1970s and early 1980s there were about 15,000 applicants for the same number of slots (54).

16. According to Rahman:

> The new sepoy continues his military training as best he can and towards the end of four years service he has the option of staying on for a full fifteen years pensionable service or of going on to the reserve for eleven years.... The normal career pattern of a member of the other ranks ensures that a bright and hardworking young man can rise in the ranks to a havildar and, if sufficiently qualified, can become a Junior Commissioned Officer. At each state he has to pass tests or courses: sepoy to lance naik, lance naik to naik, and naik to havildar.... Junior Commissioned Officers rise from the ranks and they command platoons, some thirty men in an infantry battalion. They are selected after they have qualified technically and have shown that they have the requisite educational background. In battalions where there are different class compositions they have to await a vacancy in their class. Normally a man reaches the rank of Junior Commissioned Officer after some twenty years of service, which means he is bordering on forty years of age.... (1976, 66–68).

Once officers pass through the PMA, which takes two years, they complete their baccalaureate. The officer then completes other basic courses before joining his regiment. He must pass exams to be promoted from the rank of lieutenant to captain and again to rise to the rank of major. The most ambitious officers may be selected for the staff college in Quetta; fewer still will proceed to do the War Course at the National Defence College, which only a "small band of officers" complete (71–72).

17. Col. John H. Gill, comments on an earlier draft of this volume, March 2013. See also Cohen (1984) and Schofield (2011).

18. I have personally experienced such treatment. Prior to May 2011, I received professional treatment from the Pakistan Army, which facilitated my travel to South Waziristan in July 2010 and granted me access to numerous senior Pakistani military and intelligence officials. The military and intelligence agencies also provided me with several volumes of the *Pakistan Army Green Book*. These same agencies became nonplussed when they concluded that, despite having provided me with "special access," I "treated them unfairly" in my writings. Securing a visa since then has been inordinately difficult.

19. In my experience, Pakistan Army officers—much more so than US army personnel—are extremely deferential to senior leadership even after retirement. It is rare to see junior officers disagreeing with their seniors even when these senior officers have long left the force. Necessarily, this deference stifles debate when junior officers have a different point of view and their seniors are present.

20. South Asia Foreign Area Officers in the US Army such as Gill suspect that this may well have to do with a "fear of embarrassment" should accurate assessments of the army's performance be made public (Gill review of this manuscript, March 2013). Gill is most certainly correct. When civilians have authored critical evaluations of military performance, the army seeks to suppress these reports. For example, the Hamoodur Rehman Commission Report into the causes and consequences of the 1971 war was kept from the public until 2001. The most recent report from the government-formed commission to understand the circumstances allowing bin Laden to live in the army town for years and the failure of the military to respond to the US unilateral raid on his sanctuary was made public only when it was leaked to Al Jazeera. The report was scathing of the military and the ISI although it ultimately concluded that the military and intelligence agencies were incompetent rather than complicit.

Chapter 3

1. While the partition of Bengal was also marked by ethnic cleansing and communal violence, it was significantly less intense than what occurred in the Punjab (Brass 2003).

2. The Congress was founded in Bombay (now Mumbai) in December 1885 by a group of roughly 70 male members of the westernized Indian elite, and in its early years the party made no effort to become more inclusive. Instead, the Congress focused on the "expansion of [the] elective principle in the legislative councils and greater Indianization of the administration. On the economic front, [it] developed a powerful critique of the whole gamut of colonial policies—the high land-revenue demand contributing to famines, the drain of wealth leading to general impoverishment and the use of indentured labour..." (Bose and Jalal 2004, 94).

3. Jinnah was the leader of the Muslim League from 1913 until Pakistan's independence on August 14, 1947. He became Pakistan's first governor general from August 14, 1947, until his death on September 11, 1948.

4. The word *Pakistan* is a somewhat contrived acronym coined by Chaudhury Rahmat Ali, founder of the Pakistan National Movement, while he was a student at Cambridge. As he explained in his pamphlet "Now or Never," by "PAKISTAN" its proponents "mean the five Northern units of India viz: Punjab, North-West Frontier Province (Afghan Province), Kashmir, Sind, and Baluchistan" (Ali 1933, n.p.). Thus, P is for Punjab; A is for Afghan Province, K is for Kashmir, S is for Sindh, and "Tan" is for Balochistan.

5. The United Provinces of Agra and Oudh was formed in 1877 when the presidency of Agra and the kingdom of Oudh were merged. The former United Provinces was largely coterminous with the modern Indian states of Uttar Pradesh and Uttarakhand.

6. As Indians became increasingly insistent on self-rule, the British looked for ways of diffusing the demands of the Congress and retaining its colony. In 1935, in one such effort to undermine the political power of the Congress at the all-India level, the British Parliament enacted the Government of India Act, which authorized the establishment of provincial legislative assemblies and created a central government incorporating the provinces and many of the princely states under continued British rule. The act also sought to provide for the protection of religious minorities by creating separate electorates for 19 religious and social categories (e.g., Muslims, Sikhs, Christians, Anglo-Indian, Other Backward Classes). Voters could cast a vote for candidates only in their own category. The Government of India Act of 1935 expanded the franchise by lowering land-holding requirements and substituting literacy for higher educational standards. Depending on the status of their husbands, some women were also granted the right to vote. The act also imposed a number of region-specific voting rules (Government of India Act of 1935). The 1935 law gave the provinces much more autonomy, in hopes that doing so would undercut the increasing demand for self-rule. Not only did British officials in India and in London think that such limited concessions could sufficiently appease Indian sentiment to maintain the integrity of the Raj, but they also believed that "even the prospect of provincial autonomy alone in India would be enough to pull many away from the national congress movement through the prospects of offices, jobs, and patronage" (Muldoon 2009, 177). While the motive for the act was undermining Congress' cohesion, it was nevertheless the first initiative to transfer substantial power to Indians on the basis of electoral successes. The act and ensuing elections provided the Indian National Congress, under the leadership of Jawaharlal Nehru and Mohandas Karamchand Gandhi, with an opportunity to demonstrate the legitimacy of its claim to speak on the behalf of Indians as a genuinely representative political body. To prepare for the 1937 elections, the first to be held under the new law, the Congress focused on building up its membership by establishing an all-India grass-roots presence. Its efforts paid off: in 1935 it had 473,000 members; by 1939, its rolls had expanded to 4.5 million (Brendon 2008, 394). Raj officials who had dismissed the Congress as a party of the elites were surprised by its ability to broaden its base (Muldoon 2009).

7. The Congress' victory in the 1937 elections raised numerous questions about the fate of Muslims after the transfer of power from the British to an Indian central government. Jinnah struggled to secure the Muslim League's standing as the party that spoke for Muslims as a rebuke to the Congress' claim to speak on behalf of all of India. Lord Louis Mountbatten (the last viceroy of the British Raj who oversaw the partition of the Raj and from 1947 to 1948 served as the first governor general of independent India) tried to persuade Jinnah to present a more specific vision of Pakistan, but Jinnah refused to propose exact geographical boundaries. Seeking to reinforce its claim that it spoke for all of South Asia's Muslims, the Muslim League continued to insist that South Asia's Muslims, regardless of their many differences, composed a single nation (Jalal 1990).

8. Actually, the term *prince* was imported by the British as an umbrella term for a variety of greater and lesser Indian *rajas, nawabs*, who were dependent on larger states, and even large landowners known as *zamindars*.

9. British paramountcy was represented by the viceroy or crown representative, the political department, and Britain's various local agents. Until the twentieth century, the foreign department was responsible both for foreign affairs and relations with the princely states. However, by 1914 a dedicated political department had been formed within the foreign and political department to manage relations with the states (Kooiman 1995).

10. The British established the Chamber of Princes in 1921. It included 108 high-ranking princes and 12 members who represented 127 other princely states. The viceroy presided over the council and set the agenda (Ramusack 2003, 127).

11. Indian nationalists formed the INA in 1942 in Southeast Asia. It drew initially from Indian prisoners of war who had been captured by the Japanese in the Malayan Campaign and in Singapore. Later, Indian expatriates in Malaya and Burma also joined. The first INA was short-lived, but it was revived under Subhas Chandra Bose (a Bengali), and its men fought alongside the Japanese against British and Commonwealth forces in South and Southeast Asia. Some INA members faced treason charges when they returned to India after the war, and this became a further rallying cry for independence. After independence, Nehru would not let the former INA soldiers rejoin the army. While he respected their heroism, he feared their capacity for insubordination and their political activism. The legacy of the INA is complex. While its men are heroes, they were also traitors who made enemies out of their own countrymen who were fighting with the British. They were also complicit in the war crimes of the Imperial Japanese Army. For more details, see Cohen (1963–1964).

12. According to Birdwood (1952, 305), "... The effect of the awarding of the other three tehsils to India was to offer India a railway and railhead without which she would have found it almost impossible to conduct operations in Kashmir." Birdwood's argument is simply wrong: India would have received Pathankot, the tehsil it required for these operations, even had the principle of religious affinity been applied. Such an oversight is surprising for a former chief of the Indian Army, who should have had a greater grasp of the region and of the Army's logistical requirements. Alastair Lamb, a British historian, has also consistently championed this view in his various writings. He maintains that the British, motivated by their strategic assessment of India's vulnerable northern frontier during the colonial period, envisioned Kashmir as joining India. According to Lamb, Mountbatten would have been loath to sacrifice the considerable security architecture that the British had built to fend off Russian imperial encroachment and believed that the inclusion of Kashmir within India was a necessary safeguard against Russian–Soviet penetration. Lamb also contends that Mountbatten certainly would have known that an eventual inclusion of Kashmir within the dominion of India would be contingent on the inclusion of the disputed tehsils in India's Gurdaspur award. He speculates further that British strategists advising Mountbatten would have seen India as a better guardian of the northern frontier than Pakistan (Lamb 1991, as discussed in Wirsing 1998, 25–26).

13. For concise discussion of this concept, see Peers (2008). The term *race* was used inappropriately under contemporary understandings of the word. The imperial ethnographers tended to use *caste, class,* and *race* interchangeably, although *race* tended to be used to denote a group of people who shared some kind of common heritage (linguistic, cultural, or religious) rather than common genetics. Related to this was another race-based belief that descendents of Aryans were better soldiers—a belief that disadvantaged those ethnic groups of South Asia that are not Aryan (e.g., those in South India). Other justifications for the Indian Army's focus on specific groups included arguments about unfamiliarity with combat due to prolonged periods of peace in parts of South Asia, ecological and climactic reasons for the martial prowess of some races, and strategic proximity to Britain's foes, such as Russia (Rizvi 2000a). As a result of these demand-side considerations, the British Indian Army predominantly drew personnel from the northern part of the empire and Nepal (Rizvi 2000b).

14. Edward Said's concept of Orientalism has undergone considerable criticism since he introduced it in 1978. The term generally refers to the way Westerners defined, represented, and depicted the East and themselves in relation to it. I use the term in Porter's (2009) sense, in which "Orientalism" is not monolithic but rather "a plural and shifting set of epistemological ideas, attitudes and practices" (14).

15. There was no coherent colonial army in this period. Instead, each of the three presidencies of the company (in Bengal, Bombay, and Madras) had its own army. Since the Bengal presidency stretched from Burma to the Khyber Pass, the Bengal Army was the most heavily involved in the rebellion of 1857 (for South Asians, the First War of Independence), which was centered in modern-day Uttar Pradesh.
16. The area covered by modern-day Uttar Pradesh and its environs.
17. Understandings of the rebellion of 1857 (also known as the Sepoy Mutiny of 1857) and of the First War of Indian Independence continue to evolve and be contested. See Brodkin (1972), Habib (1998), David (2002), and Callahan (2008).
18. Many of the bases Pakistan inherited were "oriented towards the frontier to the West.... [For example, the General Headquarters] was the former Northern Command of the old Indian Army, the Staff College was in Quetta, looking out upon Central Asia" (Stephen P. Cohen, personal communication, August 2009).
19. The territories that became India had largely benefited from the British policy of gradually devolving power. This began with the 1882 Self-Government Act, which fostered the development of empowered—if limited—local governance. The provinces were the next to experience democratization, beginning in 1909 and culminating in 1935 with the Government of India Act, which allowed a degree of parliamentary democracy at the provincial level. This act was a basis for the constitution of independent India. India also inherited much of the bureaucratic and governance structure of the Raj which had its capital in New Delhi (Jaffrelot 2002b). The areas that became Pakistan did not benefit from the geography of colonial parliamentarianism. Notably, those provinces that would become the core of Pakistan had the least experience with parliamentary rule. While Bengal (which in 1971 became Bangladesh) and Sindh were conquered by the British fairly early and by 1947 had significant experience with parliamentary governance, Punjab was formally conquered only in 1849. Even after it joined the Raj, the Punjab was governed by district magistrates who were responsible for everything from tax collection to the administration of justice. Balochistan, which occupies about 40 percent of Pakistan's landmass, became a British province only during the Second Afghan War (1878–1880). Whereas by 1947 much of the Raj had experienced provincial parliamentarism, electoral activity in Balochistan was confined to Quetta (Jaffrelot 2002b). The NWFP was an administrative entity created by the British in 1901 to organize the defense of the empire against a Russian advance. The British viewed both the NWFP and the Punjab through the prism of multiple layers of security interests. First, the two provinces, especially the Punjab, were the most important recruitment ground for the army. Second, they formed the primary corridor for the traditional invasion route from Central to South Asia. For these reasons—among others explained in Chapter 4—the British kept the Punjab and NWFP in relatively militarized states.

Chapter 4

1. This chapter builds upon the work in Fair (2012). Without evidence, Paris (2010, 7) writes, "The danger for the army, and for Pakistan generally, is not Talibanisation but Islamisation from Punjab-based militants and their allies." Needless to say, not only is the claim lacking in evidence, but also Paris fails to describe what he means by Islamization and why this is necessarily dangerous. His analysis suggests Islamists are more prone to hand the country to terrorists than are others.
2. I adopt the definition of Islamization offered by Nasr (2001), who describes the process of Islamization as ensconcing "Islamic norms, symbols and rhetoric in the public sphere, and in the process, it has had a notable impact on politics, policy making, law and social relations" (3).

3. These militant groups have included including the Afghan Taliban, the Lashkar-e-Taiba, and Jaish-e-Mohammad, among dozens of other groups terrorizing the region. For an example of such fears, see Paris (2010). For a countervailing view, see Schofield and Zekulin (2007).

4. Militants could obtain such materials without the assistance of the armed forces, which speaks to a greater disquiet about the spread of terrorism and radicalization in Pakistan, and state ability to counter it (Leigh 2010). These concerns about terrorist acquisition of nuclear technology or materials have intensified since late May 2011, when terrorists associated with the Pakistani Taliban launched a complex attack on a major naval base in Karachi. Pakistani journalist Syed Saleem Shahzad (2011) reported that the operation was facilitated by an al-Qaeda cell within the Pakistan Navy. (Shortly after publishing this article in the *Asia Times*, Shahzad was slain, allegedly by Pakistani intelligence agencies; Filkins 2011.) This was only one of several recent assaults on military, intelligence, police, and other federal and provincial facilities involving militant sympathizers and operatives from the ranks of the armed forces. Others include attempts to assassinate President Pervez Musharraf in 2003 and 2004 (Voice of America 2011), the 2007 suicide raid on army commandos at a high-security facility in Tarbela (Khan and Syed 2007), and the 2009 attack on Army General Headquarters by militants in military uniforms (Perlez 2009b). Many of these attacks involved civilian personnel, junior officers, or enlisted men from the army, navy, air force, police, or paramilitary organizations (Rumi 2011). Given the frequency of such attacks, Pakistanis themselves are increasingly concerned about the integrity of their national security institutions and the degree to which they have been compromised by the enemy within (Brulliard 2011). Materials pilfered from US officials and published by *WikiLeaks* have brought even classified discussions of these fears into the public domain (Leigh 2010; see also Amin 2009).

5. Haqqani (2005) notes the redaction in official published versions of this speech. For details about the lost recording of this speech, see Siddiqui (2012).

6. Minority legislators were very disturbed by this. They argued for a secular constitution, fearing, perspicaciously, that they would become the objects of persecution and discrimination. They argued for an amendment that would replace the statement "Muslims shall be enabled to order their lives... in accordance with the teachings and requirements of Islam" with "Muslims and non-Muslims shall be *equally* enabled to order their lives in accordance with their respective religions" (Shaikh 2009, 72, emphasis original).

7. The Ahmediyas view themselves as Muslims. The Ahmediya movement began at the end of the nineteenth century in British India with charismatic reformer Mirza Ghulam Ahmad (1835–1908), who claimed to be the messiah. Because this claim contradicts the essential Islamic tenet of the finality of Prophet Muhammad, other Muslims denounce Ahmediyas as apostates in Pakistan and beyond.

8. The title of this volume is significant. Ayub sought to explain that what Pakistan sought in its foreign relations were friends who would work with Pakistan rather than masters who would work through Pakistan to secure their own national goals.

9. There is considerable ambiguity implied by this phrase "Jihad-fi-sibilillah." It need not simply mean militarized struggle, as is often presumed. According to Maududi, who was an important influence for Zia, the phrase has a fairly capacious meaning and includes "any act or deed which is done for the collective well-being of mankind, by a person who has no vested interest in this world (Duniya), but seeks only to earn the pleasure and favour of Allah" (Khattab 1995, 9).

10. The Pakistan Army, like other armies, has chaplains (imams/maulvis), but the army does not make information about them public. Thus, little is known about their numbers, their credentials, or how they are recruited, among other important information.

11. According to Stephen Cohen, Zia personally explained to him that he admired the US military's chaplin corps and that this is what motivated him to upgrade the status of the unit maulvis (Stephen Cohen comments on earlier drafts, January 2013). It is instructive to compare the various roles of Islam in the Pakistan military to that of Judaism in the

Israeli Defense Forces (IDF). Pakistan and Israel share many similarities, one of which is that they are both states founded on religion and where full citizenship is contingent on religious identity. For an analysis of how the IDF mobilizes religion, see Cohen (2013).

12. The exact dates of the brigade's deployment are not publicly available, but it was withdrawn in 1988 when its last commander, Gen. Jehangir Karamat, departed. See Atlantic Council, "Pakistan Army Challenges: General Jehangir Karamat," July 1, 2009, http://www.acus.org/event/challenges-facing-pakistan-army.

13. Rashid (1996) cites a report prepared by the staff of the Senate Committee on Foreign Relations, which "has a different estimate of Pakistani troops in Saudi Arabia" (34).

14. The Pakistan Air Force (PAF) also participated in various Arab–Israeli wars. During the Yom Kippur War (also known as the Ramadan War) in 1973, PAF planes left Pakistan to support Egypt and Syria but arrived after the ceasefire. Because Syria remained in a state of war against Israel, PAF pilots become instructors there and formed the A-flight of 67 Squadron at Dumayr Air Base (*Scramble Magazine* n.d.)

15. The value of Cohen's work is that it is derived from extensive access to the Pakistan Army, including numerous interviews with officers. The limitation of his work, as he readily concedes, is that his research took place before the anti-Soviet jihad and subsequent regional and domestic developments brought about important changes in the army.

16. *Pakistaniat* is somewhat difficult to translate. Roughly it suggests that Pakistan itself is an ideology.

17. As I detail in Chapter 6, the 1971 war is considerably more complicated. West Pakistan's abusive policies toward the Bengali citizens in East Pakistan devolved into a civil war. As refugees began streaming into India, India had numerous concerns to evaluate. India began providing extensive political and military support to the insurgents, including training the Mukti Bahini, who were fighting to liberate East Pakistan. By summer 1971, India saw the insurrection as an opportunity to intervene and break up Pakistan. While India was preparing its war plans, Pakistan started the war in December when it began air strikes on Indian positions.

18. While teaching at the Lahore University of Management Sciences in summer 2010, I learned that students there do not study this pivotal conflict either.

19. It should be noted that many non-Muslim as well as Muslim countries such as Nepal, the United States, the United Kingdom, Egypt, Saudi Arabia, and the United Arab Emirates—among numerous others—send officers to Pakistan's military institutions for training. While scholars often question whether or not Pakistan Army officers deployed to the Arab Gulf states are influenced by Wahhabi teachings during their deployment, it is worth questioning whether it is Pakistan's military training institutions that are exporting highly stylized teachings of jihad. This present research cannot inveigh upon this issue, but it is worth noting for future analysis.

20. The Battle of Badr (March 624 A.D. or Ramadan, 2 AH in the Islamist calendar) was fought by the early Muslims in the Hejaz region of contemporary Saudi Arabia. It is viewed as a decisive battle of Islam's early years and represented an important turning point in the prophet's ongoing rivalry with the Quraish tribe of Mecca. Given the extent to which the Muslims were outnumbered, the victory is often seen as a result of divine intervention.

Chapter 5

1. Rais (2008, 18) concedes that the notion of strategic depth "is a widely debated issue among security experts on Pakistan. It means that Afghanistan does not allow itself to become a base to powers adversarial to Pakistan—a defensive interpretation. It also means that Pakistan will have a dominant position in Afghanistan in its rivalry with other regional powers, including preventing a Kabul–New Delhi nexus."

2. It is worth noting that the British understood South Asia and the entire Indian Ocean to make up a "single strategic region, stretching from the passes of Afghanistan through

the Tibetan buffer to northern Burma and from the Red Sea to the Strait of Malacca, with India at the center" (Garver 2001, 17). Thus, like Pakistan, independent India also inherited this strategic view of South Asia and its extended environment. However, whereas in Pakistan strategic elites adopted this strategic vision with verve; in India "it withered under Nehru's globalistic nonalignment of the 1950s" (Garver 2001, 17).

3. Persia was problematic for several reasons. Not only was it in domestic disarray, but it also had proved unable to successfully challenge Russia during Russia's various attempts to annex territory claimed by Iran. For example, the 1804–1813 war between the Persian and Russian empires ended in the Treaty of Gulistan, under which Iran ceded parts of modern-day Azerbaijan, Georgia, and Armenia to Russia. Second, and equally problematic for the British, Persia stilled claimed Herat and even laid siege to it several times during the eighteenth and nineteenth centuries—once, in 1837 and 1838, with Russian assistance. This "brought the Russians in contact with Afghanistan" (Barfield 2012, 114). Dost Mohammad was forced to call upon British assistance to repulse the Russo-Persian forces.

4. Shuja governed the Durrani Afghan state from 1803, when he ousted Shah Mahmud, to 1809, when Mahmud returned to the throne. Mahmud exiled Shuja to British India, from whence the deposed king plotted his return to power (Barfield 2010).

5. While Dost Mohammad was at first "barely able to control the region between Kabul and Ghazni, by the end of the twenty years of his second reign in 1863, he had retaken control of almost all of today's Afghanistan" (Barfield 2012, 127).

6. The following year, the British assisted Mohammad to expel the Persians from Herat. The defeat forced the Persians to finally recognize their loss of Herat and respect Afghan borders.

7. Lord Lytton, Viceroy from 1876 to 1880, first introduced the concept of a *scientific frontier* and argued that the best line of defense of British India was along the northern slope of the Hindu Kush. At that time, Indian security experts were divided into proponents of the forward and the backward approaches. The forward group "advocated that the frontier should be from Kabul through Ghazni to Kandhar [*sic*] because unless the tribal country was occupied tribesmen would continue to give trouble; river frontier was not a frontier at all; tribal area could pay the expenses of military occupation if its mineral resources were developed; and even if the policy was expensive it must be adopted for the sake of India's security" (Haq et al. 2005, 15) In contrast, the latter group "advocated that Indus should be the frontier line because the tribesmen were troublesome and fanatic and would not tolerate interference; it was difficult to fight in the mountains; and it was very expensive to have British Cantonments in the tribal territory" (ibid.). After some wavering between these schools, between 1888 and 1894 defense planners drew up a compromise boundary that they believed met the scientific requirements of defense. This scientific border between Afghanistan and India became known as the Durand Line (ibid.).

8. The British had in fact used this route to enter Afghanistan during the first Anglo-Afghan war. In the second half of the nineteenth century it was home to multiple kingdoms, one of the most important of which was the Khanate of Qalat (or Kingdom of Qalat), governed by the Khan of Qalat. In 1854 the British Indian government had concluded a treaty with the Khan under which he received £10,000 per year in exchange for permitting the British to station troops within his kingdom and agreeing to fight any internal or external forces threatening British interests (Tripodi 2011). Unfortunately, the Khan of Qalat proved unable to subdue the Marri and Bugti tribes, who continued to raid the Indian territories of Punjab and Sindh. The Disraeli government wanted to put an end to these nuisances and cement British dominance in the region.

9. This arrangement supported the Disraeli government's forward policy by helping to consolidate the British hold over Balochistan, facilitating the movement of British soldiers and material into Afghanistan, securing British access to the strategic Bolan Pass

between Balochistan and Afghanistan, and permitting the British to occupy the town of Quetta, located some 400 kilometers beyond the formal frontier (Mahajan 2002). Serbia and Montenegro declared war on Turkey in the summer of 1876, and it appeared that Russia would enter the war on the side of Serbia. Disraeli considered opening up a Central Asian front against Russia, for which it would be necessary to have access to Afghanistan and, consequently, to and through Balochistan. Disraeli's Balochistan policy was considered aggressive in some political circles (Mahajan 2002).

10. The Afghans reject the validity of the Durand Line, while Pakistan refuses to acknowledge Afghanistan's position (Barfield 2007).

11. As Barfield (2012) notes, Abdur Rahman supported many of these armed groups in order to keep the British on edge. To give his ever more oppressive state political legitimacy in spite of his close alliance with the British, "he made defense of Islam and jihad a feature of Afghan national identity when dealing with the outside world. Abdur Rahman made himself the arbiter of domestic religious and notional ideology in a way that championed his primacy while hiding his compromises" (155).

12. These were the Morley-Minto Reforms of 1909 and the Montagu-Chelmsford Reforms of 1920. The reforms moved toward ensuring constitutional rights and electoral participation for much—but not all—of the Raj.

13. In a personal communication, Thomas Barfield suggested that the British role in the Afghan Civil War of 1929 as well as their ultimate acceptance of Nadir Khan as king and provision of economic assistance and arms to his government may be an outlier. While the British did play a role in Afghan affairs at this time, their goal was not to govern Afghanistan directly but rather to ensure a friendly regime.

14. This is often referred to as Transoxiana because the Amu Darya was classically known as the Oxus River. This area lay between the Amu Darya (Oxus) in the south and the Syr Darya (in the north). It roughly corresponds to the modern-day territory encompassed by southwest Kazakhstan, southern Kyrgyzstan, Tajikistan, and Uzbekistan.

15. These claims, however, received no support from the international community: Britain insisted that all of the British–Afghanistan treaties remained binding as Pakistan was a lawful successor state (Haqqani 2005; Hussain 2005; Rubin 2002)

16. The most ardent proponent of this plan was Sardar Muhammad Daoud. Daoud was the cousin of Afghanistan's King Zahir Shah and served as prime minister before ousting the king in a coup in 1973. He argued for an independent Pakhktunistan for Pakistan's Pakhtuns who lived in NWFP (now known as Khyber Pakhtunkhwa or KP), FATA, and Balochistan, but he never clarified what—if any—relations they would have with co-ethnics in Afghanistan.

17. While Pakistan was anxious to demonstrate that it faced various threats from the Soviet Union, it was also keen to play up its strategic utility to the United States in an attempt to receive more defense supplies—as the aforecited articles by M.A. Siddiqi make clear. In the late 1970s, Pakistan's third military leader, General Zia ul Haq, again made this case to Washington. Pakistan–US defense ties had dwindled significantly following the 1965 Indo-Pakistan war, when Washington cut off military supplies to both combatants. (The United States was not enthusiastic about Zia's coup and the subsequent execution of Zulfiqar Ali Bhutto.) In 1979 the United States even applied nuclear-proliferation-related sanctions, thus precluding any US security assistance to Pakistan without a waiver. As Pakistan was heavily dependent on US systems, the lack of access to US military goods affected Pakistan much more severely than it did India. The Jimmy Carter Administration was unmoved by Zia's evocation of the threats from the Soviet Union and was in any case more concerned about developments in Iran, including the revolution and the US hostage crisis. But once the Russians crossed the Amu Darya (on Christmas Day 1979), the United States quickly shifted into gear, once again entering into a close relationship with Pakistan. While Zia was not able to get the massive assistance he sought from the Carter Administration, he was much more successful with Ronald Reagan, who oversaw

a massive economic and security assistance program for Pakistan as a part of the efforts to oust the Soviets from Afghanistan. Of course, Pakistan had begun its own Afghanistan jihad strategy long before the Soviets formally invaded Afghanistan.

18. Ironically, after 9/11, the United States sought to use the Frontier Corps as a tool to fight the Taliban without understanding its historical role in training Islamist militants (author interviews with Department of Defense officials in 2008). The results of Washington's efforts were mixed at best (Jones and Fair 2010).

19. Chishti, the commander of X Corps at the time of the coup, was responsible for the execution of Operation Fairplay, which overthrew Bhutto's government.

20. The discord between Parcham and Khalq was due to the personal animus between Karmal and Taraki but also to the factions' different approaches to reform. Parcham appreciated the lack of bureaucratic capacity to enact swift reforms and the need for gradualism. Khalq, in contrast, sought to immediately squash the existing order and banish the "backwardness of past centuries" within "the lifespan of one generation" (Maley 2002, 29; see also Magnus and Naby 2002, 118–128).

21. The delay was a result of the fact that, prior to the Soviet invasion, the United States had imposed sanctions on Pakistan for nuclear proliferation. President Carter was not persuaded of the need to change course, and even afterward he was not inclined to direct, via Pakistan, massive resources toward the jihad. But Zbigniew Brzezinski, his national security advisor, argued that the invasion mandated "a review of our policy towards Pakistan, more guarantees to it, more aid, and alas, a decision that our security policy toward Pakistan cannot be dictated by our non-proliferation policy" (Sattar 2007, 159; see also Arif 1995). In 1980, without consulting Pakistan, Washington announced an aid package that provided $400 million in economic and military aid over 18 months. Zia rejected the package because it was "'wrapped up in onerous conditions and these could affect Pakistan's pursuit of the nuclear programme thus denuding (the offer) of relevance to our defensive capacity" (Sattar 2007, 159). But with Reagan's election, US policy toward Pakistan changed. In April 1981, the United States approved a package with loans and grants totaling US$3 billion over five years (Sattar 2007).

22. The Pakistani state has made some important modifications to the FCR since 1947. Most notably, in 1999 the government extended some 365 federal laws to FATA. But the basic concept remains intact (Ali 1999).

23. From 1947 onward, the Muhajirs (people who had migrated to Pakistan from India) and Punjabis in West Pakistan tried to find some way to prevent the more numerous Bengalis of East Pakistan from reaching their true political strength. In March 1954, Governor Gen. Ghulam Mohammad dissolved the first Constituent Assembly just as it was about to come to some accommodation with the Bengalis over their demand that the Bengali language be granted official status. In an effort to offset the Bengalis' numerical supremacy and superior political coherence, Mohammad promulgated the One Unit Scheme in March 1955. Under this system, all of West Pakistan (e.g., the provinces, tribal areas, and princely states) was aggregated into One Unit, West Pakistan, in opposition to East Bengal, which was renamed East Pakistan. In June 1955 a second Constituent Assembly was elected (indirectly, via legislative councils) according to this electoral division (Jaffrelot 2002b).

Chapter 6

1. There is some debate (Whitehead 2007) about whether or not the Indian government had a signed copy of the instrument of accession in New Delhi before it began airlifting troops.

2. For a startlingly stylized account of this resolution, see the official website of the Pakistan Mission to the United Nations, "Kashmir—The History." This account emphasizes the need for the plebiscite but omits the previous two prior conditions that must be first met. While this account is selective, it is representative of how this issue is treated in Pakistani sources.

3. Notably, Operation Gibraltar was named after the early eighth-century battle led by Gen. Tariq Bin Ziyad (the Islamic conqueror of Visigoth Hispania), in which he established a beachhead at Gibraltar. Gibraltar is derived from the Arabic *Jabel al Tariq* (Rock of Tariq).

4. As Raghavan (2009) details, India's military command believed that it was running low on war stocks and pressed civilian leadership to accept the ceasefire. We now know that India's military command was incorrect and that India could have continued fighting for some time. Pakistan was supplied per American/North Atlantic Treaty Organization (NATO) standards, which meant it had about six weeks of spares and munitions. As peacetime planners often underestimate wartime requirements, it is possible that Pakistan also was running low on war materiel after three weeks of fighting (Tim Hoyt comments on this draft, April 2013).

5. Cohen (2004), in contrast, estimates that Hindus were 15 percent of East Pakistan's population, while Haqqani (2005) puts it at 12–20 percent.

6. This is in contrast to Hindi and Urdu, which are grammatically the same language. However, where the former uses a Sanskrit-based script, the latter employs a Perso-Arabic script. Over time, Hindi has increasingly drawn from the Sanskrit vocabulary and Urdu from Persian and Arabic.

7. The number of refugees is contested. Pakistan contends that there were around 3 million refugees, while Indian sources suggest 10 million (Gill 2003).

8. The report was classified until 2001, when a redacted version was published. Most scholars had assumed that the report was classified because it detailed the excesses of the army in East Pakistan, but in fact the report offers very few insights into these alleged atrocities. However, it paints a picture of Khan as an inebriated lothario and even lists the various military wives with whom he disported himself, giving their husbands' names and ranks. The enormous number of officers he allegedly cuckolded is probable cause for the military's insistence to keep the report classified. For example, the report notes that Khan not only "drank heavily and even to excess" but in addition was "far from being an austere man sexually. The number of women with whom he had illicit relations is unfortunately all too large" (Hamoodur Rehman Commission 2001, 122). It continues to lament that "even in the gravest hour of the country's difficulties, his mind was not disturbed enough to make him deviate from his usual course of debauchery" (123). The report dedicates an entire chapter to what it calls "The Moral Aspect," in which it questions the integrity of numerous army officers. The most peculiar feature of this chapter is that it details the women with whom Khan had affairs and even includes two appendices of women who visited him in his homes in Karachi and Islamabad (296–312).

9. As described later in this chapter, Pakistan prefers this concept for two general reasons. First, this conventional posture and the eternal enmity toward India justifies the army's size, inordinate privileged access to all of the state's resources, and the arrogated right to intervene politically. Second, as detailed herein, Pakistan sees its various ethnic, sectarian, and socioeconomic fault lines as potential conflicts that become active conflicts due to Indian (or sometimes other external) intervention. Since the army identifies India as the root of Pakistan's domestic insecurity, the army subordinates the country's internal threat to the external threat. This partially explains why the Pakistan Army insists on using the concept of low-intensity conflict to combat internal insurgent and terrorist organizations rather than the population-centric counterinsurgency approaches championed—for better or for worse—by the American military in recent years. If the army were to embrace the concept of population-centric counterinsurgency, it would have to reimagine the nature of the domestic conflicts it confronts.

10. There were media reports in 2013 about a newer *Green Book*. Indeed, a *Green Book 2011* has been released, which I obtained after this book was largely written. Thus I was unable to incorporate insights from that volume.

Chapter 7

1 Unfortunately, there are too few sources of data to include Pakistan's relations with Saudi Arabia in this volume. Pakistan's defense literature is surprisingly silent about the important partnership with Saudi Arabia, with the exception of anodyne references to the "Muslim world." See, e.g., El-Edroos' (1974) argument that Pakistan should enhance "cooperation with Arab states" because "the protective political and economic umbrella thus provided by the People's Republic of China and the world of Islam should permit Pakistan to concentrate on its own urgent and pressing political, economic and social problems" (32–33).

2. These various agreements were in fact conceptually linked. In forging the defense pact between Pakistan and Turkey (which laid the foundation for the Baghdad Pact/CENTO), the British and Americans aimed to link Turkey, the southernmost member of NATO, with Pakistan, the westernmost member of SEATO (US Department of State, Office of the Historian, n.d.).

3. Kashmir was infiltrated by Pakistani irregulars, who were trained and supported by the Pakistan Army (see Chapter 6).

4. According to Article 4, paragraph 1 of the Southeast Asia Collective Defense Treaty, "Each party recognizes that aggression by means of armed attack in the treaty area against any of the parties or against any state or territory which the parties by unanimous agreement may hereafter designate, would endanger its own peace and safety, and agrees that it will in that event act to meet the common danger in accordance with its constitutional processes. Measures taken under this paragraph shall be immediately reported to the Security Council of the United Nations" (Text of the Southeast Asia Collective Defense Treaty 1954, 618). For a Pakistani assessment of the costs and benefits to Pakistan from joining SEATO, see "SEATO and Pakistan" (1954).

5. I have personal experience with this dynamic. During summer 2010, while I was teaching in Lahore, I was invited to appear on CNBC Pakistan. The interview was in both Urdu and English, and the topic was US–Pakistan relations. When asked why the United States can't "be a friend like China," I playfully responded: "You mean provide you with loans not grants, subpar conventional equipment, fail to support you in any war with India…." The otherwise congenial presenter cut off the live interview in midsentence and went to commercial break. I was explicitly told that I could not discuss China in such terms. The unwillingness to challenge the military's narrative was surprising given that CNBC is a private station.

Chapter 8

1 Khan (2012a) offers the richest and most detailed accounts of Pakistan's nuclear program from its inception under Bhutto to the present. Ironically, while Khan seeks to undermine the popular contention that Pakistan acquired its nuclear program through theft and espionage, the details he provides of the extensive transfers of material and assistance from China among other sources undermine this contention mightily. For a critique of the historical interventions Khan attempts, see Fair (2013).

2. The Symington Amendment was adopted in 1976 to amend the Arms Export Control Act, which was previously known as Section 669 of the Foreign Assistance Act of 1961. This legislation prohibits US assistance to any country found to be trafficking in either nuclear enrichment technology or equipment. In contrast to Pakistani arguments that this legislation was promulgated to punish Pakistan, it was actually enacted in response to the Indian test in 1974.

3. Locks are used to prevent unauthorized activation of a nuclear weapon. Until the 1960s, mechanical combination locks were used. Since then, permissive action links (PAL), electronic devices requiring operators to enter the correct codes, have increasingly

been used. Typically, a two-person rule is employed, requiring two different codes to be entered either simultaneously or nearly so. This rule makes it nearly impossible for a weapon to be detonated by one individual. For more details on PALs and the two-person rule, among other aspects of nuclear command and control, see Feaver (1992–1993).

4. Because the adversaries' conventional forces may confound analysis of how nuclear weapons shape conflict proneness, he also controls for the conventional capabilities of both adversaries in the time series. He finds that the ratio of conventional forces remain more or less constant and thus cannot explain variation in conflict proneness over the same period (Kapur 2007, 20–22).

5. For example, if a conflict began in May 1999 and ended in July 1999, Kapur counted this conflict as lasting three dispute months. If the dispute began and ended in one month, that conflict would be counted as lasting one dispute month.

6. For analytical purposes, Kapur (2007) defines the nonnuclear period as lasting through 1989. The covert nuclear period, in his analysis, begins with the sanctions leveled against Pakistan in 1990 and extends up to the month preceding the May 1998 nuclear tests. The overt period spans May 1998 through October 2002, the last month in his dataset. Kapur performs a number of statistical tests of the data. He holds the conventional force ratios constant because he finds that, while the conventional abilities of both combatants fluctuated over time, their relative force ratios fluctuated very little. First, he examines the correlation between conventional stability and nuclear proliferation using two simple statistical tests. He cross-tabulates the nuclear proliferation status of the period in question against the tally of dispute months. For purposes of analytical ease, he defines the nuclear period as spanning 1990 through 2002, which includes both the overt and covert periods and the nonnuclear period as spanning 1972–1989. He uses a chi-square test to evaluate whether or not this distribution is significantly different from a random distribution. He finds that the expected relationship holds: the nuclear period accounts for nearly 80 percent of all dispute months, while 83 percent of all peace months occurred in the nonnuclear period. Kapur calculates the conflict rate for each period, defined by the number of conflict months divided by the total number of months in the respective period. During the nonnuclear period, the conflict rate was 0.139, compared with 0.756 in what he codes as the nuclear period. Kapur also calculates the conflict rate for all three periods, finding that the conflict rate was 0.14 in the nonnuclear phase; 0.72 during the covert period; and 0.82 during the overt nuclear period (23). Using the chi-square test, he finds that his cross-tabulations of nuclear status (nuclear vs. nonnuclear) against peace and dispute months were statistically significant at the 0.001 level. (In other words, the likelihood that this distribution occurred due to chance was less than 1 in 1,000). Notably, Pakistan was responsible for two-thirds of the militarized dispute months in this period (99 of 148 dispute months between 1972 and 2002), and in each case Pakistan's goals were revisionist. Kapur concedes that there are likely other, nonnuclear factors driving these results and cautiously suggests that nuclearization is only one "variable facilitating increased conflict in South Asia" (29).

7. Those sanctions were waived throughout the 1980s due to American national security priorities, not because Pakistan had made any significant reversal of its program. Thus, when the United States imposed sanctions in 1990, it was in fact reimposing many of the sanctions that had been suspended or waived since April 1979. As discussed already, the US decision to ignore Pakistan's proliferation was the result of a calculated decision on the part of first the Carter and then the Reagan Administration. Both presidents believed that nonproliferation goals were less important than ousting the Soviets from Afghanistan. The decision to finally reimpose proliferation-related sanctions on Pakistan in 1990 thus was more the result of evolving US security requirements than of a changed assessment of Pakistan's nuclear program. This history makes clear that an argument can be made that Pakistan's effort to develop nuclear weapons began to influence Indian and Pakistani behavior long before 1990. Second, Kapur does not contend with the growing

Pakistan-sponsored violence in India throughout the 1980s, particularly in the Punjab, where Sikh separatists fought to establish the independent Sikh state of Khalistan. Yet it is well-known that Pakistan's involvement in the Punjab insurgency was extensive, as demonstrated by the fact that the violence in the Punjab was most intense along the border (Fair 2004a, 2007, 2009a).

8. Note that Kapur's coding produces a conflict rate that is a full order of magnitude higher than the conflict rate for my nonnuclear period. Kapur's conflict rate for his combined nuclear periods (1990–2008) is 0.756; 0.72 for the covert period of 1990–1998; and 0.82 for 1998–2002. Comparing these conflict rates, it is obvious that the most important analytical difference is how Kapur and I define the nonnuclear period, and the results of our respective efforts are strikingly different. The statistical analysis I present here provides evidence to support the argument that the nonnuclear period should be defined more restrictively.

Chapter 9

1 The 2006 edition of the *Pakistan Army Green Book*, which is dedicated to terrorism, focuses on Pakistan's domestic security challenges. It alleges, however, that India, and sometimes even the United States, are behind the intense terrorist violence in Pakistan.

2. This section is drawn from Fair (2011b) with the permission of *Asia Policy*.

3. Many of these groups have been proscribed numerous times only to reemerge and operate under new names. Rather than employing the most current names under which they operate, I use the names that are likely to be most familiar to readers.

4. One long-time observer of militancy in Pakistan, Mariam Abou-Zahab, strongly discounts the claim that the TTP is a coherent alliance. She argues that the group's constituent parts are driven by local factors and constrained, in good measure, by tribal boundaries that circumscribe the leadership. Thus, she discounts the claim that the TTP is a coherent organization running the length and width of the Pakhtun belt. This view has been buttressed by my own field interviews in Pakistan in February and April 2009 and later.

5. Author discussions with US military, state, and intelligence officials throughout 2010 and earlier as well as with Indian intelligence officials in April 2010.

6. This section reproduces and expands upon Fair (2011a).

7. This paragraph draws primarily on my extensive fieldwork in Pakistan. Since December 1999, I have undertaken numerous research trips to Pakistan, Afghanistan, India, and Bangladesh to study Lashkar-e-Taiba and other militant organizations based in and operating out of Pakistan.

8. All translations by me.

9. The Quran is a book that compiles the sayings of the Prophet Muhammad as received by Allah and is thus a book of divine revelations. The Sunnah, derived from exegetical scholarship on the Quran, details the teachings and practices of Muhammad, which serve as a model for human conduct. Hadis is similar to the Sunnah but not identical to it. Hadis is a narration about the life of the Prophet.

10. Some obligations (*kifaya*) are not compulsory but merely recommended and can be obviated by other conditions (e.g., if others in the Muslim community are doing this already). In contrast, according to the manifesto, *farz-e-ein* means something that one must do. This definition is in fact debated by scholars of Islam and in particular by the Islamic scholars (ulema) belonging to Ahl-e-Hadith, the religious tradition from which Lashkar-e-Taiba emerged.

11. There are no reliable estimates for this. The census does not inquire of such things. Some surveys have included questions about confessional beliefs, but respondents may not answer such sensitive questions truthfully. C. Christine Fair, Neil Malhotra, and Jacob

N. Shapiro, drawing from a nationally representative survey of 6,000 Pakistanis, report that 8 percent of the respondents said that they were Ahl-e-Hadith (Fair et al. 2010).

12. Contrary to media reports, the organization was not the leader of relief efforts during these catastrophes (Andrabi and Das 2010). It is likely that elements of Pakistan's media knowingly or unwittingly sensationalized LeT's contribution with the outcome of fostering popular support for the organization. Many journalists are on the ISI's payroll and routinely plant stories on behalf of the ISI or characterize a story to suit the ISI's interests. As discussed in the beginning of this volume, Pakistan's intelligence agency, the ISI, has a media arm that oversees management of the Pakistani media. This bureau also monitors international coverage of Pakistan and liaises with foreign journalists and scholars working in Pakistan. This part of the ISI, along with ISPR, the army, and the Ministry of Information, facilitates travel and government meetings throughout Pakistan. Military offices provide journalists and researchers with access to the tribal areas where they can meet with military personnel engaging in operations and a host of other military and intelligence institutions in Pakistan. The military undertakes these arrangements with an expectation that journalists will report favorably in exchange for this access. Should a journalist's account vex the military, the military curtails his or her access for a limited time or perhaps indefinitely (Chisti 2011). In extremis, the government will oust foreign journalists who persistently vex the state with their accounts or, less confrontationally, the government will refuse to renew their visas when they expire. Pakistani journalists face more dire consequences: the threat of harm to themselves or to their families. Other journalists with whom I have interacted over the years report that the "agencies" can even force the papers to fire someone should their reporting prove problematic for the military and intelligence agencies. It should be noted that the ISI and the military are not the only entities interested in controlling reportage; the civilian political parties are also equally vested. While this multi-actor system can not control all reporting absolutely, it does pose significant constraints upon foreign and domestic journalists who undermine state narratives.

Chapter 10

1 Zardari's five-year tenure as president was set to end in September 2013. The parliament and provincial assemblies, which make up Pakistan's Electoral College, are required to elect a new president one month prior to the expiration of the president's term. Initially the election date was set for August 6, 2013. However, this date was too close to the Muslim holiday of Eid al-Fitr following Ramadan, the month of fasting. Thus, many of the voters would not have been able to participate. The Supreme Court ruled on July 24, 2013 to advance the elections to July 30, 2013. The PPP complained that it would not be possible to field a candidate with so little preparation time. The PPP announced its plans to boycott the election and the Awami National League choice to join (*Pakistan Express Tribune* 2013).

2. This section draws from my forthcoming work (Fair 2014).

3. I labeled those whose mother tongue is Punjabi as ethnically Punjabi. Respondents with any other mother tongue were coded as non-Punjabi.

Chapter 11

1. Comments from Amb. Husain Haqqani sent via email to the author on April 30, 2013.

REFERENCES

Abbas, Athar (Maj. Gen.). 2006. Terrorism, Its Dynamics and Response. In *Pakistan Army Green Book 2006: Terrorism*, 10–13. Rawalpindi, Pakistan: Pakistan Army General Headquarters.

Abbas, Hassan. 2009. Defining the Punjabi Taliban Network. *CTC Sentinel* 2 (April): 1–4.

——. 2011. *Reforming Pakistan's Police and Law Enforcement Infrastructure*. USIP Special Report. Online. Available at http://www.usip.org/files/resources/sr266.pdf.

——, ed. 2012. *Stabilizing Pakistan through Police Reform*. New York: Asia Society. Online. Available at http://asiasociety.org/files/pdf/as_pakistan_police_reform.pdf.

Abbottabad Commission. 2013. Report of the Abbottabad Commission. Online. Available at http://s3.documentcloud.org/documents/724833/aljazeera-bin-laden-dossier.pdf.

Abou Zahab, Mariam. 2002. The Regional Dimensions of Sectarian Conflict in Pakistan. In *Pakistan: Nationalism without a Nation*, ed. Christophe Jaffrelot, 115–130. London: Zed Books.

Abou Zahab, Mariam, and Olivier Roy. 2004. *Islamist Networks: The Afghan-Pakistan Connection*. London: C. Hurst and Co.

Adeney, Katharine. 2012. A Step towards Inclusive Federalism in Pakistan? The Politics of the 18th Amendment. *Publius* 42 (Fall): 539–65.

Ahmad, Ashfaq (Brig.). 1990. Cashing on Character. In *Pakistan Army Green Book 1990: Year of the Junior Leaders*, 105–108. Rawalpindi: Pakistan Army General Headquarters.

Ahmad, Bashir (Col.). 1963. Morale: From the Early MUSLIM Campaigns. *Pakistan Army Journal* 5, no. 2: 6–13.

Ahmad, Mumtaz. 1996. The Crescent and the Sword: Islam, the Military, and Political Legitimacy in Pakistan, 1977–1985. *Middle East Journal* 50, no. 3 (Summer): 372–386.

Ahmad, Syed Jawaid (Lt. Col.). 1992. Pakistan 1965–1971: Lessons for the Present. *Pakistan Defence Review* 4 (Dec.): 78–95.

Ahmad, Wasiuddin (Maj.) 1958. The Convulsions in Southeast Asia. *Pakistan Army Journal* 1, no. 4: 47–56.

Ahmed, Fasih. 2010. The World's Bravest Nation: In Unending Crisis, There Is Hope and Salvation Yet for Pakistan. *Newsweek Pakistan*, September 6. Online. Available at http://www.news-weekpakistan.com/index.php?option=com_content&view=article&id=64&Itemid=53.

Ahmed, Iftikhar. 2004. Islam, Democracy and Citizenship Education: An Examination of the Social Studies Curriculum in Pakistan. *Current Issues in Comparative Education* 7 (Dec.): 39–49.

Ahmed, Ishtiaq. 2013. *Pakisan the Garrison State: Origins, Evolution, Consequences 1947–2011*. Karachi: Oxford University Press.

Ahmed, Mahmud (Lt. Gen.). 2002. *Illusion of Victory: A Military History of the Indo-Pak War— 1965*. Karachi: Lexicon Publishers.

Ahmed, Muhammad Tanvir (Lt. Col.). 2002. Low Intensity Conflict Latest Challenge. In *Pakistan Army Green Book 2002: Low Intensity Conflict*, 134–42. Rawalpindi: Pakistan Army General Headquarters.

Ahmed, Munir. 2011. Pakistan Grants India "Most Favored Nation" Status. *Christian Science Monitor*, November 2. Online. Available at http://www.csmonitor.com/World/Latest-News-Wires/2011/1102/Pakistan-grants-India-most-favored-nation-status.

Ahmed, Naeem. 2007. State, Society and Terrorism: A Case Study of Pakistan after September 11, 2001. Ph.D. diss., University of Karachi. Online. Available http://prr.hec.gov.pk/thesis/2511.pdf.

Ahmed, Shafqaat (Maj. Gen.). 2008. Multidimensional Threat to the Security of Pakistan. In *Pakistan Army Green Book 2008: Future Conflict Environment*, 1–10. Rawalpindi: Pakistan Army General Headquarters.

Ahmed, Sultan. 2002. Colin Powell Tries His Hand Again. *Defence Journal* (Aug.). Online. Available at http://www.defencejournal.com/2002/august/powell.htm.

Ahsan, M. H. 2006. "'Raw is Training 600 Baluchis in Afghanitsan': Mushahid Hussain." *Boloji.com*, May 14. Online. Available at http://www.network54.com/Forum/211833/thread/1190260633/1190281489/Indian+Terrorism-+%27RAW+Is+Training+600+Baluchis+In+Afghanistan%27-+Mushahid+Hussain.

Akhtar, Asif Duraiz (Maj. Gen.). 2000. Nation Building. In *Pakistan Army Green Book 2000: Role of Pakistan Army in Nation Building*, 1–3. Rawalpindi: Pakistan Army Headquarters.

Akhtar, Khalid Mehmood (Brig.). 2002. Low Intensity Conflict and its Sources. In *Pakistan Army Green Book 2002: Low Intensity Conflict*, 43–47. Rawalpindi: Pakistan Army General Headquarters.

Akhtar, Mahmud (Lt. Col). 1993–1994. Need for National Integration in Pakistan. *Pakistan Army Journal* 34, no. 4: 108–115.

Akram, A. I. (Col.). 1964. On Infiltration. *Pakistan Army Journal* 6, no. 2: 1–4.

Akram, Muhammad (Lt. Col.). 1971. Dien Bien Phu. *Pakistan Army Journal* 13, no. 2: 29–37.

Ali, Chaudhury Muhammad. 1967. *The Emergence of Pakistan*. New York: Columbia University Press.

Ali, Chaudhury Rahmat. 1933. *Now or Never*. N.p.: Pakistan National Movement. Online. Available at http://www.columbia.edu/itc/mealac/pritchett/00islamlinks/txt_rahmatali_1933.html.

Ali, Jamshed (Brig.). 1990. India—A Super Power! Myth or Reality. *Pakistan Defence Review* 2 (Dec.): 96–107.

——. 1992. The Cultural Dimensions of Military Warfare. *Pakistan Army Journal* 33 (Sept.): 46–61.

Ali, Mohammad (Maj.). 1991. An Analytical Study of Situation in Sindh. *Pakistan Army Journal* 32 (Dec.): 78–87.

Ali, Shaheen Sardar. 1999. The Rights of Ethnic Minorities in Pakistan: A Legal Analysis. *International Journal on Minority and Group Rights* 6, nos. 1–2: 169–195.

Almeida, Cyril. 2010. Kayani Spells Out Threat Posed by Indian Doctrine. *Dawn*, February 4. Online. Available at http://archives.dawn.com/archives/44561.

Amin, Shahid M. 2000. *Pakistan's Foreign Policy: A Reappraisal*, 2d ed. Karachi: Oxford University Press.

——. 2009. A State of Denial. *Dawn*, October 21. Online. Available at http://news.dawn.com/wps/wcm/connect/dawn-content-library/dawn/news/pakistan/14-a-state-of-denial-zj-06.

Andrabi, Tahir, and Jishnu Das. 2010. In Aid We Trust: Hearts and Minds and the Pakistan Earthquake of 2005. World Bank Policy Research Working Paper No. 5440. Online. Available at http://papers.ssrn.com/sol3/papers.cfm?abstract_id=1688196.

Ansari, Massoud, and Behroz Khan. 2006. Air Force Officers Held for Attempt to Murder Musharraf with Rockets. *PakistanDefense.com*, May 11. Online. Available at http://www.defence.pk/forums/strategic-geopolitical-issues/2745-paf-personnel-busted-assasination-attempt.html.

Anwari, Masood Navid (Lt. Col.). 1988. Deterrence—Hope or Reality. *Pakistan Army Journal* 29 (March): 45–53.

Arif, K. 1984. *China Pakistan Relations, 1947–1980*. Lahore: Vanguard Books Ltd.

Arif, Khalid Mahmud (Gen.). 1995. *Working with Zia: Pakistan Power Politics, 1977–1988*. New York: Oxford University Press.

———. 2001. *Khaki Shadows: Pakistan 1947–1997*. Karachi: Oxford University Press.

Arquilla, John, and David Ronfeldt, eds. 1997. *In Athena's Camp: Preparing for Conflict in the Information Age*. Santa Monica, CA: RAND.

Art, Robert J. 1985. Between Assured Destruction and Nuclear Victory: The Case for the Mad Plus Posture. In *Nuclear Deterrence: Ethics and Strategy*, ed. Russell Hardin, Robert E. Goodin, John J. Mearsheimer, and Gerald Dworkin, 121–140. Chicago: University of Chicago Press.

Asghar, Muhammad (Maj. Gen.). 2006. The Paradoxical Dimensions of Global War on Terror and Pakistan's Response. In *Pakistan Army Green Book 2006: Terrorism*, 14–24. Rawalpindi: Pakistan Army General Headquarters.

Aziz, K. K. 1998. *Murder of History: A Critique of History Textbooks Used in Pakistan*. Lahore, Pakistan: Vanguard.

Bajwa, Asim Saleem (Maj. Gen.). 2012. Terrorist Havens in Afghanistan. *Hilal* 49 (July): 3.

Bakhtawar, Khalid (Maj.). 1990. Indian Strategic Thinking. *Pakistan Defence Review* 1 (June): 58–67.

Bano, Masooda. 2004. Unravelling "Enlightened Moderation": Musharraf Is Telling Muslim Nations to Follow Washington's Dictates. *Al-Ahram Weekly*, June 18. Online. Available at http://yaleglobal.yale.edu/content/unravelling-enlightened-moderation.

Barfield, Thomas. 2007. *The Durand Line: History, Consequences, and Future*. Report of the American Institute of Afghanistan Studies and the Hollings Center Conference, Istanbul, Turkey. Online. Available at http://www.bu.edu/aias/reports/durand_conference.pdf.

———. 2012. *Afghanistan: A Cultural and Political History*. Princeton, NJ: Princeton University Press.

Barhvi, Syed Nawab Alam (Col.). 1991. Iqbal's Concept of Jihad. *Pakistan Army Journal* 32 (Sept.): 87–97.

Barker, Kim. 2007. Pakistani Army's Stature Takes Hit. *Chicago Tribune*, October 9. Online. Available at http://articles.chicagotribune.com/2007-10-09/news/0710080407_1_islamic-militants-pakistan-al-qaeda-linked-militants/2.

Barnds, William J. 1975. China's Relations with Pakistan: Durability amidst Discontinuity. *China Quarterly* 63 (Sept.): 463–489.

Bashir, Muhammad (Capt). 1961. National Character. *Pakistan Army Journal* 3, no. 3: 47–55.

Basrur, Rajesh M. 2001. Nuclear Weapons and Indian Strategic Culture. *Journal of Peace Research* 3, no. 2: 181–198.

Bass, Gary J. 2013. *The Blood Telegram: Nixon, Kissinger, and a Forgotten Genocide*. New York: Alfred A. Knopf.

Basu, Tapan, Pradap Datta, Sumit Sarkar, Tanika Sarkar, and Sambuddha Sen. 1993. *Khaki Shorts and Saffron Flags*. New Delhi: Orient Longman.

BBC. 2007. Al-Qaeda "Rebuilding" in Pakistan. *BBC.co.uk*, January 12. Online. Available at http://news.bbc.co.uk/2/hi/south_asia/6254375.stm.

Bhutto, Zulfiqar Ali. 1979. *If I Am Assassinated*. New Delhi: Vikas Publishing House Pvt. Ltd.

Birdwood, Lord William. 1952. Kashmir. *International Affairs* 28 (July): 299–309.

Blair, Graeme, C. Christine Fair, Neil Malhotra, and Jacob N. Shapiro. 2013. Poverty and Support for Militant Politics: Evidence from Pakistan. *American Journal of Political Science* 57 (Jan.): 30–48.

Booth, Ken. 1979. *Strategy and Ethnocentrism*. New York: Holmes and Meier.

Bose, Sugata, and Ayesha Jalal. 2004. *Modern South Asia: History, Culture, Political Economy*, 2d ed. New Delhi: Oxford University Press.

Bose, Sarmila. 2011. *Dead Reckoning: Memories of the 1971 Bangladesh War*. New York: Columbia University Press.

Brass, Paul R. 2003. The Partition of India and Retributive Genocide in the Punjab, 1946–47: Means, Methods, and Purposes. *Journal of Genocide Research* 5, no. 1: 71–101.

Bradsher, Henry S. 1985. *Afghanistan and the Soviet Union*. Durham, NC: Duke University Press.

Brendon, Piers. 2008. *The Decline and Fall of the British Empire: 1781–1997*. New York: Random House.

Brodkin, E.I. 1972. The Struggle for Succession: Rebels and Loyalists in the Indian Mutiny of 1857. *Modern Asian Studies* 6: 277–290.

Brulliard, Karin. 2011. Pakistan's Top Military Officials Are Worried about Militant Collaborators in Their Ranks. *Washington Post*, May 17. Online. Available at http://www.washingtonpost.com/world/pakistani-military-worried-about-collaborators-in-its-ranks-officials-say/2011/05/27/AGgN1oCH_story.html.

Builder, Carl. 1989. *The Masks of War: American Military Styles in Strategy and Analysis*. Santa Monica, CA: RAND.

Burke, Jason. 2010. ISI Chiefs Aided Mumbai Terror Attacks: Headley. *Hindu*, October 19. Online. Available at http://www.thehindu.com/news/national/article837735.ece.

Burki, Shahid Javed. 2007. *Kashmir: A Problem in Search of a Solution*. Washington, DC: United States Institute of Peace. Available at http://www.usip.org/files/resources/PWmarch2007.pdf.

Calabrese, John. 1997. The Struggle for Security: New and Familiar Patterns in Iran–Pakistan Relations. *Journal of South Asian and Middle Eastern Studies* 21 (Fall): 61–80.

Callahan, Raymond. 2008. The Great Sepoy Mutiny. In *A Military History of India and South Asia*, ed. D. Marston and C. Sundaram, 16–33. Bloomington: Indiana University Press.

Carsen, Jessica. 2006. A Kashmiri Tie to the Terror Plot. *Time.com*, August 16. Online. Available at http://www.time.com/time/world/article/0,8599,1227651,00.html#ixzz2Z2BsMex7.

Center for Nonproliferation Studies. 1999. China's Nuclear Exports and Assistance to Pakistan. James Martin Center for Nonproliferation Studies, August. http://cns.miis.edu/archive/country_india/china/npakpos.htm.

Chadha, Vivek. 2009. India's Counterinsurgency Campaign in Mizoram. In *India and Counterinsurgency: Lessons Learned*, ed. Sumit Ganguly and David E. Fidler, 28–44. London: Routledge.

Chari, P. R. 2011. K.Subrahmanyam. Institute of Peace and Conflict Studies, February 5. Online. Available at http://www.ipcs.org/article/india/ksubrahmanyam-3325.html.

Chari, P. R., Pervaiz Iqbal Cheema, and Stephen Cohen. 2001. *Four Crises and a Peace Process*. Washington, DC: Brookings Institution.

Chaudhuri, Rudra. 2009. Why Culture Matters: Revisiting the Sino-Indian Border War of 1962. *Journal of Strategic Studies* 32, no. 6: 841–869.

Cheema, Pervaiz Iqbal. 2000. *The Politics of the Punjab Boundary Award*. Heidelberg Papers in South Asian and Comparative Politics, University of Heidelberg, Germany. Online. Available at http://archiv.ub.uni-heidelberg.de/volltextserver/volltexte/2003/4006/pdf/hpsacp1.pdf.

——. 2002. *The Armed Forces of Pakistan*. Karachi: Oxford University Press.

Cheema, Pervaiz Iqbal, and Masudul Hasan Nuri. 2005. *Tribal Areas of Pakistan: Challenges and Responses*. Islamabad, Pakistan: IPRI.

Cheema, Zafar Iqbal. 2000. Pakistan's Nuclear Use Doctrine and Command and Control. In *Planning the Unthinkable: How New Powers Will Use Nuclear, Biological, and Chemical Weapons*, ed. Peter Lavoy, Scott D. Sagan, and James J. Wirtz, 158–181. Ithaca, NY: Cornell University Press.

——. 2011. Pakistan's Posture of Minimum Credible Deterrence: Current Challenges and Future Efficacy. In *Nuclear Pakistan: Strategic Dimensions*, ed. Zulfiqar Khan, 43–84. Karachi: Oxford University Press.

Chisti, Ali K. 2011. The Intelligence and Agencies of Pakistan (Part I). *Daily Times*, February 11. Online. Available at http://www.dailytimes.com.pk/default.asp?page=2011\02\11\story_11-2-2011_pg7_20.

Chishti, Faiz Ali (Lt. Gen., Ret.). 1990. *Betrayals of Another Kind*. Cincinnati, OH: Asia Publishing House.

Chohan, Farrukh Jamshed (Col.). 1998. Morale-Motivation. *Pakistan Army Journal* 41 (Winter): 43–62.

CIA. 1947. Review of the World Situation as It Relates to the Security of the United States—Summary. Online. Available at https://www.cia.gov/library/center-for-the-study-of-intelligence/csi-publications/books-and-monographs/assessing-the-soviet-threat-the-early-cold-war-years/5563bod1.pdf.

———. 1948. Review of the World Situation as It Relates to the Secrity of the United States. Online. Available at https://www.cia.gov/library/center-for-the-study-of-intelligence/csi-publications/books-and-monographs/on-the-front-lines-of-the-cold-war-documents-on-the-intelligence-war-in-berlin-1946-to-1961/2-19.pdf.

Clarke, Ryan. 2010. *Lashkar-i-Taiba: The Fallacy of Subservient Proxies and The Future Of Islamist Terrorism In India*. Carlisle, PA: US Army War College.

Clary, Christopher. 2010. *Thinking about Pakistan's Nuclear Security in Peacetime, Crisis and War*. IDSA Occasional Paper No. 12. Online. Available at http://www.idsa.in/occasionalpapers/PakistansNuclearSecurity_2010.

Clinton, William J. 2000. Remarks by the President in Greeting to the People of Pakistan, March 25. Online. Available at http://clinton3.nara.gov/WH/New/SouthAsia/speeches/20000325.html.

Cloughley, Brian. 2002. *A History of the Pakistan Army: Wars and Insurrections*. Karachi: Oxford University Press.

CNN.com. 2012. Pakistan Reopens NATO Supply Routes to Afghanistan, *CNN.com*. July 3 Online. Available at http://www.cnn.com/2012/07/03/world/asia/us-pakistan-border-routes.

COAS. 2011. Address on the occasion of Azadi Parade 2011 at PMA Kakul. *YouTube*, 5:26, posted by "mrdanish1996," August 13. Online. Available at http://www.youtube.com/watch?v=CuzYxuSXZh8.

Cohen, Stephen P. 1963–1964. Subhas Chandra Bose and the Indian National Army. *Pacific Affairs* 36 (Winter): 411–429.

———. 1984. *The Pakistan Army*. Berkeley: University of California Press.

———. 2004. *The Idea of Pakistan*. Washington, DC: Brookings Institution Press.

———. 2011. *The Future of Pakistan*. Washington, DC: Brookings Institution Press.

———. 2013. *Shooting for a Century: The India–Pakistan Conflict*. Washington, DC: Brookings Institution Press.

Cohen, Stephen P., C. Christine Fair, Sumit Ganguly, Shaun Gregory, Aqil Shah, and Ashley J. Tellis. 2009. What's the Problem with Pakistan? Part II: The Military's Worldview. *ForeignAffairs.com*, March 31. Online. Available at http://www.foreignaffairs.com/discussions/roundtables/whats-the-problem-with-pakistan.

Cohen, Stuart A. 2013. Israel. In *Religion in the Military Worldwide, ed.* Ron E. Hassner, 114–140. Cambridge: Cambridge University Press.

Coll, Steve. 2004. *Ghost Wars: The Secret History of the CIA, Afghanistan, and bin Laden, from the Soviet Invasion to September 10, 2001*. New York: Penguin Press.

Committee to Protect Journalists. 2011. *Attacks on the Press in 2011*. Washington, DC: Brookings Institution Press. Online. Available at http://cpj.org/2012/02/attacks-on-the-press-in-2011.php.

Constable, Pamela. 2010. Pakistan's Army Chief Seeks "Stable and Friendly" Afghanistan. *Washington Post*, February 2. Online. Available at http://articles.washingtonpost.com/2010-02-02/world/36900624_1_kiyani-afghan-taliban-afghanistan.

Copland, Ian. 1991. The Princely States, the Muslim League, and the Partition of India in 1947. *International History Review* 13 (Feb.): 38–69.

Cronin, Richard. 1996. *Pakistan Aid Cutoff: US Nonproliferation and Foreign Policy Considerations*. Washington, DC: Congressional Research Service. Online. Available at http://www.fas.org/spp/starwars/crs/90-149.htm.

Cronin, Richard P., K. Alan Kronstadt, and Sharon Squassoni. 2005. *Pakistan's Nuclear Proliferation Activities and the Recommendations of the 9/11 Commission: US Policy Constraints and Options*. CRS Report for Congress No. RL32734. Washington, DC: Congressional Research Service. Online. Available at http://www.fas.org/sgp/crs/nuke/RL32745.pdf.

Daily Times. 2006. How Is Pakistan "Equal" to India? *Daily Times*, October 25. Online. Available at http://www.dailytimes.com.pk/default.asp?page=2006\10\25\story_25-10-2006_pg3_1.

——. 2012a. Kayani Wants Continuity of Democratic System. *Daily Times*, May 1. Online. Available at http://dailytimes.com.pk/default.asp?page=2012\05\01\story_1-5-2012_pg1_1.

——. 2012b. RAW, Mossad, CIA Responsible for Balochistan Situation. *Daily Times*, August 8. Online. Available at http://www.dailytimes.com.pk/default.asp?page=2012\08\08\story_8-8-2012_pg12_13.

David, Saul. 2002. *The Indian Mutiny: 1857*. London: Viking.

Davidson, Jason. 2002. The Roots of Revisionism: Fascist Italy, 1922–1939. *Security Studies* 11, no. 4: 125–159.

Dawn. 2006. Six Held for Attack on US Consulate. *Dawn*. August 19. Online. Available at http://beta.dawn.com/news/206544/six-held-for-attack-on-us-consulate.

——. 2010. Punjab Govt. Gave Rs 82m to JD: Papers. *Dawn*, June 16. Online. Available at http://news.dawn.com/wps/wcm/connect/dawn-content-library/dawn/the-newspaper/front-page/punjab-govt-gavers82m-to-jd-papers-660.

——. 2012. Kashmir a Source of Constant Indo-Pak Conflict: Khar. *Dawn*. November 22. Online. Available at http://dawn.com/2012/11/16/kashmir-a-source-of-constant-conflict-between-pakistan-india-khar/.

Denoeux, Guilain. 2002. The Forgotten Swamp: Navigating Political Islam. *Middle East Policy* 9, no. 2 (June): 56–81.

Desch, Michael C. 1998. Culture Clash: Assessing the Importance of Ideas in Security Studies. *International Security* 23, no. 1: 141–170.

Destradi, Sandra. 2012. India and Sri Lanka's Civil War: The Failure of Regional Conflict Management in South Asia. *Asian Survey* 52 (May–June): 595–616.

DeYoung, Karen. 2011. New Estimates Put Pakistan's Nuclear Arsenal at More than 100. *Washington Post*, January 31. Online. Available at http://www.washingtonpost.com/wp-dyn/content/article/2011/01/30/AR2011013004136.html.

Documentation: General Mirza Aslam Beg's Major Presentations. 1991. *Defense Journal* 17 (June/July): 39–47.

Downey, Edward F. 1959. Theory of Guerilla Warfare. *Pakistan Army Journal* 1, no. 6: 25–36.

Dreazen, Yochi J. 2011. Fear that US Can Grab Nuclear Arsenal Heightens Pakistani Anger. *National Journal*, May 9. Online. Available at http://www.nationaljournal.com/nationalsecurity/fear-that-u-s-can-grab-nuclear-arsenal-heightens-pakistani-anger-20110509?page=1&sms_ss=twitter&at_xt=4dc7c790a8ec72c6,0/.

Duffield, John, Theo Farrell, Richard Price, and Michael C. Desch. 1999. Isms and Schisms: Culturalism versus Realism in Security Studies. *International Security* 24 (Summer): 156–180.

Durrani, Asad (Maj. Gen.). 1989. Total Security—A Concept for Pakistan. *Pakistan Defence Review* 1, no. 1: 10–27.

Durrani, Umar Farooq. 2010. A Treatise on Indian Backed Psychological Warfare Against Pakistan. In *Pakistan Army Green Book 2010*, 1–10. Rawalpindi: Pakistan Army General Headquarters.

Eagleton, Clyde. 1950. The Case of Hyderabad Before the Security Council. *American Journal of International Law* 44, no. 2 (April): 277–302.

East, C.H.A. (Maj.). 1958. Guerilla Warfare. *Pakistan Army Journal* 1, no. 4: 57–66.

Economist Intelligence Unit. 2012. Pakistan Country Report: July 2012. *EIU.com*. Online. Available at http://0-www.eiu.com.library.lausys.georgetown.edu/report_dl.asp?issue_id=1589256743&mode=pdf.

Ehsan, Muhammad Ali. 2013. Changing Doctrines. *Pakistan Express Tribune,* January 6. Online. Available at http://tribune.com.pk/story/489479/changing-doctrines/.

El-Edroos, S. A. (Maj.). 1961. Infiltration—A Form of Attack. *Pakistan Army Journal* 3, no. 2: 3–15.

———. 1962. Afro-Asian Revolutionary Warfare and Our Military Thought. *Pakistan Army Journal* 4, no. 2: 26–41.

El-Edroos, S. A. (Lt. Col.). 1964a. General Vo Nguyen Giap and the Viet Nam People's Army. *Pakistan Army Journal* 6, no. 1: 10–17.

———. 1964b. Mao Tse-Tung and the Chinese People's Liberation Army (1927–1964). *Pakistan Army Journal* 6, no. 2: 8–28.

El-Edroos, S. A. (Brig). 1974. Jordan and the Arab–Israeli War: 6—October 22 1973, *Pakistan Army Journal* 15 (June): 11–35.

Evans, Alexander. 2000. The Kashmir Insurgency: As Bad as It Gets. *Small Wars & Insurgencies* 11, no. 1: pp. 69–81.

———. 2012. The United States and South Asia after Afghanistan. Asia Society Report. Online. Available at http://asiasociety.org/files/pdf/as_us_southasia.pdf.

Ewing, Katherine. 1883. The Politics of Sufism: Redefining the Saints of Pakistan. *Journal of Asian Studies* 42, no. 2 (Feb.): 251–268.

Fair, C. Christine. 2004. *The Counterterror Coalitions: Cooperation with Pakistan and India.* Santa Monica, CA: RAND.

———. 2004a. *The Historical Novels of Bhai Vir Singh: Narratives of Sikh Nationhood.* Ph.D. diss., University of Chicago.

———. 2004b. Militant Recruitment in Pakistan: Implications for Al-Qa'ida and Other Organizations. *Studies in Conflict and Terrorism* 27, no. 6 (Nov.–Dec.): 489–504.

———. 2004c. *Urban Battle Fields of South Asia: Lessons Learned from Sri Lanka, India and Pakistan.* Santa Monica, CA: RAND.

———. 2007. India and Iran: New Delhi's Balancing Act. *Washington Quarterly* 30 (Summer): 145–159.

———. 2008. The Educated Militants of Pakistan: Implications for Pakistan's Domestic Security. *Contemporary South Asia* 16 (Mar.): 93–106.

———. 2009a. Lessons from India's Experience in the Punjab, 1978–93. In *India and Counterinsurgency: Lessons Learned,* ed. Sumit Ganguly and David P. Fidler, 107–126. New York: Routledge.

———. 2009b. Militants in the Kargil Conflict: Myths, Realities, and Impacts. In *Asymmetric Warfare in South Asia: The Causes and Consequences of Kargil,* ed. Peter Lavoy, 231–257. Cambridge: Cambridge University Press.

———. 2009c. Pakistan's Own War on Terror: What the Pakistani Public Thinks. *Journal of International Affairs* 63 (Fall–Winter): 39–55.

———. 2010a. Students Islamic Movement of India and the Indian Mujahideen: An Assessment. *Asia Policy* 9 (Jan.): 101–119.

———. 2010b. "Should Pakistan Get a Nuke Deal?" *ForeignPolicy.com,* March 23. Online. Available at http://www.foreignpolicy.com/articles/2010/03/23/should_pakistan_get_a_nuke_deal.

———. 2011a. Lashkar-e-Tayiba and the Pakistani State. *Survival* 53 (Aug.): 1–23.

———. 2011b. The Militant Challenge in Pakistan. *Asia Policy* 11 (Jan.): 105–137.

———. 2011c. Why the Pakistan Army Is Here to Stay: Prospects for Civilian Governance? *International Affairs* 87 (May): 571–588.

———. 2012. Increasing Social Conservatism in the Pakistan Army: What the Data Say. *Armed Forces & Society* 38 (July): 438–462.

———. 2013. Review of Feroz Hassan Khan's *Eating Grass. Journal of Strategic Studies* 36, no. 4 (July): 624–630.

———. 2014. "Using Manpower Policies to Transform the Force and Society: The Case of the Pakistan Army," *Security Studies,* forthcoming.

Fair, C. Christine, Keith Crane, Christopher S. Chivvis, Samir Puri, and Michael Spirtas. 2010. *Pakistan: Can the United States Secure an Insecure State?* Santa Monica, CA: RAND.

Fair, C. Christine, and Seth G. Jones. 2009–2010. Pakistan's War Within. *Survival* 51 (Dec.–Jan.): 161–188.

Fair, C. Christine, Neil Malhotra, and Jacob N. Shapiro. 2010. Islam, Militancy, and Politics in Pakistan: Insights from a National Sample. *Terrorism and Political Violence* 22, no. 4: 495–521.

Fair, C. Christine, and Shuja Nawaz. 2011. The Changing Pakistan Army Officer Corps. *Journal of Strategic Studies* 34 (Feb.): 63–94.

Farrell, Theo. 2002. Constructivist Security Studies: Portrait of a Research Program. *International Studies Review* 4 (Spring): 49–72.

Farooq, Muhammad (Maj. Gen.). 2006. Extremism and Terrorism in Pakistan and How to Affect Moderation. In *Pakistan Army Green Book 2006: Terrorism*, 25–34. Rawalpindi: Pakistan Army General Headquarters.

Farooq, Umer. 2012a. General Perception. *Herald*, December 3, 39–43.

——. 2012b. The Image Makers. *Herald*, December 3, 44–45.

Farooqui, Qaisar (Maj.). 1992. Islamic Concept of Preparedness. *Pakistan Army Journal* 33 (Dec.): 10–24.

Feaver, Peter D. 1992–1993. Command and Control in Emerging Nuclear Nations. *International Security* 17 (Winter): 160–187.

Federation of American Scientists. n.d. Text of "Jihad against Jews and Crusaders, World Islamic Front Statement, 23 February 1998." Online. Available at http://www.fas.org/irp/world/para/docs/980223-fatwa.htm.

Filkins, Dexter. 2011. The Journalist and the Spies: The Murder of a Reporter Who Exposed Pakistan's Secrets. *New Yorker*, September 19. Online. Available at http://www.newyorker.com/reporting/2011/09/19/110919fa_fact_filkins.

Foster, Gregory D. 1992. A Conceptual Foundation for the Development of Strategy. In *Grand Strategy and the Decision-Making Process*, ed. James C. Gaston, 55–76. Washington, DC: National Defense University Press.

Fromkin, David. 1980. The Great Game in Asia. *Foreign Affairs* 58 (Spring): 936–951.

Gall, Carlotta, and Somni Sengupta. 2007. Pakistanis Express Ire at Army and Musharraf. *New York Times*, August 9. Online. Available at http://www.nytimes.com/2007/08/09/world/asia/09pakistan.html?pagewanted=al.

Ganguly, Sumit. 1997. *The Crisis in Kashmir: Portents of War, Hopes of Peace*. Cambridge: Cambridge University Press.

——. 2001. *Conflict Unending: India–Pakistan Tensions since 1947*. New Delhi: Oxford University Press.

——. 2008. Nuclear Stability in South Asia. *International Security* 33 (Fall): 45–70.

——, ed. 2012. *India's Foreign Policy: Retrospect and Prospect*. New York: Oxford University Press.

Ganguly, Sumit, and S. Paul Kapur. 2010. *India, Pakistan, and the Bomb: Debating Nuclear Stability in South Asia*. New York: Columbia University Press.

Garver, John W. 2001. *Protracted Contest: Sino-Indian Rivalry in the Twentieth Century*. Seattle: University of Washington Press.

Geertz, Clifford. 1973. *The Interpretation of Cultures*. New York: Basic Books.

Gell, Simeran Man Singh. 1996. The Origins of the Sikh "Look": From Guru Gobind to Dalip Singh. *History and Anthropology* 10, no. 1 (1996): 37–83.

Geo TV. 2009. Punjab Govt. Appoints Administrator for JuD. *GeoTv*, January 25. Online. Available at http://www.geo.tv/1-25-2009/33491.htm.

George F. Marshall Foundation. n.d. "The Marshall Plan." Online. Available at http://www.marshallfoundation.org/TheMarshallPlan.htm.

Ghumman, Israr Ahmad (Lt. Col.). 1990. Pakistan's Geostrategic Environment and Military System. *Pakistan Army Journal* 31 (Mar.): 26–37.

Gilani, Mukhtar Ahmad (Lt. Col.). 2003. India Was Instrumental in Starting the 1965 War. *Pakistan Army Journal* 47 (Winter): 32–37.

Giles, Gregory F., and James F. Doyle. 1996. Indian and Pakistani Views on Nuclear Deterrence. *Comparative Strategy* 5, no. 2: 135–159.

Gill, John H. 2005. India and Pakistan: A Shift in the Military Calculus? In *Strategic Asia, 2005–06: Military Modernization in an Era of Uncertainty*, ed. Ashley J. Tellis and Michael Wills, 237–267. Seattle, WA: National Bureau of Asian Research.

——. 2003. *An Atlas of the 1971: India–Pakistan War.* Washington, DC: National Defense University Press.

Giustozzi, Antonio. 2008. *Koran, Kalashnikov, and Laptop: The Neo-Taliban Insurgency in Afghanistan 2002–2007.* New York: Columbia University Press.

Glaser, Charles L. 2010. *Rational Theory of International Politics: The Logic of Competition and Cooperation.* Princeton, NJ: Princeton University Press.

Glenn, John. 2009. Realism versus Strategic Culture: Competition and Collaboration. *International Studies Review* 11: 523–551.

Global Security. n.d. I Corps. *GlobalSecurity.org.* Online. Available at http://www.globalsecurity.org/military/world/pakistan/i-corps.htm.

——. n.d. II Corps. *GlobalSecurity.org.* Online. Available at http://www.globalsecurity.org/military/world/pakistan/ii-corps.htm.

——. n.d. IV Corps. *GlobalSecurity.org.* Online. Available at http://www.globalsecurity.org/military/world/pakistan/iv-corps.htm.

——. n.d. V Corps. *GlobalSecurity.org.* Online. Available at http://www.globalsecurity.org/military/world/pakistan/v-corps.htm.

——. n.d. X Corps. *GlobalSecurity.org.* Online. Available at http://www.globalsecurity.org/military/world/pakistan/x-corps.htm.

——. n.d. XI Corps. *GlobalSecurity.org.* Online. Available at http://www.globalsecurity.org/military/world/pakistan/xi-corps.htm.

——. n.d. XII Corps. *GlobalSecurity.org.* Online. Available at http://www.globalsecurity.org/military/world/pakistan/xii-corps.htm.

——. n.d. XXX Corps. *GlobalSecurity.org.* Online. Available at http://www.globalsecurity.org/military/world/pakistan/xxx-corps.htm.

——. n.d. XXXI Corps. *GlobalSecurity.org.* Online. Available at http://www.globalsecurity.org/military/world/pakistan/xxxi-corps.htm.

University of Maryland. 2012. Global Terrorism Database. Online. Available at http://www.start.umd.edu/gtd/contact/.

Goktepe, Cihat. 2003. *British Foreign Policy towards Turkey, 1959–1965.* New York: Routledge.

Goldberg, Jeffrey, and Marc Ambinder. 2011. The Ally from Hell. *New Republic*, October 28. Online. Available at http://www.theatlantic.com/magazine/archive/2011/12/the-ally-from-hell/308730/.

Golovnina, Maria and Asim Tanveer. 2013. Leader's Death Plunges Pakistan Taliban into Dangerous Disarray. *Reuters*, November 14. Online. Available at http://news.yahoo.com/leaders-death-plunges-pakistan-taliban-dangerous-disarray-081141836.html.

Goodson, Larry P. 2001. *Afghanistan's Endless War: State Failure, Regional Politics, and the Rise of the Taliban.* Seattle: University of Washington Press.

Gopal, Anand, Mansur Khan Mahsud, and Brian Fishman. 2010. Inside Pakistan's Tribal Frontier: North Waziristan. *Foreign Policy Af-Pak Channel*, April 23. Online. Available at http://afpak.foreignpolicy.com/posts/2010/04/23/inside_pakistans_tribal_frontier_north_waziristan.

Gordon, Michael R. 1989. Nuclear Course Set by Pakistan Worrying US. *New York Times*, October 12. Online. Available at http://www.nytimes.com/1989/10/12/world/nuclear-course-set-by-pakistan-worrying-us.html.

Government of India Act of 1935. n.d. *Scribd.* Online. Available at http://www.scribd.com/doc/50556839/Government-of-India-Act-1935.

Grare, Frédéric. 2006. *Pakistan: The Myth of an Islamist Peril.* Policy Brief 45. Washington, DC: CEIP.

———. 2013. Foreign and Security Policy in Post-Election Pakistan. Carnegie Endowment for International Peace Article, May 14. Online. Available at http://carnegieendowment.org/2013/05/14/foreign-and-security-policy-in-post-election-pakistan/g3ce.

Gray, Colin. 1999. *Modern Strategy*. Oxford: Oxford University Press.

Greenberg, Michael. 1942. India's Independence and the War. *Pacific Affairs* 15 (June): 164–187.

Greenwood, Alexander. 1990. *Field-Marshal Auchinleck*. Durham, NC: Pentland Press.

Guha, Ramachandra. 2007. *India After Gandhi: The History of the World's Largest Democracy*. London: MacMillan.

Gul, Imtiaz. 2009. *The Al Qaeda Connection: The Taliban and Terror in Pakistan's Tribal Areas*. London: Penguin.

Haas, Peter M. 1992. Introduction: Epistemic Communities and International Cooperation. *International Organization* 46 (Winter): 1–35.

Habib, Irfan. 1998. The Coming of 1857. *Social Scientist* 26 (Jan.–Apr.): 6–15.

Hamoodur Rehman Commission. 2001. *The Report of the Hamoodur Rehman Commission of Inquiry into the 1971 War: As Declassified by the Government of Pakistan*. Lahore: Vanguard.

Haq, Inamul (Air Cdre Ret.). 1991. *Islamic Motivation and National Defence*. Lahore: Vanguard.

Haq, Noor ul, Rashid Ahmed Khan, and Maqsudul Hasan Nuri. 2005. *Federally Administered Tribal Areas of Pakistan*. IPRI Paper No. 10. Islamabad: Islamabad Policy Research Institute. Online. Available at http://ipripak.org/papers/federally.shtml.

Haqqani, Husain. 2005. *Pakistan: Between Mosque and Military*. Washington, DC: Carnegie Endowment for International Peace.

———. 2007. Pakistan Crisis and US Policy Options. Speech at the Heritage Foundation, Washington, DC, November 27. Online. Available at http://www.heritage.org/events/2007/11/pakistan-crisis-and-us-policy-options.

Harrison, Selig. 1980. *In Afghanistan's Shadow: Baluch Nationalism and Soviet Temptations*. Washington, DC: Carnegie Endowment for International Peace.

———. 2009. *Pakistan: State of the Union*, Washington, DC: Center for International Policy. Online. Available at http://www.ciponline.org/images/uploads/publications/pakistan_the_state_of_the_union.pdf.

Hassan, Javed Brig. 1990. *India: A Study in Profile*. Quetta: Services Book Club.

Hathaway, Robert M. 2000. Confrontation and Retreat: The US Congress and the South Asian Nuclear Tests. *Arms Control Today*, Jan.–Feb. Online. Available at http://www.armscontrol.org/act/2000_01-02/rhjf00.

Henderson, Simon. 1999. *Pakistan, Proliferation, and the Middle East*. Policy Watch No. 415. Washington, DC: Washington Institute for Near East Policy. Online. Available at http://www.washingtoninstitute.org/templateC05.php?CID=1293.

Hilali, A. Z. 1990. Pakistan's Security Problems and Options. *Pakistan Defence Review* 2 (Dec.): 46–68.

———. 2011. Strategic Dimensions of Pakistan's Nuclear Program and Its Command and Control System. In *Nuclear Pakistan: Strategic Dimensions*, ed. Zulfiqar Khan, 189–224. Karachi: Oxford University Press.

Hindu. 2011. 151227: Pakistan's F-16 Program—At Risk of Failure. *Hindu*, May 20. Online. Available at http://www.thehindu.com/news/the-india-cables/the-cables/151227-pakistans-f16-program-at-risk-of-failure/article2059832.ece.

Hoffman, Michael. 2011. Military Extrication and Temporary Democaracy: The Case of Pakistan. *Democratization* 18, no. 1: 75–99.

Howenstein, Nicholas. 2008. The Jihadi Terrain in Pakistan: An Introduction to the Sunni Jihadi Groups in Pakistan and Kashmir. Pakistan Security Research Unit, Research Report No. 1. Online. Available at http://spaces.brad.ac.uk:8080/download/attachments/748/resrep1.pdf.

Hoyt, Timothy D. 2001. Pakistani Nuclear Doctrine and the Dangers of Strategic Myopia. *Asian Survey* 41, no. 6 (Nov.–Dec.): 956–977.

Human Rights Watch. 2012. India: Abuses by Border Force Increasing: Broken Pledges by India to End Killings, Torture at Bangladeshi Border. News release, June 11. Online. Available at http://www.hrw.org/news/2012/06/11/india-abuses-border-force-increasing.

Husain, Miranda. 2011. Bahrain or Bust? *Newsweek Pakistan,* April 22. Online. Available at http://www.newsweekpakistan.com/the-take/287.

Hussain, Ishrat. 2011. *Prospects and Challenges for Increasing India-Pakistan Trade.* Washington, DC: Atlantic Council of the United States. Online. Available at http://www.acus.org/files/publication_pdfs/403/112311_ACUS_IndiaPakTrade.pdf.

Hussain, Mirza Hamid (Brig.). 2003. *The Battle Within.* Karachi: Royal Book Company.

Hussain, Rizwan. 2005. *Pakistan and the Emergence of Islamic Militancy in Afghanistan.* Burlington, VT: Ashgate.

Hussain, Zahid. 2010. *The Scorpion's Tail.* New York: Free Press.

Ifzal, Muhammad (Brig.). 2004. Concept of Limited War. In *Pakistan Army Green Book 2004: Limited War,* 13–21. Rawalpindi: Pakistan Army General Headquarters.

Ilahi, Shereen. 2003. The Radcliffe Boundary Commission and the Fate of Kashmir. *India Review* 2, no. 1: 77–102.

Indian Independence Act of 1947. n.d. Online. Original text available at http://www.legislation.gov.uk/ukpga/1947/30/pdfs/ukpga_19470030_en.pdf.

International Crisis Group. 2003. *Pakistan: The Mullahs and the Military.* Asia Report No. 49. Online. Available at http://www.crisisgroup.org/en/regions/asia/south-asia/pakistan/049-pakistan-the-mullahs-and-the-military.aspx.

——. 2004. *Building Judicial Independence in Pakistan.* Asia Report No. 86. Online. Available at http://www.crisisgroup.org/en/regions/asia/south-asia/pakistan/086-building-judicial-independence-in-pakistan.aspx.

——. 2005. *Authoritarianism and Political Party Reform in Pakistan.* Asia Report No. 102. Online. Available at http://www.crisisgroup.org/en/regions/asia/south-asia/pakistan/102-authoritarianism-and-political-party-reform-in-pakistan.aspx.

——. 2006a. *Authoritarianism and Political Party Reform in Pakistan.* Asia Report No. 102. Online. Available at http://www.crisisgroup.org/en/regions/asia/south-asia/pakistan/102-authoritarianism-and-political-party-reform-in-pakistan.aspx.

——. 2006b. *Pakistan's Tribal Areas: Appeasing the Militants.* Asia Report No. 125. Online. Available at http://www.crisisgroup.org/~/media/Files/asia/south-asia/pakistan/125_pakistans_tribal_areas___appeasing_the_militants.pdf.

——. 2007. *Pakistan: Emergency Rule or Return to Democracy?* Asia Briefing No. 70. Online. Available at http://www.crisisgroup.org/en/regions/asia/south-asia/pakistan/crisis-alert-pakistan-emergency-rule-or-return-to-democracy.aspx.

——. 2013. Drones: Myths and Reality in Pakistan. Asia Report No. 247. Online. Available at http://www.crisisgroup.org/en/regions/asia/south-asia/pakistan/247-drones-myths-and-reality-in-pakistan.aspx.

International Institute for Strategic Studies (IISS). 2007. *Nuclear Black Markets: Pakistan, A.Q. Khan and the Rise of Proliferation Networks.* London: IISS.

——. 2012. *The Military Balance 2012.* London: IISS.

Iqbal, Mohammad. 2002. *Muslim Political Thought: A Reconstruction,* edited with an introduction by Fateh Mohammad Malik. Lahore: Alhamra.

Iqbal, Mohammad Safdar (Lt. Col.). 1966. Motivation of the Pakistani Soldier. *Pakistan Army Journal* 8 (Dec.): 6–15.

Iqbal, Shahid (Maj. Gen.). 2004. Doctrinal Aspects of Limited War and Its Applicability in the Region. In *Pakistan Army Green Book 2004: Limited War,* 83–89. Rawalpindi: Pakistan Army General Headquarters.

Iqbal, Shaukat (Brig.). 2008. Present and Future Conflict Environments in Pakistan: Challenges for Pakistan Army and the Way Forward. In *Pakistan Army Green Book 2008: Future Conflict Environment,* 43–50. Rawalpindi: Pakistan Army General Headquarters.

Inter Services Public Relations (ISPR). 2011. Press Release No. PR94/2011. April 19. Online. Available at http://www.ispr.gov.pk/front/main.asp?o=t-press_release&id=1721.

———. 2012. Press Release No. PR204/2012-ISPR. September 17. Online. Available at http://www.ispr.gov.pk/front/main.asp?o=t-press_release&date=2011/9/14.

Iype, George. 2000. Bill Pussyfoots around Kashmir, CTBT with Atal. *Rediff.com*, March 21. Online. Available at http://www.rediff.com/news/2000/mar/21iype1.htm.

Jacob, J. F. R. (Lt. Gen). 1977. *Surrender at Dacca: Birth of a Nation*. New Delhi: Manohar.

Jaffrelot, Christophe. 2002a. *A History of Pakistan and Its Origins*. London: Anthem Press.

———. 2002b. India and Pakistan: Interpreting the Divergence of Two Political Trajectories. *Cambridge Review of International Affairs* 15, no. 2: 251–267.

———. 2002c. Nationalism without a Nation: Pakistan Searching for an Identity. In *Pakistan: Nationalism without a Nation?* ed. Christophe Jaffrelot, 7–47. London: Zed Books.

Jalal, Ayesha. 1985. *The Sole Spokesman: Jinnah, the Muslim League and the Demand for Pakistan*. Cambridge: Cambridge University Press.

———. 1990. *The State of Martial Rule: The Origins of Pakistan's Political Economy of Defence*. Cambridge: Cambridge University Press.

———. 2008. *Partisans of Allah*. Lahore: Sang-e-Meel.

Jamaat-ud-Dawa. 2004. *Hum Kyon Jihad Kar Rahen Hain?* [Why Are We Waging Jihad?] Lahore: Dar-ul-Andulus.

Jamal, Arif. 2009. *Shadow War: The Untold Story of Jihad in Kashmir*. New York: Melville.

Jamil, Uzma. 2011. Challenging the "Official" Story of 9/11: Community Narratives and Conspiracy Theories. *Ethnicities* 11 (June): 245–261.

Javed, Tariq (Lt. Col.). 2002. Challenges of Low Intensity Conflict and Its Response. In *Pakistan Army Green Book 2002: Low Intensity Conflict*, 128–133. Rawalpindi: Pakistan Army General Headquarters.

Jervis, Robert. 1989. *The Meaning of the Nuclear Revolution: Statecraft and the Prospect of Armageddon*. Ithaca, NY: Cornell University Press.

———. 1999. Realism, Neoliberalism, and Cooperation: Understanding the Debate. *International Security* 24, no. 1: 42–63.

Jha, Saumitra, and Steven Wilkinson. 2012. Does Combat Experience Foster Organizational Skill? Evidence from Ethnic Cleansing during the Partition of South Asia. *American Political Science Review*, 106, no. 4 (Nov.): 883–907.

Joeck, Neil. 1997. *Maintaining Nuclear Stability in South Asia*. Adelphi Paper No. 312. New York: Oxford University Press.

Joint Statement Signed by the Prime Minister of Pakistan and China. 1956. *Pakistan Horizon* 9 (Dec.): 220–222.

Johnson, Thomas H., and M. Chris Mason. 2007. Understanding the Taliban and Insurgency in Afghanistan. *Orbis* 51, no. 1: 71–89.

Johnston, Alastair Iain. 1995a. *Cultural Realism: Culture and Grand Strategy in Chinese History*. Princeton, NJ: Princeton University Press.

———. 1995b. Thinking about Strategic Culture. *International Security* 19, no. 4: 32–64.

———. 1996. Cultural Realism and Strategy in Maoist China. In *The Culture of National Security*, ed. Peter Katzenstein, 216–268. New York: Columbia University Press.

Jones, Owen Bennett. 2003. *Pakistan: Eye of the Storm*. New Haven, CT: Yale University Press.

Jones, Seth G., and C. Christine Fair. 2010. *Counterinsurgency in Pakistan*. Santa Monica, CA: RAND.

Joshi, Shashank. 2013. India's Military Instrument: A Doctrine Stillborn. *Journal of Strategic Studies* 36, no. 4 (July): 512–521.

Kamran, Tahir. 2008. Contextualizing Sectarian Militancy in Pakistan: A Case Study of Jhang. *Journal of Islamic Studies* 20, no. 1: 55–85.

Kapur, Paul S. 2003. Nuclear Proliferation, the Kargil Conflict, and South Asian Security. *Security Studies* 13, no. 1: 79–105.

———. 2007. *Dangerous Deterrent: Nuclear Weapons Proliferation and Conflict in South Asia.* Stanford, CA: Stanford University Press.

———. 2008. Ten Years of Instability in a Nuclear South Asia. *International Security* 33, no. 2: 71–94.

Karamat, Jehangir (Lt. Gen.). 1992. The Senior Commander. In *The Pakistan Army Green Book 1992: Year of the Senior Field Commander Commander*, 11–16. Rawalpindi: Pakistan Army General Headquarters.

Kargil Review Committee. 2000. *From Surprise to Reckoning: The Kargil Review Committee Report.* New Delhi: SAGE.

Kayani, General Ashfaq Pervez. Full Speech at PMA Kakul August 13th 2012. 2012. *YouTube*, posted by "SiasiTv," August 13. Online. Available at http://www.youtube.com/watch?v=7qaBNlEkxhw.

Kerr, Paul K., and Mary Beth Nikitin. 2012. Pakistan's Nuclear Weapons: Proliferation and Security Issues. CRS Report No. RK34248. Washington, DC: Congressional Research Service. Online. Available at http://www.fas.org/sgp/crs/nuke/RL34248.pdf.

Khalid, Farhat. 1988. India's Nuclear Capability and Delivery System. *Pakistan Army Journal* 29 (Mar.): 2–7.

Khalid, Zulfikar A. 1989a. Pakistan–Saudi Arabian Relations: Interests, Imperatives, Vital Links. *Pakistan Army Journal* 30 (June): 2–14.

———. 1989b. Evolution of Saudi–Pakistan Strategic Relationship 1947–1990: Military Security and Economic Factors. *Strategic Studies* 13, no. 1 (Autumn): 53–77.

Khan, Adeel. 2003. Pukhtun Ethnic Nationalism: From Separatism to Integrationism. *Asian Ethnicity* 4, no. 1: 67–83.

———. 2009. Renewed Ethnonationalist Insurgency in Balochistan, Pakistan: The Militarized State and Continuing Economic Deprivation. *Asian Survey* 49 (Nov.–Dec.): 1071–1091.

Khan, Amir Mohammad. 2004. Justice Denied. *Newsline*, December. Online. Available at *http://www.newslinemagazine.com/2004/12/justice-denied/*.

Khan, Fazal Muqeem (Maj. Gen.). 1963. *The Story of the Pakistan Army.* Karachi: Oxford University Press.

Khan, Feroz (Brig. Retd). 2012a. *Eating Grass: The Making of the Pakistani Bomb.* Stanford, CA: Stanford University Press.

———. 2012b. *Pakistan: Political Transitions and Nuclear Management.* Nonproliferation Policy Education Center. Online. Available at http://www.npolicy.org/article_file/Pakistan-Political_Transitions_and_Nuclear_Management.pdf.

Khan, Gul Hassan (Lt. Gen.). 1993. *Memoirs.* Karachi: Oxford University Press.

Khan, Ismael. 2007. Baitullah Mehsud, Pakistan's Biggest Dilemma. *Dawn*, December 31. Online. Available at http://dawn.com/news/282428/baitullah-mehsud-pakistan.

Khan, Junaid (Maj.). 2012. Living an Indian Influenced Life. *Hilal* 49 (Aug.): 28–29.

Khan, Mohammad Ayub (Gen.). 1960. Pakistan Perspective. *Foreign Affairs* 38 (July): 547–556.

———. 2006. *Friends not Masters.* Reprint. Islamabad: Mr. Books. (First edition 1967.)

Khan, Muhammad (Col. Dr.). 2009. Detrimental Effects of Extremism on Pakistani Society. *Pakistan Army Journal* 52 (Winter): 39–55.

———. 2011. Security Environment in South Asia. *Hilal* 48 (Sept.): 18–19.

Khan, Muhammad Yaqub (Maj. Gen.). 2006. Terrorism, Its Dynamics and Response Options for Pakistan. In *Pakistan Army Green Book 2006: Terrorism*, 42–54. Rawalpindi: Pakistan Army General Headquarters.

Khan, Muhammad Zafrulla, and John K. Emmerson. 1954. United States–Pakistan Mutual Defense Assistance Agreement. *Middle East Journal* 8 (Summer): 338–340.

Khan, Muqaddam, and Azaz Syed. 2007. Ex-Soldier, Brothers Held on Tarbela Attack Suspicion. *Daily Times*, September 15. Online. Available at http://www.dailytimes.com.pk/default.asp?page=2007/09/15/story_15-9-2007_pg1_7.

Khan, Rashid Ahmad. 2005. Political Developments in FATA: A Critical Perspective. In *Tribal Areas of Pakistan: Challenges and Responses*, ed. Pervaiz Iqbal Cheema and Masudul Hasan Nuri, 27–42. Islamabad: IPRI.

Khan, Sartaj. 2009. Imperialism, Religion and Class in Swat. *International Socialism* 123 (June 24). Online. Available at http://www.isj.org.uk/?id=554.

Khan, Yasmeen. 2007. *The Great Partition: The Making of India and Pakistan.* New Haven, CT: Yale University Press.

Khan, Zulfiqar. 2011. Tactical Nuclear Weapons and Pakistan's Option of Offensive-Deterrence. In *Nuclear Pakistan: Strategic Dimensions,* ed. Zulfiqar Khan, 1–42. Karachi: Oxford University Press.

Khattab, Huda, ed. 1995. Sayyid Abul A'la Mawdudid's Jihad fi Sabilillah [Jihad in Islam]. U.K.I.M. Dawah Center. Online. Available at http://www.jamaat.org/new/library/moalana%20english%20books/Typed%20books/Jihad_Fi_Sabilillah.pdf.

Kier, Elizabeth. 1995. Culture and Military Doctrine: France between the Wars. *International Security* 19, no. 4: 65–93.

Kimball, Daryl G. 2010. Pakistan Presses Case for US Nuclear Deal. Arms Control Association, April. Online. Available at http://www.armscontrol.org/act/2010_04/Pakistan.

Kohari, Alizeh. 2012. Power Projection. *Herald,* December, 51–53.

Kukreja, Veena. 2003. *Contemporary Pakistan: Political Processes, Conflicts and Crises.* New Delhi: SAGE.

Kooiman, Dick. 1995. Communalism and Indian Princely States: A Comparison with British India. *Economic and Political Weekly* 30 (Aug. 26): 2123–2133.

Korbel, Josef. 1954. *Danger in Kashmir: A Historical Survey.* Princeton, NJ: Princeton University Press.

Krebs, Ronald R. 2005. One Nation under Arms? Military Participation Policy and the Politics of Identity. *Security Studies* 14 (July–Sept.): 529–564.

——. 2006. *Fighting for Rights: Military Service and the Politics of Citizenship.* Ithaca, NY: Cornell University Press.

Krepon, Michael, and Chris Gagne. 2001. Introduction. In *The Stability–Instability Paradox: Nuclear Weapons and Brinkmanship In South Asia,* ed. Michael Krepon and Chris Gagne, 1–24. Washington, DC: Stimson Center.

Krepon, Michael, and Nate Cohn, eds. 2011. *Crisis in South Asia: Trends and Potential Consequences.* Washington, DC: Henry L. Stimson Center. Online. Available at http://www.stimson.org/images/uploads/research-pdfs/Crises_Complete.pdf.

Kroenig, Mathew. 2010. *Exporting the Bomb: Technology Transfer and the Spread of Nuclear Weapons.* Ithaca, NY: Cornell University Press.

Kronstadt, K. Alan. 2006. *Pakistan: A Chronology of Recent Affairs.* Washington, DC: Congressional Research Service. Online. Available at http://www.au.af.mil/au/awc/awcgate/crs/rs21584.pdf.

——. 2010. *Pakistan: Key Current Issues and Developments.* Washington, DC: Congressional Research Service. Online. Available at http://fpc.state.gov/documents/organization/145133.pdf.

Kumar, Arvind. 2007. Theories of Deterrence and Nuclear Deterrence in the Subcontinent. In *The India–Pakistan Nuclear Relationship: Theories of Deterrence and International Relations,* ed. E. Sridharan, 239–265. New Delhi: Routledge.

Kux, Dennis. 1992. *India and the United States: Estranged Democracies.* Washington, DC: National Defense University Press.

——. 2001. *The United States and Pakistan, 1947-2000: Disenchanted Allies.* Washington, DC: Woodrow Wilson Center Press.

Ladwig, Walter C. 2008. A Cold Start for Hot Wars? *International Security* 32, no. 3 (Winter): 158–190.

Lahore Declaration Text. 1999. Online. Available at http://cns.miis.edu/inventory/pdfs/aptlahore.pdf.

Lal, Neeta. 2012. India–Pakistan Thaw Continues. *Asia Sentinel,* April 20. Online. Available at http://www.asiasentinel.com/index.php?Itemid=225&id=4439&option=com_content&task=view.

Lall, Marie. 2008. Educate to Hate: The Use of Education in the Creation of Antagonistic National Identities in India and Pakistan. *Compare* 38 (Jan.): 103–119.

Lamb, Alastair. 1967. *The Kashmir Problem: A Historical Survey.* New York: Praeger.

———. 1991. *Kashmir: A Disputed Legacy: 1846–1990.* Hertfordshire: Roxsford Books.

Lambert, Richard D. 1950. Religion, Economics, and Violence in Bengal: Background of the Minorities Agreement. *Middle East Journal* 4 (July): 307–328.

Lambeth, Benjamin S. 2012. Airpower in India's 1999 Kargil War. *Journal of Stratgic Studies* 35, no. 3: 289–316.

Lantis, Jeffrey S., and Andrew A. Charlton. 2011. Continuity or Change? The Strategic Culture of Australia. *Comparative Strategy* 30: 291–315.

Larus, Joel. 1979. *Culture and Political-Military Behavior: The Hindus in Premodern India.* Calcutta: Minerva.

Lavoy, Peter R. 2005. Pakistan's Nuclear Doctrine. In *Prospects for Peace in South Asia*, ed. Rafiq Dossani and Henry Rowan, 280–300. Stanford, CA: Stanford University Press.

———. 2006. Pakistan's Strategic Culture. A Report Prepared for Defense Threat Reduction Agency. Online. Available at http://www.fas.org/irp/agency/dod/dtra/pakistan.pdf.

———. 2008. Islamabad's Nuclear Posture: Its Premises and Implementation. In *Pakistan's Nuclear Future: Worries beyond War*, ed. Henry Sokolski, 129–165. Carlisle: Army War College.

———. 2009. Introduction. In *Asymmetric Warfare in South Asia: The Causes and Consequences of Kargil*, ed. Peter R. Lavoy, 2–38. Cambridge: Cambridge University Press.

Leigh, David. 2010. WikiLeaks Cables Expose Pakistan Nuclear Fears: US and UK Diplomats Warn of Terrorists Getting Hold of Fissile Material and of Pakistan-India Nuclear Exchange. *Guardian*, November 30. Online. Available at http://www.guardian.co.uk/world/2010/nov/30/wikileaks-cables-pakistan-nuclear-fears.

Levin, Carl. 2009. Opening Statement of Senator Carl Levin, Senate Armed Services Committee Hearing on Afghanistan and Pakistan. Press Release, February 26. Online. Available at http://levin.senate.gov/newsroom/release.cfm?id=308740.

Li, Wei, and Dennis Tao Yang. 2005. The Great Leap Forward: Anatomy of a Central Planning Disaster. *Journal of Political Economy* 113 (Aug.): 840–877.

Lock, Edward. 2010. Refining Strategic Culture: Return of the Second Generation. *Review of International Studies* 26: 685–708.

Magnus, Ralph H., and Eden Naby. 2002. *Afghanistan: Mullah, Marx and Mujahid.* Boulder, CO: Westview.

Mahajan, Sneh. 2002. *British Foreign Policy 1874–1914: The Role of India.* London: Routledge.

Mahmood, Asif (Lt. Col.). 2000. Significance of National Integration in Nation Building. In *Pakistan Army Green Book 2000: Role of Pakistan Army in Nation Building*, 110–122. Rawalpindi: Pakistan Army General Headquarters.

Mahmud, Muneer (Brig.). 2002. Low Intensity Conflict—Historical Perspective. In *Pakistan Army Green Book 2002: Low Intensity Conflict*, 17–23. Rawalpindi: Pakistan Army General Headquarters.

Majeed, Tariq (Cdre). 1992. Weaknesses and Limitations of Indian Naval Capability. *Pakistan Defence Review* 4 (Dec.): 38–77.

Majeed, Tariq (Cdre. Retd.). 1993–1994. An Inquiry into the Causes of the India–Pakistan Wars of 1965 and 1971. *Pakistan Defence Review* 5 (Winter): 4–45.

———. 1994. Khairuddin Barbarossa: History's Most Outstanding Naval Commander. *Pakistan Army Journal* 35 (Autumn): 28–40.

Maley, William. 2002. *The Afghanistan Wars.* London: Palgrave MacMillan.

Malhotra, Jyotri. 2011. Pakistan Army on Board Trade Liberalization with India. *Business Standard*, November 21. Online. Available at http://www.business-standard.com/india/news/pakistan-armyboard-trade-liberalisationindia/456136/.

Malik, Ahmad Rashid. 2012. The New Engagement with United States. *Hilal* 48 (Feb.): 11–12.

Malik, Askari Raza (Brig). 1990. Concept of Leadership. In *Pakistan Army Green Book 1990: Year of the Junior Leaders*, 7–14. Rawalpindi: Pakistan Army General Headquarters.

Malik, Askari Raza (Maj. Gen.). 1992. The Field Commanders—A Profile. In *Pakistan Army Green Book 1992: The Year of the Senior Field Commander*, 75–82. Rawalpindi: Pakistan Army General Headquarters.

Malik, Ghulam Muhammad (Lt. Gen.). 1990. Islamic Concept of Leadership. In *Pakistan Army Green Book 1990: The Year of Junior Leaders*, 1–7. Rawalpindi: Pakistan Army General Headquarters.

Malik, Hafeez. 2002. Iran's Relations with Pakistan. *Journal of South Asian and Middle Eastern Studies* 36 (Fall): 56–71.

Malik, S.K. (Brig. Retd.). 1992a. Badr, Ohad & Khandaq: A Comparative Study. *Pakistan Army Journal* 33 (Dec.): 3–10.

——. 1992b. The Holy Prophet's Military Campaigns. *Pakistan Army Journal* 33 (Sept.): 2–12.

——. 1992c. The Holy Prophet's Defence Policy and Military Strategy. *Pakistan Army Journal* 33 (June): 2–22.

Malik, Salma. 2009. Security Sector Reforms in Pakistan: Challenges, Remedies, and Future Prospects. *South Asian Survey* 16, no. 2: 273–289.

Malik, Sondha Khan. 1963. Devotion: The Greatest Single Weapon of War. *Pakistan Army Journal* 5, no. 1: 1–3.

Mallet, Victor, and Farhan Bokhari. 2012. Pakistan: A Fragile Transition, *Financial Times*, December 19. Online. Available at http://www.ft.com/cms/s/0/fd6b21f2-494b-11e2-9 225-00144feab49a.html#axzz2ajloP4uY.

Markey, Daniel. 2007. A False Choice in Pakistan. *Foreign Affairs* 86 (July–Aug.): 85–102.

Masood, Salman. 2008. New Pakistan Army Chief Orders Military Out of Civilian Government Agencies, Reversing Musharraf Policy. *New York Times*, February 13. Online. Available at http://www.nytimes.com/2008/02/13/world/asia/13pstan.html?ref=world&_r=0.

——. 2012. C.I.A. Leaves Base in Pakistan Used for Drone Strikes. *New York Times*, December 11. Online. Available at http://www.nytimes.com/2011/12/12/world/asia/ cia-leaves-pakistan-base-used-for-drone-strikes.html.

Masood, Salman, and Eric Schmitt. 2011. Tensions Flare between US and Pakistan after Strike. *New York Times*, Nov. 26. Online. Available at http://www.nytimes.com/2011/11/27/world/ asia/pakistan-says-nato-helicopters-kill-dozens-of-soldiers.html?pagewanted=all&_r=0.

Masood, Salman, and Waqar Gillani. 2011. Blast at Pakistan Shrine Kills Dozens. *New York Times*, April 3. Online. Available at http://www.nytimes.com/2011/04/04/world/ asia/04pakistan.html?partner=rss&emc=rss.

Matinuddin, Kamal. 1994. *Tragedy of Errors (East Pakistan Crisis, 1968–1971)*. Lahore: Wajidalis.

——. 2002. *The Nuclearization of South Asia*. Karachi: Oxford University Press.

Mazzetti, Mark. 2013. *The Way of the Knife: The CIA, A Secret Army, and a War at the Ends of the Earth*. New York: Penguin Press.

McMahon, Robert J. 1994. *The Cold War on the Periphery: The United States, India and Pakistan*. New York: Columbia University Press.

Mearsheimer, John J. 2001. *The Tragedy of Great Power Politics*. New York: Norton.

Mehmud, Khalid (Maj.). 1985a. India's Global Posture. *Pakistan Army Journal* 26, no. 4: 13–24.

——. 1985b. India's Posture as a Regional Power. *Pakistan Army Journal* 26, no. 1: 2–8.

Metcalf, Barbara D. 2002. *'Traditionalist' Islamic Activism: Deoband, Tablighis, and Talibs*. Leiden, NL: International Institute for the Study of Islam in the Modern World. Online. Available at https://www.openaccess.leidenuniv.nl/bitstream/1887/10068/1/paper_metcalf.pdf.

Minority Rights Group International. 2010. *State of the World's Minorities and Indigenous Peoples—2010*. London: MRGI. Online. Available at http://www.minorityrights.org/10068/ state-of-the-worlds-minorities/state-of-the-worlds-minorities-and-indigenous-peoples-2010.html.

Mohan, C. Raja. 2004. *Crossing the Rubicon: The Shaping of India's New Foreign Policy*. New York: Palgrave MacMillan.

——. 2006. India and the Balance of Power. *Foreign Affairs* 85, no. 4: 17–32.

Moore, R. J. 1983. Jinnah and the Pakistan Demand. *Modern Asian Studies* 17, no. 4: 529–561.

Muhammad, Gul (Brig.). 2000. A Conceptual Framework for Army. In *The Pakistan Army Green Book 2000: Role of Pakistan Army in Nation Building*, 43–51. Rawalpindi: Pakistan Army General Headquarters.

Muldoon, Andrew. 2009. Politics, Intelligence and Elections in Late Colonial India: Congress and the Raj in 1937. *Journal of the Canadian Historical Association* 20, no. 2: 160–188.

Mullen, Michael (Adm.). 2011. Statement of Admiral Michael Mullen, US Navy Chairman Joint Chiefs of Staff Before the Senate Armed Services Committee on Afghanistan and Iraq, September 22. Online. Available at http://www.armed-services.senate.gov/statemnt/2011/09%20September/Mullen%2009-22-11.pdf

Murad, Asif (Brig.). 2002. Low Intensity Conflict. In *Pakistan Army Green Book 2002: Low Intensity Conflict*, 79–85. Rawalpindi: Pakistan Army General Headquarters.

Musa, Mohammad (Gen. Retd). 1983. *My Version: India–Pakistan War 1965*. Lahore: Wajidalis Ltd.

Musharraf, Pervez. 2004. A Plea for Enlightened Moderation: Muslims must Raise Themselves Up through Individual Achievement and Socioeconomic Emancipation. *Washington Post*, June 1.

——. 2006. President Address to Nation, September 19, 2001. *Our Leader-Musharraf* (blog), July 13. Online. Available at http://presidentmusharraf.wordpress.com/2006/07/13/address-19-september-2001/.

Naqvi, Anwar Shafiq (Lt. Col.). 1991. Qaid-i-Azam and Armed Forces. *Pakistan Army Journal* 32 (Mar.): 23–32.

Naqvi, Saifi Ahmad (Col.). 1994. Motivation Training in Pakistan Army. In *Pakistan Army Green Book 1994: Training in the Army*, 179–185. Rawalpindi: Pakistan Army General Headquarters.

Naqvi, Syed Shahid Abbas (Maj.). 1973. Motivation of Armed Forces: Towards Our Ideology. *Pakistan Army Journal* 15 (Dec.): 58–63.

Nasr, Seyyed Vali Reza. 2001. *Islamic Leviathan: Islam and the Making of State Power*. Oxford: Oxford University Press.

——. 2002. Islam, The State, and the Rise of Sectarian Militancy. In *Pakistan: Nationalism without a Nation*, ed. Christophe Jaffrelot, 85–114. London: Zed Books.

——. 2004. Military Rule, Islamism and Democracy in Pakistan. *Middle East Journal* 58 (Spring): 195–209.

——. 2005. National Identities and the India-Pakistan Conflict. in *The India-Pakistan Conflict: An Enduring Rivalry*, ed. T. V. Paul,178-201. Cambridge: Cambridge University Press.

Nation. 2012. Defence Day. *Nation*, September 7. Online. Available at http://www.nation.com.pk/pakistan-news-newspaper-daily-english-online/editorials/07-Sep-2012/defence-day.

National Assembly of Pakistan Official Website. n.d. http://www.na.gov.pk/en/acts-tenure.php?tenure_id=1.

National Consortium for the Study of Terrorism and Responses to Terrorism (START). (2011). Global Terrorism Database [Data file]. Online. Available at http://www.start.umd.edu/gtd.

National Defence University. n.d. Important Books to Read. Online. Available at http://www.ndu.edu.pk/SOPs/war_wing/books_list.doc.

Nawaz, Shuja. 2008a. *Crossed Swords: Pakistan, Its Army and the Wars Within*. New York: Oxford University Press.

——. 2008b. The First Kashmir War Revisited. *India Review* 7 (Apr.): 115–154.

——. 2010a. *Pakistan in the Danger Zone: A Tenuous US–Pakistan Relationship*. Washington, DC: Atlantic Council.

——. 2010b. *Kayani and Pakistan's Civil–Military Relations*. Washington, DC: Atlantic Council. Online. Available at http://www.acus.org/new_atlanticist/kayani-and-pakistans-civil-military-relations.

——. 2011. *Learning by Doing: The Pakistan Army's Experience with Counterinsurgency*. Washington, DC: Atlantic Council. Online. Available at http://www.acus.org/files/publication_pdfs/403/020111_ACUS_Nawaz_PakistanCounterinsurgency.pdf.

Nayak, Polly, and Michael Krepon. 2006. US Crisis Management in South Asia's Twin Peaks Crisis. Report No. 57. Washington, DC: Henry L. Stimson Center.

——. 2012. *The Unfinished Crisis: US Crisis Management after the 2008 Mumbai Attacks*. Washington, DC: Henry L. Stimson Center.

Nayyar, A. H., and Ahmed Salim. 2003. *The Subtle Subversion: The State of Curricula and Textbooks in Pakistan—Urdu, English, Social Studies and Civics*. Islamabad: Sustainable Development Policy Institute.

Nelson, Dean, and Ben Farmer. 2010. Hamid Karzai Held Secret Talks with Mullah Baradar in Afghanistan. *Telegraph*, March 16. Online. Available at http://www.telegraph.co.uk/news/worldnews/asia/afghanistan/7457861/Hamid-Karzai-held-secret-talks-with-Mullah-Baradar-in-Afghanistan.html.

New York Times. 1963. Kashmiri Police Quell Rioting over Theft of Mohammed's Hair. *New York Times*, December 29, p. 8.

——. 2010. Hakimullah Mehsud. *New York Times*, April 29. Online. Available at http://topics.nytimes.com/topics/reference/timestopics/people/m/hakimullah_mehsud/index.html.

Niazi, A. A. K. 1964. A New Look at Infiltration. *Pakistan Army Journal* 6 (June): 1–9.

Niazi, A. A. K (Lt. Gen.). (1998) 2009. *The Betrayal of East Pakistan*. Reprint, Karachi: Oxford University Press.

Nizamani, Haider K. 2000. *The Roots of Rhetoric: Politics of Nuclear Weapons in India and Pakistan*. Westport, CT: Praeger.

Norris, Robert, and Hans Kristensen. 2007. Nuclear Notebook: Pakistan's Nuclear Forces, 2007. *Bulletin of the Atomic Scientists* (May–June). Online. Available at http://bos.sagepub.com/content/63/3/71.full.pdf+html.

——. 2011. Nuclear Notebook: Pakistan's Nuclear Forces, 2011. *Bulletin of the Atomic Scientists* (July/Aug.). Online. Available at http://bos.sagepub.com/content/67/4/91.full.pdf+html.

Nye Jr., Joseph S., and Sean M. Lynn-Jones. 1988. International Security Studies: A Report on a Conference on the State of the Field. *International Security* 12 (Spring): 5–27.

Objectives Resolution. n.d. *pakistani.org*. Online. Available at http://www.pakistani.org/pakistan/constitution/annex_objres.html.

Outlook India. 2004. Musharraf Getting "Bad Vibes" from India Raises Plebiscite Issue Once Again. *OutlookIndia.com*, November 19. Online. Available at http://news.outlookindia.com/items.aspx?artid=262341.

Pakistan Army. 1978. *The Pakistan Army Journal* 19 (March): 3–12.

Pakistan Army. n.d. Join Pakistan Army: Men at Their Best. Online. Available at http://www.joinpakarmy.gov.pk/.

Pakistan Express Tribune. 2012. Afghanistan-Based Militants Mount Cross-Border Attack. *Pakistan Express Tribune*, July 26. Online. Available at http://tribune.com.pk/story/413139/afghanistan-based-militants-mount-cross-border-attack/.

Pakistan Express Tribune. 2013. Presidential Elections To Be Held on July 30: SC. *Pakistan Express Tribune*, July 24. Online. Available at http://tribune.com.pk/story/581281/presidential-elections-sc-asks-ecp-to-reconsider-july-30-as-election-date/.

Pakistan Institute for Peace Studies. 2008. *Pakistan Security Report 2008*. Islamabad: PIPS.

——. 2009. *PIPS Security Report 2009*. Online. Available at http://san-pips.com/index.php?action=ra&id=psr_list_1.

——. 2011. *Pakistan Security Report 2011*. Islamabad: PIPS.

——. 2012. Civilian Casualties in Armed Conflicts in Pakistan: Timeline 2012. Online. Available at http://san-pips.com/index.php?action=reports&id=tml2.

"SEATO and Pakistan." 1954. *Pakistan Horizon* 7, No. 3 (Sept.): 138–149.

Pakistan Mission to the United Nations. 2013. Kashmir—The History. Online. Available at http://www.pakun.org/kashmir/history.php.

Pakistan Supreme Court. 2002. Judgment on Constitution Petition Nos. 15, 17–24; Civil Petition No. 512 of 2002. April 27. Online. Available at http://www.supremecourt.gov.pk/web/user_files/File/JR_Detailed_Judgment_in_Referendum_Case.pdf

Pande, Aparna. 2011. *Explaining Pakistan's Foreign Policy: Escaping India*. London: Routledge.

Pant, Harsh V. 2009a. *Indian Foreign Policy in a Unipolar World*. New Delhi: Routledge.

——. 2009b. A Rising India's Search for a Foreign Policy. *Orbis* 53, no. 2: 250–264.

Pardesi, Manjeet S. 2008. The Battle for the Soul of Pakistan at Islamabad's Red Mosque. In *Treading on Hallowed Ground: Counterinsurgency in Sacred Spaces*, ed. C. Christine Fair and Sumit Ganguly, 88–116. New York: Oxford University Press.

Pardesi, Manjeet S., and Sumit Ganguly. 2010. India and Pakistan: The Origins of Their Different Politico-Military Trajectories. *India Review* 9, no. 1: 38–67.

Paris, Jonathan. 2010. *Prospects for Pakistan*. London: Legatum Institute. Online. Available at http://www.li.com/attachments/ProspectsForPakistan.pdf.

Parker, Reuben D. (Lt. Col.). 1964. Infiltration as a Form of Maneuver. *Pakistan Army Journal* 6 (June): 1–9.

Pathan, H.K. (Maj). 1963. Muhallab bin abi Sufra: His Strategy and Qualities of Generalship. *Pakistan Army Journal* 5, no. 1: 35–42.

Pattanaik, Smruti. 2012. India–Pakistan Foreign Ministers' Meet: The Hype and the Substance. *IDSA Comment*, September 17. Online. Available at http://www.idsa.in/idsacomments/IndiaPakistanForeignMinistersMeet_sspattanaik_170912.

——. 2013. India and Pakistan: Getting Along with the Peace Process. *IDSA Comment*, January 18. Online. Available at http://www.idsa.in/idsacomments/IndiaandPakistanGettingAlongwiththePeaceProcess_sspattanaik_180113.

Paul, T. V. 2005. Causes of the India–Pakistan Enduring Rivalry. In *The India–Pakistan Conflict*, ed. T. V. Paul, 3–24. Cambridge: Cambridge University Press.

PBS. Pakistan Blast Sharpens Concern on Taliban. 2010. *PBS Newshour*, April 1. Online. Available at http://www.pbs.org/newshour/bb/military/jan-june10/pakistan_01-01.html.

Peers, Douglas M. 2008. The Martial Races and the Indian Army in the Victorian Era. In *A Military History of India and South Asia*, ed. D. Marston and C. Sundaram, 34–52. Bloomington: Indiana University Press.

Perkovich, George. 1999. *India's Nuclear Bomb: The Impact on Global Proliferation*. Berkeley: University of California Press.

Perlez, Jane. 2011. Pakistan Pulls Closer to a Reluctant China. *New York Times*, October 6. Online. Available at http://www.nytimes.com/2011/10/07/world/asia/pakistan-pulls-closer-to-a-reluctant-china.html?_r=0.

——. 2009a. Landowners Still in Exile from Unstable Pakistan Area. *New York Times*, July 27. Online. Available at http://www.nytimes.com/2009/07/28/world/asia/28swat.html.

——. 2009b. Pakistan Retakes Army Headquarters; Hostages Freed. *New York Times*, October 10. Online. Available at http://www.nytimes.com/2009/10/11/world/asia/11pstan.html.

Perlez, Jane, Eric Schmitt, and Ginger Thompson. 2010. US Had Warnings on Plotter of Mumbai Attack. *New York Times*, October 17. Online. Available at http://www.nytimes.com/2010/10/17/world/asia/17headley.html?_r=1&ref=david_c_headley.

Peters, Ralph. 2006. Blood Borders: How a Better Middle East Would Look. *Armed Forces Journal*, June. Online. Available at http://www.armedforcesjournal.com/2006/06/1833899.

Peterson Institute for International Economics. 2012. Case 79-2: US v. Pakistan. Case Studies in Sanctions and Terrorism. Online. Available at http://www.iie.com/research/topics/sanctions/pakistan.cfm.

Pew Global Attitudes Project. 2012. Pakistani Public Opinion Ever More Critical of US Press Release. Online. Available at http://www.pewglobal.org/2012/06/27/pakistani-public-opinion-ever-more-critical-of-u-s/.

Pew Research Forum. 2012. Global Religious Landscape. December 12. Online. Available at http://features.pewforum.org/grl/population-number.php.

PILDAT. 2013a. 5 Years of 13th National Assembly of Pakistan: Positive Trends and Areas of Concern. Islamabad. March 29. Online. Available at http://www.pildat.org/eventsdel.asp?detid=614.

——. 2013b. A Comparative Analysis of Election Manifestoes of Major Political Parties. Islamabad. April. Islamabad. Online. Available at http://www.pildat.org/publications/publication/elections/Election2013_ManifestoesComparison.pdf.

Porter, Patrick. 2009. *Military Orientalism: Eastern War through Western Eyes*. New York: Columbia/Hurst.

Qadir, Shaukat. 2002. An Analysis of the Kargil Conflict of 1999. *RUSI Journal* 147, no. 2: 24–30.

Qazi, Shamsul Haq (Lt. Col.). 1964. A Case for Citizen Army. *Pakistan Army Journal* 6 (June): 18–25.

Qureshi, Hakeem Arshad (Maj. Gen.). 2002. *The 1971 Indo-Pak War: A Soldier's Narrative*. Karachi: Oxford University Press.

Radio Free Europe. 2006. Islamabad Links Suicide Bomber to Madrasah Attack. *Radio Free Europe*, November 8. Online. Available at http://www.globalsecurity.org/wmd/library/news/pakistan/2006/pakistan-061108-rferl01.htm.

Raghavan, Srinath. 2009. Civil–Military Relations in India: The China Crisis and After. *Journal of Strategic Studies* 32 (Feb.): 149–175.

Rahman, M. Attiqur. 1976. *Our Defence Cause: An Analysis of Pakistan's Past and Future Military Role*. London: White Lion Publishers Limited.

Rais, Rasul Bakhsh. 2008. *Afghanistan and Pakistan: Difficult Neighbors*. NBR Analysis 19 (Dec.): 13–24. Online. Available at http://www.nbr.org/publications/nbranalysis/pdf/vol19no5.pdf.

——. 2011. Afghanistan's India Lever. *Hilal* 48 (Nov.): 5–6.

Raja, Asif Jehangir (Maj.). 2012. From Editor's Desk. *Hilal* 49 (July): 3.

Raja, Muhammed Naseer (Lt. Col.). 2002. Low Intensity Conflict and Its Fallout on Pakistan. In *Pakistan Army Green Book 2002: Low Intensity Conflict*, 119–127. Rawalpindi: Pakistan Army General Headquarters.

Raman, B. 2002. Kashmir and the Pro-Bin Laden Terrorist Infrastructure in Pakistan. *Outlook*, June 17. Online. Available at http://www.outlookindia.com/article.aspx?216105.

Ramusack, Barbara N. 2003. *The Indian Princes and Their States*. Cambridge: Cambridge University Press.

Rana, Amir. 2004. *The A to Z of Jehadi Organizations in Pakistan*. Lahore: Mashal.

Rashid, Ahmed. 2000. *Taliban: Islam, Oil and the New Great Game in Central Asia*. New York: I. B. Taurus.

Rashid, Jamal. 1996. Pakistan and the Central Command. *MERIP Middle East Report* 141 (July–Aug.): 28–34.

Rassler, Don, and Vahid Brown. 2011. *The Haqqani Nexus and the Evolution of al-Qa'ida*. West Point, NY: Combating Terrorism Center.

Rassler, Don, C. Christine Fair, Anirban Gosh, and Nadia Shoeb. 2013. *The Fighters of Lashkar-e-Taiba: Recruitment, Training, Deployment and Death*. Occasional Paper, West Point Combating Terrorism Center.

Rediff. 2012. Not Again! Pakistan Rakes Up Kashmir Conflict at UNGA. *Rediff.com*, September 26. Online. Available at http://www.rediff.com/news/report/not-again-pakistan-rakes-up-kashmir-conflict-at-unga/20120926.htm.

Reetz, Dietrich. 1993. Pakistan and the Central Asia Hinterland Option: The Race for Regional Security and Development. *Journal of South Asian and Middle Eastern Studies* 17 (Fall): 28–56.

Riaz, Ali. 2002. Nations, Nation-State and Politics of Muslim Identity in South Asia. *Comparative Studies of South Asia, Africa and the Middle East* 22, nos. 1–2: 53–58.

Riedel, Bruce. 2008. Pakistan and Terror: The Eye of the Storm. *Annals of the American Academy of Political and Social Science* 618 (July): 31–45.

——. 2011. Pakistan's Jihadist Threat: Obama's Terrorism Challenge in 2012. *Daily Beast*, December 21. Online. Available at http://www.thedailybeast.com/articles/2011/12/21/pakistan-s-jihadist-threat-obama-s-terrorism-challenge-in-2012.html.

——. 2012. *Dangerous Embrace: Pakistan, America, and the Future of the Global Jihad*. Washington, DC: Brookings Institution Press.

Rizvi, Hassan Askari. 2000a. *Military, State and Society in Pakistan*. London: Palgrave.

——. 2000b. *The Military and Politics in Pakistan: 1947–1997.* Lahore, Pakistan: Sang-e-Meel Publications.

——. 2002. Pakistan's Strategic Culture. In *South Asia in 2020: Future Strategic Balances and Alliances,* ed. Michael R. Chambers, 305–328. Carlisle: Strategic Studies Institute, US Army War College.

Roach, Jason. 2013. The Growth of Islamism in the Pakistan Army. *Small Wars Journal,* January 30. Online. Available at http://smallwarsjournal.com/jrnl/art/the-growth-of-islamism-in-the-pakistan-army.

Roggio, Bill. 2006. Aftermath of the Bajaur Airstrike. *Long War Journal,* October 31. Online. Available at http://www.longwarjournal.org/archives/2006/10/aftermath_of_the_baj.php.

——. 2010. Suicide Bomber Kills 60 at Mosque in Pakistan's Northwest. *Long War Journal,* November 5. Online. Available at http://www.longwarjournal.org/archives/2010/11/suicide_bomber_kills_40.php.

Roul, Animesh. 2010. Lashkar-e-Taiba and the Strategy of "Encircling" India. *Terrorism Monitor,* October 21. Online. Available at http://www.jamestown.org/programs/gta/single/?tx_ttnews[tt_news]=37056&cHash=b2f2164427.

Rouse, Shahnaz. 2002. Elections in Pakistan. Middle East Research Information Project, October 18. Online. Available at http://www.merip.org/mero/mero101802.

Roy, Olivier. 1990. *Islam and Resistance in Afghanistan.* Cambridge: Cambridge University Press.

——. 2004. The Taliban: A Strategic Tool for Pakistan. In *Pakistan: Nationalism without a Nation,* ed. Christophe Jaffrelot, 149–160. London: Zed Books.

Rubin, Barnett R. 2002. *The Fragmentation of Afghanistan.* New Haven, CT: Yale University Press.

Rubin, Barnett R., and Ahmed Rashid. 2008. From Great Game to Grand Bargain. *Foreign Affairs* (Nov.–Dec.). Online. Available at http://www.foreignaffairs.com/articles/64604/barnett-r-rubin-and-ahmed-rashid/from-great-game-to-grand-bargain.

Rumi, Raza. 2011. The Spectre of Islamist Infiltration. *Friday Times,* May 27. Online. Available at http://www.thefridaytimes.com/27052011/page3.shtml.

Rynning, Sten, and Jens Ringsmose. 2008. Why Are Revisionist States Revisionist? Reviving Classical Realism as an Approach to Understanding International Change. *International Politics* 45: 19–39.

Sabri, Zahra. 2012. A Textbook Case. *Herald,* December, 47–50.

Saeed, Usman (Brig. Retd). 2012. Indian Interest in Afghanistan. *Hilal* 48 (June): 14–15, 19.

Sagan, Scott D., and Kenneth N. Waltz. 2002. *The Spread of Nuclear Weapons: A Debate Renewed.* New York: W. W. Norton.

Sahni, Ajai. 2012. India's Internal Security Challenges. In *India's Security Challenge at Home and Abroad.* NBR Special Report No. 39. Seattle, WA: NBR.

Sahni, Varun. 2009. A Dangerous Exercise: Brasstacks as Non-nuclear Near War. In *Nuclear Proliferation in South Asia: Crisis Behavior and the Bomb,* ed. Sumit Ganguly and S. Paul Kapur, 12–35. New York: Routledge.

Saigol, Rubina. 2003. *Becoming a Modern Nation: Educational Discourse in the Early Years of Ayub Khan (1958–64).* Islamabad: Council of Social Sciences. Online. Available at http://www.cosspak.org/monographs/monograph_rubina.pdf.

Saleem, Muhammad (Maj. Gen.). 2002. Low Intensity Conflict Conflictual Framework. In *Pakistan Army Green Book 2002: Low Intensity Conflict,* 1–8. Rawalpindi: Pakistan Army General Headquarters.

Salik, Naeem (Brig. Retd). 2009. *The Genesis of South Asia Nuclear Deterrence: Pakistan's Perspective.* Karachi: Oxford University Press.

Salik, Siddiq (Maj.Retd). 1997. *Witness to Surrender.* Dhaka: University Press Limited.

SANA. 2010. Rehman Malik Asserts He Used No Term like "Punjabi Taliban." *South Asian News Agency,* June 4. Online. Available at http://www.sananews.net/english/2010/06/04/rehman-malik-asserts-he-used-no-term-like-%E2%80%98punjabi-taliban%E2%80%99.

Sanger, David E., and Eric Schmitt. 2011. Pakistani Nuclear Arms Pose Challenge to US Policy. *New York Times*, January 31. Online. Available at http://www.nytimes.com/2011/02/01/world/asia/01policy.html?pagewanted=all.

Sarfraz, Muhammad (Brig). 1990. Our Junior Leaders. In *Pakistan Army Green Book 1990: Year of the Junior Leaders,* 23–28. Rawalpindi: Pakistan Army General Headquarters.

Sarwar, Ghulam (Col. Retd). 1995. Pakistan's Strategic and Security Perspectives. *Pakistan Army Journal* 36 (Autumn): 63–74.

Sattar, Abdul. 2007. *Pakistan's Foreign Policy 1947–2005.* Karachi: Oxford University Press.

Schaffer, Howard B., and Teresita C. Schaffer. 2011. *How Pakistan Negotiates with the United States.* Washington, DC: USIP.

Schelling, Thomas. 1960. *The Strategy of Conflict.* New York: Oxford University Press.

Schifrin, Nick, Jake Taper, and Huma Khan. 2011. Pakistan Might Allow US Access to Osama Bin Laden's Wives but Not to Compound. *ABCNews.com,* May 9. Online. Available at http://abcnews.go.com/Politics/osama-bin-laden-raid-bitter-us-split-pakistan/story?id=13561191#.UVtY3jf5WS8.

Schofield, Carey. 2011. *Inside the Pakistan Army.* London: Biteback Publishing.

Schofield, Julian, and Michael Zekulin. 2007. *Appraising the Threat of Islamist Take-Over in Pakistan.* Concordia University Research Note 34. Online. Available at http://www.ieim.uqam.ca/IMG/pdf/NOTE34.pdf.

Schofield, Victoria. 2000. *Kashmir in Conflict.* New York: I. B. Taurus.

Schweller, Randall. 1994. Bandwagoning for Profit: Bringing the Revisionist State Back In. *International Security* 19, no. 1: 72–107.

Scott, David. 2009. India's "Extended Neighborhood" Concept: Power Projection for a Rising Power. *India Review* 8, no. 3: 107–143.

Scramble Magazine. Pakistan Armed Forces. n.d. *Scramble.nl.* Online. Available at http://www.scramble.nl/pk.htm.

Sethi, Najam. 2008. Chronicle of a Result Foretold. *Friday Times.* February 15. Online. Available at http://www.najamsethi.com/chronicle-of-a-result-foretold/.

——. 2012. Last Ditch Politics. *Friday Times,* September 7. Online. Available at http://www.najamsethi.com/last-ditch-politics/.

Shafi, Mohammad (Maj.). 1963. The Effectiveness of Guerilla Warfare. *Pakistan Army Journal* 5, no. 1: 4–11.

Shah, Aqil. 2003. Pakistan's "Armored" Democracy. *Journal of Democracy* 14, no. 4 (Oct.): 26–40.

——. 2004. The Transition to "Guided" Democracy in Pakistan. In *The Asia-Pacific: A Region in Transition,* ed. Jim Rolfe, 207–219. Honolulu: Asia-Pacific Center for Security Studies.

——. 2011. Getting the Military out of Pakistani Politics: How Aiding the Army Undermines Democracy. *Foreign Affairs* 90 (May–June): 69–82.

Shah, Sayed Wiqar Ali. 2012. Political Reforms in the Federally Administered Tribal Areas of Pakistan (FATA): Will It End the Current Militancy? Heidelberg Papers in South Asian and Comparative Politics. Online. Available at http://archiv.ub.uni-heidelberg.de/volltextserver/volltexte/2012/13063/ pdf/Heidelberg_Papers_64_Ali_Shah.pdf.

Shahzad, Syed Saleem. 2011. Al-Qaeda Had Warned of Pakistan Strike. *Asia Times,* May 27. Online. Available at http://www.atimes.com/atimes/South_Asia/ME27Df06.html.

Shaikh, Farzana. 2009. *Making Sense of Pakistan.* New York: Columbia University Press.

Shanghai Daily. 2007. China Calls on Pak to Better Protect Chinese. June 27. Online. Available at http://www.shanghaidaily.com/article/?id=321184&type=National.

Shapiro, Jacob N., and C. Christine Fair. 2009–2010. Why Support Islamist Militancy? Evidence from Pakistan. *International Security* 34 (Winter): 79–118.

Shekatkar, D.B. 2009. India's Counterinsurgency Campaign in Nagaland. In *India and Counterinsurgency: Lessons Learned,* ed. Sumit Ganguly and David E. Fidler, 9–27. London: Routledge.

Siddiqa, Ayesha. 2007. *Military Inc.: Inside Pakistan's Military Economy.* London: Pluto Press.

——. 2012. Looking Back at the Lawyers' Movement. *Friday Times* 24 (March 23–29). Online. Available at http://www.thefridaytimes.com/beta2/tft/article.php?issue=20120323& page=3.

Siddiqi, Abdurrahman (Brig. Retd.). 1996. *The Military in Pakistan: Image and Reality*. Lahore: Vanguard.

Siddiqi, Aslam. 1964. *A Path for Pakistan*. Karachi: Pakistan Publishing House.

Siddiqi, M. Aslam. 1958. Can Pakistan Stay Neutral? *Pakistan Horizon* 11: 70–78.

——. 1959. US Military Aid to Pakistan. *Pakistan Horizon* 12, no. 1: 45–52.

——. 1960. *Pakistan Seeks Security*. Lahore: Longmans, Green, Pakistan Branch.

Sinno, Abdulkader. 2008. Explaining the Taliban's Ability to Mobilize the Pashtuns. In *The Taliban and the Crisis of Afghanistan*, ed. Robert D. Crews and Amin Tarzi, 59–89. Cambridge, MA: Harvard University Press.

Siddiqui, Salman. 2012. Fading Legacy: In Search of Jinnah's Missing Speech. *Pakistan Express Tribune*, August 14. Online. Available at http://tribune.com.pk/story/421817/fading-legacy-in-search-of-jinnahs-missing-speech/.

Smith, David O. (Lt. Col. Retd.). 2013. "The US Experience with Tactical Nuclear Weapons: Lessons for South Asia. Stimson. March. Online. Available at http://www.stimson.org/images/uploads/research-pdfs/David_Smith_Tactical_Nuclear_Weapons.pdf.

Snyder, Glenn. 1965. The Balance of Power and the Balance of Terror. In *The Balance of Power*, ed. Paul Seaburry, 185–201. San Francisco: Chandler.

Snyder, Jack. 1977. *The Soviet Strategic Culture: Implications for Nuclear Options*. Santa Monica, CA: RAND.

South Asia Terrorism Portal. 2012. Fatalities in Terrorist Violence in Pakistan 2003–2012. *SATP. org*, July 22. Online. Available at http://www.satp.org/satporgtp/countries/pakistan/database/casualties.htm.

Stern, Jessica. 2000. Pakistan's Jihad Culture. *Foreign Affairs* 79 (Nov.–Dec.): 115–126.

Stratfor. 2007. Pakistan and Its Army. *Stratfor Geopolitical Intelligence Report*, November 6. Online. Available at http://www.stratfor.com/weekly/pakistan_and_its_army.

Swami, Praveen. 2007. *India, Pakistan and the Secret Jihad: The Covert War in Kashmir, 1947–2005*. London: Routledge.

——. 2008. The Well-Tempered Jihad: The Politics and Practice of Post-2002 Islamist Terrorism in India. *Contemporary South Asia* 16 (Sept.): 303–322.

——. 2013. Green Books, Red Herrings and the LOC War. *Hindu*, January 16. Online. Available at http://www.thehindu.com/opinion/op-ed/green-books-red-herring-and-the-loc-war/article4310197.ece?homepage=true.

Syed, Anwar. 1969. Sino–Pakistan Relations. *Pakistan Horizon* 22 (Second Quarter): 107–119.

Syed, Anwar H. 1974. *China & Pakistan: Diplomacy of an Entente Cordiale*. Amherst: University of Massachusetts Press.

Tabbassam, Muhammad Ashraf (Maj. Gen.). 2006. Terrorism, Its Dynamics and Response. In *Pakistan Army Green Book 2006: Terrorism*, 34–41. Rawalpindi: Pakistan Army General Headquarters.

Taj, Farhat. 2008. No Class War in Swat. *News (Pakistan)*, December 18. Online. Available at http://www.khyberwatch.com/forums/showthread.php?2295-Update-on-Swat!/page49.

Tahir-Kheli, Shirin. 1974–1975. Pakhtoonistan and Its International Implications. *World Affairs* 137 (Winter): 233–245.

Talbot, Ian A. 1980. The 1946 Punjab Elections. *Modern Asian Studies* 14, no. 1: 65–91.

——. 1998. *Pakistan: A Modern History*. New York: St. Martin's Press.

——. 2002. The Punjabization of Pakistan: Myth or Reality? In *Pakistan: Nationalism without a Nation?* ed. Christophe Jaffrelot, 51–62. London: Zed Books.

——. 2007. Religion and Violence: The Historical Context for Conflict in Pakistanz. In *Religion and Violence in South Asia: Theory and Practice*, ed. John Hinnells and Richard King, 147–164. New York: Routledge.

Taliaferro, Jeffrey W. 2000–2001. Security Seeking under Anarchy: Defensive Realism Revisited. *International Security* 25 (Winter): 128–161.

Tanham, George. 1992. *Indian Strategic Thought: An Interpretive Essay.* Santa Monica, CA: RAND.

Tavernise, Sabrina. 2010. Suicide Bombers Strike Sufi Shrine in Pakistan. *New York Times,* July 1. Online. Available at http://www.nytimes.com/2010/07/02/world/asia/02pstan.html.

Tavernise, Sabrina, Richard A. Oppel Jr., and Eric Schmitt. 2009. United Militants Threaten Pakistan's Populous Heart. *New York Times,* April 13. Online. Available at http://www.nytimes.com/2009/04/14/world/asia/14punjab.html.

Tellis, Ashley J. 1997. *Stability in South Asia.* Santa Monica, CA: RAND.

——. 2008. *Pakistan and the War on Terror: Conflicted Goals, Compromised Performance.* Washington, DC: CEIP. Online. Available at http://www.carnegieendowment.org/files/tellis_pakistan_final.pdf.

Tellis, Ashley J., C. Christine Fair, and Jamison Jo Medby. 2001. *Limited Conflicts under the Nuclear Umbrella—Indian and Pakistani Lessons from the Kargil Crisis.* Santa Monica, CA: RAND.

Text of the Southeast Asia Collective Defense Treaty. 1954. Signed at Manila, the Philippines, September 8. *International Organization* 9, no. 4 (Nov.): 617–621.

Thakur, Ramesh. 2011. India and the United Nations. *Strategic Analysis* 35, no. 6: 898–905.

Tikekar, Maneesha. 2004. *Across the Wagah: An Indian's Sojourn in Pakistan.* New Delhi: Promilla.

Tinker, Hugh. 1977. Pressure, Persuasion, Decision: Factors in the Partition of the Punjab, August 1947. *Journal of Asian Studies* 35, no. 4: 695–704.

Titus, Paul. 1998. Honor the Baloch. Buy the Pashtun: Stereotypes, Social Organization and History in Western Pakistan. *Modern Asian Studies* 32 (July): 657–687.

Tiwana, Muhammad Nazar (Brig.). 2002. Low Intensity Conflict Genesis of the Concept. In *Pakistan Army Green Book 2002: Low Intensity Conflict,* 23–26. Rawalpindi: Pakistan Army General Headquarters.

Tohid, Owais. 2010. In Pakistan, Militant Attacks on Sufi Shrines on the Rise. *Christian Science Monitor,* November 5. Online. Available at http://www.csmonitor.com/World/Asia-South-Central/2010/1105/In-Pakistan-militant-attacks-on-Sufi-shrines-on-the-rise.

Tripodi, Christian. 2009. "Good for One but not the Other": The "Sandeman System" of Pacification as Applied to Baluchistan and the North-West Frontier, 1877–1947. *Journal of Military History* 73 (July): 767–802.

——. 2011. *The Edge of Empire: The British Political Officer and Tribal Administration on the North-West Frontier 1877–1947.* Farham, Surrey: Ashgate.

Yamin, Tughral (Brig. Ret.). 2011. Pakistan–US Relationship. *Hilal* 48 (Nov.): 9–10.

——. 2012. The Massacre at Salala and Its Aftermath. *Hilal* 48 (Jan.): 9–10.

University of Peshawar, Area Study Centre. 2004. *Federally Administered Tribal Areas (FATA) of Pakistan.* Peshawar: University of Peshawar Area Study Centre.

Uprety, Kishor, and Salman M.A. Salman. 2011. Legal Aspects of Sharing and Management of Transboundary Waters in South Asia: Preventing Conflicts and Promoting Cooperation. *Hydrological Sciences Journal* 56, no. 4: 641–661.

US Department of State, Office of the Historian. n.d. Milestones: 1953–1960: The Baghdad Pact (1955) and the Central Treaty Organization (CENTO). Online. Available at http://history.state.gov/milestones/1953-1960/CENTO.

US Bureau of the Census. 1950. *Statistical Abstract of the United States: 1950.* Washington, DC: US Government Printing Office.

US Department of State. 1982. Newsweek Article on Chinese Nuclear Cooperation with Pakistan (Cable 348835 to US Embassy Pakistan). December 18. Online. Available at http://www.gwu.edu/~nsarchiv/NSAEBB/NSAEBB114/index.htm.

——. 1983. The Pakistani Nuclear Program (Declassified Cable). June 23. Online. Available at http://www.gwu.edu/~nsarchiv/NSAEBB/NSAEBB114/chipak-11.pdf.

——. 2010. Designation of Falah-i-Insaniat Foundation: Media Note. November 24. Online. Available at http://www.state.gov/r/pa/prs/ps/2010/11/151931.htm.

United Nations Security Council (UNSC). 1948. Resolution 47, The India–Pakistan Question. April 21. Online. Available at http://www.un.org/ga/search/view_doc.asp?symbol=S/RES/47(1948).

Van Evera, Steven. 1999. *Causes of War: Power and the Roots of Conflict*. Ithaca, NY: Cornell University Press.

Vinayaraj, V.K. 2009. India as a Threat: Bangladeshi Perceptions. *South Asian Survey March* 16, no. 1: 101–118.

Voice of America. Two Soldiers Convicted in Musharraf Assassination Attempts. 2011. *VOA News*, December 24. Online. Available at http://www.voanews.com/english/news/a-13-2004-12-24-voa35-67335172.html.

Wadhams, Caroline, and Colin Cookman. 2009. Faces of Pakistan's Militant Leaders: In-Depth Profiles of Major Militant Commanders. Center for American Progress, July 22. Online. Available at http://www.americanprogress.org/issues/2009/07/talibanleaders.html.

Wahab, Muhammad Abdul, and Vaqar Ahmed. 2011. Foreign Assistance and Economic Growth: Evidence from Pakistan: 1972–2010. Working Paper, Munich Personal RePec Archive, University of Munich. Online Available at http://mpra.ub.uni-muenchen.de/30344/1/Foreign_Assistance_and_Economic_Growth_Evidence_from_Pakistan_1972-2010.pdf.

Waraich, Omar. 2011. Why Pakistan's Taliban Target the Muslim Majority. *Time*, April 7. Online. Available at http://www.time.com/time/world/article/0,8599,2063794,00.html.

Walker, Robin. 2006. Lt. Gen. Khalid Kidwai's CCC Address of October 2006: Pakistan's Evolution as a Nuclear Weapons State. *Strategic Insights*, November 1. Online. Available at http://www.nps.edu/academics/centers/ccc/news/kidwaiNov06.html.

Waltz, Kenneth. 1979. *Theory of International Politics*. New York: McGraw-Hill.

Waraich, Omar. 2011. US Diplomat Could Bring Down Pakistan Gov't. *Time.com*, February 9. Online. Available at http://www.time.com/time/world/article/0,8599,2047149,00.html.

Wax, Emily. 2009. India's Quiet Diplomatic Coup: Kashmir Eliminated from US Envoy's Mandate. *Washington Post*, January 30. Online. Available at http://www.washingtonpost.com/wp-dyn/content/article/2009/01/29/AR2009012903737.html.

Wazir, Maqbool. 2011. FATA Reforms: A Far Cry. *Hilal* (June): 9–10.

Wazir, M. Maqbool Khan. 2011. Geopolitics of FATA after 9/11. *IPRI Journal* 11 (Winter): 59–76.

Wei, Shao, Mao Weihua, and Wang Huazhong. 2011. Xinjiang Identifies Terror Organization. *China Daily*, August 2. Online. Available at http://usa.chinadaily.com.cn/china/2011-08/02/content_13030681.htm.

Weinbaum, Marvin G. 1991. Pakistan and Afghanistan: The Strategic Relationship. *Asian Survey* 31, no. 6: 496–511.

——. 1996. Civic Culture and Democracy in Pakistan. *Asian Survey* 36 (July): 639–654.

Weitz, Richard. 2007. Repercussions from Air Force Nuclear Weapons Incident Continue. *World Politics Review*, September 15. Online. Available at http://www.worldpoliticsreview.com/articles/1174/repercussions-from-air-force-nuclear-weapons-incident-continue.

White, Joshua T. 2008. The Shape of Frontier Rule: Governance and Transition, from the Raj to the Modern Pakistani Frontier. *Asian Security* 4, no. 3: 219–243.

Whitehead, Andrew. 2007. *A Mission in Kashmir*. London: Penguin Global.

Wirsing, Robert G. 1998. *India, Pakistan, and the Kashmir Dispute*. New York: Saint Martin's Press.

——. 2004. Political Islam, Pakistan, and the Geo-Politics of Religious Identity. In *Growth and Governance in Asia*, ed. Yoichiro Sato, 165–178. Honolulu: APCSS.

——. 2007. Hydro-Politics in South Asia: The Domestic Roots of Interstate River Rivalry. *Asian Affairs* 34, no. 1: 3–22.

Wolf-Phillips, Leslie. 1979. Constitutional Legitimacy: A Study of the Doctrine of Necessity. *Third World Quarterly* 1 (Oct.): 97–133.

Wolpert, Stanley. 1993. *A New History of India*, 4th ed. New York: Oxford University Press.

Wood, Michael J., Karen M. Douglas, and Robbie M. Sutton. 2012. Dead and Alive: Beliefs in Contradictory Conspiracy Theories. *Social Psychological and Personality Science* 3 (Nov.): 767–773.

Woodward, Bob. 2010. *Obama's Wars.* New York: Simon and Schuster.

World Bank Independent Evaluation Group. 2006. *Pakistan: Country Assistance Evaluation.* Country Evaluation and Regional Relations Report No. 34942. Online. Available at http://www.oecd.org/dataoecd/63/31/36494011.pdf.

World Bank. 2012. World Development Indicators. Online. Available at http://databank.world-bank.org/ddp/home.do?Step=3&id=4.

Yusuf, Huma. 2011. Conspiracy Fever: the US, Pakistan and Its Media. *Survival* 53 (Aug.): 95–118.

Yusufzai, Rahimullah. 2006. Return of the Taliban. *Frontline*, October 3. Online. Available at http://www.pbs.org/wgbh/pages/frontline/taliban/militants/mohammed.html.

——. 2007. The Emergence of the Pakistani Taliban. *Jane's Information Group*, December 11. Online. Available by subscription at https://janes-ihs-com.proxy.library.georgetown.edu/CustomPages/Janes/DisplayPage.aspx?DocType=News&ItemId=+++1190316.

——. 2008. A Who's Who of the Insurgency in Pakistan's North-West Frontier Province: Part One—North and South Waziristan. *Terrorism Monitor*, September 22. Online. Available at http://www.jamestown.org/programs/gta/single/?tx_ttnews[tt_news]=5169&tx_ttnews [backPid]=167&no_cache=1.

——. 2010. The Discourse on Punjabi Taliban. *News (Pakistan)*, July 6. Online. Available at http://www.memri.org/report/en/0/0/0/0/0/0/4655.htm.

Zahid, Ch. Muzaffar Ali Khan (Brig.). 1989. Counter Insurgency Operations in Erstwhile East Pakistan. *Pakistan Army Journal* 30 (June): 52–62.

Zahra-Malik, Mehreen. 2011. It's Afghanistan, Stupid: Drones and Spooks Are Not Pakistan's Real Concerns. *Time*, May 6. Online. Available at http://www.newsweekpakistan.com/the-take/312.

Zaidi, Abbas. 2008. How General Zia Has Sabotaged Lawyers' Movement from Grace. *Pak Tea House*, November 11. Online. Available at http://pakteahouse.net/2008/11/11/how-general-zia-has-sabotaged-lawyers%E2%80%99-movement-from-grave/.

Zaidi, Akbar S. 2006. Pakistan: Civil and Uncivil Society. *Economic and Political Weekly* 41 (Aug. 19): 3556–3557.

Zaman, Mohammad (Lt. Col.) 1992. Can Indian Forces Fight the Next War. *Pakistan Defence Review* 4 (Dec.): 19–37.

Zia, Muhammad (Brig.). 2002. Low Intensity Conflict. In *Pakistan Army Green Book 2002: Low Intensity Conflict*, 32–42. Rawalpindi: Pakistan Army General Headquarters.

Ziegler, Phillip. 1985. *Mountbatten.* New York: Alfred A. Knopf.

Zionts, David M. 2006. Revisionism and Its Variants: Understanding State Reactions to Foreign Policy Failure. *Security Studies* 14, no. 4: 631–657.

Zuberi, Muhammad Aslam (Maj.). 1971. The Challenge of a Nuclear India. *Pakistan Army Journal* 13 (June): 20–31.

INDEX

Note: Page numbers in italics indicate figures, maps, or tables.